PRAISE FOR *LEBANON AND TURKEY*

"This is a refreshing, lucid, and seasoned research-based analysis that is crucial to understanding a contemporary Eastern Mediterranean amid roiling shifts, what some have called 'the end of the Arab century.' A discerning survey probing deeply post-Ottoman Lebanese-Turkish relations, this book is of special importance on many levels to scholars of the Middle East but also genocide studies and the still 'hidden' history of the Great Famine on Mount Lebanon. An edifying book and deeply researched, it is written and presented with clarity and deliberation yielding illumination."

—Franck Salameh, Boston College

"Well researched, chronicled, and argued, Dr. Rabil's book stands out as a unique study, insofar as, to my knowledge, no other work has meticulously examined and scrutinized Lebanon's relationship with Turkey since Ottoman rule. The book successfully weaves together the major developments—including the overlooked Great Famine—of this relationship that helped shape modern Lebanon and continues to highlight both the chronic failures of the country's confessional system and the promise of better Lebanon–Turkey relations, against the backdrop of a fast-paced changing world order."

—Joseph Alagha, Haigazian University

"Robert G. Rabil makes clear the complicated, conflicted, and tragic history of Lebanon and its relationship with its neighbors. This compelling, insightful, and courageous book helps us understand Lebanon's tangled and contentious history with its neighbors Turkey and Syria. Lebanon is a microcosm of the Middle East, and Rabil masterfully shows how its current crisis is rooted in history."

—Robert J. Allison, author of *The Crescent Obscured: The United States and the Muslim World 1776–1815*

"Robert G. Rabil's *Lebanon and Turkey: Historical Contexts and Contemporary Realities* is a gift for those studying the history, politics, and culture of Lebanon and its important neighbor Turkey. In recent years, Turkey's foreign policy has become a frequent and serious topic of analysis for Middle Eastern scholars. This book provides an important addition to that literature. It is a unique study concentrating on Turkey's impact on the development of Lebanon from its early history to its current involvement in the country. Through archival research and interviews abroad, Dr. Rabil provides new insights into Ottoman policies leading to the Great Famine of 1915–1918, the roots of the confessional system, the growth of Arab nationalism, the Cold

War, Lebanon's civil war, and Turkey's recent and growing involvement in Lebanon and the region. This is a key contribution to filling the missing piece of the Lebanese-Turkish relationship's place in today's Middle East foreign policy puzzle. It really is a must read!"

—Lenore G. Martin, professor, Department of Political Science and International Relations, Emmanuel College

"Professor Rabil masterfully traces Turkish Middle Eastern policy from Sultan Abdul Hamid's Ottomanism to Davutoglu's Neo-Ottomanism and Erdogan's realism after the defeat of Arab popular uprisings that demonstrated the limits of Ankara's regional ambitions. Rabil's exceptional book educates students about the influence of Turkey in shaping Lebanon's sectarian alignments and guides researchers to its importance in understanding the significance of transnational ideas in exacerbating Arab countries' instability. *Lebanon and Turkey: Historical Contexts and Contemporary Realities* is an essential read for those who wish to understand Turkey's history and present to predict its future."

—Hilal Khashan, American University of Beirut

"A brilliant and highly enlightening book. Professor Rabil does an excellent job explaining how the Ottoman Empire struggled to survive by applying a policy of mass killings, starvation, and deportations in the empire's provinces that sought to become more autonomous. It is interesting how an empire resorts to cruel methods to keep itself from falling apart. Rabil's study is also relevant to understanding contemporary Russia's involvement in Ukraine. The case of the Ottoman Empire can serve as a historical paradigm to analyze powers that struggle against their own decline."

—Luis Fleischman, professor, Palm Beach State College; copresident, Palm Beach Center for Democracy and Policy Research

Lebanon and Turkey

Historical Contexts and Contemporary Realities

Robert G. Rabil

ROWMAN & LITTLEFIELD
Lanham • Boulder • New York • London

Published by Rowman & Littlefield
An imprint of The Rowman & Littlefield Publishing Group, Inc.
4501 Forbes Boulevard, Suite 200, Lanham, Maryland 20706
www.rowman.com

86-90 Paul Street, London EC2A 4NE

British Library Cataloguing in Publication Information Available

Library of Congress Cataloging-in-Publication Data

Names: Rabil, Robert G., author.
Title: Lebanon and Turkey: Historical Contexts and Contemporary Realities /
    Robert Rabil.
Description: Lanham: Rowman & Littlefield, [2024] | Includes bibliographical references
    and index. | Summary: "No empire or a regional power has helped mold the socio-
    political and religious landscape of a country as the Ottoman Empire and its heir
    (the Republic of Turkey) have helped shape modern Lebanon. Although the history
    of Lebanon and Turkish foreign policy have been the focus of a number of studies,
    no contemporary study has examined Lebanon-Turkish relations back to Ottoman
    rule of Lebanon. As such, our understanding of this historic and contemporaneous
    relationship is deficient. This text sets out to fill this gap, examining patterns and
    shifts in Lebanon-Turkey relations within the context of regional and international
    politics from Ottoman rule to Turkey's AKP-led governments. This comprehensive
    account of Lebanon-Turkey relations, grounded in layers of cultural, political,
    demographic, economic, and sectarian complexities and changes across centuries,
    analyzes the developments and dynamics that have helped shape modern Lebanon and
    its confessional system and politics. It underscores the misconceptions and lessons
    learned from this long-term relationship, locating Lebanon-Turkish relations along a
    historical continuum"— Provided by publisher.
Identifiers: LCCN 2023010093 (print) | LCCN 2023010094 (ebook) | ISBN
    9781538177501 (cloth) | ISBN 9781538177518 (paperback) | ISBN
    9781538177525 (epub)
Subjects: LCSH: Lebanon—History. | Lebanon—Relations—Turkey. |
    Turkey—Relations—Lebanon.
Classification: LCC DS80.9 .R33 2023 (print) | LCC DS80.9 (ebook) | DDC
    327.56920561—dc23/eng/20230302
LC record available at https://lccn.loc.gov/2023010093
LC ebook record available at https://lccn.loc.gov/2023010094

To my family
In memoriam
Olivia Annette Stefanovic

Contents

Note on Transliteration

The English transliteration from Arabic, Persian, and Turkish generally follows the rules of the *International Journal of Middle Eastern Studies*. Arabic or Turkish names commonly used by the *New York Times* and whose spellings are thus becoming standard retain their original form as they appeared in that newspaper. For example, Koran and Erdogan have not been transliterated as Qur'an and Erdoğan, respectively. Arabic and Turkish terms and words are italicized except for those that have become standard in their common use, such as *jihad*.

Acknowledgments

I am grateful to Florida Atlantic University's community, in particular the Schmidt College of Arts and Letters, Department of Political Science and Osher Lifelong Learning. I feel blessed to be part of a robust, caring, and intellectually agile community. I thank the faculty and staff of the Department of Political Science for their valued friendship and their scholastic and administrative support. I am thankful to my graduate students, who have never ceased to intellectually amaze and challenge me inasmuch as I have tried to challenge them. My deep appreciation goes to my lifelong learning students, whose kindness and vast repertoire of experience and knowledge only sharpens my desire to be a better human being, researcher, and instructor.

I am deeply grateful to my colleagues, professors Franck Salameh, Joseph Alagha, Asher Kaufman, Luis Fleischman, and Irving Berkowitz, for their friendship and professional support, including reviewing my manuscript and suggesting ways to improve it. I thank professors Robert Allison and Lenore Martin for their unwavering professional and personal support throughout the years. My deep appreciation goes to attorney at law and secretary general of the Christian Federation of Lebanon and the Levant, Francois Alam, for scheduling some of my interviews and driving me to many destinations in Lebanon, which were imperative to the research of this study; retired Lebanese Brigadier General Khalil Helou for sharing his experience and views on Lebanon's domestic politics and radical movements; Professor and Dean of the Faculty of Natural and Applied Sciences, Notre Dame University-Lebanon George Eid, for helping me conduct my research, including arranging interviews with retired and current Lebanese officials and religious leaders.

I am thankful to Chef du Département d'Histoire—Relations Internationales HRI, Conservateur des Archives de l'Université Saint-Joseph de Beyrouth Christian Taoutel for being so gracious in responding to my incessant requests for help, and for providing pictures of the Great Famine. I thank retired, former, and current ambassadors, including Tracy Chamoun and Mansour

Abdallah, along with former Lebanese ambassadors to Turkey, who provided me with valuable insights into Lebanon-Turkey relations. I thank members of the clergy, in particular the Maronite and Armenian clergy, who shared their views about Lebanon-Turkey relations. I thank late Professor Albert Rabil Jr., who reminded me on more than one occasion to look at Lebanon and the world through a humanistic lens.

I thank many families, including the Ghaoui, Moghabghab, and Merhebi families, for helping me in various ways to conduct my research. I am grateful to the municipal council of the city of Hazmieh, especially the president of the council Jean Asmar, for their generous welcome and support. I thank my cousins, aunts, friends, and nieces whose unwavering support was essential for completing the study. My deep appreciation goes to Dr. Paul Rabil, Dr. Michel Deaibes, Joan and Jessica Tabet, Katia Ghaoui, and Rabih Ghosn. Special thanks go to several anonymous former and current Lebanese officials and activists who helped me broaden and sharpen my analysis on Lebanon-Turkey relations.

I deeply thank my mother, Antoinette, and siblings, William and Pauline, for their unbounded love and firm belief in me, which carries me in times of doubt. I am infinitely grateful and indebted to my wife, Patricia, for her tireless, selfless, and indomitable readiness to envelop and ballast our household with unconditional love. I am eternally grateful to her for giving me no less than miracles in our children Grace and Georges, who uplift my soul, tender my gaze, enrich my thought, and nurture my life. I am perpetually in her debt for having our home feed on the energy, compassion, tender love, and amazing smiles of Nick, Olivia, Georges, and Grace. They have shown me the beauty, sanctity, and fragility of life and the importance of love and creating a safe, nourishing, and peaceful environment for all children.

I am grateful to my wife and family, to whom this book is dedicated, and to the memory of my stepdaughter Olivia Stefanovic. Olivia showed me the beauty and vagaries of life. She demonstrated the unique courage in facing the challenges of life. I compared her to the wind, which seeps through your heart unnoticed, caresses your hair on a breezy summer day, ripples your placid feelings on a glowing sunset, and shoulders your anger on a rainy day. She encapsulated life and her untimely passing has left a deep wound on our family, a scar hardly possible to hide, especially for Patricia and her father, Randy. I mourn her loss, and I pray that her memory cultivates in her siblings and loved ones the courage to fight, according to their passion and talent, for a better life for all. She expressed her feelings through art and music, the very manifestation of our world's beauty and sound of wind that whistles her memory in awe and inspiration!

I thank you and love you all!

Boca Raton, Florida
January 2023

Synopsis and Methodology

PRÉCIS

No empire or regional power has helped mold the sociopolitical and religious landscape of a country as the Ottoman Empire and its heir, the Republic of Turkey, have helped shape Lebanon. Growing up in Lebanon, I have seen the inscriptions of many past civilizations chiseled on rocks or reflected in monumental structures. But nowhere have I seen the inscription of a civilization still fresh in the collective consciousness of Lebanon as that of the Ottoman Empire. Nevertheless, never have I seen contradictions displayed in open sight patronizing and deploring Turkey as reflected by the sight of thousands of people waving Turkish flags in Tripoli and the sight of *Sahat al-Shuhada'* (Martyr's Square) in Beirut commemorating the Lebanese sent to the gallows by Ottoman authorities during World War I. Since my childhood, I wondered about the impressions of love and hate, as well as the grandeur and misery, Turkish authorities bequeathed to Lebanon.[1] These perceptions, questions, and feelings formed the ideational foundation of this study.

The territories comprising the modern state of Lebanon were both cradles of civilizations and hotbeds of conflicts. From the littoral of Lebanon, the Phoenician seafarers exported the medium of global communication and knowledge: the alphabet. Yet their city-states, from which they exported their erudition and aptitudes, came under the rule of the various Egyptian, Assyrian, Babylonian, and Persian dynasties, whose mark on history was incomplete without conquering the historical land of the Canaanites. Then the Greeks, led by the Macedonian Alexander the Great, raced their unstoppable chariots through the doors behind which the Ahiram Sarcophagus lay. Only Tyre, the purple queen of Lebanon's coast, defied the conqueror of Persopolis. At last, after seven months of siege and land and sea attacks, Tyre succumbed to Alexander the Great in 332 BCE. The victory with which Alexander III ruined, burned, and depopulated Tyre inscribed on history books the valiant efforts of its citizens.

The Greeks built on the mercantilism and erudite of the Phoenicians and made their city-states the abode of earliest democracy in the Middle East. The Hellenized heirs of the Greeks, the Romans, extended citizenship rights granted by the Greeks to the residents of their city-states to the provinces of the Roman Empire. Beirutus (Beirut) emerged as the seat of the Roman school of law and Ba'albeck as the pedestal upon which the pantheon of Roman gods was worshipped. Eastern deities became interchangeably linked with Greek and Roman gods.

Significantly, Christianity was born in the domain of the Roman Empire. Initially persecuted by Roman authorities, Christianity gradually permeated the society of the Roman elite until Roman emperor Constantine (306–337) embraced Christianity and made it the religion of the state. Christianity swept the expanse of the Roman Empire. Nevertheless, Christological controversies and dogmatic splits and schisms undercut its uniformity and the single purpose of unity with which early church fathers propagated Christianity's universal mission. Christian disputes and conflicts played out in the Byzantium Empire, the eastern half of the Roman Empire following the sacking of Rome by the Visigoths in 410 CE. Various churches, some in unison and some in discord with Rome, scattered the Levantine landscape. Mount Lebanon emerged as both a citadel and refuge for Christians, spearheaded by the Maronites and then by the various Monophysite and Uniate churches. In the meantime, the cross-pollination of Semitic and Aramean cultures with Greco-Roman culture generated a synthetic culture at ease with tradition and the openness of Hellenism.

Then amidst the power struggle between the Persian and Byzantine Empires, a new religion was born: Islam, whose spiritual, military, political, and religious expression resonated in the vast expanse of the Middle East and North Africa. This new religion not only lay the basis for empires but also attracted adherents from Christianity and other established religions. The fate of the Levant, known then by the Arabs as ***Bilad al-Sham***, was sealed when Khalid bin al-Walid, bearing the Prophet's appellation of *Sayf Allah* (Sword of God), won the battle of Yarmuk, a tributary of the Jordan, in 636 CE. Lebanon's illustrious coastal towns fell one after the other. Christians and Jews saw the Arab conquerors as liberators who would free them from the taxing policies of the Byzantines. But their religious status under Muslim rule as "People of the Book," or recipients of divine revelations, transformed them into ***dhimmis*** (protected people of the covenant). As *dhimmis* they enjoyed the protection of Islam and exemption from military service, but they had to pay a land tax and a head tax (***jizya***). Whatever citizenship rights Christians and Jews enjoyed under the Greco-Roman culture were vanquished under Islam. Society split between victor and vanquished.

Bilad al-Sham was divided into *junds* (military districts); Lebanon belonged to the Damascus *jund.*[2] As Arabization and Islamization of the area slowly yet steadily proceeded, the Christians of Mount Lebanon remained steadfast in their faith. This citadel and refuge of the persecuted also became the abode of the Druzes, a schismatic faith of Islam. The Christians, the majority of whom were Maronites, lived in northern Mount Lebanon, while the Druzes settled southern Mount Lebanon. Arab rule of *Bilad al-Sham*, as represented by the fairly moderate Umayyads (661–750) and conservative Abbasids (750–1258), was disrupted by the Fatimids. Originating in North Africa, the Fatimid Dynasty (909–1171) came to rule *Bilad al-Sham*.

Based in Cairo, the schismatic Fatimid caliphate challenged Baghdad, the seat of the Abbasid caliphate. The founder of the Fatimid caliphate claimed descent from Prophet Muhammad's daughter Fatima and gave himself out as al-Mahdi, the divinely guided Imam who went into occultation and whose return, along with 'Issa (Jesus), the Shi'ites religiously await to restore justice to earth. It was under their rule that Shi'ism scattered across Lebanon, including in Mount Lebanon. The Fatimid advent also signaled the breakup of Muslim unity as a religion and a state, following which the Crusaders coursed their way into the Holy Land.

The Maronites descended from the fastness of their mountain to welcome the Crusaders at Lebanon's coastal town al-Batroun, from which they trekked their way to Jerusalem as guides and archers for the Crusaders, reaching the contested Holy City in June 1099. The Crusaders treated the Maronites well and granted them privileges not accorded even to other Christians. The Christian towns of northern Lebanon served as defensive ramparts for the Crusader's county of Tripoli. In fact, with the coming of the Crusaders, the Maronites began to look to the West for assistance. They had lived too long in the fastness of their mountain, defending and laboring against the disabilities imposed on them by the Umayyads, Abbasids, and Fatimids. Ties with the Holy See became closer and Latin influences and practices marked the Maronite Church and liturgy. The Latinization of the Maronite rite had begun. French king and crusader Louis IX (1226–1270) feted the Maronites as a French nation and they, in turn, came to see France as *la mére du Liban*.

But the onset of this relationship with the West generated an infamous time-honored political process by which Lebanon's selfish or magnanimous desire to look beyond its border for support or help conditioned the nation to be receptive to Western interest and ambition. The political dynamics of this process peaked during Ottoman rule over Lebanon and has continued ever since. Commenting on the Maronites' contacts and relationship with the Latins, Philip Hitti emphasized:

Of all the contacts established by the Latins with the peoples of the Near East, those with the Maronites proved to be the most fruitful, the most enduring. Disabilities, particularly those imposed by the Umayyad 'Umar, the 'Abbasid al-Mutawakkil and the Fatimid al-Hakim, under which Christian minorities—at best second-class citizens—lived had conditioned them for foreign influences and rendered them especially receptive to friendly approaches from Westerners.[3]

Nevertheless, early on in their rule, the Crusaders had a tenuous hold on power in the hinterlands of the littoral of Syria, Lebanon, and Israel-Palestine, where they fortified their presence in coastal towns. Targeted by irregular yet consecutive Muslim campaigns, the anti-crusader campaign of Saladin was the most consequential. Born in Tikrit in today's Iraq to Kurdish parents in 1138, Yusuf ibn Ayyub showed an early aptitude for theology and military arts. He rose in the ranks of the Fatimid dynasty to the position of vizier, whereupon he abolished the weak and unpopular Shi'a Fatimid Caliphate in 1171 and restored Sunnism to Cairo. The singleness of purpose and assiduity with which he fought the Crusaders sparked his reputation as *Salah al-Din* (the righteousness of the faith), known concisely as Saladin. He felled Acre, Beirut, Sidon, Nazareth, Caesarea, Nablus, Jaffa, and Ashqelon like dominoes, and dealt a severe and irrecoverable blow to the Crusaders by seizing Jerusalem in October 1187.

The downfall of the Christian kingdom had enormous religio-political ripple effects. On the level of East-West relations, the defeat of the Crusaders nurtured the notion in the West that winning Muslims and bringing schismatic Christians back into union with Rome as part of the Christian universal mission was better served by pursuing peaceful missionary activities. Slowly yet steadily, Christian missionaries (Carmelites, Franciscans, Dominicans, Capuchins, Jesuits, and Protestants) burgeoned in the Levant, especially in Lebanon. The cultural and religious activities of the missionaries had tremendous impact on Lebanon's society and its relationship with Ottoman authorities. No less significant, the defeat of both the Crusaders and the Fatimids paved the way for the slave generals and soldiers of the Abbasids and Saladin's Ayyubid dynasty to found the Mamluk dynasty (1250–1516) in Egypt and Syria.

Wearing the mantle of Sunni orthodox Islam, the Mamluks uprooted the last vestiges of crusader power in Antioch (1268), Tripoli (1289), and Acre (1291). Aware of Christian support of the Crusaders and the proliferation of Muslim heterodox communities in the Levant, the Mamluks waged punitive campaigns against them, reconfiguring in the process the sectarian demography of Lebanon. Shi'ites migrated to southern Lebanon and Beka', leaving behind Christian majority areas, including in Kisrwan and Jbeil. Druzes and Christians reinforced their concentration in southern and northern Mount

Lebanon respectively. And Sunnis gradually moved into the coastal cities of Tripoli, Beirut, Sidon, and Tyre, all of which hosted an amalgam of sects. Needless to say, under Mamluk rule, Lebanon's trade and culture suffered, although the Mamluks built institutions of higher learning (*madrasahs*) and mosques, especially in Tripoli; and Christian communication with Europe was disrupted. But Mamluks' policy of annihilating or assimilating schismatic sects remained unfulfilled.

The Mamluks divided *Bilad al-Sham* into six provinces and parceled Lebanon among three of them. The province of Tripoli included North Lebanon and the coastal region from Jbeil to Ladhiqiyah (in today's Syria). The province of Safad included southern Lebanon and Tyre. And the province of Damascus included the rest: Sidon, Beirut, Ba'albeck, and the Beka'. The Mamluks enforced the practice of *Iqta'* (feudalism), known also as *Iltizam*, granting a fief in the form of tax farming rights to a ranking member or family in society as a reward for loyalty, military service, and paying due taxes. *Iqta'* played a key role in inter- and intra-relations among Lebanon's sects and between the fief holders and Ottoman authorities—a role that had tremendous ramifications for modern Lebanon.

Mamluk rule was punctuated by natural disasters, unsound and at times predatory financial policies, and Mongol invasions.[4] In 1400–1401, the Mongol hordes, led by the Turkic-Mongol leader Tamerlane, known also as Timur, devastated Aleppo, overran Hama and Homs, despoiled Beirut and Sidon, and set Damascus ablaze. Thousands perished by the sword or the flames. Timur dealt the Mamluks a severe blow from which they could not fully recover, and therefore *Bilad al-Sham* plunged into an economic and political disarray. In the meantime, a new power was taking shape in Anatolia amid the declining power of the Byzantines and Mamluks and the rising power of the Safavid Persians.

Of Asiatic Turkic stock, the Ottomans trekked their way to Anatolia, following in the footsteps of their predecessors the Seljuqs. Bearing the eponymous name of their founder, Osman, the Ottomans, little by little, enlarged their principality in Anatolia at the expanse of the Byzantines. By seizing Constantinople in 1453, the Ottomans located themselves at the geopolitical intersection of southern Europe, western Asia, and the eastern Mediterranean. It seemed as if history and fate had preordained their rise to power. Adopting the mantle of Sunni Islam, they fought in the name of their faith and for spoils. By the early sixteenth century, the rise of the Persian Shi'a Safavid dynasty choked Sunnism in Persia and ideologically challenged Sunnism in Asia minor, even among the Turks. The Ottomans had no choice but to face off the Persians. In 1514, the two armies met on the battlefield of Chaldiran, where the Persian army was defeated. Then the Ottomans turned their sights toward north Syria, where a Mamluk army, under the pretext of mediating between the two antagonists, had advanced to help the Persians and wage an attack on the Ottomans from both their southern and eastern flanks. The Ottomans discerned the Mamluk's stratagem and, in August 1516, sent their formidable force, the Janissaries, to beat the Mamluk army on the plain of Marj Dabiq, north of Aleppo. From there, the Ottoman **sultan** marched toward Damascus and Lebanon's littoral, where his force was unopposed and even welcomed, and, thereafter, continued toward Cairo.

Although the Mamluks fought valiantly, they were no match to the Ottomans, who seized Cairo in 1517 and plundered it. Mamluk rule came to an end, and the Ottomans laid claim to the Caliphate, whose seat moved to Constantinople, and thus began the reign of the Ottomans for the next four centuries in *Bilad al-Sham*.

Ottoman rule over Lebanon inherited the richness of its history, sectarian diversity, and the intricacies of its feudalism and communalism. Paradoxically, this rule played a key role in shaping both the grandeur and misery of Lebanon, drawing its geography, planting the seeds of its nationalism, enriching and enervating its culture, and determining the modulation of European involvement in its affairs, all of which gave way to modern Lebanon, where the legacy of Ottoman rule still haunts the country's contemporaneous politics.

Ottoman rule of Lebanon, broadly speaking, can be divided into four periods, each of which left its indelible impressions on shaping modern Lebanon as a state and a nation: Fakhr al-Din II Emirate, Bashir Shihab II Emirate, the **Qa'im Maqamiyah** and the **Mutasarifiyah**, and the Great Famine of World War I.

The Ottomans, in principle, preserved the Mamluk administrative division of *Bilad al-Sham*, which was based on *iqta'* (feudalism). Ottoman authorities (Sultan, Sublime Porte, or **wali**) farmed out (*talzim*) fiefs to the highest bidder of tax collection and loyal servant of the Sublime Porte (central government of Ottoman Empire). The feudal lords (holders of *iqta,' **muqata'jis***), whose rank in society ranged from emir (commander, local prince, or ruler) to *muqaddam* (chieftain, facilitator, assistant) to sheikh (tribal chief or an elder venerable man), enjoyed hereditary rights and a degree of autonomy in running the affairs of their fiefs as long as they paid their due taxes to the Porte, provided armed men to Ottoman authorities in time of need, and maintained stability in their regions. But the Ottomans redrew the borders of the provinces and districts of the Empire and changed its nomenclature. The provinces were renamed *wilayat* (plural of **wilaya**) and were divided into **sanjaks** (districts). Their sizes depended upon the strength of their military and revenue prospects. A *wali* (governor), known also as *pasha*, ruled over each province. *Bilad al-Sham* was divided into three provinces: Damascus (*al-Sham*), Aleppo, and Tripoli. Lebanon was parceled between the provinces of Tripoli and Damascus. Beirut and Sidon were constituted as districts in the province of Damascus. But in 1660, the district of Sidon was reconstituted as a province.

The Ottomans also preserved the Arab division of society by codifying it into a **millet** system comprising the Muslim community and the lower rank *dhimmi* community, whose Christian and Jewish members continued to pay the *jizya* but had a measure of freedom in handling their religious rites and affairs. Broadly speaking, Lebanon did not pose an immediate threat to the Ottoman Empire, which paid more attention to Persia, Egypt, and the Balkans. Therefore, Ottoman rule was less direct in Lebanon and Ottoman authorities bequeathed to their Lebanese vassals a measure of autonomy in handling their domestic affairs and exempted them from offering military service to the Porte. Nevertheless, conflicts among feudal lords and within feudal families over power and tax farming rights (*iltizam*), which spilled over into Ottoman corridors of power, not only preoccupied the Porte but also caused rebellions against the Porte. Significantly, the more power a feudal lord acquired the more prone the lord was to shake off Ottoman authority. No less significant, desirous of independence, the people of Mount Lebanon occasionally rebelled against Ottoman authorities.

The onset of Ottoman rule consecrated the power of the Druze Ma'n over Mount Lebanon, whose charismatic leader, Fakhr al-Din, did not support the Mamluks in the battle of Marj Dabiq. In fact, impressed by his honorable personality, Sultan Selim conferred on him the title of "Sultan of the Mountain." The Ma'n's power peaked under Emir Fakhr al-Din II (1572–1635), the paramount leader of Mount Lebanon. Through connivance, bribes, alliances, and ruthless elimination of rivals, Fakhr al-Din II considerably expanded his realm beyond the borders of Mount Lebanon. He also established commercial and military ties with the Medicis of Tuscany, which put him at loggerheads with the Ottomans. Concerned about his power, anti-Ottoman ties with the Medicis, and desire for independence from Ottoman rule, the Porte sent a punitive expedition to put him in place. Getting wind of the Ottoman mission, he fled with his retinue to Tuscany, where he self-exiled for five years (1613–1618). The Lebanese Emir was taken by European advancements in the fields of banking, judicial system, arts, trade, and military.

Upon his return to Mount Lebanon in September 1618, he set about, on the one hand, reestablishing his control over Mount Lebanon, Tripoli, Beka', Sidon, Beirut, Safed, Latakia, and parts of Palestine and Syria, and, on the other hand, introducing economic and administrative reforms he had learned about in Europe. But his tremendous expansion, coupled with ties with the Tuscans, which nearly predestined his independence from the Ottoman Empire, mobilized Ottoman authorities to move forcefully against him from land and sea. Fakhr al-Din II's fate was sealed when the Tuscans failed to come to his aid. He surrendered and was taken in chains to what is now Istanbul, where he was executed, along with three of his sons, in April 1635.

Fakhr al-Din II's execution did not remove or reverse the achievements and changes he had brought about in his realm, which were built upon by future Lebanese leaders. He introduced sericulture in Mount Lebanon, which became the mainstay of its economy. He enhanced the power of Maronite feudal families, such as al-Khazin of Kisrwan, with whom he had a close personal relationship since his childhood. He encouraged Christian peasants, especially Maronites, to migrate to Druze-majority southern Lebanon to help in silk cultivation and agricultural development. Famed for their warrior-like culture, many Druzes shied away from agricultural occupations. This coincided with Druze feudal lords inviting Christians to settle in villages along the frontiers of their territory. This initiated the process by which the demography of southern Mount Lebanon had changed. Mixed Christian-Druze villages and regions transformed the landscape in which Druzes had been the majority.

He also initiated the process by which European involvement in Lebanon became a fixture in the country's politics. Similarly, he promoted trade with Europe and invited European merchants to settle in his emirate. He established Dayr al-Qamar as the Ma'ni capital, revived Sidon as a seat of power, and promoted Beirut as a hub for trade by enlarging its port. Most importantly, he built the foundational legacy of the symbiotic Maronite-Druze relationship in Mount Lebanon, which served as the precursor to the Republic of Lebanon. Lebanese, of all religious stripes, look back in awe to Fakhr al-Din II, who grandfathered Lebanon in communal coexistence.

The legacy of the Ma'ni Emirate was inherited by the Shihab Emirate (1697–1840). Initially, the vanquishing of Ma'ni Emirate under Fakhr al-Din II ushered in a period of instability in Mount Lebanon. Related to the Ma'ns whose princely lineage ended, the Shihabs, who had established their power in Wadi al-Taym, were chosen as the heirs of the Ma'n, thereby inheriting their fiefs. But during their early rule, the Muslim Shihabs, many of whom eventually converted to Maronitism, had faced family factional feuds, which were exploited by the *walis* of Sidon, Acre, and Damascus. Moreover, dormant feuds between the Qaysi and Yemeni tribes, which can be traced to the Arab conquest of *Bilad al-Sham*, played out in Mount Lebanon. Ultimately, the Qaysis, led by the Shihabs, defeated their Yemeni challengers, led by the 'Alam al-Din, in the battle of Ain Dara in 1711, following which Yemeni-affiliated families left for Hawran.

The power of the Shihab's Emirate peaked during the reign of Emir Bashir Shihab II (1788–1850). But his rise to power was characterized by intrigues, playing one feudal family against another, assassinating his rivals, and oppressing his opponents. The first Maronite to rule Mount Lebanon, Emir Bashir, following in the footsteps of his great predecessor Fakhr al-Din II, expanded his realm and tried to centralize his rule by lording his power over Christian and Druze feudal families. Having at first subdued the Christians in northern Mount Lebanon, he turned to the Druze feudal lords in southern Mount Lebanon. One feudal lord, Bashir Jumblatt, was too strong and connected to be overcome. Emir Bashir had the *wali* of Acre lure him there, where he was decapitated, after which Emir Bashir dispossessed Druze feudal lords of their fiefs. Druze lords and commoners never forgave Emir Bashir, who also drew closer to the Maronite Church.

Yet, like Fakhr al-Din II, he pursued an enlightened religious policy. He is famed for having a mosque and a chapel in his Bayt al-Din palace. He welcomed missionaries, including Pliny Fisk, the first American missionary to land in Beirut in 1823, and made his emirate a fertile ground for higher education. Foreign travelers marveled at the natural beauty and stability of his emirate. During his visit to Mount Lebanon in 1832, renowned statesman and author Alphonse de Lamartine venerated the magnificence of Mar Mitri hill in Beirut and Hammana valley as the most beautiful of God's creation to the human eye. He wrote:

> Une des perspectives les plus belles que les hommes aient jamais eu, la chance de peindre la création de Dieu est la vallée de Hammana. Peindre ou décrire ne peut exprimer qu'un détail de l'ensemble féérique doté par le Créateur au Liban.[5]

But stability in his realm was soon to be disrupted and communal coexistence threatened for the first time in the history of Mount Lebanon by sectarianism. Muhammad Ali, the *wali* of Egypt, who had helped the Porte in the campaigns against the fundamentalist Wahhabis and the secessionist Greeks, expected Syria as a compensation for his military service. Disappointed by the Porte, Muhammad Ali decided to take over Syria by force. In 1831, he dispatched a military force commanded by his son Ibrahim Pasha to Syria. Ibrahim pasha called on Emir Bashir for help, who had a close relationship with his father. Reluctant at first, Emir Bashir eventually threw his support behind Ibrahim's campaign. The emir's forces helped the Egyptian army capture Lebanon's coastal cities before seizing Damascus. Soon, *Bilad al-Sham* fell to Egyptian rule, and Egyptian forces posed a threat to Istanbul. Recognizing the danger to their empire, Ottoman authorities prepared a counteroffensive with the support of Great Britain, which opposed Muhammad Ali on account of his close relationship with the French.

In the meantime, Ibrahim Pasha pursued a reformist agenda in Greater Syria in line with that applied in Egypt. He fought corruption, reorganized administrative structures and procedures, encouraged industry and trade, and upended the Ottomans' two-tier millet system by treating Christians and

Muslims equally. Druze feudal lords contested his rule. In 1838, a Druze rebellion began in Hawran and soon spread to the Beka' and Wadi al-Taym, where the Druzes of Mount Lebanon joined the revolt. In response, Ibrahim Pasha asked Emir Bashir to help him subdue the rebellion and distributed arms to the Christians. Emir Bashir sent a Christian armed force of four thousand, led by his son Khalil, to help Ibrahim clamp down on the rebellion. This marked the first time ever in the history of Mount Lebanon that Christians and Druzes fought on a sectarian basis, thereby planting the seeds of sectarianism that unsettled communal coexistence in Lebanon.

In order to offset his rising expenses and stabilize Mount Lebanon, Ibrahim Pasha raised taxes, monopolized silk trade, and tried to secure disarmament and military conscription, a practice rarely, if ever, employed in Mount Lebanon. This outraged all residents of his domain across the whole sectarian spectrum. A cross-sectarian insurgency erupted against him, which coincided with a naval Anglo-Austrian-Ottoman campaign attacking Beirut. In October 1840, Emir Bashir surrendered to the British, and Egyptian rule ended in Greater Syria.

This period had a lasting effect on the politics of Lebanon. Mount Lebanon became a theater for European intervention in communal affairs, Beirut emerged as the preeminent city in Lebanon, European officials, merchants, and professionals settled in Beirut, and whatever solidarity Maronites and Druzes had during their insurgency vanished with the collapse of the Shihab Emirate (1842). The murder of Jumblatt and Christian participation in the Egyptian campaign to subdue the Druze rebellion had been hardly possible to remove from the Druze collective consciousness.

In fact, the end of Bashir's rule ushered in a period of dreadful sectarianism, poignant European intervention, and unfeasible Ottoman attempts to arrest the decomposition of the Empire, all of which created a crucible for civil strife. Whereas in the past Mount Lebanon's intermittent warfare was feudal and partisan, the warfare post-1840 had become religious and denominational. A local conflict in Dayr al-Qamar set off a Christian-Druze conflagration, which spread like wildfire to the Chouf and al-Gharb areas. Most Druze feudal families, including the Jumblatts, Imads, and Nakads, joined the fight, reportedly with Turkish connivance, against Christians in mixed Christian-Druze towns. Dayr al-Qamar was set on fire in October 1841. European powers (France, Great Britain, and Russia) pressed the Porte to end the troubles and find a solution to pacify the antagonists.

The Porte came up with a plan to divide Mount Lebanon into two political and administrative districts: a northern district governed by a Christian *qa'im maqam* (sub-governor) and a southern district governed by a Druze *qa'im maqam*. Both *qa'im maqams* would answer to the *wali* of Sidon. Instead of alleviating sectarianism, the new arrangement intensified it. Both Maronites and Druzes contested the plan. Both districts had a mixed population of Druzes and Maronites, especially in al-Matn, Chouf, and al-Gharb. Whereas the Maronites sought to have jurisdiction over the Christians in the southern district, the Druzes sought their traditional right to rule over the whole mountain. More specifically, the *qa'im maqamiyah* whittled away at the power of the feudal lords, who instigated the commoners to take justice into their own hands. A new conflagration erupted in 1845.

Ottoman authorities tried to pacify Mount Lebanon, including weakening further the authority of feudal chiefs. Nevertheless, tension continued to rise until it exploded into a horrifying massacre in 1860. It's noteworthy that a letter from the people of Zahle to the French consul, Eugène Poujade, in 1843 underscored the antagonistic role played by the feudal lords, providing a bitter foretaste of what could happen on account of sectarianism. An excerpt of the letter read that "peace may well be made between the Druze peasants and the Christians but not with their leaders who will always want to have prerogatives over our brothers, which is the most impossible thing."[6]

The massacres of 1860, which are still invoked by some sectarian leaders, exposed the deep economic, social, political, and demographic grievances in Mount Lebanon, which were expressed in the language of violent sectarianism that Mount Lebanon and Damascus had never seen before. Supported by Turkish officials and employing stealthy stratagems, the Druzes, presenting a united front combining feudal lords and commoners, massacred thousands of Christians in mixed and isolated Christian-majority towns, regardless of gender or age. Kisrwan and North Lebanon, strongholds of Maronitism, were barely affected. Maronites, who had been going through a social revolution casting off the shackles of feudalism, were disunited. The Maronite Church, which supported the commoners and played a role in mobilizing Christians against Druzes, was incapable of mustering the military leadership to defend its parishioners. However, true Maronites suffered a military defeat despite their numerical strength; nevertheless, they scored a political victory thanks to European intervention.

Upon hearing about the massacres, which spread to Damascus, European powers decided to intervene militarily. France spearheaded them by sending a force to Beirut. The Porte, taken aback by the scope and breadth of the massacres, sent foreign minister Fouad Pasha with a military contingent to restore order, punish the guilty, and reorganize with the coordination of European powers the administration of Mount Lebanon. Swift Ottoman intervention was also influenced by its disposition toward the major reforms (*tanzimats*) that the Empire had been undertaking to modernize the empire and secure its territorial integrity against internal nationalist movements and European intervention. The Porte ended feudalism. Following some compromises, the leading European powers (France, Great Britain, Prussia, and Russia) signed with the Porte a new organic statute for Lebanon. The statute (*Règlement organique of June 9, 1861*) reconstituted Mount Lebanon as an autonomous region (***mutasarifiyah***) within the Ottoman Empire, headed by a non-Arab Ottoman Christian governor (*mutasarif*) vested with wide-ranging executive powers. An administrative council, including Mount Lebanon major sects, was created to counsel the governor, but had the right of veto on taxes and Ottoman military intervention in the *mutasarifiyah*. This political system established the foundation of Lebanon's confessional system. But this system also initiated the transition of feudalism based on *iltizam* to political sectarianism based in Lebanon's confessional system.

Peace was restored to Mount Lebanon, which became one of the most stable and prosperous regions of the Ottoman Empire until the dawning of World War I. In the meantime, Istanbul was facing nationalist secessionist movements, and its political elites, in the spirit of tanzimats (reforms), advocated Ottomanism, which underscored patriotism and political and social cohesion among the different ethnic and religious communities. Nevertheless, as internal and external setbacks continued to undermine the empire, a group of political reformists, the Young Turks, rebelled against the Sultan in 1908. Their initial political banner of "Liberty, Equality, and Fraternity" transformed under the leadership of an ultra-nationalist triumvirate into a political manifesto advocating centralization and Turkification of the empire and abandonment of reform, all in the interest of preventing the dissolution of the empire and preserving their powers.

Not yet confident politically, and economically and militarily weak, the new government decided to enter the Great War on the side of the Triple Alliance. The Middle East and the Balkans constituted the Ottoman Empire's theater of war. The triumvirate sent one of its own, Jamal Pasha, to take command of the Fourth Turkish army, headquartered in Damascus, to protect the eastern and southern flanks of Istanbul and seize Egypt's Suez Canal in order to disrupt British communications and troop movements. Jamal Pasha reduced the *mutasrifiyah* to ink on paper, abrogated the Capitulations, and established a military tribunal in Aley vested with full jurisdiction over Mount Lebanon and Beirut.[7]

Fearing Christian collaboration with the French and an allied landing in Beirut, Jamal Pasha pursued a harsh policy in Mount Lebanon commensurate with his moniker *al-Saffah* (the butcher). This policy became more oppressive by the day the moment Jamal Pasha's Egyptian campaign failed and Christian, especially Maronite, collaboration with the French operationalized. In response to his fears of an impending Allied landing along Lebanon's shore in collaboration with the Christians, and to the Allied Powers' blockade of the Palestine-Lebanon-Syria littoral, Jamal Pasha reinforced a blockade of

Mount Lebanon using starvation as a policy of repression. This policy went hand in hand with Jamal Pasha's oppressive measures. He detained and/or executed imaginary or real anti-Ottoman activists and employed a policy of collective punishment known dreadfully as Safar Barlik, which translated into forced conscription of Lebanese and their deportation to Anatolia to serve as forced labor.

In the meantime, the invasion of the locusts of Mount Lebanon and its attendant destruction of Mount Lebanon's sericulture, the spread of epidemics, the disruption of remittances from abroad, and the influx of Armenians into Lebanon following Ottoman's "Armenocidal" policy only worsened Jamal Pasha's policy of starvation, which developed into a deadly mass starvation. Approximately one-third of Mount Lebanon and Beirut's population perished. Having said that, designating Jamal Pasha's policy as genocidal becomes controversial when taking into account the Allied Powers' blockade of the littoral of Greater Syria and British resistance to partake in American relief efforts to help the inhabitants of Lebanon. Nevertheless, the mass starvation of Mount Lebanon, known as the Great Famine (1915–1918), and Safar Barlik, have become etched in the collective consciousness of the Lebanese, especially the Maronites and the Armenians.

Paradoxically, notwithstanding the fact that the Great Famine, in contrast to other mass killings, had caused an unparalleled number of casualties relative to population density, neither Lebanese authorities nor any religious establishment has erected a public landmark to commemorate Lebanon's most dreadful tragedy. Moreover, many official and/or religious leaders have refrained from taking up the subject publicly for fear of communal instability.

The landing of French troops in Lebanon in October 1918 and subsequent defeat of the Ottoman Empire in World War I at the hands of the Allied Powers, with support from the Arab nationalist forces of Sharif Hussein of Mecca, relieved Lebanon of the Ottoman yoke. And out of the ashes of the Ottoman Empire the modern countries of the Middle East were created in line with Great Britain and France's division of the region into spheres of influence. France helped create Greater Lebanon, whose borders roughly lined up with the Ma'n and Shehab Emirates. But the Maronite majority in Mount Lebanon dwindled to a bare plurality in Greater Lebanon. By having the mandate over Lebanon, France modeled the establishment of the country's confessional system on the *mutasarifiyah's* in order to provide representation for all sects, albeit favoring the Maronites. But the creation of independent Lebanon fostered neither a strong national identity nor a strong state, a condition that invited foreign intervention. Significantly, political sectarianism, represented by a class of sectarian political elite, more or less preserved the sociopolitical and sectarian problems that plagued Lebanon under Ottoman rule. No less significant, the political elite increased their power at the expense of that of the state.

Since Lebanon's independence in 1943, Lebanon-Turkish relations went through several phases, each of which was affected by the Cold War, Lebanon's civil war, Syria's civil war, complex Turkish relationships with Iran and Saudi Arabia, and Turkish neo-Ottomanism's approach (see below) to the Middle East. However, Turkish foreign policy, despite ideological inconsistencies in Turkish neo-Ottomanism and geopolitical variations in the Middle East and eastern Mediterranean, remained consistent in its measured (balanced) and modulated approach toward Beirut.

Notwithstanding the fact that Turkey considers Lebanon as its hinterland, Turkish national security interests and threats determined the broad outlines of Ankara's foreign policy toward Lebanon, which has been not inconsistent with the overall Ottoman policy toward Mount Lebanon. In turn, Lebanon as a nation and a state, despite some deep communal apprehensions and grievances with Turkey, has been receptive to the soft power approach of Ankara's foreign policy toward Beirut. In fact, Lebanon, shaken by a momentous economic and political crisis, has been seeking Turkish help.

During the Cold War, Lebanon had to deal not only with the Eastern-Western divide but also with what Malcolm H. Kerr illustriously described as the Arab Cold War. The rise of Nasserism shook the tenuous confessional and political balance Lebanon relied upon to secure social and communal stability. President Camille Chamoun internalized the enormous challenge Egyptian president Jamal abd al-Nasser's version of Arab nationalism posed to Lebanon. He tried to no avail to support the West without alienating Nasser and his votaries in Lebanon. His approach to the Baghdad pact (1955), Suez Crisis (1956), and Eisenhower Doctrine (1957) shaped Lebanon's relationship with Turkey. Seen through his lens, Turkey was an important regional country pragmatically needed to stem the tide of Nasserism and its attendant domestic and regional consequences for Lebanon.

The next phase in Lebanon-Turkey relations was influenced by the Arab-Israeli conflict, Lebanon's civil war (1975–1990), and the triangular Lebanon-Syria-Turkey relationship. This phase was replete with layers of domestic, regional, and international conflicts and complexities. The conflicted Syria-Turkey relationship spilled over into Lebanon at a time when the country was torn apart by a bloody civil war caused no less by systemic confessional grievances and concerns than by the Arab-Israeli conflict. Turkey, unlike Arab countries and Israel, avoided being involved in the civil war. But Turkey became concerned about Syria supporting anti-Turkish Kurdish and Armenian movements in Lebanon as instruments of pressure against Ankara. Once Ankara compellingly pacified its relationship with Damascus,

Lebanon-Turkey relations improved but remained officiated through diplomatic channels distant from warm popular support.

The Justice and Development party's assumption of power in Turkey ushered in a new phase in Ankara's foreign policy approach toward the Middle East in general and Lebanon in particular. The architect of this new foreign policy orientation was Ahmet Davutoglu, an academic who served as Turkey's minister of foreign affairs (2011–2014) and prime minister (2014–2016). Davutoglu's Strategic Depth Doctrine is an invigorated version of neo-Ottomanism, which can be traced to Turgut Özal, who served as prime minister (1983–1989) and president (1989–1993) of Turkey. Formulated against the background of the collapse of the Soviet Union, Davutoglu's doctrine grounded Turkish foreign policy in Ottoman past and heritage in the Middle East and Turkey's geostrategic location at the intersection of Asia, Europe, and the eastern Mediterranean. He defined Turkey's new foreign policy in large measure on the principle of "zero problems" with neighbors, with a focus on employing soft power.[8]

The ideological background against which Davutoglu's doctrine emerged was related to his reservations about Francis Fukuyama's *End of History* and Samuel P. Huntington's *The Clash of Civilizations*. Davutoglu perceived their international outlook as virtually perpetuating Western hegemony and exculpation from international and/or civilizational conflicts, thereby continuing the pattern of denying an international role for major non-Western countries with rich history and heritage, such as Turkey. He emphasized:

> These two contradicting approaches related to the role of civilisations in political affairs—the one Fukuyama's, which in identifying western civilisation with the fate of the human race or human history, overemphasises the role of this civilisation, the other Huntington's, which absolves western civilisation from generating conflicts and crises—are actually parts of the same picture. Huntington completes the picture drawn by Fukuyama by providing the hegemonic powers with a theoretical justification for the overall political and military strategies required to control and reshape the international system: western values and political structures have an intrinsic and irresistible universality (Fukuyama), and it is other civilisations which are responsible for the political crises and clashes (Huntington). Huntington's "the West versus the rest" polarisation is the political reflection of this picture. "The rest," it is presumed, will always need the West's guidance to reach the end of history and overcome the disorder due to geo-cultural clashes.[9]

At the heart of Davutoglu's doctrine is the transformation of Turkey, on the basis of its optimal geography and historical heritage, into a country that "should make its role of a peripheral country part of its past, and appropriate a new position: one of providing security and stability not only for itself, but also for its neighboring regions. Turkey should guarantee its own security and stability by taking on a more active, constructive role to provide order, stability and security in its environs."[10] In this respect, Davutoglu's doctrine advocated a "zero problem" foreign policy with its neighbors relying on the diplomatic and economic levers of soft power.

As a result of Turkey's new orientation, Ankara pursued a foreign policy toward Lebanon grounded in soft power, supporting Lebanon on the popular and state levels. Significantly, Turkey considerably supported the Sunni community in general and the Turkish communities in particular in Tripoli, Akkar, and northern Lebanon, as well as the dispossessed, and the Islamists. It also revived historic and cultural ties with Lebanon, while at the same time enhancing Turkish national identity among the Turkmen and fostering higher education among Sunnis in Turkish institutions.

The withdrawal of Syrian forces from Lebanon in 2005 led to deepened Turkish relations with Lebanon, reflected on the one hand by the exponential growth of pro-Turkish organizations and groups and on the other by Turkey channeling its increased support of Lebanon through state and state-affiliated civil, religious, humanitarian, and cultural institutions. The visit of Davutoglu and President Recep Tayyip Erdogan to Lebanon in 2009 and 2010, respectively, cemented Ankara's soft power approach to Lebanon at a time when Saudi Arabia had begun its political retreat from Beirut.

Eventually, the eruption of Arab uprisings and **Hezbollah**'s military involvement in the Syrian civil war on the side of the Asad regime damaged the overall Turkish relationship with Lebanon's Shi'a community. Moreover, tension intensified between the Sunni community, especially the Islamists, which supported the Syrian opposition and Turkish military involvement in Syria, and the Shi'a community, led by Hezbollah, which supported the Syrian regime. This devolved into a rhetorical war between Turkey and Hezbollah. Nevertheless, although Turkey has been accused by some Lebanese officials of funding and arming militant cells in Tripoli, this battle of words has not translated into a direct or proxy war between Turkey and its supporters, on one side, and Hezbollah and its supporters on the other. This also has not affected Turkey's humanitarian aid to Lebanon, which increased in the aftermath of the port explosion in Beirut. In fact, Turkey has been at the forefront of countries assisting Lebanon.

Notwithstanding the fact that President Erdogan has brought to the fore the inconsistency of neo-Ottomanism by becoming involved in the Syrian, Iraqi, Libyan, Cypriot, eastern Mediterranean, and **GCC**-Qatar disputes and conflicts, and thus negating the "zero problem" tenet of neo-Ottomanism, Turkey's foreign policy approach toward Lebanon has remained balanced. Turkey has not used Lebanon as a lever in its foreign policy vis-à-vis its rivals, friends, or foes. In this respect, there is, broadly speaking, a Turkish foreign policy continuum going back to Ottoman rule over Lebanon, with the noted exceptions of emirs Fakhr al-Din II and Bashir Shihab II's rule over Lebanon, whereby Mount Lebanon or Beirut, in contrast to Egypt and Persia (and the Balkans), have not posed a direct threat to Istanbul or Ankara. This is not to say that Turkey may not use its influence in Lebanon in support of its foreign policy. This remains to be seen. To be sure, however, although its influence has not extended to the state, Ankara today has legions of supporters ready to take to the streets to defend Turkey and its reputation.

THEORETICAL ANALYSIS AND TERM DESCRIPTION

The methodological approach to the study is qualitative, based on detecting and examining patterns and shifts in Lebanon-Turkey relations within the context of regional and international politics from Ottoman rule to Turkey's AKP-led (Justice and Development Party) governments. Based on historical descriptive and prescriptive analyses, the examination of these patterns and shifts chronicles the major developments and turning points in this relationship more or less through Lebanon's lens. In this respect, the study attempts to fill an academic gap because, although the history of Lebanon and Turkish foreign policy have been the focus of a number of studies, no contemporary study, to my knowledge, has examined Lebanon-Turkey relations since Ottoman rule of Lebanon.[11] As such, our understanding of this historic and contemporaneous relationship, which helped shape modern Lebanon, is deficient.

Behind this comprehensive account of Lebanon-Turkey relations, grounded in layers of cultural, political, demographic, economic, and sectarian complexities and changes across centuries, is an attempt not only to analyze the developments and dynamics that have helped shape modern Lebanon and its confessional system and politics, but also to underscore the misconceptions and lessons learned from this long-term relationship so that Lebanese can find better answers and solutions to their chronic dysfunctional political system. No less significant, locating Lebanon-Turkey relations along a historical continuum provides both Lebanese and Turks the long view to determine their future and the awareness with which to heal the collective pain of episodic communal violence and the trauma of the Great Famine (1915–1918). In this respect, the study, by examining Ottoman policy toward Lebanon within the context of the Great War, sheds light on a momentous tragedy, considered by many Lebanese as genocide by starvation, rarely studied or spoken of even though it claimed the lives of one-third of the population of Mount Lebanon and Beirut.

The corollary of the study demonstrates that Lebanon has constituted a microcosm of the Middle East, which served as a political theater for testing the methodology by which both Ottoman authorities ruled Lebanon and Turkish authorities pursued their neo-Ottomanism policy toward Lebanon. In this respect, barring certain periods of upheaval, a serrated linear trajectory of consistency has marked the Lebanon-Turkey relationship. No less significant, the study sheds light on both the scope and breadth of Turkish involvement in Lebanon and the channels through which Ankara exercises its influence in the country.

The study also provides a unique text to (a) help Lebanese undertake a collective self-critical analysis of their state and nation to address the country's dysfunctional confessional system; (b) assist initiating a Lebanese-Turkish truth and reconciliation process to surmount the trauma of the Great Famine; (c) locate Lebanon-Turkey relations within the framework of regional politics in relation to the fast-paced developments sweeping the region; (d) weigh in Turkish involvement in Lebanon on the state and communal levels in juxtaposition with foreign influence in Beirut; and (e) proffer for both nations the long view to better their relations on the popular and state levels.

Although the term *neo-Ottomanism* has been the focus of controversies and misconceptions ranging from perceptions of anti-Westernism and anti-Americanism to Islamist imperial designs, the study employs a working definition of neo-Ottomanism more specific to Davutoglu's Strategic Depth doctrine as an invigorated form of Özal's Turkey-centric neo-Ottomanism.[12] In this sense, neo-Ottomanism marked a dramatic shift from the traditional Kemalist ideology of westward-looking Turkish foreign policy, which began under Turgut Özal, and subsequently took shape under Davutoglu against the background of the collapse of the Soviet Union and the emergence of Western ideological outlooks of a new post-Soviet world order (see above). Central to Davutoglu's doctrine is Turkey's historical and geographical depth, whereby Turkey, the heir of Ottoman historical legacy, has been at the epicenter of historical events. He emphasizes:

> Geographical depth is a part of historical depth. For instance, Turkey is not just any old Mediterranean country. One important characteristic that distinguishes Turkey from say Romania or Greece is that Turkey is at the same time a Middle Eastern and a Caucasian country. Unlike Germany, Turkey is as much a European country as it is an Asian country. Indeed, Turkey is as much a Black Sea country as it is a Mediterranean one. This geographical depth places Turkey right at the centre of many geopolitical influences.[13]

Being at the epicenter of historical events, Davutoglu advocates a new influential role for Turkey predicated on reconciling its historical and geographical depth with "zero problem" with its neighbors. He notes:

> In terms of its area of influence, Turkey is a Middle Eastern, Balkan, Caucasian, Central Asian, Caspian, Mediterranean, Gulf, and Black Sea country. Given this picture, Turkey should make its role of a peripheral country part of its past, and appropriate a new position: one of providing security and stability not only for itself, but also for its neighboring regions. Turkey should guarantee its own security and stability by taking on a more active, constructive role to provide order, stability and security in its environs.[14]

However, employing Davutoglu's definition does not mean that the doctrine is free from inconsistencies relative to "zero problem" with neighbors. The Turkish foreign ministry expounded on this matter:

> Turkey wants to eliminate all the problems from her relations with neighbors or at least to minimize them as much as possible. While resolutely pursuing this policy, Turkey never puts realism aside and does not forget that "zero problems" approach represents an objective and an ideal. As a matter of fact, it is not quite possible to envisage that all problems in our region which have deep-rooted history can be solved in a short period of time.[15]

In this respect, Erdogan's disputes or conflicts with his neighbors do not negate the study's definition of neo-Ottomanism. Rather, they underscore neo-Ottomanism's inconsistency as an ordinary phenomenon in foreign relations. Moreover, the study's definition of neo-Ottomanism dovetails neatly with the AKP and Erdogan's promotion of Turkish nationalism, democracy, and Islamism. In fact, they are integral to neo-Ottomanism as demonstrated in Turkish relations with Lebanon (and other countries).[16]

It's noteworthy that neo-Ottomanism as employed in this study should not be confused with Ottomanism. Ottomanism, as a concept, emerged during the period of tanzimats (reforms, 1839–1876). It promoted equality among the multiethnic and multireligious communities of the Ottoman Empire in order to develop social cohesion to face the challenge of European nationalist ideas and growing Western involvement in the Ottoman Empire.

Similarly, the study's employment of the term "soft power" should not be only associated with intangible resources. The study employs a holistic definition of "soft power" in line with that of Joseph S. Nye Jr., who coined the term:

> Co-optive power [soft power] is the ability of a country to structure a situation so that other countries develop preferences or define their interests in ways

consistent with its own. This power tends to arise from such resources as cultural and ideological attraction as well as rules and institutions of international regimes.[17]

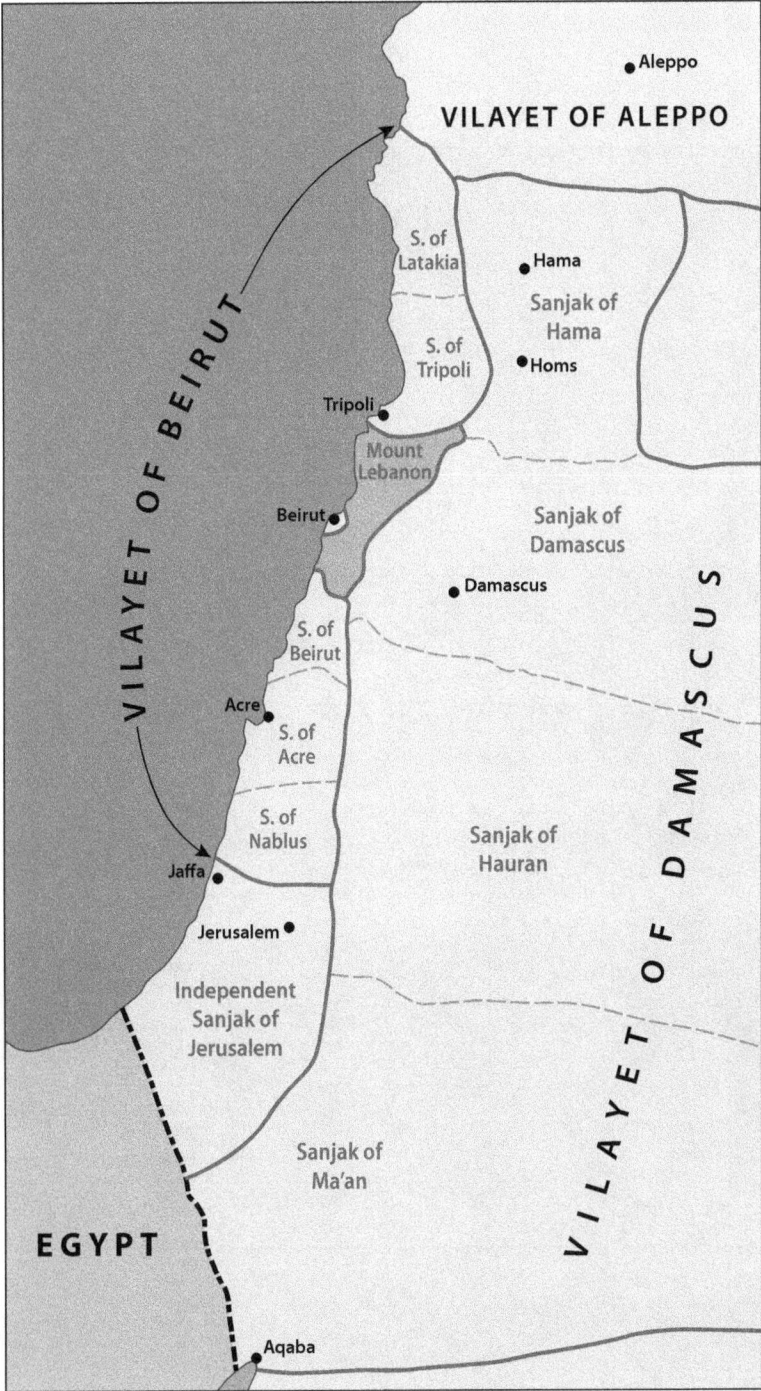

Aleppo

VILAYET OF ALEPPO

S. of
Latakia

Hama

Sanjak of
Hama

S. of
Tripoli

Homs

Tripoli

Mount
Lebanon

Sanjak of
Damascus

Beirut

Damascus

S. of
Beirut

Acre

S. of
Acre

S. of
Nablus

Jaffa

Sanjak of
Hauran

Jerusalem

Independent
Sanjak of
Jerusalem

Sanjak of
Ma'an

EGYPT

Aqaba

VILAYET OF BEIRUT

VILAYET OF DAMASCUS

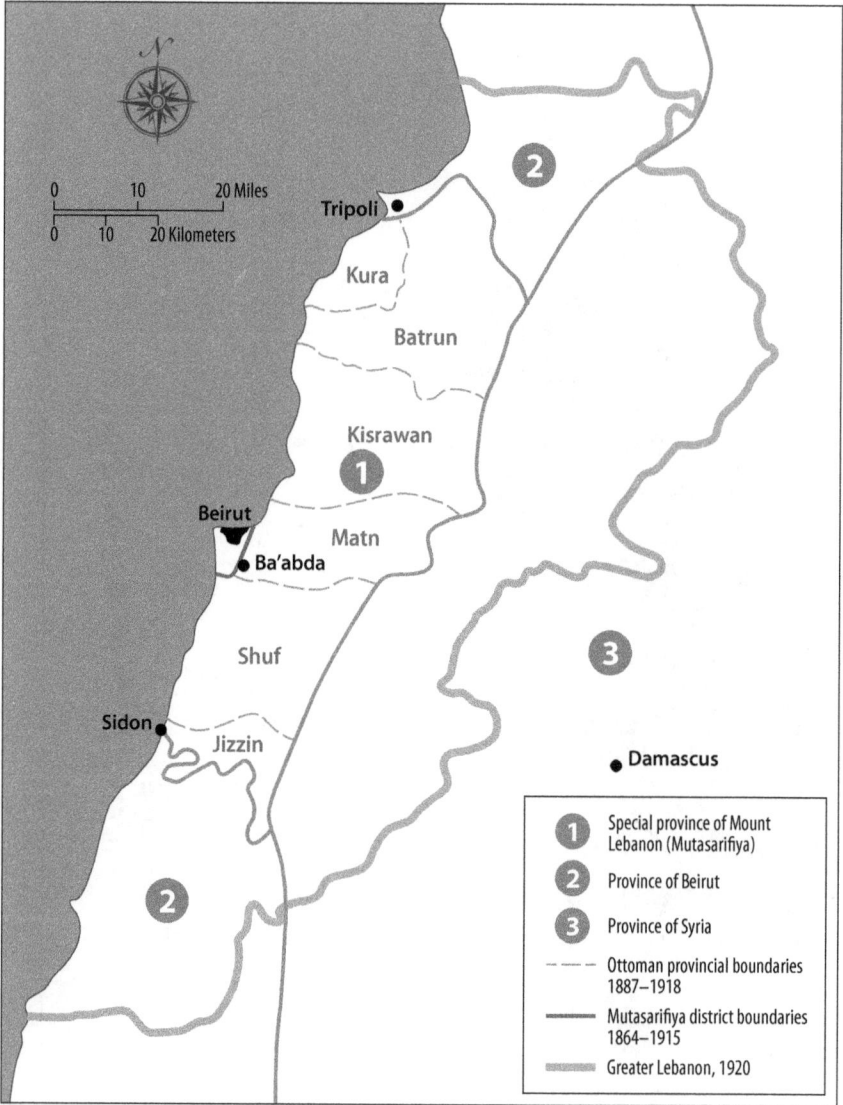

1	Special province of Mount Lebanon (Mutasarifiya)
2	Province of Beirut
3	Province of Syria
- - - - -	Ottoman provincial boundaries 1887–1918
————	Mutasarifiya district boundaries 1864–1915
▩▩▩▩	Greater Lebanon, 1920

Tripoli

Kura

Batrun

Kisrawan

1

Beirut

Matn

Ba'abda

Shuf

Sidon

Jizzin

2

2

3

Damascus

0   10   20 Miles
0   10   20 Kilometers

Chapter 1

Lebanon in History

CIVILIZATIONS, RELIGIONS, AND PEOPLES

The territories comprising Lebanon have been integral to both cradles of civilizations and hotbeds of conflicts. A Semitic people, the Canaanites, occupied the littoral of Lebanon, out of which emerged the Phoenician civilization that was held together by a string of independent Phoenician city-states from the north to the south of the country. As city-states, Tripolis (Tripoli), Byblos (Jbeil), Beirutus (Beirut), Sidon, Tyre, and Ba'albeck clustered in their glittering achievements but were weakened by their political disunity.[1] These cities exploited their hinterland for material and looked overseas for commercial opportunities. Phoenicians invented the alphabet and founded colonies in the Mediterranean, most famous of which were Carthage and Cadiz in today's Tunisia and Spain respectively.

Disunited and militarily weak, these city-states directly or indirectly succumbed to the power of Egyptian, Hittite, Assyrian, Babylonian, and Persian dynasties (1550–332 BCE). Nevertheless, it was during this period that these city-states flourished through maritime trade until their conquest by Alexander the Great in 332 BCE. Following a siege of seven months, Tyre was destroyed and thousands of its residents were either killed or sold into slavery. Following the death of Alexander the Great, historic Lebanon was incorporated in the Seleucid Empire (312–63 BCE), founded by Alexander's General Seleucus.

Before long, these city-states, under Greek tutelage, reemerged as cosmopolitan hubs enjoying within their walls Hellenistic culture and citizenship rights. Tyre and Sidon regained their status as leading port cities exporting timber, glassware, and textile colored with Phoenician purple dye. Significantly, Hellenism struck root in Lebanon's city-states. Greek philosophy, science, and literature were cultivated. But this did not mean that the

Phoenicians of Lebanon had lost their Semitic character. Hellenism gradually but easily blended with Phoenician Semitism, resulting in a Greco-Semitic cultural synthesis. Philip K. Hitti judiciously observed that the Hellenistic "cultural penetration was by no means a one-way process. The Hellenes were Orientalized, as the Orientals were Hellenized."[2] Even Hellenistic and Semitic deities became interchangeably worshipped and/or viewed. Baal became Zeus and mythical stories of Tammuz and Ashtart came to be associated with Adonis and Aphrodite.

Greek rule over Phoenicia gave way to the Hellenized Romans. In 64–63 BCE, Roman general Pompey incorporated Phoenicia and Judea in his newly established Provincia Syria. Following years of disturbances in the region, Lebanon became an integral part of the *Pax Romana* established by the Roman Empire. In fact, Roman rule and the advent of Christianity profoundly changed Lebanon's character.

The Phoenician Canaanite Semitic language became extinct as Aramaic completed its takeover of the native tongue. Nevertheless, Latin did not become the *lingua franca* during Roman rule because it was reserved to Roman officials and troops. Greek continued to prevail as the language of literature and business, continuing the trend of deepening cultural Hellenism. Roman administrative rule accorded some form of autonomy to the leading city-states of Tyre, Sidon, Tripolis, and subsequently Beirutus and Ba'albeck to run their own affairs, albeit without a role in the political matters of the Empire. Beirutus and Ba'albeck (Heliopolis) emerged as great cultural centers for the Roman Empire. Beirutus emerged as a foremost educational city during Roman rule, distinguishing itself as the eastern seat of Roman school of law. Ba'albeck, which the Greeks called Heliopolis or the city of the sun, developed into an illustrious religious city, showcasing in its acropolis the majestic temples of Jupiter and Bacchus. Conversely, Roman rule, stability, and reliable infrastructural transportation brought prosperity and population growth to the city-states, which spilled over into their hinterland and Mount Lebanon.

Significantly, Christianity was introduced to Lebanon in the first century (AD). In fact, the fame of Christ had reached Tyre and Sidon before the beginning of the apostolic message.[3] Tyre was the first seat of Christian community and church, followed by its neighbor to the north, Sidon. These seats, which evolved to become episcopal seats, were eventually destroyed by Emperor Diocletian and his colleague Maximian in the empire. Diocletian's and then Maximian's edicts not only called for the demolition of churches but also for Christians to choose between sacrifice to the gods of the empire or death.[4] Lebanon's Christians suffered from this "Great Persecution" that lasted ten years (303 CE–313 CE). Christianity, unlike other religions and cults, conflicted with Rome's conceptual political outlook. Although Rome was open to religions and cults, even adopting Hellenistic/Eastern deities, it frowned upon the Christian message of exclusive loyalty to one God. Early church fathers, even when faced with persecution, refused to sacrifice to Rome's pantheon of gods or to the emperor, whose actions to preserve peace according to Roman tradition were sanctioned by the gods.[5]

Nevertheless, despite on-and-off persecution of Christians, Christianity expanded throughout the empire, including permeating its upper class by the second century. The conversion of Emperor Constantine (272–337 CE) to Christianity marked a major turning point in the history of the church, Middle East, and Europe. Not only did persecution end and Christianity spread across the Empire; the Church became involved in political decisions. However, Christological controversies over the nature of Christ split the Middle Eastern Church and, by extension, the emerging Christian communities in Lebanon.

Once the Council of Nicea (325 CE) determined that Christ was equal with God in substance, the question arose as to how Christ could be both God and man at the same time. And if so, how are the two natures related? Nestorius, bishop of Constantinople, acknowledged two persons in Christ, implying that Christ has a dual personality. This made a distinction between the Logos (God's Word) and Jesus the man, obscuring their real union. Although the Council of Ephesus (413 CE) anathematized Nestorius's doctrinal view, a Monophysite doctrine emerged as a reaction against Nestorianism. Monophysites emphasized that Christ has one nature, a divine one. In response, the Council of Chalcedon (451 CE) affirmed its rejection of both Nestorianism and Monophysitism as heretical. The council emphasized the unity of divine and human persons in Christ, and confirmed the two distinct natures in Christ. In other words, the council concluded that Christ was truly God and truly man; Christ was of the same essence as God the Father (homoousios with God); and Christ was like man but without sin.[6]

Eventually, the Monophysites and Nestorians established independent churches in the Middle East. The Nestorian church established itself in northern Iraq and came to be known as the Assyrian Church. Out of Monophysitism emerged the Coptic Orthodox church, the Syrian (Jacobite) Orthodox church, and the Armenian Orthodox church. The Maronite Church initially embraced an offshoot of Monophysitism, the Monothelete doctrine. The Monothelete doctrine emphasized that Christ possessed both a divine and human nature but only a divine will.

Ultimately, members of these schismatic or heretic churches in the eyes of the Roman Catholic Church abjured their doctrines and entered into a union with Rome. These newly founded churches became known as the Uniate churches and included the Coptic Catholic Church, formerly Coptic Orthodox church; Syrian Catholic Church, formerly Syrian Orthodox Church; Armenian Catholic Church, formerly Armenian Orthodox Church;

Chaldean Church, formerly Assyrian Church, and Maronite Church, formerly a Monothelete Church. In addition, Protestants and Roman Latins, at a certain time, established Protestant and Roman Catholic Churches (Latin rite) in the Middle East.

It's noteworthy that following the sacking of Rome in 410 CE, Constantinople emerged as the capital of the eastern part of the Roman Empire, which became known as the Byzantine Empire. As a result of Rome's decline, the Episcopal seats of Alexandria, Antioch, and Constantinople had gained momentum. Nonetheless, the Arab conquest of the Levant and North Africa in the seventh century shifted the power of the Church to Constantinople. But this shift to the capital of the Byzantine Empire was disrupted by the theological and political disputes of the Eastern churches, thereby strengthening the spiritual hand of Roman popes, who coveted preeminence. Eastern patriarchs were averse to heeding Rome's supremacy. Moreover, whereas Eastern theological thought had been influenced by Greek philosophy, Western theology had been based more or less on Roman law. Consequently, disagreements over theological tenets led to a schism between the Western and Eastern churches. Notwithstanding clerical disputes such as over clerical celibacy, central to this schism was the question over the procession of the Holy Spirit. The Roman church, without consulting Eastern churches, added "and from the Son" to the Nicene Creed. The Creed reads: "And we believe in the Holy Spirit, the Lord, the giver of life. He proceeds from the Father and the Son." This led to a final break between the Greek Orthodox Church and the Roman Catholic Church in 1054 CE.[7] The Melkite Greek Catholic Church, known also as the Melkite Byzantine Catholic Church, was related to the Greek Orthodox Church of Antioch. Members of the church were called Melkites (imperials) because they supported the decrees of the Chalcedon Council. In the early eighteenth century, an integral part of the Greek Orthodox Church entered into communion with Rome and became known as the Melkite Greek Catholic Church. Meanwhile, the Greek Orthodox Church was no longer known as Melkite.[8]

Be that as it may, virtually all these churches have a presence in Lebanon.[9] By the fifth century, Lebanon's city-states, hinterland, and populated areas in Mount Lebanon had become Christianized. The pantheon of Semitic, Greek, and Roman gods had fallen before the monotheism of Christianity and Jesus of Nazareth.

THE ARAB CONQUEST AND THE
TRANSFORMATION OF LEBANON

Upon his death in 632 CE, Prophet Muhammad had established a new order in the Arabian Peninsula identified with a new religion, Islam. Prophet

Muhammad, a Meccan from the Quraysh tribe, received a revelation from God in the form of a holy book, the Koran. This revelation completed previous ones given to earlier prophets or messengers of God, and became the basis of Islam, a sister Abrahamic religion to Judaism and Christianity, albeit a separate one. Prophet Muhammad, who acted in the capacity of a military, political, and spiritual leader, purged the Arabian Peninsula of idols and unified its factional tribes under the banner of the universal mission of Islam. Wearing the mantle of the Prophet, his earliest successors (Abu Bakr, Omar, Uthman, and Ali, 632–661 CE), known as the rightly guided **caliphs**, expanded the realm of Islam even beyond their own imagination.

Driven by the universal mission of Islam, and incentivized by conquests and their attendant spoils, the Arabs attacked the Byzantine and Persian (Sassanian) Empires to their north and east. Both empires had been exhausted by long wars and epidemics, and their peoples burdened by taxation, harsh rule, and internal religio-political conflicts. The victory of the Arabs over the Byzantines at the battle of Yarmuk, a tributary of the Jordan River, in 636 CE sealed the fate of Lebanon, Syria, and Palestine, known by the Arabs as *Bilad al-Sham*. In many cases, Christians and Jews welcomed the Arabs as deliverers. Beirut (635 CE), Tyre, Sidon, and Jbeil (636 CE), Aleppo (637 CE), and Antioch and Jerusalem (638) fell to Arab hands with little resistance or with the aid of Christians and Jews.[10] Before long, the conquest of Syria provided an operational base from which the Arab conquerors invaded Persia in the northeast and Egypt and North Africa in the southwest.

The new Arab rulers established a societal order in the expanse of their conquered lands in which Christians and Jews, considered as "people of the Book," or the recipient of divine revelation, were given a *dhimmi* status. As dhimmis (in the protection of) they had to pay both a land tax (*kharaj*) and a poll tax (*jizya*), and in return, they enjoyed the protection of Islam and exemption from military conscription. This status has been referred to as the Pact of Omar Ibn al-Khatab, who ruled as the second caliph (634–644 CE).[11] Gone were the days whereby the residents of the Greek city-states or the provinces of the Roman Empire could acquire the citizenship of their ruler. With the onset of Muslim rule, inequality between Muslims and non-Muslims became the norm of societal life insofar as the latter did not convert to Islam.

Under Arab rule, Lebanon was included in the *jund* (military district) of Dimashq (Damascus), whose city Damascus became the capital of the first Arab Umayyad dynasty (661–750 CE). As Umayyad rule expanded and faced internal and external challenges, Umayyad rulers trusted employing Christians in their palaces and bureaucracy as a foil against internal enemies. Nevertheless, Arab rule, including that of the Abbasid dynasty (750–1258 CE), gradually engendered a transformational process Islamizing and Arabizing almost the entire regions of Mesopotamia, Levant, and North

Africa. Lebanon was a noted exception thanks in no small measure to keeping the pre-Arab Semitic, Syriac, and Aramaic nomenclatural designation of villages, plants, and theological and technical terms, and to the Druzes and Christians, particularly Maronite Christians.[12]

The origin of the Maronites is shrouded with controversy on account of the relational identification of the Maronites with the Mardaites and al-Jarajima. Maronite historians and clerics trace the origins of the Maronites to the Mardaites, known by their Arabic name al-Marada (rebels), and deny any relationship between the Mardaites and al-Jarajima.[13] Henri Lammens, among other eminent historians, believes that the Mardaites of the Byzantine historians and al-Jarajima of Arab historians are identical, contradicting Maronite historians that the Maronites were Mardaites.[14] Hailing from the Black Mountain (Amanus Mountain in Turkey's Hatay province), al-Jarajima invaded Lebanon around 666–669 CE and then in 689 CE, whereupon they occupied the highlands of northern Lebanon. Philip Hitti postulates:

> In this thinly populated region [northern Lebanon] the newcomers amalgamated with the Aramaic-speaking Christian natives and created a centre of refuge for the oppressed and disconnected from inner Syria and the maritime plain. It was probably then that they became known as Maradah (Mardaites, rebels). . . . Out of this amalgamation at this time emerged the community designated as Maronite (Mawarinah).[15]

Be that as it may, the community of believers who conglomerated around an ascetic monk, Maron, came to be known as Maronites for bearing his name as the patron saint of their church. St. Maron left Antioch, virtually the capital city of Christianity in the fifth century, for a mountain in the region of Cyrrhus in Syria, where he spent most of his monastic life. He died in 410 CE. Shortly after Maron's death, his disciples moved to a place near the Orontes River. As their numbers grew, hostility with their neighbors, among them the Jacobites, increased. In 517 CE, approximately three hundred fifty Maronite monks were slaughtered and their monastery along the Orontes was destroyed. Following this massacre, the trickle of Maronites migrating to northern Lebanon turned into a steady stream. Renewed conflicts with the Jacobites in the second half of the seventh century led more Maronites to migrate to North Lebanon, making it the hearth and home of Maronitism. This paved the way for Lebanon to become at one and the same time a citadel of and refuge for minorities and dissidents.[16]

Maronite Church fathers have been keen about Maronite historiography. According to its early fathers, the Maronite Church had been consistent in defending the Maronites against the accusation of heresy and Monothelitism, asserting its support of the decrees of Chalcedon, its unwavering orthodoxy, and its union with Rome. Most of the work of the father of Maronite historiography, Istifan al-Duwayhi, addressed the origins and orthodoxy of the Maronite Church.[17] Kamal Salibi, who examined the work of al-Duwayhi, observed:

> In *Tarikh al-Ta'ifa al-Maruniyya* Duwayhi discussed the historical and religious origins of his people and attempted to prove their unbroken orthodoxy and union with Rome. In the first part of this work, which is entitled *Nisbat al-Mawarina* (Origin of the Maronites), he dealt with the rise of the Maronite church and community and their early development until the eighth century. The second part, entitled *Radd al-tuham wa daf' ashshubah* (Answer to the accusations and disproof of the suspicions), is a polemical defense of the unbroken orthodoxy of the Maronites and their continuous attachment to the Holy See.[18]

Salibi adds that "Duwayhi set out to prove in *Nisbat al-Mawarina* that the Maronites were so called after the blessed Marun [Maron] of Cyrus, the eponymous founder of the monastery of Mar Marun on the Orontes, who died in the early fifth century, and that the monks of this monastery had always been faithfully attached to the Roman Church."[19]

Maronite attachment to their faith and their compact presence in northern Lebanon militated against both their Islamization and full Arabization. Even under the harsh rule of Abbasid caliphs such as al-Mutawakil (847–861), Maronites remained Christian in faith, maintaining Syriac as the medium of liturgy and traditional societal nomenclature. At the same time, however, they mostly lived in the fastness and often inaccessible redoubt of the mountain until the advent of the Crusaders in late eleventh century. Meanwhile, people of Lebanon disapproved of Abbasid rule (750–1258 CE), which was farthest from the more or less liberal Umayyad rule (680–750 CE). In fact, Abbasid rule was contested in Lebanon (Syria and Palestine) by dissenting vassal states until the Fatimid invasion of Lebanon's littoral in 969 CE. It was under this schismatic caliphate, the Fatimid dynasty (909–1171), that Shi'ism spread in Lebanon and the Druze religion initiated.

The founder of the Fatimid dynasty (909–1171 CE) was an Ismai'ili who claimed descent from Prophet Muhammad's daughter Fatima and proclaimed himself al-Mahdi. Considered as the divinely guided Imam who disappeared into occultation, al-Mahdi's return is expected by the Shi'a community to bring justice to earth.[20] The Fatimid dynasty was first established in Tunisia before it moved to its newly founded capital al-Qahira (Cairo). A Fatimid caliph, al-Hakim (996–1021), had given himself out as the last manifestation of the deity on earth. His confidante, Muhammad ibn Ismail al-Darazi, propagated the doctrine that al-Hakim was the last incarnation of the deity in human form. When al-Hakim died, his followers denied his death and proclaimed that he had gone into occultation, from which he will reappear on earth at the opportune time. Hounded by the people for his al-Hakim-God doctrine, and seeing his new cult attracting little, if any, adherents, al-Darazi migrated to Wadi al-Taym, at the foot of Mount Hermon (Jabal al-Sheikh), where his message struck a chord with the people there. Before long, al-Darazi died in 1019, and a missionary of the new faith, Hamza al-Labbad al-Zuzani, laid the foundational theology of the Druze religion, whose appellation derived from al-Darazi.[21]

The newcomers and adherents of the Druze religion intermingled with the indigenous Aramean population. Slowly yet steadily, in much the same vein as with the Maronites in northern Lebanon, out of the amalgamation of the newcomers and indigenous people, the Druze community flourished in southern Lebanon. As their numbers continued to grow, Druzes moved northward in Mount Lebanon, avoiding the coast. By the time the Crusaders arrived toward the end of the eleventh century, the Druzes had established their strongholds in both the Chouf area southeast of Beirut and Wadi al-Taym. In the meantime, Shi'ism thrived and spread across Lebanon thanks in large measure to the patronage of the Fatimid dynasty. The Fatimids contested the legitimacy and authority of the Abbasids, who had already been affected by dissident vassal states in Syria. With the exception of both the Maronites' northern districts of Bsharri, Batroun, and Jbeil (Byblos), and the Druzes' southern districts of Wadi al-Taym and Chouf, Shi'ism prevailed in Lebanon, including in today's Maronite stronghold of Kisrwan in Mount Lebanon.[22]

However, Fatimid ascendency took a severe blow for failing to organize a Muslim campaign to check the onslaught of the Crusaders. By February 1099, the Crusaders were in Arqa in the vicinity of Tripoli, whence they marched south toward Jerusalem, crossing Batroun, Jbeil, Beirut, Sidon, and Tyre. In Batroun, the Crusaders met the Maronites with whom they established a trustworthy relationship. Maronites served as guides and archers for the Crusader knights.[23] Following the fall of Jerusalem in late June 1099 and the establishment of the Latin kingdom of Jerusalem, the Crusaders set their sights on Lebanon's coast to establish defensive fortresses and army posts, since their eastern flank in the heartland of Syria was tenuous. They seized Tripoli in 1109, Beirut and Sidon in 1110, and finally Tyre in 1124 after a long siege.

The Frankish Crusaders granted the Maronites rights and privileges not accorded to other sects, being Christian or Muslim, including the right to possess land in the kingdom of Jerusalem. Frankish knights intermarried with Maronite locals. Significantly, it was during the reign of the Crusaders that the Maronites reportedly entered into a union with Rome, proclaiming papal supremacy. Commenting on the Crusaders-Maronite relationship and

Maronites' submission to papal authority, Matti Moosa refers to the account of the Crusader bishop and historian William of Tyre:

> The first to mention this contact was William, bishop of Tyre. . . . In a lengthy testimony William of Tyre refers to the Maronites in two contexts. He describes them as being part of the Syrian nation and as having been Monothelites for five hundred years, stating that through divine providence they renounced this heresy by professing the true faith . . . and by showing readiness to accept the teaching of the Church of Rome. William of Tyre states further . . . [Maronites] were a strong people and rendered great service to "us concerning our many and significant interests with our enemies. For this reason, our people (the Latin Crusaders) were overwhelmed with joy when these Maronites returned to the true faith," meaning the faith of the Church of Rome. . . . The first contact the Maronites made with the Crusaders was in 1099, but they did not offer their submission to the Church of Rome until the year 1182, according to William.[24]

This relationship drastically improved in a way: the Maronites came to be considered France's "children" in the Middle East, and Maronites, thereafter, earnestly called France *la mére du Liban*. In response to his warm reception at 'Akka by throngs of Maronites, the Crusader and only canonized French king, Louis IX, penned a letter in 1250 in which he described the nation established under the name of St. Maron as a party of the French nation.[25] Finally, the integration of the Maronite Church within the Catholic Roman Church was celebrated by the establishment of the Maronite College in Rome in 1584.

The Druzes, unlike the Maronites, took the side of the Damascene Sunnis against the Crusaders. Shaped no less by the harsh anti-Druze campaign against them during the infancy of their religion than by the solidarity and endurance they acquired as a compact mountainous community, the Druzes preferred the Crescent over the Latin Cross, under whose banner some slaughters were committed. For two centuries since the Crusaders' invasion of Syria, Lebanon, and Palestine, the Druzes attacked Crusaders and raided their positions in the Beka', Lebanon's coast, and northern Palestine. Successive Sunni dynasties of the Syrian interior recruited Druzes as auxiliary forces and lavished on their feudal chieftains honors and exalted military ranks. This association between the Druze chieftains and Sunni leaders paved the way, on the one hand, for the feudal chieftains to replace the traditional religious *'uqqal* (wise) as leaders of the community. On the other hand, Sunni dynasties, including the Ottoman Empire, favored the Druzes over other minorities.[26]

Conversely, the Shi'ite and Monophysite Christians had difficulty siding with either the Sunnis or the Crusaders. Inasmuch as the Shi'ites opposed the Crusaders, they contested the legitimacy and authority of the Sunni Abbasid caliphate. By the same token, inasmuch as the Monophysites opposed the Catholic Church, they frowned upon Sunni power.

By the last quarter of the twelfth century, the power of Crusaders had become precarious. Whereas internal disputes had weakened the Latin Kingdom of Jerusalem, attacks on the other crusader states had become more exacting and organized. Behind this surge of Sunni power against the Crusaders was Salah al-Din Yusuf ibn Ayyub, the scion of a noble Sunni Kurdish family, famously known as Saladin. Saladin's courage, talent, and participation in Sunni military expeditions to prevent the takeover of Egypt by the Crusaders led to his rise as commander and vizier in Fatimid Egypt. But in 1171, he abolished the feeble and unpopular Fatimid dynasty and proclaimed a return to Sunni Islam. Thereafter, he moved to Syria to unite Muslims from Mesopotamia, Syria, and Palestine (and Egypt) and led a campaign against the Crusaders. In October 1187, a month after Acre, Nablus, Jaffa, Sidon, Beirut, and Askalon had fallen, Jerusalem surrendered to Saladin. Significantly, Tyre withstood Saladin's siege.

Reinforced by fresh troops from new crusader campaigns, Acre was retaken by the Crusaders, Tyre remained defiant, and the crusader state of Tripoli (county of Tripoli) reinforced its defenses. This remained so until the advent of the Mamluk dynasty (1250–1517), which replaced Saladin's Ayyubid dynasty. The Mamluks, former Turkic and Circassian slave warriors who were key components of the Abbasid and Ayyubid armed forces, projected themselves as defenders of Islam's orthodox faith. From their capital, Cairo, Mamluks launched military expeditions to Palestine, Syria, and Lebanon to purge these lands of the Crusaders and subdue their allies and heterodox communities, especially the Maronites.

Since the advent of the Crusaders, most of the Maronites lived within the confines and on the periphery of the Crusader County of Tripoli (1102–1289 CE). Maronite *muqaddams*, chieftains, served under the Franks as their knights, allies, or vassals. The Maronites received most favorable treatment among other Uniate Christians by the Franks, and were key in defending the Crusader state.[27] The Mamluks were not ignorant about Maronite assistance to the Franks of Tripoli. In fact, before storming Tripoli the Mamluks launched successive raids into the hinterland of the County of Tripoli, ravaging the Maronite countryside. In 1283, during the last military expedition, Mamluk forces, led by Turkmen, devastated vital Maronite towns such Ihden, Baqufa, Bsharri, and al-Hadath and slaughtered their inhabitants. Once they slew the Maronites' lifeline to Tripoli, the Mamluks stormed its walls and bloodily seized it in 1289. The Mamluks took over Tyre and Acre in 1291, ending the last vestiges of Crusaders' rule and subduing the Maronites of northern Lebanon.[28]

The fate of Muslim schismatic communities fared no better. As a conservative Muslim dynasty, the Mamluk dynasty pursued a policy of religious uniformity based on Sunni orthodox Islam. Ismailis, Nusayris (Alawis), and especially Shi'ites were systematically attacked in Syria and Lebanon.[29] Their presence in the Syrian interior was virtually decimated. Shi'ite survivors fled to Lebanon, where, under the Fatimids, they comprised a plurality in many areas including Kisrwan, Beirut, Beka', and Jabal 'Amil. Druzes were considered less subversive, but their harassment of Mamluk armies during their retreat before the onslaught of Mongols in 1300, who had occupied Homs and Damascus, infuriated Mamluk authorities. Following punitive though inconclusive military expeditions, the Mamluks launched in 1305 a formidable military expedition targeting Kisrwan, which included al-Matn region and was populated by Maronites, Jacobites, Druzes, Nusayris, and Shiites. The decisive battle took place at Sawfar, a Druze stronghold lying across the Beirut-Damascus highway in Baabda district. Rebel forces, mostly Druzes, were routed. Druze villages were razed to the ground, and men, women, and children of the different religious persuasions were slaughtered. From there the Mamluk victors marched to Kisrwan, crushing and murdering the rebels and their families.[30] Survivors were dispersed. The Maronite stronghold of Jbeil was also crushed.

The Mamluks' victory was total. Mamluks divided the coastal strip from Beirut to Tripoli into fiefs administered by Turkmen families, and introduced to the hills of Kisrwan the Abu Assaf Turkmen clan to keep a watchful eye on Mount Lebanon.[31] They also parceled Lebanon into six *niyabah* (provinces), which made up Mamluk administrative Syria. The Province of Tripoli comprised North Lebanon and the coastal region from Latakia to Jbeil. The province of Safad included Southern Lebanon and Tyre. And the Province of Damascus included the rest: Sidon, Beirut, Ba'albeck, and Beka'.[32] As time passed, and relative calm held sway over Lebanon, Mamluks more or less allowed Lebanon's communities to live in relative peace as long as they observed Mamluk rules and paid their taxes.

To be sure, although they were not able to rid Lebanon of Muslim heterodox communities, Mamluks greatly weakened them and changed the demography and religious makeup of Lebanon. It was during their reign that Sunnism took root in Lebanon and replaced Shi'ism in most coastal cities. Sunni communities developed in Tripoli, Beirut, and Sidon, thanks in no small part to Mamluk suppression of Shi'ites, conversion, and influx of Sunni merchants from Syria and Egypt. Tyre remained largely Shi'ite. In the aftermath of their rout in Kisrwan, whereas most Shi'ites moved to Jabal 'Amil, Ba'albeck, and Tyre, Druzes retired to their stronghold in Wadi al-Taym and Chouf. Maronites remained largely in northern Lebanon. But a significant number of them gradually moved to Kisrwan, transforming the district into

a Maronite majority one. Henri Lammens observed that the rout and disper-
sal of Shi'ites and Druzes from Kisrwan benefited the Maronites, who in
time became a majority there.[33] Other Christian communities, Melkites, and
Jacobites scattered in Beirut, Mount Lebanon (al-Matn), northern Lebanon,
and Chouf.

Parallel to the transformation of Lebanon's demography, intra-communal
developments paved the way for profound changes in communal leaderships, especially among the Maronites. As years passed, Maronite *muqaddams* (chieftains) became subservient tax-farmers for the Mamluks (and
later Ottomans), even adopting Muslim names and titles. They neglected the
interests of their community as they curried favor with their Mamluk rulers,
thereby falling out with the Maronite clergy and their peasant community.
Consequently, the Maronite clergy began to fend for their flock against the
voraciousness and callousness of *muqaddams*. Supported by their community, the clergy, who shared the peasant roots of their flock, contested the
power of the feudal aristocracy. This contestation of power marked Maronite
social life until the Maronite Church took over the leadership of the Maronite
community during Ottoman rule. In contrast to Maronite communal fissures,
the Druze community remained faithful to the solidarity between the *'uqqal*
and feudal aristocracy.

In the meantime, broadly speaking, Lebanon under Mamluk rule experienced one of its darkest ages. Mamluks enforced the dhimmi status of
Christians and Jews, shackling them with discriminatory measures including imposing on them distinctive dress. They granted hereditary fiefdoms to
subservient feudal aristocrats, who mercilessly collected taxes. Worried about
a new European landing on Lebanon's coast, Mamluks set up a virtual iron
wall between Christians and Europeans. Maronites' contacts with France and
Rome were substantially curbed. However, in 1381 and 1404 Genoese fleets
plundered Sidon and Beirut. Thereafter, Mamluk sultans signed treaties with
European powers that allowed trade with Europe, and the Holy See permitted pilgrimage to Jerusalem. Beirut emerged as a hub for trade and a landing
for pilgrims heading toward Jerusalem. Although heavy taxes were imposed
on horses and food necessities such as sugar and salt, Lebanese communities
were efficient in tilling their lands and animal husbandry. Needless to say,
Mamluks, as former slaves, were the least cultured in the Muslim world,
known more for their ruthlessness and military power than their intellect and
wisdom. This cast a pall over Lebanon's cultural life.

Of all these debilitating sociopolitical factors, Mongol invasions of Syria
put the final nail in Mamluk rule. Following previous devastating conquests
of the Syrian interior, in 1400, Tamerlane, reportedly a descendant of the
great and brutal Mongol leader Gengiz khan, led his hordes into western
Asia, leaving in his wake scorched earth and dead bodies. He reached north

Syria in October 1400, whereupon he ravaged Aleppo, Homs, Hama, and subsequently Damascus. Thousands were put to the sword or perished by flames. Damascene skilled workers were taken to Samarkand, Tamerlane's capital, and scholars were either murdered or taken into captivity. Mongol detachments pillaged the Lebanese coast and plundered Beirut, Sidon, and Ba'albeck. Tamerlane's invasion of Syria destroyed its economy, industry, and whatever was left of its cultural life, making Mamluks' political, military, and economic recovery hardly possible.[34] This ushered in a century plagued by misrule, oppression, and corruption, rotting to the core Mamluk rule and paving the way for the newly rising Ottoman dynasty to conquer the Middle East.

Chapter 2

The Rise and Fall of Mount Lebanon Emirates

OTTOMAN CONQUEST

No doubt, the Mongol hordes of Tamerlane, which ravaged Syria and sacked Damascus, dealt a severe blow to the economy and military of the Mamluk dynasty from which it never fully recovered. Equally important, the Mamluks' misrule, oppression, corruption, and faltering trade hollowed out the authority and coffers of the dynasty. Paralleling this slow death of the Mamluk dynasty, a new dynasty had been taking shape in Anatolia, Asia Minor. Bearing the name of its founder Osman, the Ottoman dynasty nurtured its succor for conquests from the nomadic Turkic waves of central Asia, which followed in the footsteps of their Islamized kinsmen, the Seljuqs. The Seljuqs had established the Sultanate of Rum in Anatolia in 1077 on conquered Byzantine lands. Mongol invasions of Anatolia (1231–1232 and 1242–1243) incapacitated the Sultanate beyond relief, creating a power vacuum in Anatolia that was gradually filled by the Ottomans. Establishing their embryonic principality in western Asia Minor on the border of Byzantium Bithynia, the Ottomans waged incessant raids against the Byzantines. In 1354, the Ottomans seized Busra, which they made the initial capital of their rapidly growing state before conquering Constantinople in 1453 and turning it into the capital of the Ottoman Dynasty, Istanbul, and the seat of the Ottoman sultanate.

The inaugural years of the sixteenth century posed a military and religious threat to the Ottoman Empire. Persia arose as a strong state under Shah Ismail al-Safawi, who established the Safavid Dynasty and ruled it from 1501 until his death in 1524. The powerful shah proclaimed Shi'ism as state religion and began purging Sunnism from his popular bases of power. As a temporal and Shi'a spiritual leader, he also disseminated politico-religious propaganda among the Turks in Persia and Asia Minor, some of whom were receptive to his message. Wearing the mantle of Sunni Orthodox Islam, the Ottomans responded by ordering the deportation of Shi'ites from Anatolia to Greece and by mobilizing their forces along the border with Persia. Before long, hostility intensified between the two dynasties, especially after a Shi'a revolt in central Anatolia devolved into open warfare. The Ottomans defeated the Persians on the plain of Chaldiran and occupied the Safavid capital, Tabriz, in September 1514. However, the Ottomans withdrew to their capital, leaving a defeated yet still a viable Shi'ite dynasty.[1]

Significantly, this success on the battlefield raised the question of the leadership of Islam, and, by extension, the control of the Middle East. Although defeated, the Persian Empire continued its propaganda war championing Shi'ism, which only sharpened Ottoman aspiration to claim the leadership of Islam. Consequently, the Ottomans waged a vigorous war in 1516–1517 against the staggering Mamluk dynasty, occupying Egypt, Greater Syria (*Bilad al-Sham*), and western Arabia. Thereafter, the Ottomans extended their rule to the far ends of the Middle East and North Africa. Finally, the Ottoman sultans had become the leaders of Islam, championing Sunnism and ruling over the two holy cities of Mecca and Medina and the Arab world.

The conquest of Syria was swift. The decisive battle took place in August 1516 on the plain of Marj Dabiq, north of Aleppo. The Mamluks' army was routed. Not only was the Mamluk army weak, but also Mamluk *walis* (governors) switched their allegiance to the Ottomans the minute their army reached the approaches of northern Syria. A similar situation prevailed in Lebanon. Whereas the Buhtur clan of al-Gharb sided with the Mamluks, the Ma'n clan of the Chouf, led by Fakhr al-Din I, made contacts with the governors of Aleppo and Damascus, who supported the Ottomans and straddled the fence. Thereafter, Fakhr al-Din I led a delegation of Lebanese *emirs* (princes, notables) to Damascus to pay homage to his new lord and master, Sultan Selim. The sultan, impressed by the Druze emir Fakhr al-Din I, bestowed on him the title of "sultan of the mountain," and conferred to him and to other emirs their fiefs and privileges that they had under the Mamluks.[2]

Broadly speaking, the Ottomans administered *Bilad al-Sham* similarly as the Mamluks. They divided the area into *wiyalat* (provinces) and *sanjaks* (districts), headed by a *wali* (governor) called by the honorific title pasha. *Bilad al-Sham* was divided into three provinces: Damascus, Aleppo, and Tripoli. Northern Lebanon belonged to the *wilaya* of Tripoli and the rest of the country was divided between the *sanjaks* of Beirut and Sidon, which belonged to the wilaya of Damascus. In 1660, the Ottomans constituted Sidon as a wilaya.[3] The Ottomans also continued the Mamluk practice of the iqta' system (feudalism), or iltizam, which allotted tax farming rights to communal chieftains or emirs under the control of the Ottoman walis. The emirs, in turn, enjoyed a degree of autonomy in running the affairs of their fiefdoms as long as they paid their due taxes to the Sublime Porte, provided armed men to Ottoman authorities in time of need, and upheld their rule. Though the Ottoman Empire did not single out a religious community, non-Sunni Muslims were initially designated as *ra'iyah*, a term illustrative of a herd community shepherded for the benefit of the Ottoman conqueror.[4] As subjugated peoples, they faced institutional discrimination but were protected and permitted to live their own way of life so long as they observed Ottoman rule. In this respect, the Ottoman Empire codified the religiously based treatment of its subjects into a two-tier millet system comprising the privileged Muslim community and a lower *dhimmi* community made up of the "people of the Book." The *dhimmis* enjoyed the protection of Ottoman rule and a measure of a quasi-autonomous socio-religious space in which they handled their own personal status laws under the supervision of their religious authority. In return, they had to pay the *jizya* for protection and exemption from military conscription.

Commenting on this distinction in the millet system, Fawwaz Traboulsi observed:

> This distinction implied tangible differences in the relations of the two communities to the social division of labour. Generally barred from the military/administrative functions, Christians and Jews tended to specialise in commerce, finance and handicrafts. In Mount Lebanon, this uneven social location expressed itself in a Druze community dominated mainly by the tribal-warrior function and a Christian community dominated mainly by commoners, with a large peasant base. This imbalance would be largely responsible for transforming social and political conflicts into sectarian conflicts.[5]

By and large, Lebanon was parceled into fiefdoms controlled by emirs whose policies engendered power fluidity with attendant demographic and geographic changes. Inter- and intra-communal struggles for power, alliances with foreign powers, and alliances with and rebellions against Ottoman *walis* shaped the political dynamics of Lebanon, especially Mount Lebanon under Ottoman rule. During the onset of Ottoman rule, the Druze Tanukhs and the Arslans, descendants of Yemeni tribes, settled the western approaches of Beirut. The Maronite stronghold remained northern Lebanon. The Turkmen Sunni 'Assafs ruled Kisrwan and Beirut. The Kurdish Sunni Sayfas ruled Tripoli and northern Lebanon. The Sunni Shihabs (most of whom later converted to Maronitism) ruled Wadi al-Taym and southern Beka'. The Shi'a Harfushs dominated Ba'albeck and northern Beka'. And the Druze Ma'ns established their capital at Ba'aqlin and dominated the Chouf.[6]

THE RISE AND FALL OF THE MA'N EMIRATE

Favored by the Ottomans, the Ma'ns established their hegemony in Mount Lebanon, which reached its zenith under Fakhr al-Din II (1590–1635), the grandson of Fakhr al-Din I (d. 1544). A series of events, coupled with measures of intrigue, ambition, and courage, catapulted the rise of Fakhr a-Din II to the leadership of an emirate that extended far beyond the borders of Mount Lebanon. The feudal leadership of the Assafs elapsed with the passing away of their leader in 1590. The Assafs ruled Kisrwan, but following their tribute to Sultan Selim, alongside Fakhr al-Din I, Jbeil was added to their fiefdom, which flourished and attracted members of various religious communities. Nevertheless, their feudal leadership passed to the Sayfas of Tripoli (and Akkar). Of Kurdish ancestry, this feudal family expanded its fiefdom to the vicinity of Antioch and gained enough power to equal that of the pasha of Tripoli.[7] In 1584, a convoy of Janissaries, an elite Ottoman infantry, hauling taxes to Istanbul, was attacked and robbed in Djun Akkar. Enraged by the attack, the Ottomans sent a punitive expedition that ravaged the Akkar region, and thereafter pushed south to the Ma'n's Chouf to punish the Druzes, who, the Porte believed, had participated in the attack. Committed to teaching their subjects an unforgettable lesson, Ottomans killed thousands. The Ma'ni emir Qurqumaz escaped to a hardly accessible cave near Jezzin, where he died in 1585.[8]

Upon the news of Qurqumaz's passing, his wife rushed off her son Fakhr al-Din II, who was twelve years old, to Kisrwan to be in the care of the Maronite al-Khazin family. The young emir grew up nurturing hatred toward the Ottomans and fondness of Maronites. In 1590, the maternal uncle of Fakhr al-Din II, Sayf al-Din al-Tanukhi, entrusted the Chouf fiefdom to him. Driven by ambition and an innate desire to be free from Ottoman rule, Fakhr al-Din II embarked on a grand mission to rally his allies and rivals and establish his own autonomous emirate. With wit and wile, he managed to lord his authority over the emirs of Lebanon. He allied himself with the Sunni Shihabs of Wadi al-Taym and the Shi'ite Harfushs of Ba'albeck and Beka'. He forged an alliance with the Druze Arslans of al-Gharb through marriage, and deepened his relationship with the Maronites, already his benefactors. Observing the growth of Fakhr al-Din II's influence among their neighbors and coreligionists, the Druze Abu Lam' of al-Matn saccharinely joined his alliance. Consequently, his realm expanded exponentially. But he had to contend with the powerful Sayfas of Tripoli, who had taken control of Kisrwan and Beirut following the demise of the Assaf political leadership. As it turned out, the *wali* of Damascus called on Fakhr al-Din II to regain these territories. Enlisting his allies, he routed the forces of the Sayfas, and, in return, the

Ottoman wali rewarded him with the *sanjak* of Safad. He also regained the *sanjak* of Sidon, formerly held by his father, and Beirut, further expanding his realm, which now had easy access to the sea.[9]

As his power grew, Fakhr al-Din II supported the rebellion of the Kurdish leader and governor of Aleppo, Ali Janbulad (later Jumblatt), against the Ottomans in 1605–1607. Even though Janbulad was defeated, Fakhr al-Din II managed to remain in power by paying the wali of Damascus large sums of money. During the rebellion, Fakhr al-Din II came into contact with the ruling Medicis of Tuscany, who supported Janbulad. Before long, he forged good relations with the Medicis. Active in the eastern Mediterranean, Tuscany supplied Fakhr al-Din II with arms and ammunition, which significantly enhanced the power of his army. In 1608, he signed a commercial treaty with Tuscany, whose provisions included a secret military article aimed at the Ottomans.[10] Moreover, in 1611, he sent a Maronite bishop, Jirjis Ibn Marun, to Tuscany and the Holy See to negotiate an anti-Ottoman alliance.[11]

The new wali of Damascus took wind of Fakhr al-Din II's plots and convinced the Porte to take immediate action against the audacious Emir of Lebanon and end his secessionist policy. The Ottomans mustered a massive fleet and army and headed toward Mount Lebanon in 1613. While the fleet blockaded the coast, the army moved against Fakhr al-Din II's capital, Ba'aqlin. Caught in a vise and unsure of victory, he decided to flee to Tuscany onboard a French ship, which happened to be at the port of Sidon. The Ottomans stripped the Ma'ns of their fiefdoms with the exception of the Chouf.[12] Fakhr al-Din II's son Ali was entrusted with the Ma'n fiefdom, whose capital moved to Dayr al-Qamar.

During his five-year (1613–1618) self-exile, Fakhr al-Din II traveled the Italian city-states, but spent most of his time in Florence. Florence's Cosimo II (1590–1621), the Grand Duke of Tuscany, received him royally. But his expectation that the Grand Duke would organize a European expedition to forcefully reclaim his realm was a disappointing letdown. Touring Florence and other Italian city-states, Fakhr al-Din II was impressed with the liberal lifestyle of Italians compared to that of Greater Syria and with their social infrastructure, particularly the hospitals, orphanages, and museums. But what he admired the most were the banks, the local judicial system, and organization of local forces.[13]

Upon favorable political changes taking place in Istanbul and Damascus, Fakhr al-Din II decided to go home. His arrival was greeted with rejoice and fanfare. Wasting no time, he set about preparing to regain his lost territories. In a few years, with adept diplomacy and skillful military tactics, Fakhr al-Din II was able to reconstitute his army. His first order of business was to deal with his old nemeses the Sayfas. Their leader, Yusuf Sayfa, had capitalized on the absence of Fakhr al-Din II to set the Ma'ni capital of Dayr al-Qamar on fire. Before launching his military campaign against the Sayfas' armed forces, Fakhr al-Din II moved against the *muqqadams* (chieftains) of northern Lebanon to prevent them from supporting Sayfa. In 1623, Fakhr al-Din's army viciously routed the Sayfa forces, wresting control of Akkar and advancing toward Homs and Hama. He vindictively demolished the Sayfas' palaces in Akkar and later in Tripoli. Next, Fakhr al-Din II seized the Beka' from the Harfushs. In response, the wali of Damascus, Mustafa Pasha, the Harfushs, and the Sayfas joined forces against him. In November 1623, Mustafa Pasha's forces, numbering 12,000, met Fakhr al-Din II's army of 4,000 men at 'Anjar in the Beka'. Not only did Mustafa Pasha lose in the famed 'Anjar battle, but he was also taken captive by Fakhr al-Din II. He then continued to Ba'albeck, the seat of Harfush power, and destroyed it. Beset by their conflict with the Persians and internal troubles fomented by the Janissaries, Ottoman authorities conceded Fakhr al-Din II's victory and gave him back upon the release of Mustafa Pasha the *sanjaks* of Safad, 'Ajlun and Nablus.[14]

Fakhr al-Din II's victories had made him too strong and too dangerous for the Ottomans to be left to his own devices, mainly seceding from the Ottoman Empire. His lordship extended from Aleppo to Egypt, commanding a geostrategic area. His contacts with the Tuscans had become economically and militarily alarming to the Ottomans. No sooner did the Ottomans defeat the Persians in 1629 than they turned their attention to force Fakhr al-Din II into an eternal submission. In 1633, Sultan Murad IV appointed Kuchuk Ahmad Pasha as governor of Damascus, granting him the sultanate imprimatur to eliminate the Druze emir. The sultan also ordered the walis of Syria and Egypt to join Kuchuk's military campaign against Fakhr al-Din II. His son Ali led his army, numbering around 25,000, against an Ottoman army at least three times bigger and backed by a large fleet. Despite valorous attempts at stemming the onslaught of the Ottoman army, Ali fell in a battle at Wadi al-Taym, whereupon he was forthright decapitated. Fakhr al-Din II's calls to the Tuscans for help fell on deaf ears, and his allies deserted him one after the other. In a desperate act like his father before him, Fakhr al-Din II fled to a cave near Jezzin Falls. But he was discovered and taken with his three sons to Istanbul, where he was decapitated on April 13, 1635. His sons were also executed.[15]

Fakhr al-Din II was a diminutive figure but one of the greatest leaders in the history of Lebanon. He pursued a nonsectarian policy, brought prosperity and modernization to his emirate, and opened it to the Occident. Thanks to his contacts with the Italians and the French, he revived Beirut and Sidon as hubs for trade, embellished their roads, and fortified their defenses. He built a splendid castle in Beirut and one that remained unfinished in Sidon. He built a traveler's *khan* (inn) in Sidon for French merchants and invited Tuscan engineers and architects to help improve irrigation and farming in Mount Lebanon. He allowed missionaries to settle in his emirate, spearheaded by the Capuchin order. But his most enduring and consequential achievement was his introduction of the sericulture industry in Mount Lebanon, which opened up his emirate to international trade. The silk trade, coupled with prosperity and security, encouraged families from neighboring provinces, such as the Jumblatts, to migrate to Mount Lebanon. Significantly, he encouraged Christian peasants, mainly Maronites, to emigrate from North Lebanon to South Lebanon, gradually transforming the demography of Mount Lebanon whereby the hitherto exclusive Druze territory of South Lebanon became Christian-Druze mixed territory. The newcomers engaged in silk cultivation and agricultural and artisanal occupations. Christians supplanted Shi'ites in villages on the periphery of Druze territory.[16]

To many Lebanese and scholars of the Middle East, Fakhr al-Din II planted the seeds of Lebanese nationalism. His emirate was the precursor of modern Grand Liban. He also inhered in the collective consciousness of Lebanese the notion that their country cannot be isolated from the West. Commenting on Fakhr al-Din II's era, Henri Lammens observed: "Une ére de renaissance s'ouvrait pour la Syrie, plus exactement pour cette section de la Syrie qu'on pourrait déja appeler le Grand-Liban."[17] He added: "Fakhraddin, un précurseur. Mieux que personne, il comprit que la Syrie ne pouvait s'isoler, que son avenir résidait dans ses relations avec l'Occident."[18]

THE RISE OF THE SHIHAB EMIRATE AND MARONITISM

The fall of the Ma'n Emirate ushered in a period of strife and instability in Mount Lebanon. A prominent feature of the instability that prevailed was the Qaysi-Yemeni conflict. The north-Arab Qaysi and the south-Arab Yemeni tribes settled in Syria following its Arab conquest, and subsequently became bitter rivals over political power and entitlements. This conflict spilled over into Mount Lebanon and took a political dimension that split the Druze community between Qaysi and Yemeni factions. Leading the Qaysi faction, the Ma'ns, under Fakhr al-Din II, reduced the Yemeni faction to political insignificance. In the aftermath of his fall, the wali of Damascus, Kuchuk Ahmad Pasha, punished the Ma'ns by appointing Ali Alam al-Din, the leader of the Yemeni faction, as emir of southern Lebanon. However, the Chouf, Matn, Kisrwan, Jurd, and Gharb remained under the fiefdom of the Ma'n, led by Fakr al-Din's nephew Mulhim (1635–1657). Intent on doing away with Qaysi influence, Ali ordered the slaughter of the Ma'n's kinsmen the Tanukhs, who hosted him in their mansion. This caused a communal civil strife, which the Ottomans kept simmering by playing one faction against another.[19]

Eventually, Mulhim was able to recover southern Lebanon from the Alam al-Dins and restore relative peace to Mount Lebanon. Mulhim's son Ahmad (1657–1697) inherited the Ma'n Emirate upon the passing of his father. Pursuing a strategy similar to that of his grandfather Fakhr al-Din II, Ahmad tried to exploit the Ottomans' weakness and/or distractions to secure the autonomy of his realm. Incensed by his exploits, the Ottomans sent a punitive expedition to arrest him. He escaped but subsequently died without a male heir. Thereupon, the male lineage of the Ma'ns, similar to that of their kinsmen the Tanukhs before them, died out. In the meantime, the wali of Tripoli, capitalizing on the ongoing disturbances, granted the fiefdom of Jubbat Bsharri to the feudal Shi'ite Hamadah family, which they held for about a century.

Called upon by Ottoman authorities to elect a new ruler to the Ma'n Emirate, Druze and other notables held an assembly in 1697 in Simqaniyeh (near Ba'aqlin), in which they chose Bashir Shihab, a Sunni emir and relative to the Ma'n (being Ahmad's nephew) from Wadi al-Taym, as the new ruler. Their decision was transmitted through the wali of Sidon to the Porte, assuring him that the usual taxes and whatever arrears would be paid. The Porte held that Haydar, the son of Ahmad's daughter, should be the new ruler since he had a stronger claim to the emirate. But since Haydar was a minor, Bashir was declared regent. Taking his seat at Dayr al-Qamar, the former Ma'n capital, Bashir (1697–1707) auspiciously inaugurated Shihab rule, even though the walis of Damascus, Sidon, and Acre exercised significant control over his emirate. He restored relative calm to his emirate, and forged, unlike his predecessors, good relations with the walis of Sidon. He also extended his realm to Jabal 'Amil (east of Tyre) and Palestine. Upon the death of Bashir in 1707, Haydar (1707–1732) claimed the Shihab Emirate.[20]

The Ottomans approved Haydar's succession. But the new wali of Sidon had reservations about Haydar, consequent upon his tax arrears and his takeover of Jabal 'Amil. No less significant, the wali supported the Yemeni faction, which planned its comeback to Druze lordship. Eventually, Sidon's wali took over Jabal 'Amil and thereafter deposed Haydar from his Chouf fiefdom, placing in his stead Muhammad Abi Harmuch. Emir Haydar, along with Qaysi chiefs, escaped to Ghazir in Kisrwan, where they were given sanctuary by the Maronite Hubayshes. Supported by Ottoman troops, Harmuch sacked Ghazir, forcing Haydar to flee again. Harmuch then invited the Alam al-Din chiefs back to the Chouf, who had been biding their time in Damascus. Harmuch had circled the wagon of the Yemeni faction against the Qaysis, but their popular support was slim.

In response, Qaysi chiefs rallied around Haydar, who had taken up refuge with the Abi Lam' clan in the Matn district. In 1711, the forces of the leading Qaysi chiefs and their allies, including the Jumblatts, Khazins, al-Nakds, Imads, al-Maliks, and Talhuqs, joined the forces of Haydar and Lam's in Ras al-Matn, in preparation for their invasion of the Chouf. Taking heed of Haydar's plan, Harmuch and allies, including the Alam al-Dins, Arslans, and Harfuches, assembled their forces in Ayn Dara above Matn. At the same time, collaborating with Harmuch, the walis of Damascus and Sidon sent their troops to the Matn district to join Harmuch's forces in a flank attack on Haydar's forces in Ras al-Matn. Preempting their coordinated attack, Haydar attacked Harmuch's forces in Ayn Dara before the break of dawn on March 20, routing the Yemeni alliance. Harmuch was taken captive and several of Alam al-Din chiefs were killed. Losing the Ayn Dara battle before even joining it, the Ottoman walis begrudgingly accepted Haydar's *fait accompli* and messages of appeasement.[21]

The Ayn Dara battle had profound ramifications for Mount Lebanon. In the aftermath of his victory, Haydar forced the Yemenis and their allies from Mount Lebanon to Hawran in Syria. Their forced migration significantly reduced the population of the Druze community, which was compensated for by incoming Christians. Maronite migration to southern Lebanon, which gained momentum under Fakhr al-Din II, picked up speed to Druze areas. Moreover, Christian Catholics and Orthodox followed suit, establishing their new homes in mixed Christian-Druze towns and villages. No less significant, Haydar reconfigured the feudal lordships of Mount Lebanon and vicinity. For their valor and support, Haydar elevated the status of the Abi Lam's clan to the Emirate rank and appointed them as the subsidiary tax farmers (*muqata'jis*) over the Matn district.[22] The Shihabs and Abi Lam' reinforced their alliance by intermarriage, a tradition that continued to modern-day Lebanon. The Jumblatts, Talhuqs, Imads, al-Nakads, and al-Maliks were all elevated to the sheikhdom rank. The status of sheikh allowed the holder to expand his retinue and land holdings. The Jumblatts and al-Maliks consolidated their power in the Chouf and Jurd, respectively. The Arslans, unlike the Alam al-Dins, were allowed to remain in Mount Lebanon. But they were stripped of their al-Gharb fiefdom, which was given to the Talhuqs of 'Aytat. The Imads (later Yazbakis) consolidated their power in the Urqub district, and al-Nakads in the Manasif and Shahhar districts. Among the Druze sheikhdoms, the Jumblatts enjoyed the highest standing with Emir Haydar.[23] The Maronite Khazins and Hubayshes confirmed their supremacy in Kisrwan. But the Maronites of Jbeil, Batroun, and Bsharri of northern Lebanon remained under the leadership of the Shi'a Hamade clan, who as *muqaddams* did not waver or delay paying their due taxes.[24]

The defeat of the Yemeni faction and the reconfiguration of the feudal lordship in Mount Lebanon enhanced the power of the Shihabs, who, in turn, advanced the unity and cohesion of their alliance. They not only supported their feudatory subordinates but also counseled them on matters of peace and war. At the same time, they expected their *muqati'jis* (feudatories) to deliver on their collection of due taxes so that the Shihabs could hand them over to Ottoman authorities, mainly to the walis of Tripoli, Damascus, and Sidon, on time. The more territories the Shihabs acquired, the more taxes they were supposed to pay.

Upon Emir Haydar's death, his son Mulhim (1732–1754) ascended the emirate's throne. Secure in his emirate, Emir Mulhim expanded his realm by taking over the Beka', Jabal 'Amil, and Beirut. Beirut remained in the hands of Shihabs until the rise of Ahmad al-Jazzar of 'Akka (Acre). In 1754 Mulhim abdicated in favor of his brother Mansur (1754–1770), bitterly disappointing his other brother, Ahmad, who came to contest the authority of Emir Mansur. This contestation over the emirate spawned the Druze Jumblatt-Yazbaki partisanship, which came to affect the politics of Mount Lebanon for genera-tions. Whereas the powerful Jumblatts, backed by the Maronite Khazins, sup-ported Mansur, the Imads, Talhuqs, and al-Maliks, backed by the Maronite Hubayshes and Dahdahs, supported Ahmad and came to be known as the Yazbaki party.[25] This fomented intra-Druze disturbances that lasted until Mansur abdicated in favor of Mulhim's son Yusuf.

Equally important, the sons of Haydar, observing the growth of Maronite community, converted to Maronitism and were followed by their al-Lam' relatives. By the late eighteenth century Maronite ascendancy in Mount Lebanon was obvious. In fact, Emir Yusuf (1770–1788) was the first Maronite to be nominated emir of the Shihab's realm. Embroiled in conflicts with the Russians and the Christians of the Balkans, the Ottoman Porte approved Yusuf's nomination as a reliable and strong emir.[26] Clearly, constant Maronite migration to southern Lebanon and their economic prosperity, the forced migration of Yemeni Druzes to Hawran, and the conversion of the Shihabs and al-Lam' to Christianity brought about Maronites' popular and political predominance. Alternatively, the Qaysi-Yemeni conflict and subse-quently the Jumblatt-Yazbaki partisanship diminished the Druze's political predominance.

Emir Yusuf's reign was affected by the politics of the leaders of 'Akka (Acre), Zahir al-Umar (1750–1775), and Ahmad al-Jazzar (1775–1804). Initially the leader of Safad, Zahir dependably delivered his due taxes to the Ottoman government at a time when it was embroiled in a bitter conflict with Catherine II of Tsarist Russia. The sultan awarded him the fiefdoms of 'Akka, Nazareth, Tiberias, and Galilee. Covetous of power and more territo-ries, Zahir aligned himself with a renegade Egyptian Mamluk, Ali Bey, who contested the Ottomans' authority in Syria in the hope of reviving Mamluk power there. At the same time, in 1771, a Russian fleet bombarded Beirut and Sidon, which was seized by Zahir in 1772. Significantly, the Shi'a of Jabal 'Amil assisted Zahir. Heeding Ottoman calls for support, Emir Yusuf aligned himself with the wali of Damascus. In the meantime, Ottoman troops and fleet were rushed to Syria and Lebanon's coast. In 1775, Sidon was retaken, and Zahir was captured and decapitated in his capital city, 'Akka.[27]

Joining the Syrian army that fought Zahir's forces and the Russians was one ruthless former slave from Bosnia by the name of Ahmad al-Jazzar (the Butcher), who lived up to his surname. In return for his intrepid military service, the sultan rewarded him the wilaya of Sidon. Al-Jazzar fortified 'Akka, made it his capital city, and held onto Beirut, ignoring Emir Yusuf's authority. In 1780, the sultan awarded him the wilaya of Damascus. In the same year, al-Jazzar decided to punish the Shi'a of Jabal 'Amil for supporting Zahir. He led a campaign there, routed Shi'a forces, and looted their religious buildings. He suppressed local chiefs and persecuted the religious class. Many Shi'a Ulema (religious scholars) fled to Iran, Iraq, Afghanistan, and India. A few years later a group of Shi'a launched a rebellion that outlasted al-Jazzar, who died in 1804. In the interim, the Shi'a population greatly suffered, being caught between the rock of al-Jazzar and the hard place of the rebels. Their livelihood, based mainly on the industry of cotton fabrics, was virtually decimated. Shi'a recovery seemed cynically tenable.[28]

Thanks no less to his ruthlessness and his dexterity in playing one party against another than to his control of the two provinces bordering Mount Lebanon and its major ports, al-Jazzar acted as the kingmaker of Mount Lebanon's politics. This aggravated Yusuf's relationship with al-Jazzar, who terminated Yusuf's leadership by crushing his forces in Qabb Ilyas in 1788. Although Yusuf submitted to the authority of the master of 'Akka, al-Jazzar hanged him.[29] Al-Jazzar, then, determined the appointment of the next Shihab emir, Bashir al-Shihab II, whose rule was no less consequential than that of the great Fakhr al-Din II.

Broadly speaking, despite spasms of tribulations during the eighteenth century, Mount Lebanon enjoyed relative peace and prosperity under the Shihab emirs. The trend that began under the Ma'ns, whereby missionaries and traders flocked to Lebanon, had become more widespread and organized under the Shihabs. In addition, Franco-Lebanese socioeconomic relations that had been interrupted under the Mamluks continued to prosper. Missionaries expanded their presence in the Shihab's realm. Walking in the footsteps of the Capuchin's missionaries, the Jesuits, Carmelites, Franciscans and Lazarites steadfastly established themselves in the realm. Since the crowning of Maronite-Rome relations with a Maronite college in the Vatican, graduate students and missionaries helped expand literacy in the realm, though mainly

Christians profited the most. During his 1783–1785 travels across Egypt and Syria, Count and scholar C. F. Volney observed that the labor of missionaries that consisted of preaching, instructing children in catechism and the psalms, and teaching how to read and write had many advantages. He remarked,

> The most valuable advantage that has resulted from these apostolic labours, is, that the art of writing has become more common among the Maronites, and rendered them, in this country, what the Copts are in Egypt, I mean, they are in the possession of all the posts of writers, intendants, and kiayas among the Turks, and especially of those among their allies and neighbours, the Druzes.[30]

No doubt, this apostolic labor enhanced Lebanese-European relations as well. From the time Fakhr al-Din II offered a consulate to the French in Sidon and built there a khan to welcome French merchants, France's trade with the Ma'n and Shihab's emirates continued to increase. The Italians and the British also expanded their trade with the emirates. Silk, oil, raisins, wool and cotton goods, and rice and coffee from neighboring provinces were shipped from the ports of Sidon, Tripoli, and Beirut. Lebanese silk was the most prized good. Of all the communities, the Maronite community fared the best. But this did not spell sectarian conflicts among Lebanon's communities. Philip Hitti perceptively observed,

> While North Lebanon, thanks to its double contact with Italy and France, was exposed—albeit dimly—to the light of publicity, South Lebanon with its Druze and Shi'ite communities lingered in relative obscurity. None of the European travelers focused on it; none of its indigenous inhabitants recorded life as lived in it. One fact, however, is clear: Christians, Druzes and Shi'ites continued to live together in harmony and peace.[31]

In fact, Volney was surprised by the security prevailing in Mount Lebanon. He observed that despite some accidents, the inhabitants of Mount Lebanon preferred it to the most fertile plains on account of "the security they enjoy from the oppressions of the Turks. This security is esteemed so valuable a blessing by the inhabitants."[32] Similarly, he was amazed by the striking resemblance between the Druzes and Maronites. He remarked that "the Druzes in their mode of life, form of government, language and customs, bear a striking resemblance to the Maronites."[33]

EMIR BASHIR AL-SHIHAB II: THE PATH TO
INDEPENDENCE AND SECTARIANISM

If Fakhr al-Din II planted the seeds of Lebanon's nationalism, then Bashir al-Shihab II (1767–1850) virtually demarcated Lebanon's borders and set the nation on an independent path. Emir Bashir was the son of Emir Qasim, the nephew of Emir Mulhim. Qasim's claims to the Shihab Emirate were refuted by his uncles Mansur and Ahmad. Consequently, Qasim retired to Ghazir in Kisrwan, where he converted to Maronitism in 1767. Later that year, his son Bashir was born, and soon thereafter Qasim passed away. Abandoned by his wealthy family and growing up in poverty, Bashir developed a shrewd and cunning personality.

Upon reaching adulthood, Bashir left for Dayr al-Qamar, the seat of Shihab Emirate, and offered his services to his father's first cousin, Emir Yusuf. It did not take long for Bashir to distinguish himself in the court of Emir Yusuf. Apparently, both al-Jazzar and the Jumblatts took note of Bashir's ambition and shrewdness in juxtaposition to Emir Yusuf's dim leadership qualities. Al-Jazzar saddled him with ever-increasing payments of tribute, which Yusuf tried to exact from his people, provoking their ire. Commoners and feudal families, spearheaded by the Jumblatts, began to oppose him. Insecure in his position and of modest means, Bashir evaded palace intrigues until the time he married the wealthy princess Shams of Hasbayah. Thenceforth, and coinciding with growing opposition to Emir Yusuf's avarice and oppression, he became receptive to the Jumblatts' scheme of supporting him as the new emir. But in all practicalities, this was a scheme of ink on paper without the stamp of al-Jazzar. Bashir's opportunity opened up when al-Jazzar defeated Yusuf in Qabb Ilyas (see above), ending his rule. Lebanon's notables met and elected his successor Bashir, the unmistakable candidate of the Jumblatts and al-Jazzar.[34]

Bashir's election as the ruler of the Shihab's realm put him face to face with al-Jazzar, who continued to act as the kingmaker of the Shihab's emirate. Little did he know that Bashir was no puppet to his scheming strings, and that Bashir had his own vision of the emirate. Al-Jazzar on several occasions replaced Bashir with the sons of Yusuf. But the litmus test for Bashir, from the standpoint of al-Jazzar, took place when Napoleon Bonaparte invaded Egypt in 1798, and thereafter laid siege to 'Akka in 1799, the seat of al-Jazzar's government. Al-Jazzar called on Bashir for help, whereupon the latter declined under the pretext that he had no control over his people, thereby infuriating al-Jazzar. At the same time, notwithstanding warm French-Shihab relations and Bonaparte's promise of granting independence to the Shihab's emirate and control of its vital seaports, Bashir prudently turned down Bonaparte's entreaty to join him. Only some Shi'ites joined Bonaparte's forces. On the other hand, whereas Maronites rooted for Bonaparte, the Druzes were apprehensive of Bonaparte's offensive. Nevertheless, when the Ottoman grand vizier, rushing his troops from Istanbul to face off Bonaparte's forces, requested help from Bashir, the Shihab emir expeditiously obliged. In gratitude, the grand vizier summarily issued a *firman* (decree) confirming the authority of Bashir over Mount Lebanon, Wadi al-Taym, Beka', and Jabal 'Amil.[35]

Meanwhile, al-Jazzar, in cooperation with the British fleet under the command of Sir Sidney Smith, was able to fend off Bonaparte's offensive. Ottoman authorities applauded the victory of al-Jazzar as a groundbreaking achievement reversing Bonaparte's world conquest. Knowing that al-Jazzar would certainly turn on him, Bashir, with the help of Smith, arranged an audience with Grand Vizier Suleiman Pasha in Egypt. The pasha agreed to intercede for Bashir with al-Jazzar, whereupon Bashir returned to his realm. Nevertheless, Bashir faced no relief from al-Jazzar's connivance and pressure until his death in 1804.[36]

The death of al-Jazzar coincided with the turn of the nineteenth century, which dawned on a changed communal and sociopolitical landscape. The Maronite economic and demographic ascendancy in southern Lebanon presented a political challenge to the Druze leadership in their abode. Evidently, the ascendance of Maronite Shihabs to power reflected the predominance of Maronitism. Moreover, Druze factionalism and internecine fighting continued to deplete their political power. The Maronite Church had become an autonomous power with large estate, thanks in no small measure to the Ma'n and Shihab's support and *waqf* (endowments) from Maronite feudal families, such as al-Khazin of Kisrwan. No less significant, the Maronite Church, alongside missionary schools, established prominent schools that imparted general and basic knowledge of the humanities, including philosophy and literature. Trained in the humanities, priests and laypeople spearheaded the Church's opposition to the muqata'jis' power, based on maintaining virtual serfdom.[37] Contesting the power of muqata'jis, the Church had become the major supporter and benefactor of Maronite commoners, mainly peasants. Lured by the liberal policies of the Ma'ns and Shihabs and welcomed by the Maronite community, Greek Catholics from Syria, including a significant number of merchants and artisans, migrated to Mount Lebanon and Beirut.[38] Greek Catholics, along with Maronites, who benefited from the silk industry, missionary education, and trade with Europe, constituted a Christian intellectual and commercial bourgeoisie. The Shi'a reeled from al-Jazzar's devastation of Jabal 'Amil and the defeat of the Hamades in northern Lebanon. A significant number of Shi'a retreated to the Beka'. It's noteworthy that the Hamades lost the al-Dinniya and Akkar districts in northern Lebanon to the

Sunni Ra'ad clan in 1686 and to the Meri'bi clan in 1714, originally a Sunni Kurdish clan, respectively.[39]

It was against this background that Bashir set about cementing his power and reconstituting Fakhr al-Din II's vision of an independent realm. With an iron fist, he centralized his power, administered firm justice, and eliminated his rivals, including the sons of his relative Emir Yusuf. He moved his seat of government to Bayt al-Din, where he built a splendid palace. He continued the liberal policy of his ancestors by welcoming minorities and missionaries to his realm and supporting education. Druze families from Aleppo and Greek Catholics from Aleppo and Damascus migrated to Mount Lebanon, Beirut, and Zahle. The first American missionary, Pliny Fisk, set foot in Beirut in 1823, where later the Syrian Protestant College (currently American University of Beirut) was established. Bashir also sent students to Europe to further their education, particularly in the medical field.

All along, he was careful to remain in favor of the Porte and a player in the ups and downs of the triumvirate of the walis of Damascus, Tripoli, and Sidon. His chance to reinforce his power and stand in good stead with the Ottomans came in 1810 when the puritan Wahhabis, backed by the al-Saud tribe of Najd, invaded Syria in 1810. The Ottomans were already chafing at the Wahhabis' capture of the two holy cities of Mecca (1803) and Medina (1804). By invading Iraq and reaching the gates of Damascus, the Wahhabis shook the Ottoman government to the core. Commanding a force of 15,000 soldiers, Bashir rushed to support Ottoman forces and repel the invaders.[40] He also helped the Ottomans suppress an insurrection near Nablus. Although this marked a high point in his relationship with Ottoman authorities, his imposition of higher taxes on the population of his realm to finance his wars and projects enraged the commoners. Their rage soon transformed into an outbreak of violence in Antilyas in 1820, whereupon Bashir prudently and temporarily withdrew to Hawran to weather the storm.[41]

No sooner did he return to Bayt al-Din than he became involved in the disputes between the walis of Damascus and Sidon. In late 1821, he supported the wali of Sidon against his counterpart in Damascus, leading a campaign against the latter and crushing his forces in al-Mazzeh, Syria. This infuriated the Porte, who forced Bashir into exile. Bashir retired to Egypt where he was warmly received by Muhammad Ali Pasha (1805–1849), who had established himself as the strongest and most reliable vassal of the sultan. Ottoman authorities recognized his prestige following his subdual of Wahhabis in Arabia. Sharing similar dreams of supremacy independent of Ottoman diktat, the two forged a strong relationship. Eventually, Ali Pasha interceded for Bashir with the Porte to return home.[42]

Bashir returned to Lebanon with his prestige untarnished, and he quickly turned against those who plotted against him during his exile, particularly his former ally Bashir Jumblatt. Jumblatt had supported Bashir's replacement while in exile. Sensing unforgiveness despite his submission to Bashir, Jumblatt fled to Hawran. Unremitting in his anger, Bashir destroyed Jumblatt's palace in Mukhtara and confiscated his properties in the Chouf. In response, Jumblatt rallied his allies and attacked Bashir in his Bayt al-Din stronghold. But his attack was turned on its head, forcing Jumblatt and his family to escape to Damascus. Upon reaching the city, Jumblatt was arrested and taken to Acre, where he was strangled, most likely at Bashir's request.[43] With Jumblatt out of the way, Druze feudal chiefs were dispossessed of their fiefs. Some left for Damascus and Hawran, while others suffered the indignation of losing their rights and privileges, let alone some of their estates. True, the elimination of Bashir's powerful and former ally Jumblatt sanctioned the Shihab emir as the undisputed leader of his emirate; nevertheless, Jumblatt's murder had the consequential effect of undercutting Druze leadership and alienating the Druze community.

Surely, Bashir crushed Jumblatt for being a political rival and not a Druze. But the Druze community, already weakened and frowning upon Maronite predominance, began to see him as a sectarian adversary. Bashir, in much the same vein as his Shihab and Ma'n ancestors, was no sectarian ruler. His ambition and political survival guided the makeup of his alliances in a realm divided into notables and commoners regardless of sect. Sectarianism had theretofore no place in Mount Lebanon. Upon visiting Bashir's realm, statesman and author Alphonse De Lamartine observed:

> Emir Beschir is himself a Christian, and even a Catholic; or, rather, he is a type of the law in all countries professing a tolerating creed: he belongs to every official form of worship prevailing in his dominions—is a Mussulman towards Mussulmans, a Druze towards the Druzes, a Christian towards Christians. His palace contains mosques as well as a church.[44]

Nevertheless, if eliminating Jumblatt shook the harmonious Maronite-Druze communal relationship, then Bashir's alliance with Muhammad Ali during his invasion of Syria sowed sectarian discord in this relationship. Muhammad Ali had assisted the sultan in fighting the Greeks (and before that the Wahhabis) who had clamored for their independence, and, in return for his services, he asked for Syria as a reward. The sultan declined his request, which made Muhammad Ali more committed to expanding his powers and securing independence from Ottoman lordship. In autumn 1831, he sent his troops, commanded by his son Ibrahim Pasha, to conquer Syria. By late November, Ibrahim had besieged Acre. The invasion of Palestine had immediate repercussions for the Shihab's emirate. Bashir was known as Muhammad Ali's ally and friend. Perhaps the Druzes saw in the Egyptian invasion the opportunity they were waiting for to avenge the murder of their leader Jumblatt or, an opportunity to gain favor with the sultan by standing by him so that he could restore their leadership over Mount Lebanon. Druze chieftains joined the Ottoman army to check the advance of Egyptian troops. On the other hand, Christians, including in Syria, rooted for the incoming Egyptian troops. Be that as it may, scattered troubles broke out between Maronites and Druzes in Mount Lebanon.[45]

As resistance to Ibrahim Pasha intensified, he called on Bashir for support. Bashir prevaricated, fearing, on the one hand, Druze escalation of troubles in Mount Lebanon and vicinity, and on the other hand, Muslim dissension because Ibrahim Pasha had promised legal equality for Christians and Muslims. Whatever his concerns, Bashir brushed them aside upon receiving a stern letter from Muhammad Ali. Bashir threw in his lot with Ibrahim Pasha. Bashir's troops fought alongside those of Ibrahim Pasha in the battles over 'Akka, Beirut, Tripoli, Homs, and Damascus. Zahleh was made a depot of arms and provisions for Egyptian forces. As promised, upon conquering each town, Ibrahim Pasha removed the long-standing restrictions imposed on Christians and Jews. And, with the help of Bashir, Ibrahim rapidly held sway over Syria, unnerving not only the Ottomans but also the British. The British feared that Muhammad Ali, supported by the French, could threaten their interest in Asia Minor and the Indian subcontinent.[46]

At first, Ibrahim Pasha established a more or less fair and efficient administration in Syria, which he ruled directly with the help of Bashir's sons. Emir Bashir, under the suzerainty of Ibrahim Pasha, continued to administer his own expanded emirate. Lamartine observed that the chief towns of Beirut, Sidon, Tripoli, Jaffa, and Acre were conjointly occupied by Bashir's and Ibrahim Pasha's troops. Lamartine also observed that should the situation change, Bashir would forsake Ibrahim Pasha. He grimly remarked that "were Ibrahim to be defeated at Homs, the Emir Beschir might possibly cut off his retreat, and annihilate the remains of the Egyptian army."[47]

But it did not take long for the Egyptian occupation of Syria to become costly, save maintaining the readiness of the Egyptian army and reinforcing the northern frontiers against Ottoman forces. Syria was an impoverished province, buffeted by troubles and misrule. And the Ottomans were by no means disposed to let go of their occupied provinces. Muhammad Ali ordered his son to raise taxes, take control of the silk industry including in Mount Lebanon, and disarm and conscript the population. Rebellions broke out in 1834 in Palestine, Tripoli, and Lattakia region. Ibrahim Pasha, with help from Bashir, put them down. Meanwhile, Ibrahim Pasha abolished the autonomy of Shi'a chieftains in Jabal 'Amil, putting the district under the authority of Emir Bashir. In 1836, upset with the overbearing rule of Bashir's son, the Shi'a rebelled. Fearing renewed fighting with the Ottomans, Ibrahim Pasha, in late 1837, ordered additional Druze conscription in the Egyptian army from Hawran, and called on Bashir to conscript Druze and Christians.

In 1838, Hawran's Druzes rebelled and were able to repel an Egyptian military expedition sent by Ibrahim Pasha to suppress them. They also called on their co-religionists for help. In response, the Druzes of Wadi al-Taym rebelled, supported by Druzes from Mount Lebanon. These rebellions coincided with the smoldering violence in Jabal 'Amil. Beset by these enduring rebellions, Ibrahim Pasha asked Bashir to organize a Christian force and to assist him in crushing the rebellion in Hawran and Wadi al-Taym. Bashir was placed in a very difficult novel situation. Never before had a Ma'n or Shibab emir participated in a confrontation between Druzes and Maronites, or for that matter, between two sects. This went against the grain of long-standing traditional policy in Mount Lebanon. Furthermore, Bashir was already looked upon by the Druzes as a Christian adversary since the murder of Bashir Jumblatt. Eventually, unable to avoid this predicament, Bashir led a force of 4,000 Maronites and joined Ibrahim Pasha's forces in suppressing the Druze rebels. This consequential event planted the seeds of sectarianism and Maronite-Druze feud.[48]

Equally important, Muslims and Druzes were disturbed by the reforms of Ibrahim Pasha and the concessions he gave to European traders that benefited the Christians. Not only were Christians to be treated on an equal footing with the Muslims, but also Christians emerged as the beneficiaries of concessions made as part of elaborate capitulations with European powers. Maronites and Greek Catholics controlled most businesses in Beirut, which emerged as a trade hub in the Levant.[49] Other factors also simmered sectarian tension. Druze *'uqqals* (wise religious men) and commoners stood in solidarity with their muqata'jis, who frowned upon the steady loss of their privileges in favor of Christian muqata'jis and the emerging class of a Christian intellectual-commercial bourgeoisie. Conversely, Christian muqata'jis frowned upon the growing power of the Maronite Church, which, thanks to its support of Emir Bashir, and by extension Ibrahim Pasha, further expanded its political and economic power as the largest landholder in Mount Lebanon.

No sooner were the rebellions tamed than the Ottomans led a military campaign in the spring of 1839 to defeat the Egyptian army in Syria. Ibrahim Pasha's forces met the Ottoman forces at Nizib in Syria, not too far from the Iraqi border. To the consternation and shock of European powers, Ibrahim Pasha dealt a severe blow to the sultan's army, and appeared close to proclaim the death knell of the Ottoman seat of power in Istanbul. Immediately thereafter, Great Britain, Russia, Austria, and Prussia decided to intervene to prevent the breakup of the Ottoman Empire. Since France continued to support Muhammad Ali, the aforementioned powers gave Muhammad Ali an ultimatum according to which he could only keep the hereditary wilayas of Egypt and Acre or face grim consequences. Backing their ultimatum with a show of force, on August 11, 1840, British and Austrian warships reached the shores of Beirut.

In the meantime, British and Ottoman emissaries had been making diplomatic rounds to rally Lebanese opposition to Ibrahim Pasha. Already the Druzes and Shi'ites had seen their revolts suppressed by Ibrahim Pasha and his enforcer Emir Bashir and were disposed to reignite their rebellion under opportune circumstances. Significantly, the Maronites had shifted to the opposition. Concerned about a new military campaign and/or revolt against his Egyptian army in the Levant, Muhammad Ali ordered his son to disarm the Maronites. He feared that Maronites could join the Druzes and Shi'ites in a revolt against his army, as Britain had hoped. Ibrahim Pasha had armed the Maronites and, in appreciation of their services in suppressing the revolts in Hawran and Wadi al-Taym, promised them to keep the arms and not to raise their taxes. Muhammad Ali also felt that disarming Maronites and Druzes was a crucial preliminary step to conscript them. Maronites were enraged.

Emir Bashir found himself again in a difficult situation that he could not circle the wagons around, and opted to obey Muhammad Ali's orders. He called on the Maronite, Druze, and Greek Catholic inhabitants of Dayr al-Qamar to disarm as a first step to disarm other towns, given the reputation of Dayr al-Qamar as the most armed town in Mount Lebanon. Little did he know that his orders would instantaneously bring about intercommunal solidarity, expressed by a solemn oath to oppose disarmament and restore independence to Mount Lebanon and its hinterland. Soon enough, the revolt in Day al-Qamar spread like wildfire throughout the Shihab Emirate. At the same time, British, Austrian, and Ottoman warships bombarded Beirut, the headquarters of Egyptian operations, and moved to land troops at Jounieh, north of Beirut, to support the rebels. In October 1840, the Egyptian army withdrew to Acre, and Emir Bashir, abandoned even by his ardent supporters, including the Maronite Church, surrendered to the British. He was exiled to Malta, whence he moved to Istanbul, where he died in 1850.[50]

The ouster of Bashir brought to an end the rule of the longest-serving emir, whose reign aspired for independence and demarcated the geographic contours of modern Lebanon. His reign also witnessed the introduction of sectarianism and foreign involvement, which became fixtures in Lebanon's politics. Reflecting on the momentous life of Bashir, Lammens remarked: "Une légende se formera autour de son nom, comme autour de la mémoire de son prèdécesser ma'nide, don't sa carrière et sa chute rappellent la vie mouvementée."[51]

Chapter 3

Sectarian Violence and Mount Lebanon Autonomy

SECTARIAN VIOLENCE AND THE *QA'IM MAQAMIYAH*

The fall of Bashir II's rule ushered in a period of instability whereby a conflation of internal and external factors brought an end to the Shihab Emirate. Britain and Austria, which played a key role in ending Muhammad Ali's rule in the Levant, had become influential there and vexed the Ottomans. Britain swayed the appointment of Bashir Shihab III as the new Shihab Emir. Bashir III, unlike his predecessor, was incompetent and no kingmaker in internal politics. During his brief domain (1840–1842), sociopolitical and sectarian tensions were intensified following an interregnum of intercommunal solidarity to oust Emir Bashir II. No sooner had he succeeded to the emirate than Druze and other feudal chiefs who had been forced from the Shihab's realm during Bashir II and Egyptian rule began to return home. Led by the sons of Bashir Jumblatt and backed by the British and Ottomans, they immediately began to lay claim to their feudal estates and privileges. They were also joined by Druze chiefs who suffered the loss of estates and rights under Bashir II.

Bashir III was neither ready to meet their demands nor able to blunt their actions. Furthermore, Bashir III also unsuccessfully tried to reduce the power of Christian feudal chiefs. Meanwhile, Christians who had acquired Druze estates under Bashir II rejected out of hand Druze demands of restitution. In addition, Christians who lived in original Druze districts refused to resubmit to Druze judicial power, short of the death penalty. All along, Maronite Patriarch Yusuf Hubaysh (1823–1845) continued to press his case to the sultan that a Shihab Maronite emir be appointed for life as ruler of Mount Lebanon, assisted by a Maronite *mudabbir* (secretary) and twelve councilors representing the different sects. All of this infuriated Druze chieftains and deepened Druze ill-feeling toward Maronites, tracing it back to the murder of Bashir Jumblatt and Maronite participation in the suppression of Druze revolts in Hawran and Wadi al-Taym. Whatever solidarity Maronites and Druzes had shared to oust Emir Bashir II completely vanished.

It was against this background that an incident in early 1841 seemed to trigger the first Maronite-Druze clashes, laying bare the political and socioeconomic asymmetry between the two communities that pushed them to mobilize and subsequently clash along confessional lines. Reportedly a Maronite from Dayr al-Qamar shot a partridge on the property of a Druze from al-Nakad family in neighboring Ba'aqlin. This led to a quarrel that devolved into a clash between the Christians of Day al-Qamar and the Nakads, supported by the Jumblatts and the Imads. Seventeen Druzes from Ba'aqlin were killed. Although Patriarch Hubaysh sent a delegation to the Chouf to express regret and settle the issue, the Druze chieftains dissimulated accepting Christian apologies and stealthily prepared for revenge. Belying their response to attend a meeting summoned by Bashir III in Dayr al-Qamar, the Druzes assailed the town and set it on fire on October 14. Soon clashes spread to other towns in the Chouf district where Druze fighters gained the upper hand, and fleeing Maronites were attacked by Ottoman troops. Conversely, the Druze attack on Zahle, the main Christian town in the Beka', was repelled by the town's Greek Catholics, who were assisted by the Shi'a from Ba'albeck.

Both Bashir III and Patriarch Hubaysh called on Christians to support their co-religionists and upon Ottoman authorities to stop the fighting. A Christian offensive from Ba'abda backfired, leading Druzes to plunder more Christian villages under the indulgent eyes of the Ottomans. Christians either failed or hesitated to relieve Emir Bashir III, who was under siege in his Dayr al-Qamar's palace. Greek Orthodox, unlike Greek Catholics, were reluctant to rally around Maronites; and Christian *muqata'jis* halfheartedly supported their co-religionists. Capitalizing on Christian discord, Druzes stormed Bashir's palace and mishandled him. It was then that Ottoman authorities finally, under pressure from France, Britain, and Russia, decided to stop the fighting.

The Ottomans were eager to abolish local autonomy in their provinces, especially in Mount Lebanon, as part of a series of Ottoman reforms, known collectively as the *tanzimat* (1839–1876), to centralize and modernize the Ottoman Empire. As such, the Ottomans were keen on demonstrating to the European powers that Maronite-Druze reconciliation was hardly possible, and therefore their self-rule was a recipe for further deadly troubles. In January 1842, the Porte declared the end of the Shihab Emirate, deposed Bashir III, and sent him off to Istanbul. He appointed Umar Pasha as governor of Mount Lebanon, and commissioned Mustapha Pasha to find out the causes of troubles and devise measures to restore order. The Ottomans had triumphed in establishing their direct rule over Mount Lebanon, reflecting the collapse of Maronite-Druze solidarity upon which the autonomy of Mount Lebanon had historically rested.[1]

Umar Pasha set up his headquarters at the Shihab's palace in Bayt al-Din, and set about, in full cooperation with Mustapha Pasha, to prove to European powers the paramountcy of Ottoman direct rule over Mount Lebanon. He tried to gain the loyalty of both Maronites and Druzes, but to no avail. He returned to the Druze feudal chiefs their privileges and estates, which had been appropriated by the Shihab Emirs. But the Druzes clamored for their self-rule, perceiving that they were the chief party that overthrew Bashir III. Druze commoners continued to stand in solidarity with their feudal chiefs. Alternatively, Umar Pasha tried to ingratiate himself with both Christian feudal chiefs and commoners. Whereas the feudal chiefs supported him, Christian commoners, encouraged by the Maronite Church, favored the reconstitution of the Shihab Emirate. At the same time, Umar and Mustapha Pashas devised a plan to show European powers that Ottoman direct rule over Mount Lebanon had popular backing. They sent agents to collect signatures on a petition praising Ottoman rule and asking the Porte to prevent the return of the Shihabs. Druze feudal chiefs were more or less indifferent about the petition. Maronite feudal chiefs, unlike the Maronite Church and to its chagrin, supported the petition. Commenting on Maronite feudal chiefs' capitulation to Ottoman designs, British Colonel Charles Henry Churchill, who surveyed the unfolding of events in Mount Lebanon emphasized:

> Such was the venality and pusillanimity of the Christian aristocracy, that numbers were gained over by the most ordinary presents, such as pelisses or shawls, and, utterly regardless of past experience or future consequences, to vote for the permanent supremacy over them, of those very beings who had but one short month before been reveling in their blood and trampling on their religion.[2]

At the same time, foreign involvement in Mount Lebanon's affairs peaked and made Umar Pasha's task of securing the loyalty of Mount Lebanon's communities hardly possible. To be sure, from Umar Pasha and Mustapha Pasha's standpoint, securing the loyalty of Maronite and Druze communities did not mean securing the peace between them. In fact, the more the two communities were at loggerheads, the better the Ottomans could make the case to European powers that their direct rule over Mount Lebanon was essential for securing peace there. Colonel Churchill emphasized:

> A more unhappy choice could not possibly have been made. It soon appeared that his [Mustapha Pasha] sole object was to inflame still farther the unhappy

dissensions which already existed, and to excite the feelings of the Mohammedan sects in such a manner as to increase with tenfold energy their ordinary antipathy to the Christians.[3]

All along, the French and Austrians championed the protection of Maronites and Uniate Catholics, Russia the protection of Greek Orthodox, and Britain the protection of the Druzes. Although Britain, unlike France, was a recent actor in Mount Lebanon's communal politics, it managed through its dexterous consul in Beirut, Colonel Hugh Rose, to draw the Druzes into an alliance under which terms Britain would safeguard Druze interests, and Druzes, for their part, would uphold British policy. As gestures of goodwill, Druzes welcomed to their districts Protestant missionaries, while Britain supplied Druzes with arms. No doubt, the Anglo-Druze alliance extinguished hopes of Maronite-Druze solidarity. Conversely, the Maronites threw in their lot with the French, who initially toiled to keep Maronites and Druzes away from British influence. But following the Anglo-Druze alliance, the French focused on Catholics. No less significant, European missionaries deepened the sectarian schism among Mount Lebanon's communities. Catholic missionaries incited Christian Catholics against the Druzes, and Protestant missionaries drew the ire of Maronite and Greek Orthodox clergy for expanding their missionary activities. Maronite clergy considered Protestants as heretics, and the Orthodox clergy, egged on by the Russian consulate in Beirut, tried to keep their flock away from British and American Protestant teaching and activities.[4]

Meanwhile, Umar Pasha was getting angry with the Druzes for their dwindling support. Significantly, he was disappointed with the Anglo-Druze alliance for not supporting the results of his petition, citing, along other European powers, Ottoman intimidation and corruption. In fact, the proposal of the Porte to maintain direct rule in Mount Lebanon was rejected by most European powers, which called for the establishment of a new form of government. The Maronite Church and Druzes applauded the position of European powers, although for different reasons, infuriating Umar Pasha. Before long, as Druze opposition to Umar Pasha intensified, Umar Pasha, on April 6, 1942, ordered the arrest of Druze chiefs who had come upon his invitation for dinner in Bayt al-Din. The arrest of the most prominent Druze chiefs drove the Druzes to rebellion.[5]

In an attempt to rally a strong force and knowing Maronite opposition to Umar Pasha, the Druzes appealed to the Maronite Patriarch to recreate a Maronite-Druze alliance as they did against Ibrahim Pasha. The Druzes promised to agree to the reconstitution of the Shihab Emirate and to compensate Christians for their losses in the 1841 clashes. However, suspicion and hostility between the two communities scuttled their reunion. At this point, the Druzes of Hawran and Wadi al-Taym, led by Shibli al-'Aryan, a veteran leader of the uprising against Ibrahim Pasha, decided to act alone. They swiftly advanced into the Chouf, and by the end of November al-'Aryan stormed his way to Bayt al-Din and put Umar Pasha under siege. Startled by the swift Druze advance, As'ad Pasha, who had replaced Mustapha Pasha as commissioner extraordinaire, sent emissaries to negotiate al-'Aryan's withdrawal from the Chouf. Eventually, As'ad Pasha was taken aback by al-'Aryan's audacious demands that needed to be met before his withdrawal, which included (a) the immediate dismissal of Umar Pasha, (b) the release of Druze chiefs from prison, and (c) exemption of Mount Lebanon from conscription and disarmament, as well as exemption from taxation for three years.[6]

Acknowledging that a face-saving compromise to uphold Ottoman authority with the Druzes was unfeasible, As'ad Pasha designed a plan whereby he would send a military expedition of Turkish and Albanian troops from Sidon to Dayr al-Qamar to attack al-'Aryan forces from the rear; concurrently, Umar Pasha's garrison, assisted by Maronite cavalry, would attack them headlong. The plan was successful, and Asa'd Pasha won the day. Druze chiefs fled to Hawran, Druze fighters shabbily dispersed in various directions, and al-'Aryan surrendered.[7]

Parallel to these developments, European powers had been haggling among themselves and negotiating with the Porte what form of government should be established in Mount Lebanon. Finally, the Porte agreed on a compromise plan introduced by the Austrian chancellor, Prince Metternich. Mount Lebanon would be divided into two districts, a northern district under a Christian *qa'im maqam* (sub-governor), and a southern district under a Druze qa'im maqam. Both qa'im maqams would be under the authority of the Sidon *wali* residing in Beirut. The Beirut-Damascus road marked the division line between the two districts. Although the French and the Maronite Church supported the appointment of a Shihab as qa'im maqam, Emir Haydar abu al-Lam' was appointed in a compromise with the British and the Porte, who refused the return of Shihabs. Similarly, although a number of Druze sheikhs and the British advocated for a Jumblatt as a qa'im maqam, Emir Ahmad Arslan was appointed in a compromise with the Porte and the Druze Yazbaki faction who were concerned about Jumblatt's prospective supremacy in the Druze district.[8]

In principle, this political division made sense by having a Maronite administer the original abode of the Christians in northern Mount Lebanon and a Druze administer the original abode of the Druzes in southern Lebanon. In practice, however, this division was a recipe for further sectarian strife by deepening religious cleavages and grievances. The two *qa'im maqamiyahs* had a mixed population. Many Druzes lived among Christians in

Matn, the southernmost district of the Christian qa'im maqamiyah, while many Christians lived among Druzes in Chouf and al-Gharb in the Druze qa'im maqamiyah. Dayr al-Qamar, enjoying a special administration, was a Christian stronghold in the heart of the Druze qa'im maqamiyah.[9] Moreover, the original plan stipulated that each qa'im maqam would be responsible for his own co-religionists, which meant that the boundary between the two administrative districts was more illusory than practical. As such, the Christian qa'im maqam would be responsible for his co-religionists in the Druze district, undercutting the authority of Druze feudal chiefs, and vice versa.

Taking note of this problem, the Porte resolved to limit the jurisdiction of each qa'im maqam to his own district. France and Emir Haydar opposed the decision of the Porte, with the latter claiming full jurisdiction over all Christians including those living in the Druze district. Moreover, Emir Haydar was not happy with the exclusion of Jbeil from his district following the Russian appeal to the Porte to carve out an independent Greek Orthodox district. Haydar's claim, supported by the French Consul in Beirut, Prosper Bourée, was rejected by Emir Arslan and Colonel Rose, both of whom advocated for the principle of territorial jurisdiction. Unable to resolve the impasse, As'ad Pasha appealed to the Porte to send a high-ranking envoy to mediate among European powers and find a solution. The Porte obliged and sent Khalil Pasha, the admiral of the Ottoman fleet.

Upon his arrival to Beirut in June 1844, Khalil Pasha set about finessing a solution to a virtually intractable problem based on socioeconomic and political grievances expressed in religious terms. Equally important, European involvement in inter- and intra-communal politics exacerbated sectarian tensions. Before long, Khalil Pasha decided that the Shihabs would not return to power and that the question of jurisdiction in mixed districts would be settled by having two agents (*wakil*), one Christian and one Druze, chosen by their respective communities with the approval of the local qa'im maqam, but each responsible to the qa'im maqam of his sect. He also specified the indemnity that the Druzes had to pay to the Christians for losses suffered in 1841.[10]

Druze chiefs were not happy with Khalil Pasha's decisions, perceiving them as undercutting their judicial prerogatives. They also refused to pay any indemnity to the Christians unless they were under their jurisdiction. No less significant, the two communities were barely on speaking terms, thereby making Khalil Pasha's arrangements hardly possible. Broadly speaking, it was taboo for a Maronite, even in a mixed area, to speak with a Druze. Ominously, in early February 1845, the Druze chiefs held a general meeting in Mukhtara, the seat of Jumblatt's power, which was attended by their rival faction, the Yazbakis. This raised the fears of the Christians, let alone the Ottomans and the French and Austrian consuls, about the purpose of the meeting. Although Colonel Rose tried to assuage their fears that the Druze chiefs were not preparing for battle, Christians began taking military precautions and Ottoman authorities rushed reinforcements to the Chouf to prevent an outbreak of violence. The Maronite Patriarch angrily declared that "the blow must be struck, and he who strikes first will have two chances to one in his favour."[11]

Soon, fears of a renewed confrontation were confirmed as clashes between Maronites and Druzes swept Mount Lebanon like wildfire. Christians, as previously, lacked a united front. Maronite feudal chiefs had been concerned about growing peasant mobilization against feudal aristocracy in conjunction with support from the Maronite Church and its ascendancy. Moreover, Greek Orthodox, unlike Greek Catholics, leaned more toward helping the Druzes.[12] Nevertheless, Maronites would have been able to gain the upper hand in their confrontation with the Druzes had it not been for Ottoman military involvement on the side of the Druzes. Wajihi Pasha, who replaced Umar Pasha, either stood idly by or took part in the fighting when Druzes were painted into a corner. He obstructed the movement of Christians, while allowing the Druzes to move freely. He defended the Druzes in Mukhtara, al-Matn, Qurnayel, and other areas either by blockading Christian reinforcements or repelling Christian attacks. By May, the Ottomans changed the tide of war in favor of the Druzes. All along, villages were burned and plundered, and fleeing villagers robbed, beaten, or even killed.[13]

A juxtaposition of a memorandum by the Christians of Zahle to the French consul, Eugène Poujade, with a letter from Druze chief Sa'id Jumblatt to another Druze chief, Hamoud al-Nakad, during the civil strife of 1840s emphasized the Ottoman role in the civil strife and the contentious socio-economic and religious ramifications for communal coexistence. The memorandum read:

> The Druze came to attack us . . . our Christians turned against them and routed them . . . When the Turks saw that we were the victors, they sent us Gebran-Aura, Cassem and Mustapha-Aga [Ottoman officers] with soldiers who shot at us; we then withdrew. At the same time, other Druzes attacked the Christians camped in Ras al-Matn and defeated them. The pasha did not hurry to stop the vanquishers of Christians; on the contrary, he let them burn the whole Matn. When he saw us defeat the Druzes he made his soldiers stop us. According to our reports, it seems positive that the Druzes are only coming to war on us because they are forced to do so by their *maqata'jis* [feudal chiefs]. . . . Indeed, as long as the chiefs have pretensions, privileges, immunities, Lebanon will not be able to enjoy peace. . . . Lebanon is not the property of the Druzes; it is ours. The Druzes are refugees whom we were kind enough to welcome when they fled Egypt after the murder of the impostor Hakim . . . they are foreigners. . . . Peace

may well be made between the Druze peasants and the Christians but not with their leaders who will always want to have prerogatives on our brothers, which is the most impossible thing.[14]

The letter read:

Illustrious Brother . . . venerable Sheikh Hamoud. You have no doubt learned what the nation of Christian infidels did at home in the Chouf; if the Porte and his troops had not rescued us, they would have dispersed us. Now we and the other Druze gatherings have been allowed by his Excellency the illustrious Daoud-Pasha [Commander of Ottoman forces in Mount Lebanon] to fall upon the Christian nation and annihilate it. In accordance with this authorization, it is your duty to stand up immediately with your men, to fall upon the Chahar and Dubbieh Christians, to burn their houses. . . . Fear not. The troops who are in Abbey, have the order to help you; so this is the time to take the opportunity to annihilate this perverse nation. May God protect you.[15]

This memorandum and the letter make clear that the Ottomans assisted the Druzes in their confrontation with the Christians. The memorandum claims that Druze peasants would not wage war against Christians were it not for the Druze feudal chiefs. Significantly, the memorandum asserts that peace would not be possible so long as Druze feudal chiefs have prerogatives over Christians. No less significant, on a grim note, whereas Christians perceived the Druzes as strangers to the land, preeminent Druze leader Jumblatt described the Christian community as an infidel nation to be annihilated.

Finally, coming under heavy pressure from European consuls, Wajihi Pasha intervened to stop the fighting. In early June, he summoned Druze and Christian chiefs to Beirut to end the hostilities. Wajihi Pasha, along with the British and Russian consuls, blamed the Christians for the violence. The French consul, Poujade, recognizing Wajihi Pasha's partiality to the Druzes, demanded his immediate replacement. With no agreement in sight and violence in mixed districts unabated, the Porte, under pressure from European powers, sent Ottoman Foreign Minister Shakib Effendi to bring about a settlement.

Once in Beirut in September 1845, Shakib Effendi began in earnest fulfilling a plan he already hatched before his departure to pacify Mount Lebanon. He urged European consuls (British, French, Austrian, Russian, and Prussian) not to meddle in local affairs; insisted that Europeans, especially missionaries, residing in Mount Lebanon move temporarily to Beirut; placed under arrest most Christian and Druze chiefs; indemnified Christians for some of their losses due to them; and ordered the disarmament of Mount Lebanon. Once he followed through on his plan, he turned to settle the central question of Mount Lebanon's administration. His settlement, as represented by an organic law known by his name the *Règlement* of Shakib Effendi, was communicated to European consuls on October 29 and became effective upon its publication.[16]

Mount Lebanon (and its hinterlands) would remain divided into two districts, each headed by qa'im maqam appointed and removed by the Sidon wali. Each qa'im maqam would preside over a *majlis* (council) consisting of a deputy qa'im maqam, a judge, and an adviser for each of the Maronite, Druze, Sunni, Greek Catholic, and Greek Orthodox sects. The Shi'a had only an adviser since the Sunni judge would adjudicate for both Sunnis and Shi'ites. The majlis would decide on the assessment, distribution, and collection of taxes and on hearing judicial cases referred by the qa'im maqam. Fiscal matters would require unanimity from the majlis. Absent unanimity, the Sidon wali would decide as he saw fit. Settlement of judicial cases did not need the majlis' unanimity. They would be heard by the judge of the sect to which the contending parties belonged. Should the cases involve contending parties from different sects, then the judges of the respective sects would jointly adjudicate the cases. Dayr al-Qamar would retain a special administration under the Sidon wali, who would have the last word in all public appointments.[17] No doubt, the Règlement was written in the spirit of the tanzimat to centralize the Ottoman Empire.

As the previous arrangement, Shakib Effendi's Règlement was great in principle but vulnerable in practice. The Règlement actually undercut Mount Lebanon's feudal system by vesting in the councils most prerogatives that belonged to the feudal chiefs. No sooner Shakib Effendi left for Istanbul than both Christian and Druze feudal chiefs tried to obstruct the application of the organic law, to the chagrin of peasants. Christian peasants, in particular, supported the Règlement because not only it undermined the jurisdiction power of feudal chiefs, but also gave them a representative voice in the majlis. Furthermore, European councils resumed their involvement in local affairs, deepening inter- and intra-communal schisms. Commenting on the relationship between European powers and Mount Lebanon's communities, Richard Edwards underlined: "We know rightly or wrongly that in Syria we look at the Greek Orthodox as the protégés of Russia, the Greek Catholics as the protégés of Austria, the Maronites as the faithful of France, and the Druze as the humble servants of England."[18]

Clearly, the obstruction of the Règlement intensified the rift between Maronite feudal chiefs, on one side, and the Maronite Church and peasants, on the other. Maronite peasants had been chafing at their feudal chiefs (the Khazins, Dahdahs, Hubayshes, and Dahers) for their lordship over them; and most recently, for their virtual collusion with the Druzes by not supporting the Christians in the civil strife. Essentially, whatever mutual links the two parties had under the pretext of Maronite solidarity were severed when Bulus Mas'ad was elected as Patriarch in 1854. Born of peasant stock and known for his antipathy toward the feudal class, Patriarch Mas'ad brought the Maronite clergy into a firm alliance with the peasants.[19] This unsettled Christian relations in Kisrwan and north Lebanon and paved the way for a peasant rebellion against the feudal lords of the Mountain.

Similarly, factionalism among the Druzes intensified as the rival clans the Jumblatts and Yazbakis began regrouping their camps, with European powers egging on one side against the other. Meanwhile, Druze tension with Ottoman authorities built up over the latter's opposition to the preeminence of feudal chief Sa'id Jumblatt in juxtaposition to that of the Druze qa'im maqam. In 1852, this tension climaxed into a Druze rebellion against the Ottomans when the Porte called for a general conscription of the Druzes. Nevertheless, the Crimean war (1853–1856), in which the Ottomans fought the Russians, brought the Ottomans close to the Druzes. The Ottomans appreciated the effort of the Druze qa'im maqam, Amin Arslan, to organize a Druze contingent to fight on the side of the Ottomans. This rapprochement burgeoned when Kurshid Pasha became the new wali of Sidon in 1857. Residing in Beirut, Kurshid Pasha made no effort to conceal his partiality to the Druzes, to the chagrin of Christians.

By 1858, Mount Lebanon and its hinterlands had become a cauldron of simmering socioeconomic, political, and inter- and intra-communal tensions on the cusp of boiling over into a crucible of war. The split in the Maronite community of Kisrwan and northern Lebanon between the feudal chiefs and their supporters, on one side, and the Maronite Church and peasants, on the other, deepened and became invariably compounded. The preeminent Khazin feudal family of Kisrwan opposed the Christian qa'im maqam Bashir Ahmad Abu al-lam', who replaced his kinsman Haydar Abu al-Lam' following his death in 1854. Initially, the Khazins had disdained the appointment of Bashir Ahmad as qa'im maqam for being what they considered of lesser stature. Then they opposed him for his harsh administrative rulings, including arresting some of them. Worried about the trend of their diminishing power since the rule of Emir Bashir II, the Khazins rallied other feudal families and waged a campaign against Bashir Ahmad, supporting his rival kinsman Bashir Assaf Abu al-Lam'. In response, Bashir Ahmad solicited the help of the Maronite clergy and peasants, championing their causes. Before long, European consuls became involved. No sooner had the French and Austrian consuls supported Bashir Ahmad than the British consul supported Bashir Assaf, further polarizing the Christian community.

It was against this background that the peasants' social mobilization, with support from the Maronite clergy, against the Christian feudal aristocracy took an active turn. Young men in each village organized themselves to defend their community against the injustices of the feudal aristocracy, in particular the Khazin family whose oppression had become notoriously unbearable:

> For [the Khazins] no longer took any account of their subjects, nor even of the leading persons among them. They would say that the peasant and his posses-sions belonged to them, showing not the slightest regard for him. The most insignificant of the Khazins would insult the most reputable of the people, not to mention killing or imprisoning them and such like.[20]

As it turned out, mediation between the Khazins and the peasants failed. This coincided with the nomination of Tanius Shahin as the leader of the peasant movement. Shahin, a half-literate muleteer from Ajaltun, Kisrwan, defied the perceptions of both his supporters and detractors, including European consuls who considered him a ruffian with questionable character. Strong and ambitious, exuding an air of superiority, Shahin toured the countryside and aroused the anti-feudal feelings of the villagers. His speeches reflected both the injustices of the feudal aristocracy and notions of the liberal political climate ushered in by the reforms of Muhammad Ali and Ottoman tanzimat. Shahin's speeches struck a deep chord with the peasants, who treated him like a hero. And he played his role to a fault. Before long, the Kisrwan peasant revolt, led by Shahin, began in earnest in January 1859. The Khazins' entreat-ies with Kurshid Pasha for intervention not only did not go anywhere, but fur-ther incited the peasant movement. Shahin, assisted by village peasant chiefs, chased the Khazins out of their homes.[21] Neither Ottoman authorities nor the Maronite clergy, who were tacitly supporting the revolt, came to the rescue of the Khazins. By early spring, the Khazins had been evicted from Kisrwan.[22]

The wave of peasant euphoric victory revived the hopes of Christian peas-ants in Druze districts. But here the Druze peasants, encouraged by their *'uqqals*, were too distrustful of their Christian neighbors to make common cause with them and rise against the Druze feudal chiefs. The sectarian hos-tilities of the 1840s were too fresh in their mind and constantly evoked by scattered religiously inspired incidents throughout the 1850s, about which Ottoman authorities did nothing. In fact, Christian-Druze sectarian polariza-tion continued to intensify until an incident apparently triggered the worst sectarian massacre in the history of Mount Lebanon.

THE 1860 MASSACRES

Eyewitness accounts, including by Protestant missionary Henry H. Jessup and British Colonel Charles Henry Churchill, provided vivid details of the political climate and wanton actions committed by the antagonists, especially the Druzes in complicity with Khurshid Pasha. On August 30, 1859, a quarrel between a Christian and a Druze boy in Beit Mirri, a village nine miles east of Beirut, evolved into a Maronite-Druze bloody affray in which the Druzes were beaten with a great loss of life.[23] Chafing at their defeat, Druzes began preparing for war, whereupon the Maronites followed suit. The harsh snowy weather of Mount Lebanon apparently offered the two communities enough time to better prepare and arm, while Ottoman authorities stood idly by. Jessup expounded the situation:

> All through the fall and winter, both sides hastened their preparations. The government of Beirut could have stopped these movements at any moment, and prohibited the importation of arms and ammunition. But for some reason they did not interfere.[24]

But Maronites' preparations and bravado were no match to Druze's stealthy preparations and treachery. Druze sheikhs took the unusual step of spending the winter of 1859–1860 in Beirut, where they held long and frequent meetings with Ottoman authorities. As it turned out, the Ottomans armed the Druzes and planned with them how to bring Christians to their knees.[25] By early May, scattered violence broke out throughout the Druze districts, while at the same time Druze feudal chief Sa'id Jumblatt held constant assemblies with his co-religionists. Jessup illustrated:

> The air was thick with the news of outrage and murder: two Christians killed at Owaly bridge near Sidon, four Druzes killed at Medairij on the Damascus road, three Christians at Jisr el Kadi bridge; two Moslems at Juneh north of Dog River near Beirut; muleteers carrying flour to Deir el Komr stopped by the Druzes, the highroad everywhere dangerous. The Druse leader, Said Beg Jumblatt, held constant councils, and his adherents poured in from all quarters.[26]

As violence and agitation increased in the Chouf, Jezzin, and Dayr al-Qamar, the Christians there appealed to their co-religionists in Kisrwan. The strongman of Kisrwan Shahin responded that he could send 50,000 men to help them should the need arise. This response immediately transformed during the early days of hostilities, as Colonel Churchill perceived, into an inflated and bombastic appeal transmitted through letters by the Maronite clergy and leaders to the Christians of Druze districts, calling on them to rise fearlessly against their oppressors and promising them immediate assistance. Colonel Churchill emphasized that the men of Zahle, Dayr al-Qamar, Jezzin, Hasbayah, and Rashayah "were told to be of good cheer; this was a war of religion."[27]

Nevertheless, Christian families were overwhelmed by fear and decided to seek refuge in Christian strongholds such as Dayr al-Qamar, Zahleh, and Jezzin. Armed Druzes robbed some of them on their way and then proceeded to plunder and burn their homes. In late May, the Christians of the 'Urqub district were attacked by the Druzes while on their way to Zahleh. In response, on May 27, a Christian force of 3,000 men from Zahleh advanced to Ayn Darah in 'Urqub to punish the Druzes there. They were met on the Damascus Road by a Druze force of 600 men, who defeated them. The victorious Druzes, then, entered al-Matn district through Medairij on the Beirut-Damascus road and pillaged and burned Christian villages there. Approximately sixty villages in this district were destroyed in a month.[28] Jessup and Colonel Churchill were of one mind about the disposition of Maronites and Druzes. The Maronites, though brave and imbued with a fighting spirit, lacked good leaders, command leadership, and discipline, resulting in confusion and defeat on battlegrounds. The Druzes, on the contrary, had skillful and daring leaders, were disciplined, planned treacherously, and fought mercilessly.[29]

The Christian defeat in Ayn Dara and the plunder of al-Matn's villages only increased the panic with which the Christians of Baabda and Gharb districts were seized. The mixed districts were jostling with armed Druzes crisscrossing the villages. Ominously, Druzes from Hawran, upon the request of Sa'id Jumblatt, had come to join their co-religionists of Mount Lebanon in their confrontation with the Christians, and were parading their battle-ready outfits. Whereas Christians were terrified, Druzes were trumpeting their clarion call for slaughter. American missionary Jessup, who was living then in 'Abbieh luridly described the agitated political climate:

> We made an American flag to hoist over the mission premises as a protection in case the hordes from Hauran should invade this district, for we had no fear from the Lebanon Druses. The whole population were in a state of apprehension. Bodies of armed Druses, horse and foot, marched from village to village, singing their weird song, "Ma hala, Ma hala, kotl en Nasara!" "How sweet, how sweet, to kill the Christians."[30]

Fearing an attack on Baabda and al-Hadath on the outskirts of Beirut, home of Shihab emirs, Maronite leaders from Kisrwan sent a force of 300 men to protect them. On May 29, Kurshid Pasha, who had placed a regiment of Ottoman troops in Hazmieh straddling the Beirut-Damascus road along the approaches to the aforementioned towns, called on the Shihab emirs to send back the reinforcement force as he would protect them. Once the Shihab emirs obliged and the force withdrew, concerted Druze forces, acting on a signal from the Ottomans, stormed the towns and set them on fire. A Turkish irregular cavalry participated in the plunder of the Christian towns before pursuing the Christian families who had already fled. Christian males and females, who had not been killed or molested respectively, were cut to pieces by Turkish irregulars after they robbed them and violated the females.[31] Immediately thereafter, Druzes from different directions hauled on their mules and donkeys whatever was left from the unscorched plunder, particularly the paraphernalia and silk crops of the towns' sericulture, which served as their economic mainstay. As the pillage continued unabated, Kurshid Pasha's regiment stood idly by. In fact, once the pillage was satisfactorily completed, Kurshid Pasha received Druze chiefs in Beirut with hearty congratulations.[32]

As news traveled of the plunder and carnage, Christian families from neighboring towns began fleeing to Beirut by the seashore. Colonel Churchill described their dreadful journey:

> [They] were suddenly intercepted by the Druzes and Turks, and cut to pieces; the latter sparing neither woman nor child. The gardens around Beyrout now became hourly thronged with masses of unhappy fugitives, lying about under the trees in all directions, some bleeding, some naked, all in the last stages of destitution.[33]

Shaken by the influx of suffering Christians to Beirut, the European community immediately organized a program of relief work. On June 1, European consuls, alarmed by the conduct of Kurshid Pasha, visited him in Hazmieh and urged him to stop the hostilities. Kurshid Pasha "expressed his anxious desire to suppress the hostilities," blamed the Christians for buying and distributing arms "as the cause of the war," and called on the consuls "to do all their power to restrain the Maronites from sending assistance to their countrymen." He also declared that he "on his part would give orders to the Druzes to cease their warfare."[34]

In the meantime, murders had taken place near Dayr al-Qamar in the Chouf district. On May 23, a Christian convent was burned near Dayr al-Qamar and the head priest was slaughtered in his bed. The Christians of Day al-Qamar took the fatal decision to remain neutral, and expressed their desire for coexistence to both Druzes and Ottomans. Reassured of their safety by Ottoman officials, they mistakenly felt protected by the Turkish garrison deployed near their town. Therefore, they made no preparation for battle.

By this time, Sa'id Jumblatt had become the Druze warlord, and Druzes had been eyeing Dayr al-Qamar as a thorn in their flesh. No less significant, Jumblatt had come to know about an intercepted letter in which Maronite bishops boasted to the Christians of Zahleh and Dayr al-Qamr that they could muster an army of 50,000 strong men in contrast to the Druze's 12,000, and that this was a war of religion. This only whetted his resolve to bring about a final solution to the Christians of the Druze Mountain by uprooting them and killing all adult males.[35] In late May, the Christians of Dayr al-Qamar woke up to their naivete when they discovered that the water supply to their town had been cut off and the approaches to the town had been intersected with Druze barricades. On June 1, 1860, the day Kurshid Pasha declared that he would order the Druzes to cease their warfare, a Druze force of 4,000 men, comprising the Jumblatts, Imads, Nakads, and Hamadis, furiously descended on the town. Some Turkish soldiers joined their ranks, and Ottoman officials refused to intervene. Unprepared for battle and overwhelmed by the assailants, Dayr al-Qamar surrendered the next day to the Druzes, whereupon they burned 130 houses and then withdrew. Ottoman officials then visited the town and ironically upbraided the Christians for being rebels and disturbers of public peace, with the objective of getting the French involved. The Ottoman officer in charge, Tahir Pasha, commander of the Turkish troops in Beirut, advised that what happened to them was just a chastisement for their insubordination, a lesson he hoped they would learn from. Then he assuaged their fears by stating that Dayr al-Qamar was as safe as Constantinople.[36]

Pursuant to his plan, Jumblatt dispatched an emissary with a letter to the Christians of Jezzin informing them that they were under his protection and no harm would befall them. No sooner did the emissary leave the town carrying a letter from Jezzin's residents expressing their gratitude to Jumblatt than a Druze force of 2,000 men advancing from the Chouf, led by Jumblatt's kinsman Selim Jumblatt, assailed the town. The assailants killed every male they came across. Panic-stricken, Christians fled the town, which was set on fire. The Druzes pursued them, massacring 1,200 men in the space of two miles. Joined by Christian fugitives from nearby villages, survivors of the Jezzin massacre rushed toward Sidon. They were waylaid by a Druze gang all the way to the gates of Sidon, whose Muslim population refused to let them in. The butchery resumed, leaving behind more than 300 bodies strewn along the shores of Sidon. Women and girls were either slain or violated, including by a horde of Sunnis and Shi'ites who hurried off to join the orgy of hell.[37] Terrorized by Sidon Muslims, the remaining fugitives and Christian residents of the city were saved by the arrival of a British ship *Firefly*, whose gallant officer restored order to the city.[38] Clearly, Christians underestimated Muslim envy and grievances against them. Thanks to Ottoman tanzimat (reform decrees) of 1839 and 1856, which recognized the principle of equality between Christians and Muslims, Christians had prospered and became influential with close cultural, commercial, and political contacts with Europe. This infuriated the once officially predominant Muslim community, and spread, in the perceptive words of Kamal Salibi, a wave of fanaticism across Ottoman provinces.[39] Obviously, the Druze's war against Christians, which (as we shall see) spilled over into Damascus, was also considered by aggrieved Muslims as a Muslim war in defense of Islam's prerogatives and privileges. No wonder Muslims supported the Druzes, and Ottoman garrisons, let alone Kurshid Pasha, implicitly or explicitly colluded with the Druzes.

Meanwhile, Druze gangs roamed the countryside for a week, plundering villages, burning houses, and murdering Christian laggards. Monasteries and nunneries, which also received letters from Sa'id Jumblatt promising protection, were also treacherously plundered. Nuns were mishandled and humiliatingly denuded. Priests were slaughtered. Thirty monks of the wealthy Meshmoushy convent were slaughtered, and the precious belongings of the convent were stolen before it was set on fire.[40]

Thereafter, Sa'id Jumblatt set his eyes on the Christians of Hasbayah and Rashayah in Wadi al-Taym, which at the time belonged to the *wilaya* of Damascus. This mixed Druze and Christian region had been under the feudal jurisdiction of the Sunni Shihab emirs. However, Nayifa Jumblatt, sister of Druze leader Sa'id Jumblatt, carried a lot of influence in the region. Once hostilities began in the Chouf, the Shihabs, led by Emir Sa'd al-Din Shihab of Hasbayah, appealed to Ottoman authorities to maintain the peace in Wadi al-Taym. Christians there had been worried about ongoing Druze preparations for war. Their inquiry about these activities received reassurances from Osman Bey, the commander of the Ottoman garrison in Hasbayah. Nevertheless, as these preparations continued unabated, in late May, Christians from villages neighboring Hasbayah poured into the town with their cattle and belongings. They felt secure being admitted to the grand quadrangle of the town's Serail next to the Turkish garrison.[41]

However, their feeling of security was short-lived. On June 3, the Christians of Hasbayah awoke to see the Druzes circling the heights of their town. They appealed to Osman Bey for help. But he told them to fight and he would support them if necessary. A few hundred young men advanced to meet the raiding Druzes, only to be swiftly routed. They retreated to the Grand Serail. Immediately thereafter, the Druzes controlled the town and burned the Christian houses. At this grave moment, Osman Bey went to see Sitt [lady] Nayifa, who "demanded an unconditional surrender on the part of the Christians and the delivering up of their arms."[42] Sitt Nayifa also gave her consent to Osman Bey to give the "Christians a written guarantee, pledging the faith of the government for their personal safety."[43]

The following day, Sitt Nayifa accompanied Osman Bey to the Serail, where the Christians surrendered their arms. Also on this fateful day, a Druze force of 1,500 men attacked Rashayah, north of Hasbayah. The treacherous scenario of Jezzin was copycatted. The people of Rashayah were assured of safety, only to be taken by surprise the next day. Yet they fought gallantly until they ran out of ammunition, whereupon they rushed to the town's Serail to secure the protection of the Ottoman garrison there. For several days, the Christians sheltered in the Serails of Hasbayah and Rashayah were not allowed to venture out. Afflicted by hunger and anxiety, they prostrated themselves before Osman Bey, pleading for help.

Meanwhile, European consuls in Damascus and the Greek Orthodox clergy appealed to Ahmad Pasha, the wali of Damascus, to arrange the safe transport of the Christians in Hasbayah and Rashayah to Damascus. A little hesitant at first, Ahmad Pasha obliged and sent his own aide-de-camp with an order to a Druze, Sheikh Kenj al-Amad, in the Beka' to go to Hasbayah and execute the instructions of the order. Dreadfully, Sheikh Kenj had been for fortnight pillaging Christian villages and murdering Christians in the Beka'. Anyway, upon receiving the order, he set forth to Karaoun, a village near Wadi al-Taym. He "assembled the Christians there, congratulated them on their approaching safety, and at the head of 150 horses, took them on with him to Hasbeya."[44]

On the way to Hasbayah, he was joined by Ali Hamadi, a lieutenant of Sa'id Jumblatt, who had been in Mukhtara and instructed to proceed to Hasbayah with a reinforcement of 300 men. They reached Hasbayah on June 10, whereupon the Christians of Karaoun joined their co-religionists. Osman Bey read Ahmad Pasha's order to the relief, tearful eyes, and cheers of the Christians. They were elated that by tomorrow they would be safe in Damascus. While they were getting prepared for departure, the two Druze sheikhs went to Sitt Nayifa, most likely to reaffirm her brother's instructions. Hamadi made the presumptuous appeal that since Sa'id Jumblatt was inflexible, a woman's heart could relent, and asked Sitt Nayifa, "Are the Christians to be massacred? . . . Think of their families, the widows and the orphan babes, and take compassion." "Impossible!" she exclaimed, "impossible; my brother's orders are peremptory and explicit . . . not a Christian is to be left alive from seven to seventy years."[45]

By the time they went back to the Serail, throngs of Druzes cordoned off the Serail. Upon the order of Osman Bey, trumpets sounded and Turkish soldiers rushed to the buildings of the Serail, savagely forcing the perturbed Christians to the central court. Then the gates of Serail were thrown open:

> The Druzes rushed in with a loud yell. . . . And now the butchery began. The Druzes, from their standing place, first fired a general volley, and then sprung on the Christians with yatagans, hatchets and bill-hooks. The first victim was Yoosef Reis, the confidential secretary of the Emir Saad-e-deen. He clung to the knees of Osman Bey . . . the ruffian kicked him with his foot on the mouth, and sent him staggering. He was seized and cut up piece-meal. . . . The Emir Saad-e-deen was next decapitated. . . . By degrees the moving mass was hewn into. Many had their noses, ears and lips cut off, and were otherwise horribly mutilated, before the final blow was given. . . . A few Christians, at first, tried to escape by the gate. The Turkish soldiers seized them, stripped their clothes off

them, and delivered them over to the Druzes; in more than one instance indeed despatching them themselves.[46]

By the time the slaughter took a reprieve, approximately 1,000 Christians, many of whom were Greek Orthodox, had been murdered. An hour after sunset, Sitt Nayifa went to the Serail and "for a long time feasted her eyes on the ghastly sight. Several hundred mangled corpses lay heaped up over each other before her." She exclaimed: "Well done my good and faithful Druzes . . . this is just what I expected from you."[47]

In the meantime, the Druzes from Hawran, amounting to 3,000 men, led by Ismail al-Atrash, advanced across the Anti-Lebanon into Wadi al-Taym, murdering Christians they had come across. On their way, they passed through Khanekin, a Muslim town employing Christians who had fled there. They slaughtered them all. On June 11, they reached Rashayah, where 150 Christians and many members of the Shihab family were still at the Serail. The Muslim Shihabs had trusted Turkish protection. By the time al-Atrash's force arrived, Druzes had already thronged before the Serail. Soon, as in Hasbayah, upon the order of the Turkish officer in charge, the gates of the Serail were thrown open and the joint Druze forces rushed in. The butchery began and ended only when all Christians there were slaughtered. Neither a young nor an old Shihab survived.[48] Their crime was their close relationship with the Christians.

Then, the joint forces of Wadi al-Taym and Hawran Druzes, amounting to 5,000 men, proceeded to the Beka' to wipe out whatever was left of unharmed Christian villages there. Sunni and Shi'ite tribesmen participated in the plunder and hunting of Christians like wild beasts. By mid-June, the Druzes were in complete control of the Chouf, Wadi al-Taym and the Beka'. Dayr al-Qamar and Ba'abda were brought to their knees. The Christians of Gharb and Jurd were spared in exchange for large sums of money paid to their Druze feudal lords. Only Zahleh remained unconquered in the heart of the Beka'. Zahleh had a deserved reputation of bravery, and was known as the shield of Christians.

The majority Greek Catholic stronghold of the Beka' dug in its heels and began preparations for battle. Recognizing the magnitude of the odds against them, they appealed to the Christian leaders of Kisrwan and northern Lebanon, who had been more talk than action. Although commanding large Christian forces, Tanius Shahin and another emerging leader from Ehdin, Yusuf Karam had been stationary. Perhaps their intentions were unresolved, blurred by Druze treachery, Ottoman false assurances and promises, European wishful thinking, and/or pure selfishness. Be that as it may, the much vaunted 50,000-strong force stood shamelessly in inaction. Alternatively, the Christian feudal chiefs clearly wanted no contest with their Druze counterparts, who had been in contact with them during the peasant rebellion. Colonel Churchill perceptively cast the situation into sharp relief: "The triumph of the Druzes was that of feudalism."[49]

Before long, the Druze forces reached the approaches of Zahleh and encamped two miles from the town. They were joined by Sunnis and Shi'ites. Perceiving the gathering storm, Zahleh elders appealed to European consuls to intercede with Kurhsid Pasha so that he would send a garrison to maintain the peace. Eventually, a Turkish garrison was sent, but encamped two hours distance from Zahleh. As if the script of treachery were replicated, Turkish officials met with Druze leaders, not to broker peace but to preside over another orgy of hell. Seeing no help coming soon, the Christians of Zahleh decided to take matters into their own hands and pursue an offensive approach. On June 14, 200 horsemen and 600 foot fighters sallied forth in the plain of the Beka' to charge their enemies. Following a fierce encounter, the Zahleh fighters were routed. They reassembled their forces, and the next day they again sallied forth but with a larger force. They were for a second time defeated. In the meantime, Ottoman officials asked the Christians of Zahleh to surrender their arms and therefore be in the protection of the imperial army. The majority decided to trust their own arms, a judicious decision for, if the recent past was an indication, had they given up their arms, they would have been massacred en masse.[50]

Eventually, the Druzes attacked on June 18, 1860. The Christians of Zahleh defended their town valiantly, trusting that Yusuf Karam had advanced to assist them in time. But help never came, and Zahleh was overwhelmed. Females were spared, but males, with the exception of infants, were slaughtered. Zahleh was set on fire. Some managed to escape to the mountains, whence they headed to the Maronite districts. During the unfolding massacre, Turkish troops either assisted the Druzes or laughed off the carnage. The fall of Zahleh reverberated with chills among Christians and with cheerful excitement among the Druzes and their Sunni and Shi'ite supporters.[51]

Now came the turn of Dayr al-Qamar. Although humbled, Dayr al-Qamar remained a thorn in the flesh of Sa'id Jumblatt (and the Nakads) that had to be removed. Jumblatt had been preparing for this deadly extraction. As Zahleh burned, Druze detachments left for Dayr al-Qamar on June 19. The following day, they attacked Dayr al-Qamar, to the consternation of its Christian residents. Seized with panic, Christian families approximating 1,200 persons rushed to the Serail, where the officer in charge admitted them. Meanwhile, Druze forces pillaged the town and set flame to Christian houses. No one who came across the raiding Druzes was saved, regardless of age or gender. Priests and monks were slaughtered on their altars. Turkish troops stood guard over the plunder. Then, leading Druze forces, Ali Hamadi, Jumblatt's enforcer, approached the Serail and called on the Turkish official to open the gates. Though he did not open the gates for the Druzes, he pointed to a low wall that could be easily jumped over. Instantly, Druzes clambered over the wall and rushed to the court of the Serail. Women were separated from their husbands and sons, and the horrors of Hasbayah were reenacted with deadly gusto. Those who managed to hide were dragged out by Turkish troops and delivered to the Druzes. Colonel Churchill described: "For six long hours the infernal work went on. The blood at length rose above the ankles, flowed along the gutters, gushed out of the water spouts, and gurgled through the streets."[52]

The Turkish officer in charge, acting like an imperial Nero, was seen sitting "smoking his pipe, the bowl resting on a corpse, and the stream of blood running beneath him into the inner court."[53] Not a body was buried. What remained of the male population of Dayr al-Qamar were 2,200 bodies heaped on top of each other.[54]

The sunrise of the next day magnified the pain reflected on the fear-stricken faces of the approximately 2,000 widows and orphans, who tightly assembled in a mass of jerking heads. The Abou Nakad sheikhs came and callously shepherded them down to Damour, the seaside town between Beirut and Sidon. The littoral of Lebanon from Damour and Tyre had become strewn with Christian fugitives taunted and threatened by angry Sunnis and Shi'ites. British and French ships carried them over to Beirut, which rustled with ominous feelings. Threatened by angry Muslim mobs, Christian families fled to the north or by sea to Egypt or Greece. European consuls now worried about a Druze attack on Kisrwan, which they reportedly entertained. Having no faith in Kurshid Pasha's impartiality or eagerness to protect the Christians, European consuls decided to address a letter to Sa'id Jumblatt and other Druze chiefs, making them responsible for any future aggression against the Christians.[55]

Clearly, the Druzes and the Turks had accomplished their objectives by vanquishing the Christians in the Druze mixed districts. The Druzes had completely controlled southern Mount Lebanon, let alone projected their influence over the whole country, and the Ottomans had subdued the Christians and shown European powers that Maronite-Druze coexistence in Mount Lebanon was hardly possible without Turkish lordship. In less than four weeks, more than 11,000 Christians had been killed, a few thousand died from deprivation, and approximately 100,000 had become homeless.[56] The swiftness with which the massacres of 1860 took place outpaced any European actionable plan. Fundamentally, the time had come for Kurshid Pasha to impose his peace and wrap up the joint Druze-Turkish victory far from European involvement.

On July 6, Khurshid Pasha summoned the Christian and Druze leaders to Beirut and imposed on them a peace proposal, which was immediately accepted. Virtually, the proposal was about sweeping under the rug the misfortunes and consequences of the sectarian strife and charging Kurshid Pasha with reestablishing order and justice. The past was to be forgotten, plunder not to be restored, and indemnity not to be paid. Clearly, the peace proposal secured the Druzes' victory. Christian leaders signed off on the proposal no less on account of their defeat than to protect their feudal jurisdiction. Khurshid Pasha treated the matter as an internal one, and he, therefore, excluded European involvement.[57] From his standpoint, there was no reason for European powers to be involved since both Christians and Druzes signed off on the peace proposal.

However, Khurshid Pasha's peace proposal did not see the light of day. On July 9, Lebanon's sectarian strife spilled over into Damascus, which had been bristling with Muslims' antipathy toward Christians. Muhammad Ali's reforms and the egalitarian provisions of Ottoman tanzimat, which benefited and elevated Christian social status, had obviously taken an immeasurable toll on Muslim pride and conceit. Encouraged by Druze victories, Muslims had been taunting, harassing, insulting, and threatening Christians, including Europeans, daily. European consuls, perceptively seeing the situation in Damascus as a powder keg, repeatedly appealed in vain to Ahmad Pasha, the wali of Damascus.[58]

The butchery began when three young Muslims were arrested for trampling over crosses and insulting Christians. An infuriated mob, armed with guns, pistols, swords, and battle-axes, gathered and raided the Christian quarter of Damascus, shouting "kill them, butcher them, plunder, burn, leave not one alive, fear nothing, the soldiers will not touch us."[59] The plunder first began, followed by stealing Christian belongings; then the butchery commenced. Christians were slaughtered in their houses and on their streets. Priests were murdered in their churches, including European missionaries. Christians who tried to escape were forced back by Turkish soldiers. Ahmad Pasha stood idly by, while his troops either feasted on the carnage or participated in it. The die of exterminating the whole Christian population of Damascus had been cast. But the illustrious Algerian Emir Abd al-Kadir, who was in exile along with his loyal retinue in Damascus for fighting the French army in Algeria, took the lead in facing off the blood-soaked mob, whose number swelled by fresh Druze, Kurd, and Arab fanatics. He saved as many as he could by escorting them to his house and safe houses, which were guarded by his own troops. Europeans, including consuls and missionaries, rushed to his house for safety. By the end of this horrific day, al-Kadir had saved 12,000 souls. Sadly, 7,000 Christians had perished, including 1,000 in the Franciscan convent. Many women and girls were violated. Some were killed, and some were married off by Muslims.[60]

As news of the Damascus massacre spread, Christians in Palestine and Syria were seized by panic. Reports had circulated among the Muslim communities there that the Sultan himself had issued the orders to execute the Christian infidels. Christians hurried off to pay large sums of protection money to Turkish officials and Muslim Sheikhs, while others embraced Islam to save themselves. Whole Christian villages in Palestine embraced Islam.[61] As in Mount Lebanon, Turkish complicity in the massacre astounded European consuls. In a letter, dated July 18, 1860, addressed from the British consul in Damascus, M. Brant, to his counterpart in Beirut, M. Moore, Brant stressed:

> I have to communicate to you today the most awful news on the burning and looting of the Christian quarter. Very few houses until that moment have escaped the flames, which continue to be ravaged. The conduct of the pasha was sovereignly shameful; he demonstrated that he is deprived of all the quality of a governor, and he did not appear anywhere. The soldiers, instead of preventing looting, gave their assistance; and, with such a man at the head of affairs, one cannot say when evil will stop.[62]

THE *MUTASARIFIYAH*: THE FOUNDATION OF THE CONFESSIONAL SYSTEM

Once the news of the massacre reached European capitals, European powers immediately put pressure on the Porte to restore order and prepared their fleet to depart for Beirut.[63] Upon hearing the news of the carnage in Damascus on July 16, the French were the first to instantly order 7,000 troops to leave for Beirut under the command of General Charles-Marie-Napoléon de Beaufort d'Hautpoul. Fearing a European armed intervention, the Porte dispatched to Beirut Foreign Minister Fouad Pasha, vesting in him full executive powers to resolve the affairs in Mount Lebanon and Damascus. Fouad Pasha arrived in Beirut on July 17. He promised the people of Lebanon expeditious justice and straightaway left for Damascus to restore order.

Immediately following his arrival in Damascus on July 29, Fouad Pasha arrested all leading Turkish officers and hundreds of Muslim sheikhs and notables. Following a rigid investigation, he dealt sternly with all of those who participated, committed, or were complicit in the massacres. Ahmad Pasha, wali of Damascus, was shot along with Osman Bey and two other officers who presided over the Hasbayah massacre. One hundred and seventeen army and police officers were shot. Four hundred Muslims were either imprisoned or exiled. And fifty-six leading sheikhs and notables were hanged and eleven exiled. No less significant, Fouad Pasha enforced military conscription in Damascus, which had been exempted since the Arab conquest.[64]

Fouad Pasha returned to Beirut on September 11, whereupon he prepared to meet General d'Hautpoul, who had arrived in Beirut on August 16. French troops moved into the mixed districts of Mount Lebanon, comforting the Christians and overawing the Druzes, many of whom fled to Hawran. Moreover, British and other European ships had already anchored near the shore of Beirut. In the meantime, Fouad Pasha received a critically worded memorandum from British Admiral W. F. Martin, in which he called for redressing the enormities that took place against the Christians and punishing all guilty actors, including Khurshid Pasha. Otherwise, Admiral Martin threatened that "the Turkish government will have no claims to consideration if it should not do voluntary and ample justice. The matter will probably be taken out of their hands if they exhibit any indication of shortcomings."[65]

Without delay, Fouad Pasha arrested Khurshid Pasha and his leading officers. He also summoned forty-seven Druze chieftains to Beirut. Sa'id Jumblatt, along with thirteen others, obeyed the summon and were placed under arrest, while the others escaped to Hawran. All of them were convicted. Turkish officers were sentenced to life imprisonment, and the Druze chieftains to death. But executing these sentences was hardly possible. Punishing the Druze leaders was tantamount to punishing the whole Druze community for the civil war, something Fouad Pasha was reluctant to do because he apparently believed that both Christians and Druzes may have been more or less equally responsible. Eventually, all Turkish and Druze prisoners were released from prisons, and on May 11, 1861, Sa'id Jumblatt died in prison of tuberculosis. In the meantime, Fouad Pasha set his eyes on punishing the lower-rank leaders and commoners who participated in the carnage. He asked a special Christian commission to come up with a list of major offenders. The commission submitted to him a list of 4,600 Druzes and 360 Sunnis and Shi'ites, which he found too large. A revised list was resubmitted, ascribing to 1,200 Druzes principal guilt, who were ultimately arrested. But, again, trying and sentencing them was hardly possible because rarely one witness, if any, was ready to testify against them. Correspondingly, most were released, and 240 were temporarily exiled to Tripoli (Libya), who eventually returned home. This completed Fouad Pasha's judicial dispensation of Ottoman justice.[66]

In contrast to the fairly swift judicial dispensation, the political dispensation of a settlement proved more tedious and cumbersome. An international commission representing Lord Dufferin and Claneboye for Britain, M. Beclard for France, M. Novikoff for Russia, M. Weckbecker for Austria, M. De Rehfuss for Prussia, and Fouad Pasha for the Porte was organized to investigate the massacres and plan a new government for Lebanon. The commission had twenty-five meetings, with the first held October 5, 1860, and the last on March 25, 1861. Concerns among and between European Powers, intensified by Fouad Pasha's politicking, militated against further executing perpetrators of the massacres and coming to a swift agreement. To be sure, many were condemned and forced into temporary exile. Significantly, Britain was worried about French occupation of Lebanon becoming permanent. Although Lord Dufferin acknowledged that Turkish officers had participated in the massacres and British policy had been strongly pro-Turkish, he rejected France's proposal of restoring the Lebanese Emirate. Conversely, France, along other powers, rejected British proposals.[67]

Finally, a statute about governing Lebanon, born out of compromise, was agreed upon on June 9, 1861. The statute, known as the *Règlement Organique*, reconstituted Lebanon as an autonomous province (*mutasarifiyah*) headed by a governor-general (*mutasarif*) under the guarantee of the Porte and European Powers (France, Britain, Austria, Prussia, Russia, and later by Italy in 1867). Preceding the signing of the statute, General d'Hautpoul and French troops began leaving Lebanon on June 5 and the last French soldier left Beirut on June 8.

The Règlement had seventeen articles that reorganized Lebanon. Minor revisions were added to the statute in September 1864, which remained in force until the outbreak of WWI. The statute stripped Lebanon of Beirut, Sidon, Tripoli, Beka', and Wadi al-Taym regions. The major ports of Beirut, Sidon, and Tripoli were placed under direct Ottoman rule. The Ma'n and Shihab's Lebanon was reduced to Mount Lebanon under the mutasarifiyah. The *mutasarif* was now to be an Ottoman Catholic Christian subject, but not Lebanese, appointed by the Porte in consultation with the signatory powers. The mutasarif was responsible directly to the Porte, and his tenure was extended from three to five renewable years. He was to be assisted by an administrative council of twelve elected members representing the religious communities: Four Maronites, three Druzes, two Greek Orthodox, one Greek Catholic, one Sunni, and one Shi'ite.[68] The mutasarifiyah was divided into seven administrative districts, each of which headed by a qa'im maqam appointed by the mutasarif and hailing from the prevalent religious denomination. Each district was subdivided into sub-districts headed by special administrative councils. Finally, the people of every village in the mutasarifiyah were to elect a village headsman, or sheikh, whose official appointment was to be approved by the *mutasarif*. These village sheikhs were to elect the members of the administrative council.[69]

Significantly, the Règlement abolished feudalism and conferred equal rights on all individuals. Taxes were collected to meet the mutasarifiyah's budget, and only surplus, if any, was to be sent to Istanbul. Turkish troops were not deployed in the mutasarifiyah, which was exempt from military conscription. The mutasarifiyah had its own judiciary and a local gendarmerie to preserve order under the supervision of the *mutasarif*.[70]

Dawud Pasha, an Armenian Catholic from Istanbul, and director of Posts and Telegraphs in the Ottoman capital, was appointed as the first governor (*mutasarif*).[71] He took Bashir II's Bayt al-Din palace as his seat of power in the summer and Baabda in the winter. He published for the first time a Lebanese official gazette. Dawud Pasha was a capable and enlightened governor who worked hard to maintain cordial peace in Mount Lebanon and fuel its prosperity. He pacified the Christian-Druze mixed districts and thwarted feudal opposition to his rule by absorbing members of the feudal aristocracy in his administration.

He faced opposition in northern Mount Lebanon, which escaped the civil war. Yusuf Karam, supported by members of the Maronite clergy and later by France, was not happy with the non-nativity of the governor and the broad powers with which he was vested at the expense of that of Christians. Dawud Pasha tried to conciliate him by offering him various high posts, including the qa'im maqamiyah of Jezzin. He spurned them and agitated against the governor, who exiled him to Egypt. He was allowed to return to his native Ehdin in the north in late 1864 on the condition that he remained at peace with Dawud Pasha's government. But in January 1866 he again rebelled against the government. Supporters of Karam in Kisrwan had refused to pay their taxes, forcing Dawud Pasha to take disciplinary actions against them. Karam came to their assistance, leading a Maronite rebellion against the governor. Turkish troops were sent to fight the rebels upon the request of Dawud Pasha. Neither the clergy nor France came to Karam's support. Eventually, his rebellion was suppressed, and he was forced into permanent exile in late January 1867. He died in exile in Naples in April 1889.

During his term as governor, Dawud Pasha weathered discontent and sectarian animosity by diplomacy and adeptness rarely seen in Ottoman political circles in Lebanon. Insight into his approach to governance was illustrated in an address he delivered to the notables of Lebanon on Easter in 1863:

> A doctor fell sick, and called in a fellow physician and said to him, "we are three, you, I, and the disease. If you will help me, we will conquer the disease. If you help the disease you will conquer me." So we in Lebanon are three; you, the people, I, the ruler, and the traditional animosity of races in Lebanon. Help me and we shall conquer it. Help it, and you will ruin me and yourselves together.[72]

Dawud Pasha's achievements were not limited to his politics. During his term, the Beirut-Damascus highway was completed in 1863, becoming the major artery in the country connecting most villages. He also built a road linking Dayr al-Qamar with Beirut, which reemerged as a hub for trade. He sponsored a high school in 'Abbieh that bore his name. Missionary work, besides the relief work missionaries had taken upon their shoulder to help casualties of the 1860 civil strife, resumed with vigor. Several governors succeeded Dawud Pasha, but none rose to his level of efficacy, devotion, and honesty.[73] Yet despite corruption, incompetence, truncated geography, and loss of its major ports, Mount Lebanon enjoyed stability and flourished culturally and economically.

Agriculture flourished, silk factories proliferated, and sericulture boomed, becoming again the mainstay of Mount Lebanon's economy. Stability, efficient public services, and good roads promoted domestic and international trade. But nowhere was the prosperity of Lebanon near the cultural awakening of the country under the mutasarifiyah. Missionary activities played a key role in this awakening. American Protestant missionaries crowned their educational work with the establishment of the Syrian Protestant College (today the American University of Beirut) in 1866; and their French Jesuit counterparts with the establishment of Saint Joseph University in 1875. Jesuit and Sisters schools proliferated, including the Sisters of Nazareth of Lyons, Sisters of the Holy Family, and Sisters of the Good Shepherd.[74] The Knights of St. John founded the Johanniter Hospital on a hillside near Ras Beirut. Theophilus Waldmeier, a German Swiss, established the first sanatorium for treating the mentally ill in 1897 in al-Asfuriyeh, Hazmieh.

Mount Lebanon became a paradigm of the best governed and most prosperous province in the Near East. It earned the proverbial saying: Happy is he who possesses even a goat's enclosure in Mount Lebanon. Referring to Lebanon after the application of the Règlement Organique, Lord Dufferin wrote in 1887,

> Within a couple of years after these arrangements [provisions of *Règlement*] had been carried into effect, blood feuds entirely ceased, and from that time until the present day the Lebanon has been the most peaceful, the most contented, and the most prosperous province of the Ottoman dominion.[75]

But this development and prosperity Mount Lebanon had experienced came to an ominous screeching halt when the Ottoman Empire entered World War I, casting a deadly pall over the country.

Chapter 4

The Great Famine: 1915–1918

THE YOUNG TURKS AND THE GREAT WAR

The stability and prosperity of Mount Lebanon under the *mutasarifiyah* began to show signs of distress in the early twentieth century. Despite the fact that the successors of Dawud Pasha, with the exception of Rustum Pasha (1873–1883), had been more interested in pleasing the Porte than promoting the welfare of Mount Lebanon, the mercantilism and resourcefulness of Mount Lebanon's population sustained its reputation as one of the most stable and prosperous provinces of the Ottoman Empire. But in July 1908 the capital of the empire was shaken by an armed rebellion led by a political reform movement known as the Young Turks. The seeds of this revolution go back to 1889, when the Young Turks' secret organization the Committee of Union and Progress (CUP) was formed to introduce reform in the spirit of *tanzimats*, including constitutionalism, as an alternative to the autocracy of the sultans. Comprising initially an assorted group of secular intellectuals, activists, and army officers from various Turkish, Greek Arab, Jewish, and Armenian backgrounds, the Young Turks raised the banner of "Liberty, equality, and fraternity" as the motto of their movement.[1]

The Young Turks forced Sultan Abd al-Hamid II (1876–1909) to restore the constitution of 1876. The sultan had issued the constitution in 1876, which pledged freedom and equality for all Ottoman subjects, freedom of the press, and popular representation through a bicameral parliament. However, no sooner had the ink on the document dried than the sultan abolished whatever reforms had been issued, increased state censorship, and suspended the constitution in 1878. Apparently, in much the same vein as in 1876–1878, he planned in 1909 to suppress the revolution of the Young Turks and bury the constitution. Nonetheless, his scheme was detected and he was deposed.

His brother Mehmed V (1909–1918) was brought from confinement and enthroned as sultan, although the Young Turks wielded power.

As it turned out, the celebration and the auspicious promises with which the Young Turks were received soon turned bitter as their policies and plans foundered. Notwithstanding the political schisms among the Young Turks, their vision of rallying all national and religious communities of the empire into one Ottoman grouping backfired by enhancing separatist movements. At the same time, European powers, exploiting Ottoman weakness, continued to seize Ottoman territories. Austria, which had occupied Bosnia since 1878, annexed it outright. Bulgaria, which had been autonomous, declared its independence in 1908. The Greek-majority island of Crete entered into a union with Greece. Italy occupied Tripoli (Libya), which was ceded formally by the Ottomans to Italy in 1912. Arab nationalism gained momentum, and the Armenian question over reforms was again raised not the least by the Russians (see below). On top of that, the Ottoman army disastrously lost the Balkan War (1912–1913), whereby the Balkan League (Bulgaria, Serbia, Greece, and Montenegro) seized most of the European territories of the Ottoman Empire.

It was against this background that an ultra-nationalist group of army officers among the Young Turks carried out a coup d'état and seized power in 1913. A triumvirate consisting of Talaat Pasha as Minister of the Interior, Enver Pasha as Minister of War, and Jamal Pasha as Minister of the Navy held the reins of power in Istanbul. These new leaders of the Young Turks abandoned any notion of reform and committed themselves as much to arresting the dissolution of the Ottoman Empire as to maintaining their personal powers by pursuing any means justifying their end. Commenting on the failed Ottoman ideal of the Young Turks and the rise to power and praxis of the triumvirate, American Ambassador to the Ottoman Empire Henry Morgenthau wrote in his biography:

In a speech in Liberty Square, Saloniki, in July, 1908, Enver Pasha, who was popularly regarded as the chivalrous young leader of this insurrection against a century-old tyranny, had eloquently declared that, "To-day arbitrary government has disappeared. We are all brothers. There were no longer in Turkey Bulgarians, Greeks, Servians, Rumanians, Mussulmans, Jews. Under the same blue sky we are all proud Ottomans." That statement represented the Young Turk ideal for the new Turkish state, but it was an ideal which it was evidently beyond their ability to translate into reality. The races which had been maltreated and massacred for centuries by the Turks could not transform themselves into brothers. . . . Above all, the destructive wars and the loss of great sections of the Turkish Empire had destroyed the prestige of the new democracy. . . . Thus the Young Turks had disappeared as a positive regenerative force, but they still existed as a political machine. Their leaders, Talaat, Enver, and Djemal, had long since abandoned any expectation of reforming their state . . . [They] had added to their system a detail . . . that of assassination and judicial murder.[2]

Before long, as the dark cloud of an impending world war hovered over Europe, the triumvirate faced the difficult decision as to whether to stay neutral or join a camp to the brewing conflict. Initially, the Ottoman Empire was neutral as hostilities and tensions between the Triple Entente (France, Russia, and England) and the Triple Alliance (Germany, Austria-Hungary, and Italy) exploded into a war among Europe's great powers in August 1914. But remaining neutral was no longer an option for the triumvirate, especially Talaat and Enver Pashas. The Turkish Empire was in dire straits politically, militarily, and economically. Constantinople was virtually broke and its army disarrayed. Significantly, the triumvirate, yet politically vulnerable, feared a coup, similar to the one they had carried out, to oust them from power. These Young Turk leaders recognized the urgent need of a great European power to keep their empire viable and their rule unmolested. In other words, they recognized that absent outside support, it was not a question of whether but when their regime would collapse.

Some years back, Britain would have been the ultimate choice. But London's occupation of Egypt in 1882, failure to support Constantinople in the Balkan War, and shrinking investment in the Ottoman Empire made that choice hardly possible. By the same token, France had expanded its influence in the Levant and exploited the much-hated capitulations to weaken Ottoman rule there. Germany, on the other hand, had no colonial ambition in the empire and expressed its readiness to support the empire, including reorganizing its army. But the definitive factor that determined the triumvirate's choice and ultimately their side in the Great War was Russia. Ottomans considered Russians as their historic enemies, most responsible for dismembering the Ottoman Empire, and most desirous of possessing Constantinople, the former seat of Byzantine power. Significantly, they frowned upon Russian involvement in the Armenian Question over reforms, which could lead to the secession of the Armenian-inhabited eastern provinces bordering Russia.

The Armenians of the Ottoman Empire had had a precarious life under Turkish rule, often associated with the tyrannical reign of Sultan Abd al-Hamid, who massacred thousands of Armenians. Following the Balkan Wars and the instability that prevailed in the Balkans, European powers focused on the Eastern Question as a means of pursuing coercive diplomacy with the Ottoman Empire.[3] Russia, under the pretext of instability in the eastern provinces of the Ottoman Empire, encouraged and sponsored Armenian reforms to safeguard the Armenian Nation. In February 1914, Russian-Turkish negotiations culminated in an agreement under which the Sublime Porte would implement reforms under European controls in the

Armenian-inhabited provinces.[4] The reforms or the terms of the agreement bring to mind those that underwrote Mount Lebanon's mutasarifiyah, with the exception that the latter was a distant Ottoman province far from the seat of power. Though the agreement was a bitter pill to swallow, the Sublime Porte honored its promise and jointly with Russia announced the reforms in a communiqué addressed to the great powers. Admittedly, the Sublime Porte neither forgot nor forgave the Armenians for inviting foreign meddling in Turkish domestic affairs, and perceived the Armenians as a fifth column paving the way for the secession of the eastern provinces of the empire.[5]

Commenting on the reason Turkey allied itself with Germany during the Great War, American ambassador to Constantinople Morgenthau observed:

> Russia was the historic enemy, the nation which had given freedom to Bulgaria and Rumania, which had been most active in dismembering the Ottoman Empire, and which regarded herself as the power that was ultimately to possess Constantinople. This fear of Russia, I cannot too much insist, was one factor which, above everything else, was forcing Turkey into the arms of Germany.[6]

Conversely, inasmuch as Turkey needed Germany, Germany needed Turkey. Turkey commanded a geostrategic location most imperative to Germany's ability to disrupt the Triple Entente, known also as the Allied Powers. Ambassador Morgenthau expounded:

> There was only one way in which Germany could make valueless the Franco-Russian alliance; this was by obtaining Turkey as an ally. With Turkey on her side, Germany would close the Dardanelles, the only practical line of communication between Russia and her Western allies; this simple act would deprive the Czar's army of war munitions, destroy Russia economically by stopping her grain exports, her greatest source of wealth, and thus detach Russia from her partners in the World War.[7]

Before long, thanks in no small measure to the adept diplomacy of Germany's ambassador to Constantinople, Baron Hans Von Wagenheim, and Talaat Pasha and Enver Pasha's urgent need to uphold the solvency of their empire and reorganize its decrepit army and navy, Germany came to influence Turkey's politics and virtually control its army and navy. During a meeting in August 1914 between Wangenheim and Morgenthau, the former boasted to the latter: "We now control both the Turkish army and navy."[8] In fact, it was German-commanded Turkish warships that bombarded the ports of Odessa, Sebastopol, and Novorossiysk on October 29, 1914, that led to Turkey's entry into the Great War. On November 2, Russia declared war on the Ottoman Empire, followed by Great Britain and France on November 5. A week later, Constantinople formally declared war on the Entente allies. On November

13, the sultan, considered as the caliph, the spiritual and temporal ruler of the Muslim *Umma* (community), issued a declaration of war, which was more of an appeal for a holy war, **jihad**, against the infidels. Soon afterward, Turkey's senior cleric, Sheikh al-Islam, issued a proclamation, summoning the Muslim world to rally around the caliph and rise up against France, Great Britain, and Russia, the enemies of Islam. He concluded his proclamation: "The chief of the believers, the Caliph, invites you all as Moslems to join in the Holy War!"[9]

REPRESSION AS A STATE POLICY

As the drumbeat of war grew louder, the triumvirate decided to send one of its own, Jamal Pasha, secretary of the navy, to take command of the Fourth Turkish Army, headquartered in Damascus. Hailed as the savior of Egypt by members of the Turkish cabinet and other influential Turkish people who assembled at Haidar Pasha's railroad station to bid him farewell, Jamal Pasha declared before embarking on the train: "I shall not return to Constantinople until I have conquered Egypt!"[10]

The Ottoman Empire's theater of war included the Balkans and the Middle East. The Levant (Lebanon-Palestine-Syria) was crucial for protecting the eastern and southern approaches to the Anatolian heartland, but also as the launchpad to the Ottoman campaign against Britain in Egypt. Seizing Egypt's Suez Canal would cut British communications with East Africa, India, and Asia, and prevent British troops from reaching the Mediterranean and Europe, thereby helping Germany breach the Entente's western front.

Parallel to the importance of controlling the Suez Canal was the closing of the Dardanelles Strait, known also as the Strait of Gallipoli. The Dardanelles is a narrow waterway in northwestern Turkey, making up part of the border between Europe and Asia. It connects the Aegean Sea to the Sea of Marmara and to the Black Sea via the Bosporus Strait. As Germany's hope of a short, decisive war was blunted mainly by Russian forces sweeping triumphantly through Galicia and standing ready to cross the Carpathians into Austria-Hungary, closing the Dardanelles had become strategically important to neutralize Russia's navy and army and undermine its economy. On September 27, 1914, the Ottoman Empire, acting at the behest of its German ally, closed the Dardanelles.

This simple yet calculated tactic of war had serious ramifications for Russia and its allies, leading to the defeat of the former. Ambassador Morgenthau observed:

Few Americans realize, even to-day, what an overwhelming influence this act wielded upon future military operations. Yet the fact that the war has lasted for so many years is explained by this closing of the Dardanelles. For this is the element in the situation that separated Russia from her allies that, in less than a year, led to her defeat and collapse, which, in turn, was the reason why the Russian revolution became possible. . . . This was the narrow gate through which the surplus products of 175,000,000 people reached Europe, and nine tenths of all Russian exports and imports had gone this way for years. By suddenly closing it, Germany destroyed Russia both as an economic and military power. By shutting off the exports of Russian grain, she deprived Russia of the financial power essential to successful warfare. What was perhaps even more fatal, she prevented England and France from getting munitions to the Russian battle front in sufficient quantity to stem the German onslaught.[11]

It was against this background of controlling waterways and sea lanes that the Allied Powers held a naval conference in Paris in December 1914 to design a plan to control maritime traffic in the Mediterranean and blockade the coasts of Syria, Mount Lebanon, and Palestine. The blockade was meant to prevent the Ottoman navy from using vital sea lanes, to prevent the Ottoman army from receiving supplies and materiel, and to restrict enemy naval maneuvering. In fact, the British, by December 1914, had already deployed ships along the coasts of Palestine, Lebanon, Syria, and Sinai to control the eastern Mediterranean and protect the Suez Canal against an attack by the Triple Alliance, also known as Central Powers. More specifically, HMS *Doris*, a British Eclipse-class cruiser commanded by Captain Frank Larken, received orders to patrol off Alexandretta (at the time on the Syrian coast) and interdict supplies on the Hejaz railway. Meanwhile, similar operations in the same area were carried out by the Russian cruiser *Askold* and French cruiser *Requin*. On December 16, HMS *Doris* anchored along the coast of Jaffa and conducted an aerial reconnaissance. Then it destroyed Turkish communications lines. Two days later, British troops landed ashore and destroyed more than two miles of telegraph line (wire, insulators, and posts). Thereafter, *Doris* departed for a final pass around the Beirut coast, where intelligence officer Lieutenant H. "Pirie Gordon secured further intelligence from some French Dominican friars before the ship returned to Egypt."[12]

Along with trying to control the eastern Mediterranean and affect a naval blockade of the Syrian-Lebanese-Palestinian coast, the British were also the first to initiate intelligence-gathering operations in Greater Syria.[13] On January 16, 1915, British intelligence officer Captain Lewen B. Weldon arrived in Port Sa'id to undertake the mission of cooperating with French seaplanes to allocate agents behind Turkish lines. Weldon expounded in his book *Hard Lying* that "At that time we knew that there were many people in Palestine and Syria who were willing to help us with information of enemy movements, etc., if we could arrange some system for collecting their news. The only way of doing this was to land agents on the coast behind Turkish positions, and to pick them up again when they had found out all our friends had to tell them."[14] The British commandeered the *Aenne Rickmers*, a confiscated German ship, carrying two French seaplanes and manned by French, British, and Greeks.

Meanwhile, on December 7, 1914, Jamal Pasha arrived in Damascus, whereupon he immediately took command of the Ottoman Fourth Army and served as military governor of Greater Syria. He set about preparing his plan to attack British forces stationed along the Suez Canal, and making sure that the local population would not cooperate with Allied forces. He worried about French and British intelligence operations, especially among the Christians and foreign missionaries in Greater Syria in general and Lebanon in particular. He also doubly worried about an Allied landing on the coast of Greater Syria, especially at Beirut, with help from the local population. A few days after his arrival, on December 11, he issued an ominous memorandum to the people of Lebanon warning them against cooperating with or showing affection toward Allied forces:

In order to protect the honor, life and properties of families, I call upon the people of Lebanon, in the event the enemy tried to make any attempt against the shores of Lebanon and Beirut, to place themselves under the flag of the Ottoman's Fourth Army and to participate with the Military Detachment in self-sacrifice to scuttle the actions of the enemy. In order to achieve this goal, actions must be taken in accordance with the orders of the Commander of the Military Detachment and in fulfilling his requests. Should any Lebanese, whoever he may be, try to compromise the safety of the Empire and public security by any modicum action or any show of empathy and affection towards our French, British and Russian enemies, will be instantly prosecuted before the Customary War Office to receive his punishment. Given that the Commander of the Military Detachment Muhammad Rida Bey will in another proclamation list all matters, actions and movements that are detrimental to the welfare of the Empire, I warn all families to totally avoid them. The Government will occupy all institutions and offices belonging to our enemy states in Mount Lebanon and transform them into national and scientific institutes to promote Lebanese culture. . . . In conclusion, I ask God, the most glorified and exalted, to confer upon Lebanon happiness and wellbeing, and guide it in the path of stability and success.

Commander of the Ottoman Fourth Army and Secretary of the Navy, December 11, 1914.[15]

Jamal Pasha's infamous reputation as a cruel official preceded him. US Ambassador Morgenthau observed on his insidious qualities: "after a momentary meeting, I was not surprised to hear that Djemal was a man with whom assassination and judicial murder were all part of the day's work."[16] In fact, Jamal Pasha's cruel actions in Lebanon earned him the nickname of *al-Saffah* (the Butcher). His memorandum prefigured the harsh way by which he would rule Lebanon. To be sure, however, prior to the advent of Jamal Pasha to Damascus, Ottoman authorities had already pursued a callous policy in Lebanon meant to reinforce their rule there, to circumscribe the movements of the local population, and to disrupt the work of foreign officials, missionaries, and institutions belonging to enemy states.

A report from the archives of the Jesuit Fathers reveals that "from August, horses, mules, camels, everything was requisitioned. The railways were reserved for Ottoman military transport. The locomotives (for lack of coal) were supplied with wood from mulberry trees and Lebanese forests."[17] On September 9, the Ottoman government declared unilaterally the abrogation of all Capitulations. Although the decree was signed into law in December 1914, it was put into effect in Lebanon the moment the declaration was made. Article one of the decree read:

> The confessional and personal protection of the government of France and other foreign countries, initiated from the old eras, of foreign Catholics has been annulled. The right of protection that France had from the afore-mentioned eras of clerics of French persuasion and of foreign and Latin institutions has also been revoked. Accordingly, consuls can no longer intercede in the Ottoman state especially in the blessed areas of denominational matters and disciplines.[18]

On November 8, 1914, Deputy Director of the Police Othman Bey ordered the rector of Saint Joseph University, Père Gérard de Martimprey S. J., to shut down the university and give him the keys. Père Martimprey rushed to see the wali of Beirut to get a stay order. The wali coldly told him: "I am sorry for what happened to you, but you have the misfortune of being the ally of our traditional enemies, and it is the war."[19] Before long, in late November, Ottoman authorities ordered French and English residents of Beirut to leave the city by sea, and appropriated foreign schools there to transform them into Ottoman ones. An entry in the diary of a Jesuit father indicates that on November 24 "the qaimaqam has said that all public utility establishments (orphanages, schools, hospitals) held by foreigners would run by Ottomans, and to let go of all foreigners and their employees."[20] This order, followed by similar ones, which deprived Lebanon's already tenuous health-care system of foreign health-care employees and volunteers, be they physicians, pharmacists, and nurses, had a terrible impact on public health, as we shall see.

This systematic policy to shut down all foreign official and unofficial work and establishments belonging to enemy states, and by extension sever the extensive contacts between the local population, especially Christians, and foreign institutions and subjects, was complemented by a centralized administrative policy. Upon his arrival, Jamal Pasha reorganized the administration of Mount Lebanon and Beirut. He centralized their administrative locations by moving them to Aley, east of Beirut. He revoked the judicial power of Mount Lebanon's court of law at Baabda over all but minor cases and placed adjudication of law under the jurisdiction of the military tribunal established at Aley. He gave the Ottoman military, under the command of Muhammad Rida Bey, full jurisdiction over Mount Lebanon and Beirut.

Next, he prepared his military campaign against the British to take over the Suez Canal. In January 1915, Jamal Pasha initiated his campaign. Leading the Ottoman Fourth Army, he crossed Mount Lebanon and moved south toward Beersheba in Palestine, where he established a field headquarters. Thereafter, he marched across the Sinai Peninsula and engaged British forces along the Suez Canal. However, his offensive was fleeting and was rapidly repelled. In the meantime, Allied forces, led by the British, began bombarding the Dardanelles, with the objective of breaking through Turkish fortifications all the way through the Sea of Marmara and Bosporus straits. Ottoman authorities feared that Constantinople would fall and Russia would be reinvigorated to revive a successful campaign against Turkey. A grim and bleak atmosphere gripped Constantinople. American Ambassador Morgenthau observed:

> At that time there was no force which the Turks feared so greatly as they feared the British fleet. . . . The possibility of British success was one of the most familiar topics of discussion, and the weight of opinion, both lay and professional, inclined in favour of the Allied fleets. Talaat told me that an attempt to force the straits would succeed—it only depended on England's willingness to sacrifice a few ships. The real reason why Turkey had sent a force against Egypt, Talaat added, was to divert England from making an attack on the Gallipoli peninsula.[21]

No doubt, the failure of Jamal Pasha's offensive in Egypt and the fear of Allied forces breaking through the Dardanelles waterway heightened Jamal Pasha's concern about an Allied landing on the Lebanese coast with the help of Christians. Jamal Pasha deeply distrusted the Christian communities, especially the Maronite community, for their close relationships with Western powers, particularly France.

No less significant, Allied fleets patrolling the coast of Lebanon and Syria reinforced his belief that an Allied invasion of Beirut was only a matter of time. By early 1915, the French navy had maintained a constant presence off the coast of Beirut, enforcing a blockade limited to patrolling the coast and seizing contraband. This fed his paranoia about French-Christian conspiracies against Ottoman rule. In fact, Allied intelligence-gathering operations and placing agents behind Turkish lines had expanded and become better organized by mid-1915. Of great importance was the French occupation of the island of Arwad on August 31, 1915. Located around two miles offshore of the Syrian port of Tartous and approximately twenty miles from Tripoli, Arwad's strategic location was ideal as an operational center for the Allied intelligence operations off the Lebanon-Syria littoral. The French installed a military garrison on the island, and its governor, Albert Trabaud, organized a team of French and Lebanese personnel whose main task was intelligence gathering. The French also set up the "Agence des Affaires de Syrie" to cooperate with British and French naval authorities operating out of Port Sa'id.[22]

The French seizure of Arwad Island, preceded by intelligence-gathering operations by the Allied forces, coupled with aerial reconnaissance and occasional bombardment of Turkish positions along the Lebanese-Syrian littoral,[23] deeply heightened Jamal Pasha's fear of both an Allied landing along the littoral and of conspiracies against his rule. Correspondingly, he set about tightening his security measures over Mount Lebanon and Beirut to bring the people there into total submission so as to prevent an insurrection, sever their contacts with the allied forces, nip in the bud any real or illusory conspiracy against him, and deprive a potential Allied landing at Beirut of any popular support. He gradually but steadily widened his dragnet of orders to corral and incapacitate the people of Mount Lebanon and Beirut even to the point of mass murder by starvation.

By the summer of 1915, Jamal Pasha had effectively reduced the *mutasarifiyah's règlement organique* into no more than ink on paper. He had already introduced martial law in Mount Lebanon and thanks to his emergency powers, real political and military power in Mount Lebanon and Beirut rested in the hands of Colonel Muhammad Rida Bey. Moreover, Jamal Pasha, fearing a revolt in the fastness of Mount Lebanon, had deployed thousands of Anatolian soldiers mostly in Mount Lebanon to enforce martial law.[24] Unhappy with becoming a figurehead, Mount Lebanon's governor, Ohannes Kouyoumdjian Pasha, who had been in office since 1912, resigned from his post in early June and returned to Constantinople. He was the last Catholic governor of Mount Lebanon. He was replaced by an acting governor, Muhammad Halim Bey, until September, and then by Ali Munif Bey as the new governor, whose position was no more than a facade to the diktat of Jamal Pasha and his enforcer, Colonel Rida Bey.

Of all leaders who vexed Jamal Pasha, the most irksome were the French sympathizers and the Christian clergy and their missionary allies, in particular the Maronite clergy headed by Maronite Patriarch Elias Huwayek. Early in the war, Jamal Pasha sought to relocate the patriarch from his seat in Bkirki to Damascus so he could be placed under better surveillance. Emir Shakib Arslan, a Druze from Mount Lebanon's Chouf district, got wind of Jamal Pasha's directive, and interceded on behalf of the patriarch with Jamal Pasha. He convinced Jamal Pasha that relocating the patriarch, a subtle way of exile, would incite the Maronite community against the Ottomans.[25]

Following his humiliating military campaign in Egypt, Jamal Pasha, gripped by anger and fixated on conspiracies, ordered a perusal of official documents seized in the French consulates in Beirut and Damascus. At the beginning of the war, France closed its Beirut consulate and placed it under the protection of US consul Stanley Hollis. Ottoman officials learned that some potentially incriminating documents were stored in the consulate. In violation of international law, they broke into the consulate and seized the documents. American Ambassador Morgenthau strongly protested Ottoman illegal entry of the French consulate under US protection and demanded in vain that the seized documents be returned. Meanwhile, brushing aside any form of judicial process, Jamal Pasha unwaveringly signed off the order to execute Father Yusuf Hayek, a Mount Lebanon Maronite priest, for exchanging correspondence with Paul Deschanel, a future president and then president of the French Parliament. Father Hayek was hanged in Damascus on March 22, 1915.[26] No doubt, Jamal Pasha's order to execute Father Hayek was a stern message to the Maronite Church that any correspondence with Entente powers would be seen as treason and penalized by capital punishment.

Then, unfazed by American protests, Jamal Pasha ordered the arrests of individuals suspected of conspiring with French authorities. The evidence, as it turned out, consisted of prewar correspondence with French authorities to help Lebanon secure its independence from the Ottoman Empire, but also of underground nationalist activities revealing that the "army was honeycombed with revolutionary cells, that England and France had agents in the country to provoke a revolt, that an Allied landing on the Syrian coast was impending."[27] The suspects were taken to the infamous Aley Military Tribunal, where they were tortured and interrogated before being prosecuted. They were found guilty of treason. Eleven men were sentenced to death, two to life in prison, and forty-five who managed to escape to death in absentia. Although the suspects pleaded their innocence, they were executed by hanging in Beirut on August 21, 1915.[28]

Never failing to live up to his moniker al-Saffah, Jamal Pasha's ruthlessness was put saliently and regularly on display as more orders of arrests, deportations, forced labor (see below), and executions were carried out, save the horrendous and deadly blockade of Mount Lebanon. More trials were conducted at Aley as more arrests in Beirut, Mount Lebanon, and Damascus were undertaken under the pretext of flimsy suspicions. Prosecution of the suspects took months, yet no intercession on behalf of the suspects stayed their execution. The first to be executed was Jospeh Hani, a well-known Christian resident of Beirut who was publicly hanged on April 5, 1916. A month later, on May 6, twenty-one victims of respected and distinguished backgrounds were sent to the gallows, seven in Damascus and fourteen in Beirut. The day is still commemorated in both Lebanon and Syria as Martyrs' Day, and Beirut renamed the square where the victims were hanged as Martyrs' Square (*Sahat al-Shuhada'*).[29] The charges against them, as published in *al-Sharq*, a newly founded Arabic daily dedicated to supporting Jamal Pasha's policies, were defined as "treasonable participation in activities of which the aims were to separate Syria, Palestine and Iraq from the Ottoman Sultanate and to constitute them into an independent State."[30]

In the meantime, in January 1915, Jamal Pasha, apparently swayed by the Germans, forced the clergy and all religious figures affiliated with European congregations from Lebanon. He ordered their swift departure from Beirut port. An entry in the Jesuits' archives read:

> We are on a small boat built for about fifty people, almost 500 religious men and women from all congregations, Jesuits, Marists, Lazarists, Dominicans, Capuchins, Franciscans . . . the trip will be horrible, the price too . . . hardly had the boat weighed anchor from the port of Beirut, a joyful Ave Maria escaped from all mouths and hearts. Marie had saved her children from the hand of the Turkish-German barbarians.[31]

Getting wind of the Ottomans' harsh treatment of the Jesuits, Ambassador Morgenthau inquired about their welfare from the American consul in Beirut, Stanly Hollis. In response, Hollis wrote a letter to Ambassador Morgenthau, dated January 20, 1915, in which he pointed out:

> Jesuit University at Beirut was closed and confiscated by the Government; all the priests were expelled from the University premises, and a large part of the furniture was taken by the Government. The French Medical Faculty at Beirut was also confiscated by the Turkish Government, and the surgical instruments were commandeered and transported to Damascus. In fact, all the establishments belonging to the Jesuits in Beirut were confiscated; all the French and British Fathers were expelled from the country. The Ottoman Fathers and those who belong to non-belligerent states were allowed to remain in Beirut.[32]

Jamal Pasha also expelled British, French, and Russian nationals from Beirut and Mount Lebanon. Most of these nationals and missionaries had worked in the educational or medical fields, and their departure gutted many of the foundational social services in Mount Lebanon's communities. Indigenous Christian churches and some missionaries were allowed to continue their clerical and charitable work as long as they served Ottoman orders and policies. But as the war progressed, their survival as institutions and individuals became premised on the whims of Ottoman officials who saw enemies and conspirators in every corner of Mount Lebanon and who struggled to maintain their power in a calamitous war.

THE GREAT FAMINE: MASS STARVATION

Yet the most devastating measure taken against the people of Mount Lebanon, especially the Maronites, was Jamal Pasha's blockade of Mount Lebanon. By February–March 1915, Jamal Pasha began issuing orders to ration and control the food supply there in order to maintain food and grain reserves to feed his soldiers as part of the imperial war effort. His initial orders were ad hoc and disjointed, such as limiting the weight of a loaf of bread, banning the export of olives, prohibiting the shipment of sugar out of Beirut, and limiting the export of cereals and wheat to Mount Lebanon. But two major developments turned Jamal Pasha's initial orders into a systematic blockade policy used as a means both for completely controlling the food supply in Mount Lebanon and Beirut and political subjugation.

In late February 1915, following a season of drought in Greater Syria, swarms of locusts appeared in the skies of Palestine and began to double in number and move toward Beirut and Mount Lebanon. In early April, locusts virtually obscured the sun over Beirut and invaded the city.[33] The scene of destruction wrought over Beirut by the locust invasion unfolded in a biblical imagery manifesting the wrath of God over a population feeling already unmoored by the ramifications of the Great War. Locusts continued their earth-scorching invasion toward Mount Lebanon and Syria, leaving in their wake parched, barren lands. In a short period of time, the greenery of Mount Lebanon disappeared as the locusts devoured flowers, plants, leaves, and tree buds. Beehives were attacked and honey and bees were eaten. By early summer the entire food crop was destroyed. Wheat virtually disappeared from Mount Lebanon and Beirut.[34] No less significant, locusts stripped mulberry trees, killed silkworms, and destroyed Mount Lebanon's sericulture. As already mentioned, sericulture, since the nineteenth century, made up the mainstay of Mount Lebanon's economy. As a result, Mount Lebanon, unlike other areas in Greater Syria, suffered doubly from the locust invasion since the rural population invested more in sericulture than in subsistence crops, thereby losing both their income and produce.[35] By early May, people had begun to die from hunger. Famine first struck Beirut and the coastal areas, then rapidly crept up toward Mount Lebanon.

In the meantime, although they formally announced their blockade of the entire eastern Mediterranean in an effort to cut the supplies to the Ottomans in summer 1915, the Allied forces had already enforced a firm blockade of the Palestine-Lebanon-Syria littoral in March.[36] No vessel was allowed to berth along the coast of Greater Syria, let alone come near to its shore. Travel from and to Beirut ceased, remittances from abroad stopped, and foodstuff had become a rare commodity. The blockade shut down all supply lines to the coastal region of Greater Syria, causing prices to skyrocket. More specifically, having a fragile and transactional economy reliant on global capitalism, Mount Lebanon's and Beirut's economy immediately collapsed and people could no longer earn a livelihood. Whereas locusts destroyed sericulture, the major pillar of the economy, the blockade halted income from remittances and wrecked tourism and trade, the other minor pillars of the economy. What also helped drive the process of mass pauperization was the Ottoman government's war economic policy that introduced a banking moratorium and paper money, which had little if any value. Not only did Beirut and Mount Lebanon lack food to feed their people; people had no income to buy whatever foodstuff was available at staggering prices.

Conversely, fearing an impending Allied landing, Jamal Pasha responded by reinforcing his blockade of Mount Lebanon. He cordoned off Mount Lebanon from the Beka' Valley, the breadbasket of Lebanon, along with Palestine, and Syria. He restricted the transport of livestock and livestock-related products, which were scarce in Mount Lebanon; prohibited the export of cereal and wheat to Mount Lebanon; and enforced a blanket control of crops, especially wheat. He controlled the destiny and quantity of wheat delivered to bakeries in Mount Lebanon to make bread, and determined its distribution. His priority was feeding his troops and battering the Christians into moribund submission. Apparently, Enver Pasha, who visited Jamal Pasha, shared his concerns and plans. A letter by Father Ronzevalle S. J., dated May 21, 1915, illustrated the desperate condition of both Beirut and Mount Lebanon:

> We learn that since the passage of d'Enver Pasha, the attitude of Jamal Pasha has become quite hostile to Christians and Francophiles. Enver Pasha went so far as to say: "If the French came, they would only find rocks." It seems that the blockade of Lebanon has started. We can no longer hold onto it, we are literally dying of hunger. In Achkout [a village in Kisrwan, Mount Lebanon] in two months, we saw 97 inhabitants die of hunger out of 450 that they are. Many other villages have lost a quarter, a third and even a half of their inhabitants. Food no longer enters Lebanon . . . absolute prohibition not to introduce anything from Beirut or Beka' although cereals abound there. All Christians in Lebanon, especially the Maronites, are there under terror.[37]

By fall 1915, news of the impending famine disaster befalling Mount Lebanon and Beirut, along with information that Ottoman authorities had formally abolished Mount Lebanon's autonomy and special status in October 1915, had reached the Americans and Allied forces. In fact, the economic situation had deteriorated so much that Reverend Howard Bliss, president of the Syrian Protestant College (SPC) in Beirut, wrote a forewarning letter to Ambassador Morgenthau dated October 5, 1915, in which he underlined that "there is great suffering, and there will be still greater suffering this coming winter."[38] By 1916, Jamal Pasha's blockade had depleted Beirut and Mount Lebanon of foodstuff and essential crops, causing a widespread starvation made worse by profiteering and a poor transportation system. Merchants hoarded wheat and flour, and transportation within the empire was hampered by both the government prioritizing the military use of the few accessible rail lines in the empire as part of the war effort and by fuel shortages.[39] Even a loaf of bread was getting hard to get, although the Ottoman government tried to secure wheat at a fair price and penalize profiteering.[40]

Apparently, Jamal Pasha's blockade of Mount Lebanon was both a response to the Entente's blockade of the coastal region of Greater Syria and a reflection of the growth in his distrust of Lebanese communities in Beirut and Mount Lebanon, notably the Maronite community. Nevertheless, the Maronite Church was not cowed into submission. The Maronite Church, under the leadership of its patriarch, Huwayek, mustered all its resources to help alleviate the suffering of Lebanese. Significantly, notwithstanding Jamal Pasha's warning to the Church not to communicate with the French, Patriarch Huwayek designated Father Boulos Akl as the point man for the Church's secret relationship with French authorities, tasking him with providing them with intelligence on the overall condition in Mount Lebanon and Beirut and supervising joint efforts to smuggle food and money into those areas. In May 1916, Patriarch Huwayek desperately appealed to the French to help the Lebanese population, claiming they were in imminent danger of extinction.[41] In the same month, according to a French intelligence report, Jamal Pasha had allegedly boasted, "We have rid ourselves of the Armenians by the sword. We shall do away with the Lebanese by famine."[42]

On October 3, 1916, Father Akl sent a letter to a French intelligence agent on Arwad Island describing the desperate situation in Mount Lebanon and asking the agent to send relief funds as soon as possible to save people from near death. Father Akl cried out: "Oh how miserable the people of Lebanon are. You may be sure my friend that if these people have to sustain this for another two or three months, none of them will survive."[43]

Two weeks later on October 16, Father Akl wrote a detailed intelligence report on the social, economic, political, and military condition in Lebanon to a French intelligence agent on Arwad Island.[44] He underscored that

a. the situation had become worse, for the blockade was strictly enforced, and that wheat had disappeared, explaining that efforts by Ottoman authorities to provide wheat and foodstuff to the general population had been hampered by corruption, profiteering, lack of transportation, and soaring prices;[45]

b. the poor and most of the middle class had perished, and that those of the higher class were mortgaging their properties and selling their belongings, including their shoes to survive;

c. Jamal Pasha's position had become shaky, and that he came to Beirut to get certificates of "good conduct and innocence" from Muslim sheikhs and dignitaries and Christian priests to cover up his oppressive deeds and to condemn Sharif Hussein of Mecca for his disparaging and critical attitude;[46]

d. local government, gendarmes, and Ottoman soldiers had taken advantage of the desperate situation in Lebanon to swindle money and commit unspeakable injustice;

e. Ottoman soldiers had become weak, and their numbers continued to decrease due to disease and scarcity of food, and that talks of their rebellion, mutiny, and desertion were often heard;

f. Druzes of Hawran had rebelled and Shi'a families were causing trouble for the government;

g. Ottoman soldiers were strictly enforcing the blockade from all sides of Mount Lebanon and by all methods;

h. Ottoman soldiers, for unknown reasons, had stopped working on fortifications and trenches;

i. Ottoman paper money had continued to depreciate, and that Ottoman officials were forcing the exchange of paper money for coins by all means; and

j. disease had increased and spread, killing many Lebanese, and that there were no medicine, food, doctors, or people to bury the dead.

Significantly, Father Akl inquired in his letter about French plans to liberate Mount Lebanon, underscoring the urgency of launching the campaign before the advent of winter. He wrote,

> So please inform us of what is happening. Is relief near? We have always been awaiting this hour. A small campaign of 20,000 is enough to restore these mountains, the treasure of love and attachment, to the mother of the oppressed before the arrival of winter which will undoubtedly wash away what is left of us.[47]

Father Akl's intelligence report was not overstated. The situation in Mount Lebanon and Beirut had become virtually a death trap. Famine and malnutrition triggered a wave of epidemics that worsened the already desperate condition in the land of the cedars. By summer 1916, cholera, malaria, and typhoid spread throughout Mount Lebanon and Beirut. By September 1916, smallpox had attacked those who had survived the famine and other epidemics, and brought to an almost screeching halt the charitable and dispensary work of religious establishments. Writing in his diary in September 1916, Father Angélil S. J. stressed that smallpox had come with violence, completing the adversities of the war, locusts, famine, and other plagues. He added that this epidemic had been aggravated by malpractice and lack of care and medicine. He despondently concluded his diary's entry: "Nothing is more profound than the heart of a missionary powerless to rescue misery and condemned to see so many calamities. Death is more desirable for him."[48] Father Paul Mattern wrote on October 2, 1916, that "the misery is extreme in Lebanon. Many are dying from starvation. In one day in Beirut we collected 50 dead persons from the streets."[49]

No less significant, among the first overseas news outlets to take note of the famine was the *New York Times*, which featured an article on September 16, 1916, based on an American woman's reportage. Illustrating images of misery, starvation, and death, the article read, "We passed women and children lying by the roadside with closed eyes and ghastly pale faces. It was a common thing to find people searching garbage heaps for orange peels or other refuse, and eating it greedily when found. Everywhere women could be seen seeking edible weeds among the grass along the roads."[50]

It's noteworthy that some districts, especially Maronite majority districts, fared more poorly than others, clearly on account of the strict and harsh Ottoman measures against the Maronites. An American who journeyed across Lebanon reported in a letter the "hell of famine" inflicting the country. Her letter, compiled in the Jesuits' archives, detailed the severity of the famine in Lebanon's various districts. Penning the letter on October 13, 1916, she observed:

> The traveler in the villages of Kesrouan [Maronite majority district] discovers corpses on the side of the roads and in the woods. The famine in this part of Lebanon is particularly severe since the government, for reasons known to all, used harsh methods against the Lebanese. In the district of Jezzine, the few well-off families have managed to feed the hungry. In South Lebanon at Ibaa and Jarjouh, the situation is not very bad. In the Chouf, the situation is difficult but better than in Kesrouan. . . . On the coast, in Saida and Beirut, the children go to the kitchens of the Americans and ask to drink the water from the washed dishes, in the ultimate hope to find a few grains of rice or a few leftovers. Sometimes children go through the trash cans to find orange peelings which they eat despite the dirt and grime. Sometimes as I walk through the streets, I

see children who open their mouths like hungry chicks, but no one gives them anything to eat.[51]

The extent to which the severity of the famine affected the various districts of Lebanon are borne out by letters in the Jesuits' archives, one of which described that "the districts that suffered the most are Kesrouan, Metn and Batroun [Maronite majority districts] where villages have no more inhabitants. The absence of medicine, physicians, and pharmacists, all requisitioned by the Turkish army, is total."[52]

Apparently, neither the plague nor the starvation snuffing out the lives of Lebanese effected a change in Ottoman attitude or policy. Jamal Pasha was spiteful and indifferent toward the Lebanese. Responding to an account about the ravages of famine in Lebanon by a committee charged with helping the hungry, Jamal Pasha said: "As long as . . . the Lebanese will not eat each other, they can still bless God."[53] Enver Pasha may not have been as emphatic as Jamal Pasha, but he definitely was a coauthor of Lebanon's starvation as a war strategy. According to a letter received from the Jesuits of Aleppo, Enver Pasha had given firm orders not to allow wheat or cereals of any kind to enter Lebanon. The letter underscored that "the goal of Enver Pasha is to exterminate the Lebanese people as a punishment for their sympathy for France."[54] No less significant, Ottoman authorities not only continued to strictly enforce the blockade but also made smuggling and illegal import of flour to Mount Lebanon punishable by death.[55]

Dreadfully, the more desperate the condition of Lebanon's districts had become, the more Ottoman authorities adopted harsh measures to hermetically suck the air out of Beirut and Mount Lebanon. In October 1916, Ottoman authorities made exemptions of military conscription almost impossible. Back in August 1914, Ottoman authorities had distributed red posters to local officials to post on the doors of government buildings and houses of worship. The posters were emblazoned with two green crescent moons, one crossed by a sword and the other by a gun. Below the crescent moons, large letters read "SAFAR BARLIK," a call for arms and forced conscription. Although some in Beirut answered the call, many fled to Mount Lebanon to evade conscription. At the time, Mount Lebanon had a special autonomous status exempting men from military service.

But as the war progressed and the Ottoman military position began to deteriorate, Ottoman authorities in the fall of 1916 critically restricted conscription exemption (*badal askari*) and extended Safar Barlik to Mount Lebanon, which lost its special status. Mainly high-ranking civil servants, *Qadis* (judges) and *ulema* (Islamic scholars) were exempted, and the age bracket for conscription had increased to sixty in Beirut. Men in Mount Lebanon between the ages of twenty-five and forty-five years old were called for military service. Runaways were threatened with capital punishment, though they could invoke the law of redemption and accordingly pay forty Turkish lira to buy their freedom. In late October, the Ottomans issued a new directive abolishing the law of redemption and ordering a general call for military service even for those who had paid the badal askari. The only exemption that the Ottomans allowed entailed the provision of 15,000 kilos of wheat to Ottoman soldiers, something that was outright impossible.[56] To be sure, Ottoman conscription was more or less haphazardly and incrementally expanded, subsequently devolving into an improvised, arbitrary act executed ad hoc by Turkish officers. As a result, the conscription piled up the inventory of catastrophes gripping Mount Lebanon and Beirut. An entry in the Jesuits' archive in 1917 pointed out:

Young Lebanese are subject to the service of the Turkish army. Many are obliged to serve without uniforms; they are allowed to wear their civilian clothes. They are made to work in building roads and digging trenches. They actually became in the service of the Turkish soldiers themselves. Those who try to desert risk their lives.[57]

By 1917 and until the landing of French troops in Beirut in October 1918, plague and starvation had caused an unimaginable measure of human misery in Mount Lebanon and Beirut, expanding the circle of death and forcing individuals to commit appalling acts to survive. Father Paul Mattern, in his diary entry on March 10, 1917, stressed that typhoid had taken a huge toll on young men and women between the ages of seventeen and forty years old. He also reflected in another entry that between 1916 and 1918 the corpses filled the streets of Beirut, which were collected several times a day and deposited in mass pits in remote areas, often by the sea.[58] Other entries spoke of families dying in their own homes and being eaten by rats. Even cannibalism was cited. An entry detailing a striking measure of misery illustrated that "a man from Maalacat Damour, after the death of his wife, having nothing left to eat, decided to kill his two dying children, aged 8 and 10, to feed on them. He made a fricassee in the evening, boiled the flesh in a pot, and buried the bones in the interior of the house. When questioned, he answered: I am hungry."[59]

ARMENIAN GENOCIDE, THE GREAT FAMINE, AND AMERICAN RELIEF EFFORTS

Armenians had not been strangers to tragedies. Following its defeat in the Russo-Turkish War (1877–1878), the Ottoman Empire lost most of its Balkan territories. The Congress of Berlin (1878) sanctioned the independence of Serbia, Romania, and Montenegro, and designated Bulgaria as a semi-independent principality. Austria-Hungary occupied Bosnia-Herzegovina. Grievances over the outcome of the Congress of Berlin festered and eventually led to the Balkans War (1912–1913). Feeling humiliated and imputed as the "sick man of Europe," the multiethnic and multireligious empire strove to stem the tide of nationalism that swept its provinces.

Of particular concern to the Ottomans was prospective Armenian nationalism, compounded by an Ottoman fear of an Armenian-Russian cooperation that could turn Eastern Anatolia, the heartland of the Turkish Empire and where most Armenians lived, into a restive region. Though protected under the Ottoman millet system, Armenians, as second-class citizens, had faced institutional discrimination, double taxation, land usurpation, and systematic harassment by Kurds and Circassians. In fact, the Sublime Porte at the Congress of Berlin had agreed to respond to Armenian calls for civil reform, ensure the safety of Armenians, and protect their properties. However, the Porte did not institute any enforcement mechanism, and harbored a deep resentment against the Armenians. Sultan Abdul Hamid II (1876–1909) took exception with the Armenians, sending a delegation to the Congress of Berlin to lobby for Armenian civil reform and safety. The Ottomans believed that Armenian nationalism constituted a serious threat to the territorial integrity of the empire, and that Armenians served as a tool in the hands of European powers to weaken the empire and meddle in its internal affairs. Ambassador Morgenthau observed:

> He [Sultan Abdul Hamid] believed, rightly or wrongly, that Armenians, like the Rumanians, the Bulgarians, the Greeks, and the Serbians, aspired to restore their independent medieval nation, and he knew that Europe and America sympathized with this ambition. The Treaty of Berlin, which had definitely ended the Turco-Russian War, contained an article which gave European powers a protecting hand over the Armenians. How could the Sultan free himself permanently from this danger?[60]

This Ottoman attitude and European concern about Armenians paradoxically led to both the emergence of the Armenian question in international diplomacy and to harsher Ottoman measures against them. As the Ottoman Empire continued to decline and Armenians continued to strive for civil reform and equal treatment, Sultan Abdul Hamid established in 1891 an irregular force, the Hamidiye regiments, composed mainly from Kurdish tribes, to suppress what he considered the subversive acts of the Armenians. Sanctioned by the sultan, attacks against Armenians and their properties gradually escalated into widespread massacres from 1895 until 1897. Approximately 200,000 Armenians were murdered by Ottoman soldiers, Muslim mobs, and the

Hamidiye regiments, bereaving 50,000 Armenian children.[61] Ottoman atrocities committed against the Armenians, which became known as the Hamidian massacres, elicited European leaders to hurl various epithets at Sultan Abdul Hamid, including the infamous term coined by English Statesman William E. Gladstone: "the great assassin."

The assumption of the CUP of power resolved neither the festered grievances in the Balkans nor the hostile Ottoman attitude toward the Armenians. Notwithstanding that Greece, Serbia, Montenegro, and Bulgaria had acquired their independence, many of their nationalists remained under Ottoman rule. Counseled by Russia, the aforementioned states formed the Balkan League and declared war on the Ottoman Empire in October 1912. Lasting approximately eight months, the war concluded by readjusting the boundaries of the former European territories of the Ottoman Empire. But rivalries among the Balkan League's countries led to the second Balkan war in June 1913. Marked by nationalist fervor, ethnic cleansing, and definitive loss of Ottoman territories, the Balkan wars reinforced the determination of the Young Turks to Turkify the empire to prevent its disintegration. So despite their initial promises of universal brotherhood, the Young Turks shared Sultan Abdul Hamid's view that the Armenians posed a serious threat to the territorial integrity of the Turkish heartland. Ambassador Morgenthau remarked, "And now the Young Turks, who had adopted so many of Abdul Hamid's ideas, also made his Armenian policy their own. Their passion for Turkifying the nation seemed to demand logically the extermination of all Christians— Greeks, Syrians and Armenians."[62]

Moreover, as already discussed, Armenians' drive to solicit the Armenian Reforms agreement under the sponsorship of Russia and implementation of reforms under European supervision in the six Eastern Armenian–inhabited Anatolian provinces not only infuriated the Young Turks but also alienated the Sublime Porte (see above). Clearly, the Young Turks never forgave the Armenians for asking for European controls over the implementation of reforms. No sooner did the Great War begin than the Young Turks suspended the reforms and moved to systematically pursue premeditated measures to deal once and for all with the Armenian Question. Unfolding events served as justifications for Ottoman policies.

As the Great War ground on in the first months, the Young Turks were concerned about two principal fronts: the Russian-Turkish front and the Dardanelles. Initially, the Russians advanced along the Russian-Turkish front and defeated the Turkish army. But the Germans came to the rescue and counterattacked, repelling the Russians. As the Russian army was withdrawing to the Caucuses, Armenians in villages along the front line fled alongside the Russian army. Although the majority of Armenians remained in their villages along the Russian-Turkish border and did not support the Russian army, including Armenian-Russians, reports from Ottoman and German officials spoke of Armenian participation in the Russian assault and Armenian savagery exacted on Muslims.[63] Clearly, these events provided the Young Turks, especially Talaat Pasha, the interior minister, with the pretext to begin their systematic policy to put an end to the Armenian Question.

To be sure, in the fall of 1914, Ottoman authorities began repressing the Armenians, especially in Eastern Anatolia, by applying harsh measures against them. Ottoman authorities issued orders to conscript Armenians aged twenty to forty-two years old, making their exemption from military service hardly possible and their evasion of military service a capital punishment. They also confiscated Armenian carts and animals (horses, mules, sheep, and oxen), and collected most of their provision and harvest (wheat, flour, barley, oil, and dairy products). Then in February and March 1915, Ottoman authorities ordered Armenians to turn in all their arms. All along, Armenians were harassed, robbed, beaten, and at times killed by Ottoman soldiers and Kurds.[64]

During this time, in several meetings with Armenian Patriarch Zaven Der Yeghiayan, Ottoman officials, including interior minister Talaat Pasha, denied any premeditated policy to collectively punish or exterminate the Armenians. However, official denials and lies were exposed following the Armenian uprising in Van province in early April 1915 when the Turkish government dropped all attempts to conceal its genocidal policy toward the Armenians. No sooner did the Armenians of Van revolt against their oppressors than the Turkish government ordered a mass arrest of Armenians in Constantinople, including intellectuals and professionals. Significantly, Armenian officials in the Turkish government were dismissed, and soldiers were disarmed and led either to slaughter or to forced labor.[65] Shocked by the mass arrest in the capital and the news of massacring Armenian soldiers who loyally served their fatherland, a high-level Armenian delegation went to see Grand Vizier Halim Pasha and Interior Minister Talaat Pasha. Responding to the delegation's measured outcry, Talaat Pasha said, "All those Armenians who either through the pen, their words, or their work have endeavored or may endeavor in the future to build an Armenia, are considered the enemies of the state, and, in times such as these, they have to be dispersed."[66]

By early May, the trickle of Armenians who were deported from the Armenian-inhabited provinces had become a deluge. Clearly the Ottoman order was to transport them across the Syrian Desert to the area in Mesopotamia lying between Aleppo and Mosul. The deportation of the Armenians without their belongings constituted the crux of Ottoman policy to put an end to the Armenian Question. Patriarch Yeghiayan described Ottoman "Armenocidal" policy as a hellish plan "Armenia without Armenians," beginning with disarming the Armenians, terrifying them by exiling most Armenian men including their leaders and compelling the rest into forced labor, and then ending the Armenian Question, once and for all, by deporting them, many of whom were women, children, and elderly, on foot for one or two months across an area where it was hardly possible for them to survive.[67]

After several unsuccessful attempts to see Interior Minister Talaat Pasha, Patriarch Yeghiayan finally saw him on September 19, 1915. Responding to Patriarch Yeghiayan's questions and appeals for help to prevent further Armenian misery, Talaat Pasha emphasized,

> The Armenians themselves caused this situation, I am the one who knows best their internal affairs. We knew everything! We knew about the decisions they had taken, that for as long as the Ottoman Army was not defeated, they would assume a waiting stance, and, in the event of [the army's] defeat, they would stage a revolution. They also decided to help Russia. Every day they were piling weapons, bombs. . . . But when they started actively collaborating with the enemy, causing a part of the country to fall in their hands, we could no longer remain silent. . . . I used to love the Armenians, because I considered them an element useful to the country. But the opposite turned out to be the case. Naturally, I love the fatherland more than I love the Armenians.[68]

Aleppo was the largest destination of the Armenian exodus. Armenian survivors arrived there emaciated, destitute, and psychologically injured. They were placed in camps that became breeding grounds for contagious diseases, including typhus and smallpox.[69] Commenting on what happened to Armenian deportees and the spread of epidemics, an eyewitness account by a senior Turkish officer Rafael de Nogales revealed:

> On every hand were groups of famished walking skeletons, whose lives were flickering out one by one in the crowded streets or on the innumerable plots of grounds covered with filth which were their only lodging places. Despoiled of everything, sometimes even of clothing, those wretches of both sexes and all ages crawled along begging and spreading the germs of typhus everywhere. In Aleppo alone, it seems that more than thirty-five thousand persons perished from that disease during the brief period from August, 1916, to August, 1917.[70]

According to the American consul general in Aleppo, 150,000 Armenian refugees had arrived in the area around Aleppo, Damascus, and Dayr al-Zur in early 1915.[71] The spread of contagious diseases and the unprecedented number of Christian refugees settling in Syria affected the Syrians' perception of the new refugees.[72] Many Armenians decided to migrate to Lebanon. Despite the harsh conditions in Mount Lebanon and Beirut, Maronite patriarch Huwayek welcomed Armenian survivors of Ottoman atrocities, defiantly declaring, "The piece of bread that we have, we will share it with our Armenian brothers."[73] But local authorities and some local leaders were not as welcoming to Armenians. Initially, most Armenian refugees lived in the ghettos of Beirut, and a number of them were ordered to convert to Islam.[74] Before long, many of them moved to Bourj Hammoud, an eastern suburb of Beirut, where they came to comprise the majority of the population.[75] Dedicated to keeping the memory of the Armenian genocide fresh in the Armenian collective consciousness and to tracing their origins, Armenian refugees named most of the streets of Bourj Hammoud after the names of regions and cities, such as Cilicia, Adana, Van, Marash, and Sis, from which they were deported.[76]

As the Great War ground on, the number of Armenian orphans and Armenians who moved to Lebanon from Syria increased. Paradoxically, Jamal Pasha, in contrast to his triumvirate's colleagues, refused to plan or participate in any plan to massacre Armenians once in Syria. In fact, he tried to help them, including giving them rations of food, as long as they stayed within the borders of Greater Syria. Armenian Patriarch Yeghiayan recollected:

> I consider it necessary to state that, in the area under Jemal Pasha's rule . . .
> the Armenian deportees lived more comfortably than in the other areas.
> . . . Jemal Pasha did not want to execute this decision [massacre and extermi-
> nate Armenians], and the Armenians within the boundaries of Syria were not
> massacred. . . . Jemal Pasha treated the Arabs of Syria more severely than he
> did the Armenians, to whom he suggested temporarily adopting Islam until the
> storm subsided.[77]

Patriarch Yeghiayan's recollection is corroborated by Bayard Dodge, a faculty member and subsequently president of the Syrian Protestant College, who handled most of the American relief efforts to Mount Lebanon and Beirut (see below). Dodge underscored in his book *The American University of Beirut* that "Fortunately for the Armenians, Ahmad Jamal Pasha proved to be their friend, so that once they were transported to his territory, they were at least free from massacre, if not from exposure and hunger."[78]

Jamal Pasha also took an interest in helping Armenian orphans. Ottoman authorities turned the Collége Francaise D'Anturah in Mount Lebanon's Kisrwan district, which the Turks had taken over, into an orphanage for Armenian, Kurdish, and Turkish orphans, with the former comprising the majority of orphans. In 1916, Jamal Pasha brought a well-known Turkish feminist, Halidé Edib, to manage the orphanage and reorganize Mount Lebanon's educational system. Although the orphanage faced serious delinquencies, it was transformed into a well-kept home for approximately 1,200 children by the fall of 1917. Responding to Edib's objection over giving Armenian children Muslim names, Jamal Pasha emphasized:

Do you believe that by turning a few hundred Armenian boys and girls Moslem I think I benefit my race? You have seen the Armenian orphanages in Damascus run by Armenians. There is no more room in those; there is no more money to open another Armenian orphanage, and only Moslems are allowed. I send to this institution any wandering waif who passes into Syria from the regions where the tragedy took place. . . . When I hear of wandering and starving children, I send them to Aintourah. I have to keep them alive. I do not care how. I cannot bear to see them die in the streets.[79]

Notwithstanding Jamal Pasha's lenient treatment of Armenians in contrast to that of Arabs of Greater Syria and Lebanese Christians, Armenians fared no better than other communities in Mount Lebanon and Beirut. Disease and starvation did not discriminate according to race, religion, or gender, although the Maronite districts of Mount Lebanon suffered the most. Significantly, the Armenian genocide reconfigured how the allied powers and United States perceived the ongoing tragedy befalling Lebanon. The scale and swiftness with which the Armenian massacres were carried out raised fears among the allied powers and the United States that Lebanese too, especially Christians, had been singled out for annihilation. These fears were deepened and corroborated by media, intelligence, and local reports that thousands of Lebanese had been dying daily from disease and starvation.[80] Consequently, the United States and France, whether on the individual or the governmental levels, sought to help both the Lebanese and Armenian refugees. American Ambassador Morgenthau was among the first to report on the Armenian massacres and petition his government to create a committee to help the Armenian refugees. In a telegram to the US secretary of state dated September 3, 1915, Ambassador Morgenthau wrote:

Destruction of Armenian race is progressing rapidly . . . will you suggest to Cleveland Dodge, Charles Crane, John R. Mott, Stephen Wise, and others to form committee to raise funds and provide means to save some of the Armenians and assist the poorer ones to emigrate.[81]

Upon receiving Ambassador Morgenthau's urgent plea for assistance, President Woodrow Wilson called upon his adviser, Cleveland H. Dodge, to form the American Committee for Armenian and Syrian Relief (**ACASR**) to help Armenians and other Christian minorities who were being forcibly deported, starved, or killed in a systematic premeditated campaign by the Turkish government. On September 16, 1915, the ACASR was officially launched in New York under the leadership of James L. Barton and Cleveland H. Dodge. Dodge's son, Bayard Dodge, who was on the faculty of the Syrian Protestant College, supervised the receipt and distribution of funds. The Turkish government recognized ACASR as a relief agency and more or less did not obstruct its work. By 1918, ACASR had raised eleven million dollars. From October 15, 1915, to September 1, 1917, ACASR had delivered to its relief committees $4,255,420.60, including $642,762.53 to the Beirut relief committee.[82] By July 1, 1921, ACASR had distributed $90 million, including $12,527,000 to Syria and Palestine.[83]

Contribution to ACASR was not confined to individuals. The American Red Cross and Rockefeller Foundation also contributed funds to ACASR, and the American government played an active role in helping provide funds and foodstuffs.[84] At the behest of His Holiness the Pope, the king of Spain contacted the American government to help Christians, "especially of those at Mount Lebanon and Jerusalem, of which more than a hundred thousand have perished from hunger."[85] In early May 1917, Assistant Secretary of State William Phillips informed the Spanish Ambassador in Washington that relief supplies had been sent on US collier *Caesar* to Asia Minor via Spain.[86]

It's noteworthy that Great Britain objected to the US State Department authorizing the American Committee for Armenian and Syrian Relief to transmit individual remittances to non-enemy subjects in the Ottoman Empire. Great Britain considered all subjects of the Ottoman Empire as enemy subjects. In August 1917, the US State Department sent a telegram to the ACASR informing them that

> The [US State] Department recognizes your Committee as authorized to transmit relief funds to persons, other than enemy subjects, in Turkey. . . . In general it may be said that individual remittances may be transmitted so long as these do not exceed $125 per person per month. . . . It is further understood that these funds shall be transmitted only through the Société de Banque Suisse at Geneva.[87]

In response to this American effort, on December 3, 1917, British Ambassador Cecil Spring Rice sent a telegram to Assistant Secretary of State William Phillips, emphasizing:

> The Foreign Office pointed out to us that, as the United States of America are not nominally at war with Turkey, the condition as to non-enemy destination is quite without effect in the case in question. They further point out that, as far as His Majesty's Government are concerned, *all* subjects of the Ottoman Empire, of whatever race or religion, are enemy subjects, and that funds transmitted to these people will eventually tend to help Turkey to prolong the war.[88]

After careful consideration, the US State Department disagreed with the letter and spirit of the British government's text. On December 18, 1917, Assistant Secretary of State Phillips sent a telegram to British Ambassador Spring Rice in which Phillips underscored:

The grounds upon which we have based our policy in this respect seem to us to be sound, not only from the humanitarian point of view but from that of expediency as well. We feel that the material benefit to the Turkish government is insignificant compared to the moral and political advantage to our own cause which must result from helping these starving races within reasonable limits.[89]

No less significant, President Wilson was active in mobilizing American public opinion to help Armenian and Syrian peoples. On October 29, 1917, President Wilson issued a memorandum in which he made a special appeal to the American public to help the "stricken Armenian and Syrian peoples." He wrote:

Reports indicate that of orphans alone there are more than 40,000, besides women and other dependent children, reaching a total of more than 2,000,000 destitute survivors. The situation is so distressing as to make a special appeal to the sympathies of all. In view of the urgent need I call again upon the people of the United States to make further contributions as they feel disposed, in their sympathy and generosity for the aid of these suffering peoples. Contributions may be made through the American Red Cross, Washington, D.C. or direct to the American Committee for Armenian and Syrian Relief, Cleveland H. Dodge, treasurer, One Madison Avenue, New York City.[90]

The American Red Cross had established a chapter in Beirut in 1909. During the early months of the Great War, the faculty of SPC played a key role in supervising and organizing the American Red Cross's relief efforts. The American Red Cross cooperated with the municipality of Beirut. But its work in Beirut was suspended in August 1915 upon the order of wali Azmi Bey of Beirut, reportedly for reasons of distrust and/or resentment. Nevertheless, its work in Beirut was mostly taken over by the American Committee for Armenian and Syrian Relief. Significantly, in November 1916, the wali of Mount Lebanon, Ali Munif Bey, allowed the American Red Cross to resume its activities in Mount Lebanon.[91]

No doubt, had it not been for Jamal Pasha, neither the American Red Cross nor ACASR would have been able to operate in Greater Syria (Lebanon, Palestine, and Syria). Significantly, he supported the faculty and students of SPC, including their key role in organizing and supervising the activities of both the American Red Cross and ACASR. President of Syrian Protestant College Howard Bliss pursued an honest and transparent policy with the Turks, who came to trust him. He also gained the confidence of the Muslim community in Beirut, including its religious establishment. Jamal Pasha appreciated and came to trust the college's doctors and medical students, who served in frontline hospitals and attended to Turkish casualties, as well as helped to treat and contain the spread of epidemics. The college also provided dental care to Turkish officials. Correspondingly, Jamal Pasha, along with Turkish officials, granted the college many concessions. He furnished the college with wheat and other supplies at military prices, permitted British professors to continue their work, and released most of the Lebanese teachers from military service.[92]

Even when the United States entered the war in April 1917 on the side of the Allies, the college more or less continued to operate in a normal way. According to Bayard Dodge, "This good fortune was due to the fact that the United States had decided not to declare war against Turkey and Jamal Pasha was glad to interpret the decision in a way favorable to the College."[93]

In parallel to American relief efforts, French relief efforts were mostly confined to smuggling money and foodstuffs to Lebanon's coast via Arwad Island. Lebanese emigrants sent money to Maronite Bishop Yusuf Daryan, who was central in collecting relief funds in Egypt. The French then forwarded the money to French intelligence in Arwad Island, whose main contact was father Boulos Akl. Father Akl, under the cover of night, would smuggle the money by boat to Lebanon. Money for the most part was smuggled as gold to the Maronite Patriarchate, which would exchange it for Turkish bank notes and distribute them across Mount Lebanon.[94] But the money sent was too little to make a substantial difference. Father Akl consistently asked for more, including a loan from the French government.

Certainly, American and French relief efforts saved thousands; nevertheless, they were not enough to meet the critical need of starving Lebanese. By the time the Ottomans were defeated and the French landed in Beirut on October 7, 1918, approximately 200,000 had perished from famine and disease.[95] Lebanese at last breathed the fresh air of freedom from the long-lasting Turkish rule.

This dark chapter in Lebanon's history has left an indelible impression of the Turks in the collective consciousness of the Lebanese, in particular among the Maronite and Armenian communities of Lebanon. In fact, both communities believe that Turkish authorities had committed genocide by starving the population of Mount Lebanon and Beirut. Known interchangeably in popular culture as the Great Famine or Safar Barlik, this tragic history has become a folk tale about Turkish oppression. It was also depicted in a historic war and musical film released in 1967 bearing the title *Safar Barlik*. The film was directed by Henry Barakat and starred famous popular singers and actors including Fairuz, Nasri Shamseddine, Assi Rahbani, Berj Fazlian, Salah Tizani, and Salwa Haddad.[96]

If history is any indication, the famine in Beirut and Mount Lebanon is a tragic and living history for many Lebanese, and recognition of that history should act as a form of reconciliation and as a lesson against repeating the atrocities of the past. Recognizing its painful history will also serve as a domestic and international warning of how the politics of war can lead to needless slaughter, whether willingly or unwillingly. Ironically, whereas the Great Famine is etched in the collective memory of many Lebanese, its commemorative representation is absent from Lebanon's public landscape. Neither the government of Lebanon nor a political party nor a religious denomination has erected a statue or a sculpture to commemorate the Great Famine. This was left to a young artist, Yazan Halwani, famed as a street artist focusing on identity, to unveil the Memory Tree monument in Beirut in 2018 to commemorate the Great Famine.[97] It is the first memorial to ever be erected to the tragedy more than one hundred years later.

To be sure, although the Maronite Church affirms that Turkish authorities had committed genocide in Mount Lebanon and Beirut, senior members of the Maronite clergy have intimated better relations with Turkey based on mutual respect, reciprocal friendship, deference to each country's sovereignty, and admission of responsibility for the Great Famine. They favor a truth and reconciliation commission to help heal the trauma of the Great Famine and bring about a popular reconciliation to surmount its legacy. When asked about the Maronite Church's attitude toward Turkey and the Great Famine, a Maronite bishop emphasized that

> Lebanon needs to have friendly relations with all regional countries, for conflicts do not resolve any outstanding issue. It behooves Lebanon and Turkey to have a truth and reconciliation commission so that both nations can come to grips with what happened and therefore work together to heal the trauma of the Great Famine. The Church does not seek prosecution for past crimes or blame the current Turkish leadership. We need to collectively surmount the legacy of the Great famine so that all Lebanese communities can enjoy a warm relationship with the Turkish people devoid of regrets or resentments.[98]

The recent US recognition of the Armenian genocide should open up opportunities to acknowledge other atrocities from this period, including the pain and suffering Lebanese experienced at the hands of the Ottomans during the same period. American president Joseph Biden emphasized that the recognition of such events is "not to cast blame, but to ensure that what happened is never repeated."

Chapter 5

Inheriting the Confessional System

ARAB NATIONALISM, GREATER SYRIA, AND THE MANDATE

No doubt the emergence of Arab nationalism weakened the hold of the Ottoman Empire on its Arab provinces, paving the way for Arab rebellion against Istanbul and alliance with Great Britain. Significantly, Arab nationalism went through several developmental phases that influenced its attitudinal ideology toward the Ottoman Empire, European powers, and Lebanon.

Initially, the ideational base out of which Arab nationalism grew had its earliest expression in the thoughts articulated by certain activist Muslim intellectuals in response to their growing awareness of the weakness of the Muslim world before European military and political challenges. Those intellectuals opposed European encroachment upon the Arab world, which was under Ottoman Muslim rule. Jamal al-Din al-Afghani (1839–1897), a Persian by birth, regarded religion as a temporal political force that would bring about Muslim unity. He preached "Muslim unity and solidarity in the face of European encroachments."[1] Although al-Afghani transformed Islam into an ideology of a proto-nationalist type that took the form of pan-Islamism, his pan-Islamist concept emphasized building a new consciousness of Muslim solidarity against colonialism.[2]

Muhammad Abdu (1849–1905), a pupil of al-Afghani, shared the latter's views but went a step further to advocate the freeing of the Muslim mind from the fetters of tradition.[3] H. A. R. Gibb noted that Abdu worked for the "purification of Islam from corrupting influences and practices, . . . and the defense of Islam against European influences and Christian attacks."[4] Abdu believed that Islam is an all-embracing system, and sought to revitalize it through cultural activity, which included modernizing the Arabic language. His goal was to affirm that modern culture was not incompatible with Islam "as long as it does not encroach upon the latter's claim to be an all-embracing system."[5]

Rashid Rida (1865–1935), a pupil of Abdu who was born in Syria and settled in Egypt, expressed his dissatisfaction with the state of Islam at the time and his desire to reform it. Rida emphasized Arab solidarity (*asabiyah*), which rested on the Arabic language and Arab centrality in Islam. But in contrast to Abdu, Rida worked for a puritanical revival of Islam. Sylvia Haim noted the connection between Rida, al-Afghani, and Abdu that was premised on Islamic reform through the *Salafiyah* movement (the return to the ways of the pious ancestors). She remarked that "it is in the arguments of the *Salafiyya* that we may trace the first intellectual burgeoning of Arab nationalism."[6]

Abd al-Rahman al-Kawakibi (1849–1902), another follower of Abdu and a Syrian like Rida, who settled in Egypt in 1898, opposed Ottoman as well as European rule over the Arab world (by 1882 Egypt had become a British colony). Kawakibi argued that Ottoman tyranny had caused the decline of Muslim civilization and the stagnation of Islam. He emphasized that Arabs (of the Arabian Peninsula) only can effect the regeneration of Islam. He envisioned an Islamic union spiritually led by an Arab caliph residing in Mecca.[7]

These activists played something of a nationalist role as they revitalized an Islamic movement directed against foreign domination, emphasizing pan-Arab sentiment. But as Bassam Tibi rightly observed, the movement must be considered an inherent part of the nationalist movement in the Middle East, although in the minds of its own protagonists they were not nationalist but Muslim.[8]

This revitalized Islamic movement planted the seeds of pan-Arabist thought, but its role eventually crumbled before the rising tide of secular nationalism, inaugurated indirectly by the Lebanese Christians' national literary renaissance, which ushered in the second and more explicit phase in the development of the Arab nationalist idea. The Arabic literary awakening was the consequence of two related factors: missionary activities and the reforms of Muhammad Ali. As European powers continued to make political and economic inroads in the Ottoman Empire, particularly in the nineteenth century, they supported their penetration with missionary activities in the Arab Middle East. The cultural and political ideas spread by these missionaries appealed to many in the multinational and multireligious Ottoman Empire, especially to the Lebanese Christians. The political climate under which the Christian missions operated improved drastically when the reforms of Muhammad Ali emancipated the Christians in Lebanon and Syria (1831–1840). The emancipation changed the social structure of Lebanon and Syria and significantly opened them up to Western influence.

The Americans and French led the missionary activities. But whereas the French pursued a colonialist policy, the Americans, who entertained no colonial ideas, were more interested in revitalizing the Arabic language in order to popularize their religious activities. An unintended consequence of revitalizing the Arabic language was the inauguration of a national literary awakening. It was the literary work of Christian scholars, such as Nasif al-Yaziji (1800–1871), Faris al-Shidyaq (1805–1887), and Butrus al-Bustani (1819–1883), that revived the Arab national culture, thereby arousing national consciousness. According to George Antonius, Ibrahim al-Yaziji (1847–1905), the son of Nasif, was the first Arab nationalist author to compose a poem eulogizing Arab achievements, denouncing sectarian strife, and inciting Arab insurgency against the Turks.[9]

This trend of cultural nationalism was reinforced by the establishment of the Syrian Protestant College in Beirut in 1866 (later the American University of Beirut), which graduated the first generation of secular Arab nationalists. Although cultural nationalism emphasized the existence of an Arab "nation," it did not call for an independent state. For the Christians, Arab cultural nationalism served as the best means to transcend their minority status, and at the same time to undermine Arab loyalty to the Ottoman Empire, which was predicated on a religious (Muslim) identity. This set in motion a growing desire for articulating pan-Arab and anti-Ottoman sentiments. Negib Azoury, a Christian Arab, founded a secret society called *La Ligue de la Patrie Arabe* in Paris in 1904; then a year later published his book *Le Reveil de la Nation Arabe dans L'Asie Turque*. Much in the same vein as Nasif al-Yaziji, Azoury declared the existence of an Arab nation and called for the creation of an Arab empire in the Middle East, not including Egypt, for Azoury did not consider the Egyptians as Arabs.[10]

Meanwhile, the Ottoman state was experiencing a steep decline in its power in large measure due to the activities of the nationalist (separatist) movements in its Balkan territories. In response, as already mentioned (see chapter 4), a group of Turkish reformers known as the Young Turks revolted against the Sultan (1908) and set about to reform the empire and arrest its decomposition. Turkish nationalism and centralization of the empire were to be the main vehicles of reform. The Arabs of the empire perceived the process of Turkification, which intimated the superiority of Turkish elements above all other elements in the empire, as an open attack on their identity, language, and race. Consequently, they organized several secret societies with a pan-Arabist orientation. Thus, ironically, the Turks strengthened the movement of pan-Arab, nationalist thought.

Among the most important secret societies were *Al-Jam'iyyat al-Arabiyya al-Fatat* (the young Arab society) and *Jam'iyyat al-Ahd* (the society of the covenant). Al-Fatat was founded in Paris in 1911 by Syrian students and in 1913 its headquarters were moved to Damascus. Al-Ahd was founded in Istanbul in 1913 and was composed entirely of Arab army officers, the majority of whom were Iraqis.[11] Al-Fatat took a leading role in organizing an Arab congress in Paris in 1913. All the participants agreed on the reality of an "Arab nation" distinct from other nations, which "only included the Arabic-speaking Asiatic portion of the Ottoman Empire."[12] Egypt was not included in the "Arab nation." At this point, one could conclude that the seeds of the concept of Greater Syria, as the core of the "Arab nation," were sown in this congress. These seeds evolved during World War I and in light of its aftermath to constitute the crux of the Greater Syria concept.

When the Ottoman Empire entered World War I against the British and the French, Arab nationalists faced the inescapable dilemma of having to choose sides. This dilemma marked the third phase in the development of the Arab nationalist idea. Harsh Ottoman rule in Syria and Lebanon helped the Arab nationalists in their decision to break away from their Turkish masters. Members of al-Fatat approached Sharif Hussein, the Hashimite ruler of Hijaz, to form an alliance with them and to lead the uprising. Meanwhile, Hussein had established contacts with the British, who had significant interest and influence in all the Arab lands. Between 1915 and 1916, letters were exchanged between Henry McMahon, the British High Commissioner for Egypt and Sudan, and Sharif Hussein (known as the Hussein-McMahon Correspondence). In these letters, the British, in vaguely worded promises, offered Sharif Hussein a guarantee of his right to rule Arabia and other Arab lands of the Ottoman Empire if he consented to commit his forces on the side of the war efforts of the Allies.[13]

This British promise to Hussein was substantially contravened by a counter-pledge in the form of a secret agreement between Russia, France, and Britain (the Sykes-Picot Agreement), according to which Britain and France were to divide the Arab territories of the Ottoman Empire among themselves after the war. Under the agreement, France was to have a great part of Syria and Lebanon, Britain was to have Iraq in addition to the port cities of Haifa and Acre, while parts of Palestine were to be placed under an international administration.[14] Another pledge that raised controversy between the Arab nationalists and Britain was the Balfour Declaration. On November 2, 1917, Great Britain issued the Balfour Declaration in the form of a letter addressed to Lord Rothschild. The letter made it known that "His Majesty's Government views with favor the establishment in Palestine of a national home for the Jewish people."[15]

Coming on the heels of the Sykes-Picot treaty revelations, Arab nationalists were greatly disturbed by the declaration. They perceived the Balfour promise as nonbinding and invalidated by the British guarantees to Sharif Hussein. According to the British, the correspondence had excluded Palestine from the territories promised to the Arabs.[16] Despite this misunderstanding, the Arab nationalists fought alongside the British. Prince Faisal, the son of Sharif Hussein, led the Arab revolt that ended triumphantly in Damascus in the fall of 1918, whereupon he established his Arab Military Government. But after driving the Turks out, the British divided the former Ottoman territory of the Arab parts of Asia, with the exception of the Arabian Peninsula, into three military administrations (see below), keeping one under their control and giving the other two to Faisal and the French. This greatly disappointed the Arab nationalists, who expected to rule over all these Arab lands.

Consequently, since the Arabian Peninsula remained outside the British division, the Arab nationalists began to focus their political efforts on the remaining land mass that was subjected to this British division and that extended from the Mediterranean in the west to Iraq in the east. This land mass was referred to as "Syria" under the Ottomans and known in general as Bilad al-Sham by the Arab population (after the Arab conquest in the seventh century). Since the Ottomans structured this land mass, "Syria," into administrative divisions, one of which was called the Province (*wilaya*) of Syria, the whole region was subsequently referred to by many Arabs as Greater Syria as well. Greater Syria comprised what are today Syria, Lebanon, Jordan, Israel, and the Palestinian territories. It was within this context that the Arab nationalists began to infuse into the geographical concept of Greater Syria a political meaning, reinforcing it, on the one hand, by the cultural bonds asserted by Arab cultural nationalism, and, on the other, by the sheer political weight of the fact that Arab nationalism had emerged from Greater Syria. The Arab nationalists actualized this by their responses to the unfolding events consequent upon British and French political maneuvering in the region.

Fearing French colonial ambitions in Lebanon and Syria and suspicious of British intentions, Faisal sought to strengthen his regime. He declared his kingdom the Arab Syrian Government and sought to enlist Zionist support. Faisal met the Zionist leader, Chaim Weizman, in Aqaba and later met with other Zionist leaders in London to discuss Arab-Jewish cooperation. As a result, a historic agreement was born in January 1919 that was "mindful of the racial kinship and ancient bonds existing between the Arabs and the Jewish people, and realizing that the surest means of working out the consummation of their national aspirations is through the closest possible collaboration in the development of the Arab State and Palestine."[17] Nonetheless, in an addendum to the agreement, Faisal made its implementation conditional upon the Arabs obtaining their independence.[18]

Apparently Faisal signed the agreement hoping to enlist not only Jewish economic potential in building his state but also Jewish influence with Great Britain to vitiate France's claim to the control of Syria. He also hoped that

Zionist political influence could help secure international support for Arab self-determination.

Scores of Arab nationalists strongly rejected Faisal's agreement with the Zionists, in which Arab recognition of a Jewish national home in Palestine was affirmed and Jewish immigration into it encouraged. Concomitantly, Arab political activity in Palestine converged with that of Syria. A significant number of Palestinian nationalists had already proclaimed their loyalty to the Arab government in Damascus and denounced the Balfour Declaration. In February 1919, Palestinian delegates to a political meeting, referred to as the First Palestinian National Congress, endorsed by a majority a position that considered "Palestine as part of Syria as it has never been separated from it at any time."[19] This position reflected more a concern over the future of Palestine than over the issue of unity with Syria. The underlying assumption was that Palestine, as part of Greater Syria, referred to as "Southern Syria," under the rule of King Faisal, would provide the best reason for invalidating Zionist claims and British rule.

Taking note of Arab nationalist aspirations and concerned with the future of the French and British military administrations in Syria, Faisal attended the Paris Peace Conference and made the case for the independence and unity of Greater Syria. He laid special emphasis on the cultural, geographical, and economic factors that bonded the Arabs of Greater Syria together.[20] Faisal also proposed that a commission of inquiry be sent to Syria and Palestine to find out the aspirations of the population. President Woodrow Wilson endorsed the proposal, with the result that an American commission, known as the King-Crane Commission, toured Syria and Palestine in June and July of 1919. Upon his return to Damascus in May, Faisal, with the cooperation of al-Fatat (which had transformed itself into the Arab Independence Party), called for a general congress to prepare themselves for the commission of inquiry. The General Syrian Congress, known in Arabic as the *Al-Mu'tamar as-Suri al-Am*, was convened in July and was attended by delegates from Lebanon and Palestine.

The congress passed resolutions calling for the independence of Syria with its boundaries covering the land mass of Greater Syria, and asking to maintain the unity of the country whereby Lebanon and Palestine remain inseparable parts of Syria. The congress did not recognize any French governmental right to any part of Syria. In addition, the congress rejected the "claims of the Zionists for the establishment of a Jewish commonwealth in that part of southern Syria which is known as Palestine."[21] After soliciting opinion from the local population and witnessing the events of the General Syrian Congress, the King-Crane Commission issued a report that supported some of the resolutions of the General Syrian Congress. It recommended that Palestine and Lebanon remain united with Syria, and that Syria be placed for a limited time under either an American or a British mandate. Though the commission expressed sympathy for the Jewish cause, it recommended restrictions on Jewish immigration and against the project of making Palestine distinctly a Jewish commonwealth.[22]

The resolutions of the Syrian General Congress, along with the recommendations of the King-Crane Commission, constituted a watershed in Syria's history, for they enabled the idea of Greater Syria to crystallize as a single political community in the minds of many Arab nationalists. In fact, many Arab nationalists saw in Greater Syria's unity a timeless pretext for intervening in Lebanese and Palestinian affairs. However, the Syrian General Congress and the King-Crane Commission meant little to Britain and especially to France. In an effort to evade a clash with France over Syria and keep its commitments under Sykes-Picot, Britain decided to withdraw its troops from Syria and Lebanon in September 1919. Faisal and the Syrian nationalists got wind of Britain's intentions, particularly at a time when France had dramatically increased the number of its troops in the region. At the urging of Syrian nationalists, Faisal convened another congress in March 1920, at which the call for unity and independence was reiterated.

In the meantime, preceding the landing on October 7, 1918, of the French naval division at Beirut, on December 11, 1917, General Edmund Allenby, commander of the British "Egyptian Expeditionary Force," entered Jerusalem. By September 1918, General Allenby had occupied Palestine and moved to conquer Lebanon and Syria. Arab troops under the leadership of Emir Faisal, son of Sharif Husayn of Mecca, supported General Allenby. By the end of October, the whole of Syria and Lebanon had fallen into the hands of the Allies. Tripoli was the last town to fall.

In late October, General Allenby drew the broad lines of the military administration of the former Ottoman provinces. He divided the occupied territories into three zones more or less in line with the British-French agreement, Sykes-Picot, which divided Ottoman territories in the Middle East into spheres of influence. His division included a British South Zone (Palestine), an Arab East Zone (Syrian interior) and French North Zone (Lebanon and Coastal Syria). When Cilicia came to be called the North Zone, Lebanon and Coastal Syria became known as the West Zone.[23]

Meanwhile, Turkey had signed at Lemnos Island an armistice effecting an immediate demobilization of all its troops. Subsequently, the military administration transitioned into a mandate system over Lebanon and Syria by France and over Palestine and Iraq by Britain. In fact, the Allied powers had decided to meet at San Remo, Italy, in April, to decide the fate of the former Ottoman territories. At San Remo, the Allies accorded Britain mandatory jurisdiction over Palestine and Iraq, and France over Syria and Lebanon. The 1920 San Remo conference officiated this transition by considering France and Britain the rightful heirs to the partitioned Ottoman Empire. Before long, Turkey signed the treaty of Sèvres renouncing its rights to the mandated areas.

The mandate system was a novel feature in international affairs. Simply put, it operated under the pretext that Britain and France, which had the mandate over Palestine, Iraq, Syria, and Lebanon, would rule the peoples of these areas until they were ready to rule themselves. This sheer colonial disposition, expressed in a noble concept new to imperial designs, was expounded in Article 22 of the covenant of the League of Nations:

> Certain communities formerly belonging to the Turkish Empire have reached a stage of development where their existence as independent nations can be provisionally recognized subject to the rendering of administrative advice and assistance by a Mandatory until such time as they are able to stand alone. The wishes of these communities must be a principal consideration in the selection of the Mandatory.[24]

On the face of it, the ostensible purpose of these mandates was to promote the well-being and the development of the indigenous population so as to prepare them to rule themselves and meet the challenges of the modern world. With this international recognition of their rights in Syria, the French moved in on Damascus and dethroned Faisal.

On July 24, 1922, the League of Nations officially approved the British and French mandates and incorporated the Balfour Declaration in the charter of the British Mandate.[25] Not only was Greater Syria dismantled and Arab independence denied, but also the foundation was laid for securing the establishment of a national Jewish home in Palestine. France and Britain had fashioned a new political map in the Middle East roughly conforming to the imperial arrangements of Sykes-Picot. This division made a lasting impression on Arab nationalism. It idealized the concept of Greater Syria as a historic reality by an act of historical retrojection from the present into the past to prove Greater Syria's political viability. To many Arab nationalists the thinking went as follows: had Greater Syria not been a united political community, it would not have been divided.

Evidently, the mandate clashed with the aspirations of Arab nationalists who had severed their relationship with the Ottoman Empire and supported the Allies', especially the British, war effort. Their anti-colonial activities affected inter- and intra-communal relations within and beyond the borders of the mandated areas. Consequently, Arab nationalists had become as much against Turkey and colonial powers as against Lebanon nationalism, especially as advocated by Lebanese Christians.

ARAB NATIONALISM AND GREATER LEBANON

On September 1, 1920, French High Commissioner Henri Gouraud proclaimed the establishment of the State of Greater Lebanon:

> Before all the peoples of Mount-Lebanon gathered here, people of all religions, who were once neighbors, but who shall from this day forward be united under the auspices of a single nation, rooted in its past, eminent in its future; at the foot of these majestic mountains, which in prevailing as the impregnable stronghold of your country's faith and freedom, have shaped your nation's strength; on the shores of this mythical sea, which has been witness to the triremes of Phoenicia, Greece, and Rome, and which once carried across the universe your subtle, skillful, and eloquent forefathers; Today this same sea is joyfully bringing you confirmation of a great and old friendship, and the good fortune of French peace; Before all of these witnesses to your aspirations, your struggles, and your victory, and in sharing your pride, I solemnly proclaim Greater Lebanon, and in the name of the French Republic, I salute her in her grandeur and in her power, from Nahr el-Kebir to the gates of Palestine and to the peaks of the Anti-Lebanon.[26]

This seminal statement in the history of modern Lebanon, which was hailed by some, vilified by some, and condemned by others, cast a pall of ambiguity over the national identity of Lebanon from the outset of its creation. To the Maronites, the statement pronounced the long-standing cultural and political kinship, mythical and/or constructed, between them and France, earnestly called "La mére du Liban." It expressed the toil of the Maronite Church, which worked industriously to create an exclusive Christian national identity, separate from Arabism. It also intimated the national aspirations of the Maronites, as expressed in Phoenicianism and Lebanonism, whose symbols, thanks to non-clerical Francophones, permeated the collective heritage of the nation.

Tracing the beginning of its relationship with the Maronites to the Crusaders, France, by the beginning of the nineteenth century, had begun to systematically attempt to acculturate Christian society along French intellectual and cultural lines. Acting in the capacity of France's cultural arm, the French Jesuit order established a chain of schools, and most important, Saint Joseph University in 1875 in Beirut, which soon evolved into the nodal cultural center linking Beirut to Paris. It was there that Henri Lammens planted the ideological seeds of a separate Christian identity.[27]

Influenced by the intellectual atmosphere at Saint Joseph University, Maronite graduates drew the Phoenician ancestral link to a separate Christian identity, which found its expression in modern Greater Lebanon. Among them was Yusuf al-Saouda, who unequivocally spoke about the Phoenician origins of the Lebanese people, while glorifying Phoenician culture and Lebanon's heritage. He asserted:

> Every nation has a strong desire to return to its roots by drawing from the well of its past to its present the glory of its pedigree. Italy is proud to be the heir of mighty Rome with its victories, its glory and its banner. The Greeks glorify their lineage to the important dynasty of personalities of the Iliad with its poets and philosophers. The civilized world thanks Italy and Greece and respects their descendants and the greatness of their forefathers. . . . As a nation is proud of its roots and draws its good virtues from its good progeny, so is Lebanon proud to remember and remind us that it is the cradle of civilization in the world. It was born at the slopes of its mountain and ripened on its shores, and from there, the Phoenicians carried it to the four corners of the earth. The same as Europe has to be committed to Italy and Greece it also has to be committed to a land that is the teacher of Rome and the mother of Greece.[28]

This perspective of the glory and contribution of Phoenicia to Western civilization, not the least the invention and dissemination of the alphabet by the mercantilistic Phoenicians, which were embodied in Lebanon's cultural heritage and collective identity, became the mantle of Phoenicianists in early-twentieth-century Lebanon. Among others Michel Chiha and Charles Corm, the doyen of Phoenicianism, standardized and routinized Lebanon's Western orientation and national identity as an aspect of Phoenicianism. In 1919, Corm began publishing *La Revue Phenicienne*, which became the mouthpiece of the intellectual and political activity of the Phoenician idea, and subsequently, inspired by Maurice Barres, wrote *La Montagne Inspirée*, which was regarded by many as the apotheosis of Phoenicianism.[29]

Parallel to this intellectual effort to reify Lebanon's Phoenician myth of origin and national character uniqueness, the assiduous work of the Maronite Church to create a separate non-Arab Christian identity culminated in providing the political foundation to the Phoenician idea in Greater Lebanon. This was illustrated by the decisive role played by Maronite Patriarch Elyas Huwayek in creating Greater Lebanon. The patriarch (E. P. Hoyek) headed the Lebanese delegation to the Peace Conference in Versailles, where he called for the creation of Greater Lebanon as a separate Christian entity. He justified his claim on the grounds of the Phoenician idea.[30]

As such, Gouraud's statement not only materialized the national aspirations of the Maronite Church and the Phoenicianists, but also helped Lebanonize the Phoenician myth of origin, even though non-Christian communities rejected such notions.

Paradoxically, the creation of Greater Lebanon was an attempt to typify historical and/or mythical Phoenicia; nevertheless, Greater Lebanon reduced the majority of the Maronites to a slim plurality in the new state. Mount

Lebanon, the abode of the majority of Maronites, was not economically viable as a political entity without the coastal cities, out of which shores the Phoenician seafarers set out. Correspondingly, the fertile Beka' region and the regions around the coastal cities of Tripoli, Sidon, and Tyre, with their large Sunni and Shi'a communities, were added to the Mountain to form Greater Lebanon.[31] This condition posed a challenge to the supporters of Greater Lebanon, as many in the new state were then neither predisposed nor ready to identify with the national concept of Greater Lebanon (see below). Consequently, Lebanonism grew from and in response to Phoenicianism. But in contrast to Phoenicianism, whose appeal was confined to a Christian base, Lebanonism, as it was locally referred to, promoted patriotism and Lebanese nationalism. It is with the objective of transcending an essentially Christian Phoenicianism so as to appeal to the Muslim community that Lebanonism concerned itself with an inclusive Lebanese national idea. At the base of the myth of this national idea, born in the time of ancient Phoenicia, was the theme, articulated by Said Akl, of an immemorial "Lebanese People." In other words, the Lebanese constituted a sui generis endogenous and complete nation, which seduced and transmuted (Lebanonized) all invaders. As Franck Salameh remarked, "being 'simply Lebanese' would come to constitute one of the foundational tenets of Lebanonism, and the phrase 'Lebanon is Lebanon, free of labels and epithets extrinsic to its nature' would emerge as the movement's lapidary motto."[32]

Initially, the Muslims rejected out of hand the national concept of Greater Lebanon. The Sunni community, being socially and politically more advantaged than the Shi'a and Druze communities, led the opposition against the formation of Greater Lebanon. The Sunni leadership, which supported King Faisal as ruler of Bilad al-Sham (Greater Syria), had been furious with the French who forced the self-proclaimed monarch from Damascus once they had the mandate over Syria. These Arab nationalists believed that Greater Lebanon was severed from Syria and thus advanced union with the latter. But their initial opposition was temporized by internal and external factors during the mandate, yielding a compromise in the form of an unwritten national pact (Mithaq Watani) that became the cornerstone of Lebanon's confessional system.

INHERITING THE *MUTASARIFIYAH:* THE CONFESSIONAL SYSTEM, LEBANON'S NATIONAL IDENTITY, AND THE NATIONAL PACT

Once the French had the mandate over Lebanon, they set about laying the foundation for its political structure. They issued a series of decrees, among which were the creation of a Representative Council, an electoral law, and a constitution in 1926, all of which served to shape Lebanon's confessional system. At the heart of this system was the apportionment of representation in the council and the administration of the new state on a confessional basis, where every religious community (seventeen altogether) would be represented according to its demography.[33] In fact, this system was a revised version of the political structure that existed during the *Mutasarifiyah* in Mount Lebanon (1861–1920) during Ottoman rule, which thanks to French intervention solidified Maronite political power.[34]

The Sunni elite, most of whom were unionists (Arab Nationalists advocating a union with Syria) from the three major coastal cities of Tripoli, Beirut, and Sidon, led, in the words of Farid el-Khazen, an "organized, systematic effort" against the attachment of their territories to Greater Lebanon, an effort far from being "an act of desperation by local notables disenchanted with the state of affairs that prevailed during the mandate."[35] They organized a series of conferences in which they reiterated their rejection of the fait accompli of Greater Lebanon and petitioned the French High Commissioner about their grievances. Simultaneously, they tried to coordinate their efforts with Arab nationalists in Syria, namely the National Bloc leaders.[36]

But a combination of internal and external factors tempered the singleness of purpose and assiduity with which they pursued their political activism. Generally speaking, four factors affected the political outlook of the Sunni elite. First, the political leadership had become concerned about the growing reality, endurance, and legitimizing role of services rendered by the mandate's institutions. This was reflected by the leadership petitioning the High Commissioner, demanding equal treatment between the territories. No less significant was their concern about the bearing of the census taken in 1932, which favored the Christians, on the distribution of political power and citizenship in the new state.[37]

Second, the Maronite Church by the 1930s had become more or less critical of French policies, demanding Lebanon's full independence.[38] This position caused a thaw in the icy relationship between the Church and the National Bloc leaders. Sunni elite frowned upon this budding political rapprochement, fearing a weakening of their "unionist" position.[39]

Third, the Maronite leadership, represented by Beshara al-Khoury, began advocating a pro-Arab policy in the late 1930s, which was neither incompatible with the position of the Maronite Church nor with Christian elites calling for a Christian-Muslim national understanding. The growing base of this development within the Christian community helped ease Christian-Sunni tensions.[40]

Finally, the Sunni leadership grew disenchanted and disillusioned with the policies of the National Bloc leaders. They felt betrayed by the National

Bloc leaders negotiating a treaty with France that did not include the disputed territories added to Lebanon.[41] The cumulative effect of all of this tempered Sunni rejectionism and reinforced a trend advocated by Sunni leader Riad al-Solh that an independent Lebanon could bring about internal unity as a precondition to Arab unity.[42]

Consequently, Khoury and Solh found in each other an ally to support their national vision. The corollary of this alliance was the birth of the National Pact as a political formula for Lebanon's confessional system and problematic national identity. While political power would be distributed along religious (confessional) lines according to the 1932 census,[43] Lebanon's identity would be characterized by an "Arab face" and manifested by the slogan "No East, No West."[44] Nonetheless, the birth of the National Pact, which actually put the last nail in the coffin of the French mandate, would have been hardly possible without propitious regional developments.

The French position in the Levant had been steadily deteriorating. They, unlike the British, clashed caustically with Arab nationalists. Their position took a detrimental turn when the Vichy government assumed power and the Free French under de Gaulle sought to control Syria and Lebanon. Circumscribed by few resources, the Free French needed British military assistance, as well as support from the local nationalists, to retake control. Consequently, in 1941, they promised full independence to Syria and Lebanon. But once the Vichy forces were defeated, the Free French were no longer willing to live up to their promise. Prodded by British-French rivalry, the British, under Major General Edward Louis Spears in the Levant, supported the nationalists by trying to force the French from the Levant.[45] In fact, in June 1942, a British-sponsored meeting in Cairo between Khoury, Syrian president Jamil Mardam, and Egyptian Prime Minister Mustafa Nahas Pasha engendered an Arab blessing for Lebanon's independence.[46] Upon the enunciation of the National Pact in October 1943, the French arrested Lebanese leaders, including Solh and Khoury, in Rashaya. The British responded by threatening to declare martial law. Recognizing their untenable situation, the French released the nationalists on November 22, 1943. This momentous day has been celebrated as Lebanon's independence day.

Reinforcing the National Pact, the newly independent state adopted the constitution designed by the French, though with slight variations, to accommodate the heterogeneous population. Modeled after the constitution of the French Third Republic, it provides for a parliamentary republican order. The parliament is elected by the people every four years, and the parliament in turn elects the president of the republic for a period of six years. The president, in consultation with parliament, designates the prime minister and the ministers, who would constitute a cabinet responsible constitutionally to the parliament. The National Pact, together with the constitution, provided the framework for Lebanon's confessional system.

No doubt, Maronite-Sunni cooperation in the shadow of British and Arab support proved decisive in creating the National Pact, which actualized independence. Nevertheless, other communities, especially the Shi'a community given its demographic significance, had little, if any, role in the process of concluding the National Pact. Considered as a heterodox community by the Sunni Ottoman Empire, the Shi'a community was denied official recognition as a separate religious community in the empire, thereby facing debilitating discrimination. At a great political and socioeconomic disadvantage from other communities at the beginning of the twentieth century, the Shi'a community had been led by Zu'ama (local notables basing their leadership on the control of patron-client relationships in the community) who were more interested in maintaining the feudal system, which supported their traditional clan leadership. The Zu'ama viewed their representation in the parliament as a means by which they could maintain their patron-client relationships. Moreover, their participation early on in the institutions of Greater Lebanon was eased by the French premeditated policy toward the Shi'a that officially recognized the Shi'a community as an independent sect and sanctioned the Ja'afari school of jurisprudence as a governing body for Shi'a religious affairs.[47] Previously, deprived of privileges accruing to recognized religious communities in the Ottoman Empire, the Shi'a had to suffer the indignation of submitting to Sunni Hanafi juridical law as a legal recourse for their personal status issues.

This lack of influence was illustrated by the reality that the Greek Orthodox and Greek Catholic communities continued to contest the position of the speaker of the parliament after the National Pact was established. In fact, in 1946, the Greek Orthodox Habib Abu Chahla was elected as speaker. Afterward, only Shi'a have occupied this position. But all this does not mean that Shi'ites were not involved in some religious, social, and/or political activism. Some were Arab nationalists who supported King Faisal and opposed the French, while others joined secular and leftist parties. For example, the preeminent Zai'm of the South (Jabal 'Amil), Kamil al-As'ad, opposed initially the French mandate and supported union with Syria. Similarly, the Shi'a notables of the Haydar family in the Beka' supported King Faisal and actively opposed the French. On the other hand, the 'Usayran family supported Greater Lebanon and became identified with the Lebanese nationalist movement. But by the late 1920s widespread support in the wider Shi'a community in both Jabal 'Amil and the Beka' for Greater Lebanon became visible as many Shi'a notables began to recognize the political value of being a considerable community in Lebanon, rather than a minority in the larger Sunni Arab world.[48] Simultaneously, the founding of Shi'a institutions enhanced the power of religious scholars and served as a vehicle for integration into the Lebanese state.[49]

Evidently, the National Pact helped bring about under special circumstances communal conciliation, and to some extent unity. But it neither fostered nor forged a national identity. It was based on a compromise guided by the false assumptions that Muslims would "Arabize" the Christians while Christians would "Lebanonize" Muslims. This also is not to say that the National Pact was supported by a majority of Christians and Muslims. Emile Edde, a rival of Khoury for the presidency, represented a deep current with variant impulses within the Maronite community, ranging from the belief of organic affiliation with the West to Christian humanist character. Besides opposing Arabism and espousing the idea of Phoenician origin, Edde advocated a smaller Lebanon, where Christians would constitute a majority.[50] Similarly, Muslim elites, such as Abdul Hamid Karame of Tripoli and Salim Salam of Beirut, had acquiesced to the pact and independent Lebanon not out of conviction but rather out of resignation; they felt betrayed by the National Bloc leaders. This left a strong impulse of Syrian irredentism within the Muslim community were Syria's position on Lebanon changed. No less significant, the National Pact was concluded by Muslim and Christian elites, leaving the masses either alienated from the process of national conciliation or torn by the hybridity and multiplicity of nationalist, Syrian, and pan-Arab ideologies.[51]

Commenting on the National Pact, Georges Naccache, editor of the pro-Edde *Le Jour*, published an article titled "Deus Negations Ne Font Pas Une Nation." He wrote:

> What kind of unity can one derive from such formula? It is easy to see what half the Lebanese do not want. And it is easy to see what the other half do not want. But what the two halves actually both want—that one cannot see. . . . The Lebanon that they stitched together was a homeland made up of two fifth columns. . . . And in toiling to spurn both East and West, our leaders ended up losing their bearings. . . . The folly was in having elevated a compromise to the level of a state doctrine . . . in having believed that two "No's" can, in politics, produce a "Yes." . . . A state is not the same as a double negative.[52]

On the other hand, remarking, in hindsight, on its historical legacy, Farid el-Khazen wrote:

> Despite its shortcomings and "reactionary" confessional character, the National Pact, based on the very concept of dissent, was liberal in substance and was the last remnant of the liberal age in Arab politics that came to an end at the hands of military dictators and self-styled revolutionaries. Nonetheless, with Lebanon's disintegration and emergence of a variety of post-war pacts, ranging

from federation formulas to "Islamic solutions," the 1943 National Pact was, and is, an indispensable preliminary working paper without which the reshaping of Lebanon's future is impossible.[53]

Significantly, the emergence of Greater Lebanon and its independence were no panacea to heal the sociopolitical and sectarian problems that plagued Lebanon under Ottoman rule. In fact, being a weak state, Lebanon has invited foreign intervention despite the national motto of "No East/No West." Lebanon's identity has remained contested. Most importantly, the feudal leadership, which was based on tax farming under Ottoman rule, has transformed into a feudal sectarian political leadership that deepened sectarianism in Lebanon and led the country to sectarian violence. As Dr. Yusri Hazran aptly argued religious or communal pluralism does not categorically lead to political sectarianism. The development of political sectarianism or sectarian violence has been organically linked to elites' political behaviors and interests. As such, sectarianism takes the form of the instrumental exploitation of a religious or communal identity, whereby sectarianism is first and foremost a product of the elites' quest for power.[54]

No less significant, the sectarian political elite have increased their power at the expense of that of the state. The confessional system has become a fodder of spoils for the class of confessional/sectarian elite who nurtured a patronage system that permeated Lebanese society. It's clear that independent Lebanon was born of and a growth of the *Mutasarifiyah*. As we shall see in the forthcoming chapters, Lebanon-Turkey relations have fluctuated and been dictated by domestic and regional considerations and concerns that to some extent played out in much the same way as Ottoman-Lebanese relations but under a different regional order.

The pictures show Lebanese from Mount Lebanon suffering and/or dying from the Great Famine (1915–1918). After its agriculture and sericulture economy were devastated by a locust invasion, Mount Lebanon suffered from the Allied powers' blockade of the entire eastern Mediterranean to cut off supplies to the Ottomans. In response, Ottoman authorities sealed off Mount Lebanon and Beirut to prevent Christian collaboration with the Allies and an Allied landing in Beirut. Lacking foodstuff and medicine, Mount Lebanon and Beirut succumbed to a deadly famine intensified by widespread epidemics. Approximately one-third of the population of Mount Lebanon died from what came to be known as the Great Famine. Broadly overlooked, the Great Famine, in relation to population density, caused one of history's worst man-made mass starvations.

Credit: Archives de l'Université Saint-Joseph de Beyrouth / Collection Ibrahim Naoum Kanaan, *Le Peuple Libanais dans la tourmente de la Grande Guerre 1914–1918*. C. Taoutel et P. Wittouck, PUSJ, 2017.

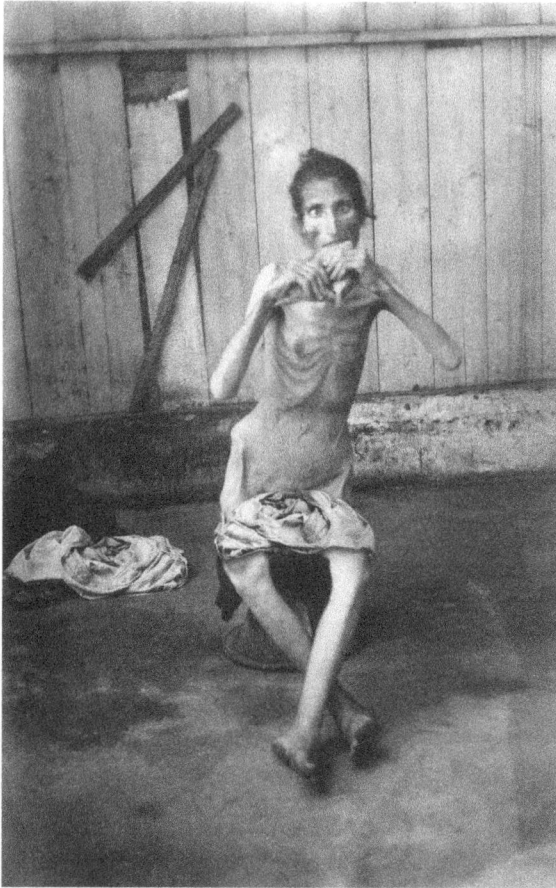

The pictures show Lebanese from Mount Lebanon suffering and/or dying from the Great Famine (1915–1918). After its agriculture and sericulture economy were devastated by a locust invasion, Mount Lebanon suffered from the Allied powers' blockade of the entire eastern Mediterranean to cut off supplies to the Ottomans. In response, Ottoman authorities sealed off Mount Lebanon and Beirut to prevent Christian collaboration with the Allies and an Allied landing in Beirut. Lacking foodstuff and medicine, Mount Lebanon and Beirut succumbed to a deadly famine intensified by widespread epidemics. Approximately one-third of the population of Mount Lebanon died from what came to be known as the Great Famine. Broadly overlooked, the Great Famine, in relation to population density, caused one of history's worst man-made mass starvations.

Credit: Archives de l'Université Saint-Joseph de Beyrouth / Collection Ibrahim Naoum Kanaan, *Le Peuple Libanais dans la tourmente de la Grande Guerre 1914–1918*. C. Taoutel et P. Wittouck, PUSJ, 2017.

The pictures show Lebanese from Mount Lebanon suffering and/or dying from the Great Famine (1915–1918). After its agriculture and sericulture economy were devastated by a locust invasion, Mount Lebanon suffered from the Allied powers' blockade of the entire eastern Mediterranean to cut off supplies to the Ottomans. In response, Ottoman authorities sealed off Mount Lebanon and Beirut to prevent Christian collaboration with the Allies and an Allied landing in Beirut. Lacking foodstuff and medicine, Mount Lebanon and Beirut succumbed to a deadly famine intensified by widespread epidemics. Approximately one-third of the population of Mount Lebanon died from what came to be known as the Great Famine. Broadly overlooked, the Great Famine, in relation to population density, caused one of history's worst man-made mass starvations.

Credit: Archives de l'Université Saint-Joseph de Beyrouth / Collection Ibrahim Naoum Kanaan, *Le Peuple Libanais dans la tourmente de la Grande Guerre 1914–1918.* C. Taoutel et P. Wittouck, PUSJ, 2017.

The pictures show Lebanese from Mount Lebanon suffering and/or dying from the Great Famine (1915–1918). After its agriculture and sericulture economy were devastated by a locust invasion, Mount Lebanon suffered from the Allied powers' blockade of the entire eastern Mediterranean to cut off supplies to the Ottomans. In response, Ottoman authorities sealed off Mount Lebanon and Beirut to prevent Christian collaboration with the Allies and an Allied landing in Beirut. Lacking foodstuff and medicine, Mount Lebanon and Beirut succumbed to a deadly famine intensified by widespread epidemics. Approximately one-third of the population of Mount Lebanon died from what came to be known as the Great Famine. Broadly overlooked, the Great Famine, in relation to population density, caused one of history's worst man-made mass starvations.

Credit: Archives de l'Université Saint-Joseph de Beyrouth / Collection Ibrahim Naoum Kanaan, Le Peuple Libanais dans la tourmente de la Grande Guerre 1914–1918. C. Taoutel et P. Wittouck, PUSJ, 2017.

Ottoman Cemetery of Hazmieh was the official graveyard of Ottoman governors [*Mutasarifs*] of Mount Lebanon and their relatives. I resided in Hazmieh, where I served in the Red Cross during Lebanon's civil war.

Credit: Robert Rabil

Mezher Palace, Hammana. The Mezher family ruled the area as Druze Muqaddams under Ottoman rule.

Credit: Pierre Bou-Jabbour

Martyr's Square in downtown Beirut commemorates the Lebanese martyrs executed by Ottoman authorities on May 6, 1916, for supporting independence from Ottoman rule and having contacts with the Allies.

Credit: Robert Rabil

Memory Tree, Beirut. The Memory Tree was commissioned by Université Saint-Joseph de Beyrouth and writer Toufic Salame. It is the only monument commemorating the victims of the Great Famine (1915–1918). Erected a century after the Great Famine, the Memory Tree was designed by Yazan Halwani.

Credit: Robert Rabil

My great-grandmother and father. Great-Grandmother Mounira was among the survivors of the Great Famine.
Credit: Robert Rabil

My siblings and cousins. The background of the picture shows Hammana's silk factory, which shuttered during World War I. Sericulture was the mainstay of Mount Lebanon's economy.

Credit: Robert Rabil

Chapter 6

The Cold War and the Rise of Nasserism

LEBANON, TURKEY, AND THE RISE OF NASSERISM

A state and a nation more or less shaped by sectarianism, weak national identity, and a bitter taste of Ottoman legacy, Lebanon had initially no desire to forge a warm relationship with Turkey. With the exception of some Sunnis who resented the abolition of the Caliphate in 1923, virtually most Lebanese did not aspire to have cordial relations with Turkey, the heir of the Ottoman Empire. Notwithstanding the appeal of Arab nationalism, many Lebanese still harbored strong anti-Turkish feelings. Ottoman's starvation of Mount Lebanon and Beirut was fresh in the collective consciousness of many Lebanese. Moreover, the small but active Armenian community, which had managed to escape to Lebanon following the Armenian genocide committed by the Turks during WWI, has been a vocal critic of Turkey and Turkish policies. No less significant, the Shi'a of Lebanon had no love for Turkey. The Shi'a community, besides being stigmatized as a heterodox community under Ottoman rule, had to observe a Sunni juridical school rather than its own Ja'afari Twelver school of Islam. Shi'ites strongly resented what they considered as a Turkish systemic denigration of their community.

This attitude did not change during the administration of Beshara al-Khoury (1943–1952). Lebanon's first president pursued, broadly speaking, a foreign policy in line with the National Pact and Lebanon's identity as characterized by an "Arab face" and manifested by the slogan "No East, No West." In fact, thanks in no small part to the Khoury-Solh arrangement (see previous chapter) and the support each of them lent to the other, the republic's early years weathered the heterogeneous impulses of a heterogeneous society. The admission of Lebanon to the newly founded Arab League in 1945 legitimized

Arab official recognition of the country's independent status. Christian concerns about "Arabization" of Lebanon were mitigated by the Arab League's recognition, and Muslim concerns about a Hashemite's Greater Syria union scheme, supported by Britain, were alleviated by membership in the league.[1]

Similarly, the emergence of a mercantilistic Lebanon at the hands of Christian oligarchs did not alienate the Muslim traditional leadership, which benefited either from the capitalist economy or from the confessional system that maintained feudalism as a means to sustain patron-client relationships. No less significant, the merchant republic enjoyed a proverbial freedom and stability at a time when Arab societies were succumbing to military dictatorships. But the winds of change had begun to blow. Coinciding with the emergence of the Cold War, Lebanon was buffeted by domestic and international troubles and setbacks that slipped the country into a civil strife in 1958. During this time, Lebanon's relationship with Turkey was principally influenced by the rise of Egyptian president Jamal Abd al-Nasser's brand of Arab nationalism, best known as Nasserism.

Lebanon's domestic politics had become critically polarized when President Khoury managed to renew his presidential term. A broad anti-Khoury coalition, bringing together cross-ideological and cross-sectarian politicians, emerged. Led by the Maronite and Druze leaders Camille Chamoun and Kamal Jumblatt respectively, the coalition was adamant about bringing down Khoury's second state.[2] Before long, as opposition grew, President Khoury resigned and Camille Chamoun, supported by the broad anti-Khoury coalition, known then as the National Socialist Front, was elected president on September 23, 1952.

No sooner did Chamoun assume the helm of the presidency than he had a falling out with Jumblatt, the man of the Left and founder of the Progressive Socialist Party.[3] Notwithstanding the domestic issues that helped alienate the former political allies, President Chamoun's foreign policy served as the final nail in the coffin of Chamoun-Jumblatt relationship and Chamoun–National Socialist Front relationship and their Nasserist allies. Central to these rifts had been President Chamoun's approach to the Baghdad Pact (1955), Suez Crisis (1956), and Eisenhower Doctrine (1957), which shaped his presidency and Lebanon's relationship with Turkey.

As already mentioned, even after Lebanon's independence from France in 1943, many Lebanese of various religious stripes maintained their negative outlook toward Turkey. Moreover, several Lebanese communities, spearheaded by the Sunni community, strongly resented Turkish recognition of Israel in 1950, a country not recognized by and technically at war with Lebanon. However, the rise of Nasserism in the 1950s, as a pan-Arab movement led by Egyptian president Jamal Abd al-Nasser, temporarily moved the two countries closer together. President Chamoun felt threatened by

Nasser's wave of pan-Arabism that swamped the country's anti-Maronite camp, led by Leftists, Marxists, and pro-Palestinian activists. As the leader of the Christian community, President Chamoun considered Nasserism a direct threat to Lebanon's informal dissociation from the Arab-Israeli conflict, to Maronite hegemony over the state, and to his growing relationship with the United States.[4]

In fact, the emergence of Nasser as the charismatic champion of Arab nationalism sent shockwaves throughout the Arab world. His bombastic rhetoric, populist style, and charismatic appeal notwithstanding, Nasser's opposition to the Baghdad Pact (1955) and vicarious triumph without firing a shot in the 1956 Suez Crisis consecrated his Arab nationalist leadership in the eyes of Arab masses. His "Nasserist" Arab unity movement, referred to locally as *al-Harakah al-Nassiriyah* (The Nasserite Movement or Nasserism), resuscitated dormant pan-Arab impulses and sentiments no less in Beirut than in any other Arab capital. Lebanese Muslims zealously supported Nasser, the long-awaited pan-Arab potent leader.

This compelling political force posed a serious challenge to Lebanon's Christian leadership. Though President Chamoun tried to walk a fine line trying to accommodate Nasser without being swallowed by him, he soon internalized the enormity of Nasser's challenge to the regional order in general and to Lebanon in particular. The strand of Nasser's nationalism turned any modicum of cooperation with the West into an act of sedition. Not only did Nasserism identify with the bloc of non-aligned countries, but also with Third World revolutionary (anti-colonial) movements. Chamoun described Nasser as a power-hungry, expansionist dictator. At the same time, he accused Muslim leaders like Saib Salam and Abdallah Yafi among others, and Druze leader Kamal Jumblatt as partisans of Nasser, blindly following his directives.[5]

Similarly, Washington and London considered Nasserism as a threat to the Western camp for being in tacit alliance with the Soviet camp. In response, they instigated a defense alliance in the Middle East led by Turkey to prevent Soviet penetration of the heartland of the Middle East. Turkey negotiated a security agreement with Iraq in 1955, known as the Baghdad Pact, which Iran and Pakistan later joined. Nasser, considering the pact as a new form of colonialism of the Middle East under the pretext of a security alliance, attacked the pact.

Chamoun initially expressed concerns about joining the Baghdad Pact, as he tried to play a mediating role between the pro-Western and pro-Nasser protagonists. But as the threat became immediate to his rule, Chamoun sided with the pro-Western axis led by Iraq and Turkey in the Middle East. Counteracting Nasser's opposition to and capitalizing on Chamoun's support of the Baghdad Pact, Turkish prime minister Adnan Menderes visited

Lebanon in 1955 to promote the pact. However, strong domestic opposition to the pact led to the downfall of the Lebanese government and to Lebanon not signing off on the pact. Nevertheless, President Chamoun refused to sign a defense pact established by Egypt, Saudi Arabia, and Syria in March 1955 as a response to the Baghdad Pact.[6]

Yet when Great Britain, France, and Israel seized the Suez Canal in response to its nationalization by President Nasser in 1956, Lebanon, Turkey, and Arab states opposed publicly the Anglo-French-Israeli invasion of Egypt, albeit for different reasons. This, however, did not sooth the ire Nasser had for Chamoun for his support of Western powers and Turkey as a NATO member. In fact, Nasser attacked Chamoun for refusing to break off diplomatic relations with Great Britain and France, as Egypt and its ally Syria had done. Facing domestic and regional opposition, Chamoun looked up to Turkey as a country sharing his concerns about Nasserism and their alliance with the Left. In April 1956, President Chamoun made an official visit to Turkey, where the leaders of the two countries issued a joint declaration emphasizing their common views about Middle East developments.[7]

In the meantime, opposition to President Chamoun grew as other politicians from across Lebanon's sectarian spectrum joined the National Socialist Front, which transitioned into the National Union Front. Furthermore, Nasser and his Syrian allies intensified both their support of the National Union Front and opposition to Chamoun. It was against this background of domestic and regional opposition to his rule that Chamoun decided to endorse the Eisenhower Doctrine.

THE EISENHOWER DOCTRINE AND LEBANON'S CIVIL STRIFE

President Dwight D. Eisenhower announced the Eisenhower Doctrine in January 1957, which was approved by Congress in March of the same year. Under the Eisenhower Doctrine, "a country could request American economic assistance and/or aid from U.S. military forces if it was being threatened by armed aggression from another state." Eisenhower singled out the Soviet threat in his doctrine by authorizing the commitment of US forces "to secure and protect the territorial integrity and political independence of such nations, requesting such aid against overt armed aggression from any nation controlled by international communism."[8]

At the time, Washington feared a total Soviet victory in the Middle East. In January 1957, Secretary of State John Foster Dulles addressed Congress, stressing that "it would be a major disaster for the nations and peoples of the Middle East, and indeed for all the world, including the United States, if that area were to fall into the grip of international communism." He added that the United States "must do whatever it properly can to assist the nations of the Middle East to maintain their independence."[9] The Eisenhower administration had its way when Congress passed the joint resolution in March 1957, henceforth known as the Eisenhower Doctrine, conceding to the administration request that

> The president is authorized to . . . employ the armed forces of the United States as he deems necessary to secure and protect the territorial integrity and political independence of any such nation or group of nations requesting such aid against overt armed aggression from any nation controlled by International Communism.[10]

President Chamoun endorsed the Eisenhower Doctrine in February 1957 following President Eisenhower's confirmation to the Lebanese president that the United States would respect the sovereignty of Lebanon and defend it against any threat to its independence and territory.[11]

The US president sent Ambassador James P. Richards to the Middle East to inaugurate the new doctrine. Whereas Syria refused to receive the ambassador, the Chamoun administration met for three days with the ambassador on March 14, 15, and 16, 1957. On the last day, President Chamoun, in addition to reiterating his endorsement of the Eisenhower Doctrine, concluded an agreement with Ambassador Richards according to which the United States would help Lebanon politically, economically, and militarily in return for Beirut supporting Washington and its allies in the region.[12] Soon, Iraq endorsed the doctrine.

Consequently, domestic opposition swelled. Nevertheless, Lebanon's parliament approved the doctrine, sparking calls by the National Union Front and its allies for the government to resign. President Chamoun sensed a coming civil strife no less sought by the National Union Front than by Egypt and Syria, which had been supplying arms to the opposition. Furthermore, Egypt and Syria had been preparing for their unity under the name of the United Arab Republic (UAR), which was actualized in February 1958.

The union helped crystallize the applicability of the Nasserist vision of Arab unity for Nasser's supporters in Lebanon, who began agitating to integrate Lebanon in Nasser's Pan-Arab system. Remarking on the dire situation, Kamal Salibi wrote:

> When Syria relinquished her independent existence and united with Egypt in February 1958, the Lebanese Moslem enthusiasm for the union broke all bounds. The last traces of Moslem unity to Lebanon seemed suddenly to disappear, and it was soon clear that the Lebanese Republic stood in danger.[13]

Lebanon had become a tinderbox waiting to explode. On May 8, 1958, the journalist Nassib al-Matni was assassinated, thereby igniting the fuse of domestic explosion. The National Union Front called for a general strike, whereupon a number of people were killed. Thereafter, the strike rapidly transformed into civil strife. The army, led by General Fouad Shehab, stood by, mainly protecting public places. Chamoun invoked the Eisenhower Doctrine and requested military assistance from President Eisenhower. A heated debate ensued in the US congress because some congress members believed that it was not communist threats but domestic issues that lay at the heart of Lebanon's civil strife.[14]

Significantly, in late May, President Chamoun's political position had become tenuous when Maronite Patriarch Boutros Boulos al-Meouchi censured the president and sent words to foreign ambassadors, including the American ambassador, that the strife was the result of domestic issues and not the outcome of the UAR's meddling in Lebanon's domestic affairs, as the Chamoun's government had depicted. The patriarch was no less furious with Chamoun breaking Lebanon's regional neutrality than with his rapprochement with Turkey.[15]

Be that as it may, President Chamoun and his Christian allies, the Phalange, stood their ground.[16] Ultimately, the American military intervention took place only after a violent Arab nationalist coup d'état overthrew the pro-British Hashemite monarchy, whereupon Hashemite family members and the prime minister of Iraq were murdered. Fearing the crisis would spiral out of control, and given the flow of arms and Arab volunteers into Lebanon from Syria, US Marines were dispatched to Lebanon in July to stabilize the country.[17]

Commenting on President Chamoun's pro-Western stance and cooperation with Turkey, a senior Lebanese official and former ambassador to Turkey underscored what he considered "the Wolf theory under which pretext President Chamoun had to ally Lebanon with the United States and Turkey." According to this theory, the ambassador emphasized "that strident pan-Arabism, Islam and Communism all came in the wolf's skin of Arab solidarity to devour Lebanon."[18] When asked about Patriarch Meouchi's anti-Chamoun stance, the ambassador assertively responded that "the Patriarch had to hedge the position of his community because being a minority in the Middle East the Maronites could not afford siding with the losing side." He underlined the proverbial anecdote: "You cannot put all your eggs in one basket."[19]

The US Marines helped restore calm to the streets of Beirut, and American Ambassador Robert Murphy mediated between the antagonistic parties to defuse the crisis. General Fouad Chehab was elected president by the parliament on July 31, 1958, and Rashid Karami, an opposition leader, formed a government as prime minister on September 24, 1958. The United States supported the government of Karami and completed the withdrawal of its troops by the end of October. Whereas President Chehab reinforced the power of state institutions and tried to maintain a pro-Arab yet a neutral position in Arab politics, the Karami government kept a distance from the Menderes government.[20]

To the unsusceptible eye, the crisis was over. To Jumblatt, the true revolutionary man of the left, the "revolution ended where it should not have ended."[21] As far as he was concerned "the true causes of the recent Lebanese revolution still stand and cannot be treated except by means that are revolutionary in spirit and program."[22] This was so telling before the spark of civil war in 1975, reflecting both the precarious nature of the Republic and Jumblatt's conviction of revolutionary change.

TURKEY'S RAPPROCHEMENT
WITH THE ARAB WORLD

Before long, in May 1960, the Turkish military, led by General Cemal Gürsel, overthrew the Menderes government, with the objective of reinforcing the democratic process and improving the country's relations with the Arab world. The military accused the Menderes government of often violating the democratic process and acting as a vessel for Western interests in the Middle East. Civilian rule was eventually restored following parliamentary elections in October 1961, though General Gürsel remained president until 1966. And the country, though remaining devoted to NATO commitments, pursued a balanced relationship with the Arab world, supporting Arab causes, such as the Palestinian cause, without alienating the West or Israel. In 1965, the Turkish foreign ministry expressed an interest in the predicament of Palestinian refugees and emphasized that its relationship with "Israel would not develop in the direction which would be against the interests of the Arab countries."[23] With regard to Lebanon during the 1960s and early 1970s before the onset of the civil war, Ferenc A. Váli observed that "Turkey's rapport with Lebanon was exceedingly good. Both Beirut and Amman shared Ankara's full confidence."[24]

No doubt, Arab leaders discerned and welcomed Turkey's policy of rapprochement with the Arab world, which, broadly speaking, refrained from intervening in inter- or intra-Arab conflicts and regional conflicts until the 1990 Gulf War. During the events leading up to the 1967 War, Turkey did not take a position on Egypt blocking the Gulf of Aqaba to Israeli shipping, and declared that NATO bases in Turkey would not be used in the event of war. Following the war, the Turkish foreign ministry declared its opposition to territorial gains by the use of force and sent humanitarian aid to the Arab states of Egypt, Syria, and Jordan, which had suffered huge losses in the war. At the same time, as Michael Bishku observed, Turkey never labeled Israel an "aggressor."[25]

Turkey's rapprochement with the Arab world continued slowly yet steadily. In September 1969, Turkey participated as an observer in the first summit of the Organization of Islamic Countries (**OIC**), held in Rabat, Morocco. The OIC sought to organize a response both to the status of Jerusalem after Israel seized the Old City and the eastern part of Jerusalem in the 1967 Six-Day War and to the arson of al-Aqsa mosque. And in much the same vein as during the 1967 war, Turkey informed the United States not to use its military bases in Turkey to aid Israel during the 1973 Arab-Israeli war.[26] By the mid-1970s, Turkey sought to deepen its relationship with the Arab world.

In 1974, Ankara invaded Cyprus following a coup d'état meant to integrate Cyprus with Greece against the wishes of Turkish Cypriots who constituted approximately 19 percent of the population.[27] Pressured, in no small measure, by the Greek-American lobby, US Congress imposed an arms embargo on Turkey. The American embargo convinced Ankara to pursue more or less an independent foreign policy in the Middle East and to improve its relationships with the regional countries.[28] Ankara supported Arab resolutions in the United Nations critical of Israel. Significantly, in November 1975, Turkey, in concert with the entire Arab world, supported UN General Assembly Resolution 3379 equating Zionism with racism. In October 1979, Turkey sanctioned the opening of a Palestine Liberation Organization (**PLO**) representative's office in the capital, whereby the head of the PLO mission, similar to that of Israel, held the rank of chargé d'affaires.

In the words of Váli, Turkey, in its rapprochement with the Arab world, pursued a policy of "benevolent neutrality" as "diplomacy at its best" since Turkey was "able to express sympathies toward the Arab states involved in the war without offending Israel."[29] This was, broadly speaking, the case with Lebanon until the eruption of the country's civil war and its ramifications for the region in general and Syria and Turkey in particular.

Chapter 7

Lebanon's Civil War, Syria, and Turkey

THE POLITICAL BACKGROUND AND DYNAMICS OF LEBANON'S CIVIL WAR

Kamal Jumblatt's warning that "the true causes of the recent Lebanese revolution [1958] still stand and cannot be treated except by means that are revolutionary in spirit and program," began to ring louder and louder in late 1960s and 1970s. Lebanon's stability, which rested on a delicate balance of power among the confessional groups since the crisis of 1958, was disrupted when the Palestinians residing in Lebanon had become an additional actor in the country. The Palestinian question had become grafted onto Lebanon's domestic problems. The country's Sunni and Druze leadership supported the Palestinians and considered the Palestinian question as the Arab cause par excellence in the Arab world, thereby making reforms of the political system inseparable from the Palestinian question.

The number of Palestinians in Lebanon had increased dramatically to approximately 300,000 following their defeat at the hands of the Hashemite regime in Jordan's civil war in 1970. The bulk of the PLO moved out of Jordan to Lebanon via Syria. Soon, given the geographic contiguity of Lebanon with Israel, the PLO and other Palestinian organizations reinforced their presence in southern Lebanon. In 1969, the PLO military's presence in Lebanon was enhanced following the Cairo Agreement, which provided extraterritorial rights for the PLO, particularly in the Palestinian refugee camps. Southern Lebanon had become infamously known as "Fatahland," a designation bearing the name of the PLO's military wing, Fatah.[1]

Already before 1970, PLO attacks on Israel were leading to severe retaliations. In December 1968, Israel raided Beirut International Airport and blew up thirteen Lebanese airplanes, precipitating the fall of the government. Undeterred, the PLO increased its infiltration and sabotage activities in Israel, instigating harsh Israeli counterattacks that made parts of southern Lebanon uninhabitable. This had two immediate bearings on Lebanon's politics. First, the accelerated flight of the indigent Shi'a inhabitants of southern Lebanon to the slums around a predominantly Sunni West Beirut led to the destabilizing of the homogenous religious societal composition of that part of the capital and set in motion an irreversible radicalization of the Muslim community. Second, the Muslim and Christian communities had become dangerously polarized. Whereas the leadership of the Muslim community supported the PLO and criticized the weakness and neutrality of the army in the face of Israel's aggression, the leadership of the Christian community opposed the very presence of the PLO on Lebanese soil.[2]

This polarization was compounded by grave internal disagreements about power sharing and Lebanon's identity. Jumblatt, who led the Lebanese National Movement (LNM), the mainstay of the Muslim camp, abhorred Maronite privileges in Lebanon and sought to overthrow Maronite hegemony over the Lebanese system. In fact, the LNM's Reform Program, announced in August 1975, aimed at changing the political system. It proposed complete secularization by eliminating sectarianism from the whole system and opening the three highest offices in the land to all communities.[3] Significantly, Jumblatt perceived the Maronites as central players in a US and Zionist conspiracy against Lebanon and the Arabs in general. According to him, the Maronites strove to cut Lebanon off from its Arab surroundings in the hope of creating a "Christian Zion" called Lebanon, serving to undermine Arab unity. Thus, according to Jumblatt, the "battle of the National Movement was to save Lebanon and its Arabism and to reaffirm Lebanon's commitment to the Palestinian cause, foiling the Phalangist conspiracy."[4] Jumblatt, in the name of Arabism, was recruiting the PLO to fight his war against the Christians. This posture was grist for the mill of the PLO, which eventually became a decisive player in Lebanon's civil war.

This created two diametrically opposed political camps. The Muslim camp sought to alter the status quo and to gain political advantage, moving Lebanon unequivocally in the direction of pan-Arabism. The Christian camp sought to maintain the status quo and keep Lebanon out of the Arab-Israeli conflict, thereby preserving their political predominance. Before long, the civil war broke out in April 1975, initiating a process of dividing Lebanon along heavily armed sectarian lines, with many Christian and Muslim villages and towns sacked and cleansed along confessional lines. Fronted by the PLO, and outgunning and outmanning the Christian camp, the Muslim camp gained the upper hand and threatened the Christian camp with defeat.[5] The potential defeat of the Christian camp posed security threats to Syria, Israel, and the

United States. Syria frowned upon a Muslim-PLO potential victory, which could either provoke a Christian declaration of independence or an Israeli intervention on their behalf. Israel feared a Muslim-PLO victory, which could turn Lebanon into a PLO citadel across Israel's border. The United States perceived a win by the Muslim-PLO camp as a win for the Soviet Union, which supported them.

Ironically, the three countries, despite their mutual antagonism and/or animosity vis-à-vis each other, shared the concern about the potential defeat of the Christian camp. Consequently, they reached an oral agreement, known as the Red Line agreement, under which Syrian troops would enter Lebanon to separate the combatants and press for a cease-fire, paving the way for a political settlement.[6] On the night of May 31, 1976, Syrian armored columns crossed the border into Lebanon.

LEBANON-SYRIA-TURKEY
TRIANGULAR RELATIONSHIP

Syrian entry into Lebanon brought an initial truce among the antagonists. But this truce rested on a weak political twig that before long collapsed, and, therefore, Lebanon's civil war not only resumed, but also involved new actors. To be sure, Damascus's military presence in Lebanon enhanced its power in Beirut; nevertheless, it created new dynamics affecting Lebanon's relationship with Israel, and Syria's relationship with both Israel and Turkey. The Christian leadership, led by Bashir Gemayel, established a strong relationship with Israel to the chagrin and infuriation of Syria's president, Hafiz al-Asad. This new alliance stemmed from Bashir's realization that Lebanon's sovereignty could not be restored so long as Syrian and Palestinian troops remained on its soil and from his recognition that without American or Israeli intervention his forces could not evict Syrian and Palestinian forces from Lebanon. Chafing over the Maronites' close cooperation with Israel, Syria decided to whittle away at Maronite power and began a process of rapprochement with the Muslims and Palestinians. Significantly, President Asad cultivated a strong relationship with the Shi'a community, notably with Imam Musa al-Sadr, at the expense of its traditional leadership, the Zu'ama. Admittedly, despite the fact that members of the Shi'a community had been active in pan-Arab, leftist, and Palestinian groups and organizations, the community, broadly speaking, until the second half of the 1970s, did not project the sociopolitical power commensurate with its growing number.

Initially, Turkey supported neither the Christian leadership as during the Chamoun era nor the National Movement. More specifically, Turkey, unlike certain Arab countries, avoided being involved in the civil war by not providing weapons to the antagonists. However, as the civil war (1975–1990) continued unabated, Turkey became concerned about its adverse relationship with Syria and its support of Lebanon's Kurds and the Armenians, who shared strong opposition to Turkey.

Turkey's relationship with Syria intensified during the Cold War when Turkey and Iraq concluded the Baghdad Pact. Soon thereafter Britain, Pakistan, and Iran joined the pact, respectively on April 4, September 23, and November 3, 1955. Egyptian president Nasser opposed the Baghdad Pact (see previous chapter) and frustrated any attempt by the Western powers to bring Damascus into the pact's alliance. President Nasser had the Ba'thists, leftists, and communists as allies in Syria, who shared his belief that the pact was an imperialist plot to recolonize the Arab world under the pretext of a defense alliance. Turkey frowned upon the activities of the Ba'thists. They opposed the pact, then the Eisenhower Doctrine, while at the same time marshalling Syrian political forces to unite Egypt and Syria. Syria appeared to be growing more anti-Western by the day.

Significantly, Turkey became worried about Syria's improved relationship with the Soviet Union. Not only did Syria receive military aid from the Soviet Union; it also allowed Moscow to deploy missiles on Syrian territories. Turkey perceived Syrian militarization and deployment of Soviet missiles as a direct threat to its national security. Eventually, in early September 1957, Turkey mobilized 33,000 troops along its border with Syria, describing its maneuver as a preventative measure. Contrariwise, Soviet Foreign Minister Andrei A. Gromyko saw Turkish deployment as a "threat of armed intervention in the internal affairs of Syria."[7] The next day, on September 11, President Nasser decided to send Egyptian troops and arms to support Syrian forces.[8] This led to an increased tension between the Soviet Union and Syria, on one side, and Turkey and United States, on the other. Soviet leader Nikita S. Khrushchev cautioned Turkey against any act of aggression against Syria. In turn, US Secretary of State John Foster Dulles warned the Soviet Union that an attack on Turkey would mean that the United States would attack Soviet territory.[9]

Unexpectedly, on October 29, 1957, Khrushchev attended a reception held at the Turkish embassy in Moscow, where he held talks with Turkish officials, among others. Apparently, Khrushchev's visit defused the crisis. In November, Turkey began to withdraw its troops from the Syrian-Turkish border.[10]

Admittedly, the resolution of the Syrian-Turkish crisis did not improve their relationship. Historically, notwithstanding the chronic friction over smuggling across Syria-Turkey's 835-mile-long border, Syrian grievances with Turkey revolved around two main issues. Syria had irredentist claims over the Turkish province of Hatay (Alexandretta). In June 1939, following a referendum organized by the French mandate over Syria, Hatay was transferred to Turkish sovereignty. Syria disputed the referendum as rigged, considering it a French appeasement of Turkey to side with the allies against Nazi Germany.[11] The other grievance was over the usage of the waters of the Asi (Orontes), Tigris, and Euphrates Rivers. This became a highly combustible issue when Turkey launched its ambitious water project the Southeastern Anatolia Project (GAP) in the early 1980s. In response, President Hafiz al-Asad of Syria began supporting anti-Turkish Armenians and Kurds as a leverage against Turkey.

SYRIA, LEBANON'S ARMENIANS AND KURDS, AND TURKEY

Amid Lebanon's civil war, the country had little, if any, official diplomatic channels with Turkey. It was Syria and some confessional groups that punctuated Lebanon's relationship with Turkey. Of utmost importance to Turkey had been Syria's support of what Ankara considered the radical factions of the Kurdish and Armenian communities in Lebanon.

Kurdish warriors and clans came to Lebanon throughout its history. Some were sent to Lebanon by dynasties to safeguard their rule there against aggressors, and some settled in Lebanon to escape persecution by their opponents. Clannish Kurdish chiefs became feudal lords under the Mamluks and thereafter under the Ottomans. For example, the Banu-Sayfa clan came during Mamluk rule and settled in Tripoli and Akkar. Their leader, Yusuf ibn-Sayfa, became a feudal lord more powerful than the Turkish pasha in mid-sixteenth century. The kingmakers of the Druze community, the Jumblatts, settled in the Chouf in the seventeenth century. They trace their ancestry to Kurdish chief Ali Janbulad, who usurped the *wilaya* of Aleppo and entered into an alliance with Fakhr al-Din II, who rebelled against the Ottomans.[12] Fearing Ottoman retribution, Janbulad's tribesmen migrated to Lebanon. However, these clans were "Lebanonized" and became integral parts of Lebanon's established confessional communities and/or feudal lordships.

Notwithstanding the presence of some Kurdish families who lived in Lebanon since Ottoman rule, Kurdish migration to Lebanon took place mainly between the 1920s and 1960s. Following the suppression of the Kurdish-led rebellion of Sheikh Said in Turkey in 1925, Kurds migrated to Syria and Lebanon. During the late 1950s and 1960s, Kurds in Syria, facing state discrimination and economic discontent, moved to Lebanon for a better life. Most Kurds lived in Beirut and its suburbs.[13] They were among the lower classes in Lebanon's society, and many of them lacked citizenship, which exacerbated their economic condition by depriving them of the infamous patronage system that doled out employment opportunities and services in return for votes. Given that confessional Lebanon had done only one census in 1932, it is estimated that in the early 1980s Kurds numbered between 60,000 and 90,000.

The majority being Sunnis, Kurds supported Sunni leadership. During the 1940s and 1950s, they supported Prime Ministers Riad and Sami al-Sulh, who helped naturalize hundreds of Kurdish families. In the 1960s and early 1970s, they supported Prime Minister Saeb Salam, scion of a wealthy notable family. However, Salam lent his support to naturalized Kurds who voted for him. A significant number of Kurds shifted their loyalty to the Druze leader and head of the Progressive Socialist party, Kamal Jumblatt, who provided the Kurds "under-study" identification cards. Issued in 1962, these cards were used as documents for traveling and for registering Kurdish children in public schools. But these cards did not confer on the Kurds citizenship rights. Fearing a disruption of demographic balance, Maronite Christians more or less opposed granting citizenship to Palestinian and Kurdish Sunnis.[14]

During the first years of the civil war (1975–1990) Kurds supported the National Movement, becoming members chiefly of the Sunni Murabitoun and the Lebanese Communist party. They also fought alongside the PLO and the Popular Front for the Liberation of Palestine (**PFLP**), which trained them. The Phalange purged them, along with the Palestinians, from East Beirut. Meanwhile, Kurds were cautious in their relationship with Syria, whose troops moved into Lebanon in 1976. Syrian *Mukhabarat* (intelligence) had considerable influence in the country.[15] True, Kurds became politicized and joined Lebanese parties; nevertheless, they also supported the Kurdish leader in Iraq, Mustafa Barzani, and his Kurdish Democratic party. Barzani's struggle for Kurdish independence appealed to the Kurds of Lebanon, who established an affiliate party, the Kurdish Democratic Party in Lebanon (al-Hizb al-Dimuqrati al-Kurdi fi Lubnan-al-Parti). Despite their support of the Sunni community, Kurds were either ignored or discriminated against within the community until the election of Rafiq Hariri as prime minister in the 1990s. Kurdish causes were rarely championed by Sunni leaders. It was against this background in the 1980s that many Kurds began to support the Kurdistan Worker's Party (PKK) under the leadership of Abdullah Ocalan, whose charisma and struggle for Kurdish nationalism against powerful Turkey struck a nationalist chord among Lebanon's Kurds.

As the PKK expanded its military activities outside of Turkey, President Asad welcomed Ocalan in Damascus and helped the PKK set up a training camp in Lebanon's Beka' valley. The PKK found in the PLO and the PFLP nationalist allies as both Kurds and Palestinians fought for their self-determination. In fact, before and during Israel's invasion of Lebanon in 1982, both Syria and the PLO militarily supported the PKK and their Lebanese allies, who fought against Israel.[16] As it turned out, The PLO was forced from Lebanon to Tunis and Israel withdrew to its buffer zone in southern Lebanon in 1984 until its complete withdrawal in 2000. Clearly, Israel's victory was short-lived and Syria emerged as the hegemonic power in Lebanon. President Asad kept harboring the PKK in the Beka' valley and supported it mainly as a leverage tool against Turkey until the Adana agreement of October 1998.[17]

During the 1980s, Turkey continued its policy of noninvolvement in Lebanon's civil war. Conversely, Syria's influence in Lebanon, with the exception of the Christian heartland mainly in East Beirut, North Matn, and Kisrwan, proscribed Turkish cooperation with any political or sectarian group. Nevertheless, Turkish intelligence often visited anti-Syria Christian East Beirut to pry information on the PKK and radical Armenians. At the time, East Beirut was battered by internecine squabbling among Christian political and militia leaders, especially following the 1982 assassination of Bashir Gemayel, president-elect and leader of the Lebanese Forces. As a result, rudimentary contacts between Turkish officials and Christian leaders went nowhere and were nipped in the bud when Syria (and Saudi Arabia) mediated the end of the civil war in 1990, which practically ushered in Syrian occupation of Lebanon until 2005.[18]

By the late 1980s, Turkish frustration with Syria intensified at a time Ankara had considered readjusting its pro-Arab tilt in the region. Neither the Arab world nor the PLO supported Ankara's Cypriot policy; and none of them empathized with the predicament of Bulgaria's Turkish minority, many of whom fled to Turkey. Moreover, Turkish negotiations with both Syria and Iraq over the water issue had reached a dead end. It was against this backdrop that Iraq invaded Kuwait and drove the final nail in Arab solidarity. The US-led coalition to extract Iraq from Kuwait was supported not only by most Arab countries but also by Turkey and Israel. Alternatively, Iraq was not the only loser in the first Gulf War; the PLO, which supported Iraq's invasion of Kuwait, lost significant Arab support, undercutting the political weight the Palestine cause had laid on the Arab and Turkish relations with Israel. Consequently, by the early 1990s, Israel-Turkey relations improved quite drastically and before long transformed into a strategic relationship, which was manifested by a capacious military and intelligence agreement between the two countries in 1996.[19]

Coming on the heels of Turkey accusing Syria of aggression and threatening self-defense measures, the strategic Israeli-Turkish agreement was looked upon by Syria as the most dangerous threat facing the Arabs. Similarly, Ankara asserted that Syrian-Turkish relations would normalize only should Syria cease its support of the PKK and turn Ocalan over to Turkish authorities.[20] In 1998, seeing no considerable change in Syria's behavior, Turkey threatened Syria and massed its troops along the Syrian border. Facing two powerful technically allied enemies on his country's border, President Asad capitulated to Ankara's demands and signed the Adana agreement. As a result, he expelled Ocalan from Lebanon and Syria, recognized the PKK as a terrorist organization, and agreed to end all forms of support to it. Ocalan was later captured in Kenya and repatriated to Turkey, where he remains a prisoner.[21]

No doubt, Syrian occupation of Lebanon affected Lebanese-Turkish relations. But with the PKK expelled from Lebanon and Syrian-Turkish relations slowly improving, the dawn of a new era in Lebanese-Turkish relations began to appear on the horizon. In the meantime, some Kurds, who were active with the PKK, left Lebanon for Iraqi Kurdistan, which had become a virtually autonomous region following the first Gulf War. Some Kurds left for Europe, especially Germany, where a significant Kurdish community from Turkey lives. The remaining Kurds in Lebanon shifted their loyalty to late prime minister Rafiq Hariri, who promulgated the naturalization decree in 1994. A majority of Kurds, especially in Beirut, looked up to him as their champion.[22] However, even though the majority of Kurds who remained in Lebanon became naturalized and began to actively engage the system to better their sociopolitical and economic lives, the Kurdish community as a whole has not benefited from the confessional system and its spoils as have other communities.

The Armenians, on the other hand, fared much better as a community than the Kurdish one. In much the same vein as the Kurds, the Armenians had a long history in Lebanon. The Armenian trek in the direction of Lebanon began following the downfall of the Armenian kingdom of Cilicia in 1375. A group of Armenians settled in Tripoli and northern Lebanon among the Christians of Ehdin, Zgharta, and Ghazir. Eventually, these Armenians were assimilated by the native populations.[23] The next small waves of Armenian migrants to Lebanon took place mainly during the reigns of Ma'ni Emir Fakhr al-Din II (1590–1635) and Shehabi Emir Bashir II (1788–1840). Both emirs expanded their territories, sought separation from Ottoman rule, and pursued economic and political policies, including welcoming religious minorities, which helped prosper Lebanon. Both emirs had affinity with Christians.

Discriminated by the Ottomans and virtually persecuted by their native churches, Catholic Armenian defectors found a welcoming abode among the Maronites of Lebanon. Both the Maronite Church and Maronite feudal lords welcomed Armenians. The Khazin feudal lords of the district of Kisrwan welcomed Syrian, Greek, and Armenian Catholics, bestowing on them money and lands. Consequently, the district of Kisrwan prospered. The Maronite Church, after its union with Rome, interceded with the Vatican to formally recognize the Armenian Catholic Church as part of the Roman Catholic Church, which took place in 1742. In 1771, the Armenians built the monastery of Bzommar, which housed the Catholicos-Patriarch, the head of the Armenian Catholic Church. The monastery became the oldest extant Armenian institution in Lebanon and an enduring symbol of the Armenian's ecclesiastical and communal bond with Lebanon.[24]

In the mid-to-late nineteenth century, some professional and handymen Armenians were attracted by Beirut's emergence as a prosperous hub of trade and education. No less significant, a number of Armenians fled to Lebanon during the Hamidian Armenian massacres (1894–1897). But the major influx of Armenians to Lebanon took place after the Armenian genocide in Turkey during WWI and immediately after the independence of the Republic of Turkey.[25] Armenians were broadly welcomed, even though Lebanon had been reeling from the WWI famine. Maronite Patriach Elias Huwayek, who played a key role in creating Greater Lebanon in 1920, opened his arms to the Armenian refugees and famously said, "The piece of bread that we have, we will share it with our Armenian brothers." This warm welcome was perceived by some as more of a tactical move by the patriarch to maintain Christian plurality in Lebanon than an altruistic gesture, given that Armenians were Christians.

Another significant wave of Armenian migration to Lebanon took place in 1939 when France ceded the Sanjak (province) of Alexandretta (Hatay) to Turkey, prompting the province's Armenians to flee to Lebanon.[26] Other smaller waves of Armenian migration to Lebanon, similar to those of the Kurds, trickled from Syria during the 1950s and early 1960s in search of a better life.

The Armenians, unlike the Kurds, were fairly quick to thrive in Lebanon's society. They made a qualitative identity shift from refugees as a nation temporarily in exile in Lebanon to perceive Lebanon as their fatherland, without forsaking the Armenian cause. They were easily integrated as a minority in Lebanon's confessional system. They have also prospered as an assimilated minority in Lebanon's multi-sectarian social fabric and assumed economic and political influence in clustered neighborhoods and cities. They constitute a majority in Beirut's eastern suburb of Bourj Hammoud and Beirut's neighborhood of Khalil-Badaoui. They constitute a large community in north Matn, and they have a plurality in the Beka' city of Anjar. They are also found in different suburbs of Beirut and Kisrwan villages.[27] In the early 1980s, the Armenian population of Lebanon was estimated between 160,000 and 180,000, bearing in mind that a few thousand left Lebanon during the early years of the civil war. Though the Armenian clergy is widely respected and has a strong religious and social leverage, Armenians have been politically represented by three parties: the Armenian Revolutionary Federation (Tashnag), Social Democrat Hunchakian Party (Hunchak), and Armenian Democratic Liberal Party (Ramgavar Party). Though doctrinally socialist, the Tashnag party is deeply nationalist and the strongest of the three parties in Lebanon. Whereas the Hunchak party is Marxist yet nationalist, the Ramgavar party is liberal and nationalist.[28] Notwithstanding their different ideologies, the three parties have been unified in their opposition to Turkey.

Although Christians and the plurality of them lived in Christian areas, Armenians sought to have cordial relations with all denominations. In fact, during the civil war (1975–1990), the Armenian political leadership embraced what Ohannes Geukjian termed a policy of positive neutrality.[29] Aware of the potential dangers of the war with respect to "Lebanon in general and the Armenian community in particular," the political leadership decided "to face these potential threats with a united position and bear the socio-economic and political consequences of its stance."[30] This caused tension with the political leadership of the Christian Phalange party and the National Liberal party. A few skirmishes took place in Khalil-Badaoui and Bourj Hamoud. However, whatever tension the Armenians had with the Phalange dissipated as members of the community joined the ranks of the two major Christian parties and fought the PLO and the National Movement. Moreover, despite the policy of positive neutrality, the Armenian churches provided humanitarian aid, shelter, and financial resources to the Christian war effort.[31]

The Armenians also did not want to sever their relations with Syria, especially after Syrian troops moved into Lebanon in 1976. In principle, their policy of positive neutrality also included Syria. Not only did Armenians live in Syria; they also lived in Lebanese territories controlled by Syria and its allies. However, despite their strong opposition to Turkey, the political leadership of Armenians avoided being involved in Syria's proxy war against Turkey. President Asad mainly supported the Armenian Secret Army for the Liberation of Armenia (ASALA), which had carried out terror acts against Turkish institutions, diplomats, and citizens. Reportedly, following its invasion of Lebanon in 1982, Israel provided Turkey with documentary evidence that ASALA members received training at PLO bases in Lebanon.[32]

In much the same vein as with the PKK, Syria, following its capitulation to Turkey in 1998 and in line with the Adana agreement, stopped supporting ASALA and other radical Armenian Marxists. Significantly, it was under Syrian occupation of Lebanon that the Armenian political leadership, through its Armenian bloc in the Lebanese parliament, put forth a bill that the legislature unanimously approved on April 4, 1997, calling for the commemoration of the eighty-second anniversary of the Armenian Genocide perpetrated by the Ottoman Turkish government. Three years later, on May 11, 2000, the Lebanese parliament recognized and condemned the genocide perpetrated against the Armenian people and expressed its complete solidarity with demands of its Armenian citizens. Lebanon was the first Arab country to recognize the Armenian genocide.[33] Lebanon's recognition infuriated Turkey.

But Ankara had little if any influence with the political leadership, parties, or religious communities to oppose or protest Beirut's recognition of the Armenian genocide. This condition slowly yet steadily changed as Turkey made inroads in Lebanon's society.

Chapter 8

Planting the Seeds of Change

TURKEY'S STRATEGIC DEPTH
DOCTRINE AND LEBANON

With the expulsion of the PKK from Syria and Lebanon, Syrian-Turkish relations steadily improved after 1999 and, by extension, Lebanon-Turkish relations since Syria dominated Lebanon. No less significant, the arrest of Ocalan and the assumption of power of Bashar al-Asad in 2000 incentivized better relations between the two countries. In fact, in January 2004, President Asad with his wife Asma made a historic visit to Turkey. The leadership of both countries signed economic agreements, including removing travel visas. President Asad also implicitly relinquished his claim to the Hatay province.

However, Turkey remained consistent in its foreign policy approach of avoiding inter– and intra–Middle East conflicts insofar as they did not threaten its national security. Ankara remained indifferent to Beirut's sectarian and regional problems. But the ascension of the Justice and Development Party (AKP) to power in 2002 ushered in a new foreign policy approach toward the Middle East.

The architect of Turkey's new foreign policy approach was Ahmet Davutoglu, who proposed a new "Strategic Depth Doctrine" in response to Turkey's challenges and prospects vis-à-vis the emerging new post–Cold War international order. Once a close associate of AKP leader Recep Tayyip Erdogan, Davutoglu based his doctrine on the following points: (a) Turkey should transform itself into a global power, based on its unique geostrategic position and Ottoman legacy; (b) Turkey should pursue a "zero problem" foreign policy with its neighbors and thus enhance its stature; (c) Turkey should change its foreign policy orientation from that of a security-oriented country to that of an economic-oriented one; (d) Turkey should play the role of mediator in conflicts, especially in the Middle East; and (e) Turkey should promote an "Alliance of Civilization" as an alternative to the theory of "Clash of Civilizations."[1] This new approach marked a qualitative shift in Turkish foreign policy, which was based on the securitization of Turkish Middle East foreign policy. In the words of F. Stephen Larrabee and Ian O. Lesser: "With some exceptions, Turks tend to see the Middle East more as a sphere of risk than as a sphere of opportunity."[2] Whereas Turkey perceived threats to its national security as the main driver (and securitization) of its Middle East foreign policy, Turkey's new approach relied more on the principle of "zero problem" with neighbors and on the diplomatic and economic levers of soft power to pursue the objectives of its national security.

Clearly, Davutoglu's doctrine is an invigorated form of neo-Ottomanism, which can be traced to Turgut Özal, who served as prime minister (1983–1989) and president (1989–1993) of Turkey. During his period in power, Turkey witnessed critical changes on the domestic and foreign policy levels, which highlighted the inviability of the state's doctrine of Kemalism. The cumulative effect of Kurdish nationalism and insurgency, the first Gulf War (1990–1991), and the independence of central Asian countries following the disintegration of the Soviet Union shaped the ideological background against which Özal's neo-Ottomanism was expressed. In other words, neo-Ottomanism was born as a response to the inviability of Kemalism in meeting Turkey's domestic and foreign challenges. Kemalism, the eponymous name of the founder (father) of modern Turkey Mustafa Kemal (Attaturk), based Turkey's state ideology on the principle of "one country, one language, and one nation." Kemalism, as its founder aspired, was designed to detach the newly founded Turkish Republic from its Ottoman past, Muslim culture and religion; modernize and acculturate Turkey along Western lines including embracing Laicism; and define national identity as purely Turkish in reference to a shared language, common values and history, and the will to share a future.[3] In this respect, Kemalism was Turkey-centric.

However, Kemalism's failure to assimilate the Kurds, incapacity and/or disinterest to gauge the regional and global ramifications of the Gulf War (1990–1991), uneven economic development, weak democracy, and distance from Muslims including Turkish communities in newly independent Asian states led Özal and like-minded academics and officials to rehabilitate Turkey's state doctrine and chart a new domestic and foreign policy course for the country. Theirs was neo-Ottomanism. Neo-Ottomanists supported an active and diversified foreign policy in line with the country's historical heritage, a commitment to Turkish communities abroad, an even development throughout Turkey, and democratization of Turkey. In the words of M. Ataman, "One of the most significant steps taken by Özal toward democratization of the state was 'demilitarization and civilianization' of the state administration." Given then the preponderance power of the military, neo-Ottomanists believed that for "a democracy to be effective, some mecha-nisms of civilian control over the military have to be established."[4]

Introduced as a term by leading Turkish columnist and academic Cengiz Candar, and popularized in the West initially by David Barchard for examin-ing the ties between Turkey and the West, neo-Ottomanism developed into an unofficial state doctrine, albeit with contradictions, under Davutoglu's Strategic Depth doctrine. At the heart of Davutoglu's doctrine is the trans-formation of Turkey, on the basis of its optimal geography and historical heritage, into a country that "should make its role of a peripheral country part of its past, and appropriate a new position: one of providing security and stability not only for itself, but also for its neighboring regions. Turkey should guarantee its own security and stability by taking on a more active, constructive role to provide order, stability and security in its environs."[5] In sum, Turkey should capitalize on its history and geographical depth, which places Ankara at the heart of geopolitical developments, to play an active and constructive trans-regional role (since Turkey is a Middle Eastern, Balkan, Caspian, Mediterranean, Gulf, and Black Sea country) to guarantee both its security and stability and those of its neighbors using the diplomatic and economic levers of soft power.

As a result of its new foreign policy orientation, Ankara developed a keen interest in Beirut grounded no less in Ankara's "Strategic Depth" doctrine than in common culture, history, and Islamist ideology as embraced by the Islamist party **al-Jama'a al-Islamiyah** (Islamic Association). However, Syrian occupation of Lebanon, despite warm Syrian-Turkish relations, cir-cumscribed close Turkish cooperation and contacts with the political and sectarian leadership of Lebanon. Turkish-Lebanese relations were executed on an official and conventional basis, and bilateral relations between the two countries gained momentum following the visit of Lebanon's Prime Minister Rafiq Hariri to Turkey in 2004. Ironically, whereas Hariri's visit to Ankara gave momentum to Lebanon-Turkish bilateral relations, his assassination in February 2005 and subsequent forced withdrawal of Syrian troops from Lebanon doubled that momentum in unconstrained ways.

The assassination of Hariri provoked a national outcry against the Syrian occupation of Lebanon. It was at this critical juncture in Lebanon's history that many Lebanese from across the country's political and sectarian spec-trum joined hands to clamor for democracy and Syria's withdrawal from the country. This mass demonstration, labeled "Cedar Revolution," all but crushed the Syrian order in Lebanon, prompting Damascus to withdraw its troops after almost three decades of Machiavellian Syrian politics and reign of terror.[6] Initially, senior Syrian officials were implicated in the massive car bombing that killed Hariri and twenty-one others in Beirut. But after years of investigations by a UN-backed tribunal, Special Tribunal for Lebanon, in the Netherlands, four Hezbollah operatives were charged with the murder, but only one, Salim Ayyash, was convicted of participating in a conspiracy to carry out the bombing.[7]

The Turkish attitude toward Syrian implication in the murder and withdrawal of its troops from Lebanon was ambivalent. Notwithstanding international pressure on Syria to withdraw from Lebanon, President Ahmet Sezer, to the consternation of the international community, especially United States and France, did not cancel his scheduled visit to Damascus in April 2005. Besides appreciating President Sezer's visit to Damascus, President Asad perceived the visit as an unambiguous Turkish show of support for the Syrian regime at such a critical time, save a demonstrable readiness to stand by Syria and improve Syrian-Turkish relations. Yet, President Sezer called on his Syrian counterpart to pull out his troops from Lebanon by the end of April 2005 in line with UNSCR 1559.[8]

Conversely, the withdrawal of Syrian troops from Lebanon removed serious societal, sectarian, and political impediments to better Lebanese-Turkish relations. Acting on its Strategic Depth doctrine, Turkey's interest in Lebanon was manifested during the Hezbollah-Israel conflagration in summer 2006.[9] Turkish leaders criticized Israel's massive bombings of urban areas and the country's infrastructure, and large popular demonstrations against Israel's bombings of both Gaza and Lebanon took place in Diyarbakir province.[10] Significantly, Turkey played an active role in bringing about a cease-fire, and following the adoption of UNSCR 1701, which ended the war and expanded the mandate and membership of the United Nations Interim Force in Lebanon (UNIFIL), Turkey contributed 1,000 army personnel to the peacekeeping and monitoring mission.[11] At the same time, the Turkish government, in concert with the Turkish Emergency agency, provided significant humanitarian aid to Lebanon. The Turkish Red Crescent and civil society organizations were also quick in organizing aid campaigns to Lebanon.[12] It's noteworthy that Turkey also contributed financially to the UN-backed Special Tribunal for Lebanon.

Turkey's unbiased support of Lebanon, irrespective of political or sectarian groups and communities, did not go unnoticed by many Lebanese. In fact, Lebanese from across the country's sectarian spectrum, with the exception of the Armenian community and some Christians, appreciated Turkish support and began viewing Ankara's rapprochement with Beirut more warmly than ever before.[13]

According to the Turkish Ministry of Foreign Affairs, Turkey "has always attached importance to the stability, security and prosperity of Lebanon." This Turkish view was amplified by Foreign Minister Davutoglu during his visit to Lebanon in 2009. Interestingly enough, Davutoglu's visit was made within the context of not only his Strategic Depth doctrine of "peaceful neighborhood" policy but also of reviving historic ties with Lebanon in general, and cultural identity ties with the country's Turkmen communities.

Addressing the Turkish parliament before his visit to Lebanon in the aftermath of the parliament's decision to extend the mission of Turkish troops in UNIFIL, Davutoglu said that "preserving peace in Lebanon is one of Turkey's responsibilities as part of our country's historical obligations." In reference to the parliament's decision to extend the mission of Turkish troops as part of UNIFIL, he said that the decision "should not be seen as having a solely military value but should be considered as a reflection of Turkey's stance in the region." He underscored that "relations between Turkey and Lebanon can be seen as an outset of Turkey's foreign policy for the Middle East."[14]

Davutoglu was received with open arms during his visit to Lebanon on July 30 and 31. He met with most political leaders, including the president and representatives of most political parties. He emphasized Lebanon's key role for regional stability and his eagerness to contribute to the stalled efforts to form a coalition government. He also visited the Turkish contingent serving as part of UNIFIL. Significantly, Davutoglu was able to conduct talks with the two opposing camps dominating Lebanon's politics, the pro-Western March 14 camp led by then prime minister designate Saad Hariri and the pro-Syrian, pro-Iranian "Resistance" camp led by Hezbollah.

DISCOVERING LEBANON'S TURKISH COMMUNITIES AND APPLICATION OF SOFT POWER

Clearly, Davutoglu's original foreign policy approach also relied on establishing and deepening a vast network of personal and formal contacts across the political spectrum. More specifically, it reflected an approach meant to develop strong relationships based as much on common "cultural identity" as on ideological affinity and strategic considerations.[15] In this respect, Davutoglu visited Ottoman landmarks and local Turkish-speaking communities whose presence in Lebanon was barely known to Ankara. Ankara discovered these communities by happenstance. A private in the army from the village of Qawashra in the northern region of Akkar was heard speaking Turkish by his commander, who took him to the Turkish Embassy in 1989. The private, Halit Esad, introduced himself to Ambassador Ibrahim Dicleli as a Turkmen from Qawashra. This piqued the interest of the ambassador, who invited the elders and prominent figures of Qawashra to the embassy. In turn, the ambassador visited Qawashra, whose residents welcomed him as a prodigal son. Soon Ambassador Dicleli established a personal and institutional relationship with the villagers of Qawashra, who introduced him to the other Turkmen communities in Tripoli, Akkar, and Ba'albeck.[16] But it was not until the AKP assumed power that Ankara began systematically supporting and cultivating a strong relationship with the Turkish communities of Lebanon. Initially, this relationship was confined to the Turkish Embassy and the Turkish contingent in the UNIFIL. Thereafter, the relationship steadily deepened as Turkey began to improve the living standards of the Turkmens, to strengthen their bonds with Turkey, and to underscore their cultural identity as a matter of pride and heritage.[17]

Significantly, during his trip to Lebanon, Davutoglu visited the Turkish communities in Akkar region, who cheerfully welcomed him, chanting "Long Live Turkey." In his speech to the Qawashra community, Davutoglu declared: "You are the bridge of friendship between Lebanon and Turkey. We will always stand by you as we also do for our Palestinian brothers in Gaza. When you are in peace and prosperity, we are also at peace. Your problem is our problem."[18]

Davutoglu promised the Turkmen in Akkar that Turkey will continue aiding the Turkish communities in Lebanon. He visited a centuries-old Mevlevi lodge then being restored at Ankara's expense, attended a performance by whirling dervishes, and cut the red ribbon for the opening ceremony of a Turkish-built hospital with a capacity to serve as many as 20,000 patients annually.[19] In the same year, the Turkish Red Crescent constructed a prefabricated high school building in Akkar. No doubt, Davutoglu's visit to Lebanon was a turning point in Lebanon-Turkish relations, reflecting the commitment of Turkey to buttress its presence in Lebanon as an aspect of its regional policy. Yet the major turning point in those relations took place when former prime minister and president Erdogan visited the villages of Qawashra and Aydamun in the Akkar region in November 2010. The crowd welcoming Erdogan constituted then the largest demonstration in the history of Lebanon.

In his speech, Erdogan addressed the Turkmen: "My Turkmen brothers living in this region provide a friendship bridge for us and Lebanon. I believe that my Turkmen brothers will continue supporting the peace in Lebanon."[20] During his visit, a public ceremony was held for a school built in Aydamun by the Turkish Cooperation and Coordination Agency (**TIKA**).[21] Moreover, Erdogan, welcomed by a large crowd, cut the ceremonial ribbon for the opening of the Turkish hospital in Sidon, which the government of Turkey had pledged to build following the 2006 summer conflagration between Hezbollah and Israel.[22]

Certainly, Erdogan's visit cemented Ankara's approach toward and deep interest in Lebanon and in its Turkish communities. Correspondingly, Ankara's humanitarian, logistical, cultural, and educational aid systematically increased to Lebanon's Turkish communities.[23] Significantly, Beirut Yunus Emre Turkish Culture Center was opened in 2013 and TIKA Lebanon Coordination Office opened its doors in 2014. These two organizations, in coordination with the Turkish Embassy in Beirut, worked to improve the living standards of the Turkish communities and protect their cultural identity. Complementing their work, the Presidency for Turks Abroad and Related Communities, an agency of the prime minister's office, offered scholarships to Lebanese students and helped establish and/or organize civil society organizations, all for the benefit of bettering Lebanon-Turkey relations and deepening the Turkish communities' bond with Turkey, save enhancing Turkish culture and language.[24] In the words of a former Lebanese ambassador to Turkey, "Lebanese who have studied in Turkey have become Turkey's shield and economic, cultural and political bridge to Lebanon." For example, Khaled Omar Tadmori, who received Turkish scholarships to study in Turkey has led a campaign funded mainly by Turkey to restore and reconstruct Mamluk and Ottoman landmarks. In 2004, he was elected member of the Tripoli City Council, Municipality of Tripoli. He has been a member and representative of the Turkish Foundation for the Protection and Promotion of the Environmental and Cultural Heritage (CEKUL). His restoration of Ottoman landmarks, coupled with his urban planning in Tripoli, has earned him the respect and gratitude of many in Tripoli and northern Lebanon, and by extension, much gratitude to Turkey and its leadership.[25]

Moreover, Turkey has offered Turkish citizenship to ethnic Turkmen and Turks. Notably, following the explosion of Beirut's port (see chapter 9), President Erdogan instructed his foreign ministry and the Turkish Embassy in Lebanon to grant Turkish citizenship to any ethnic Turkmen or Turk who expresses a desire to become Turkish.[26] Reinforcing its soft power on the official level, Turkey signed several agreements with Lebanon, most important of which were creating a free trade zone between the two countries, waiving customs duties, and waiving entry visas to both nationals visiting each other's country.[27]

Chapter 9

Arab Uprisings and Regional Geopolitics

SYRIA'S CIVIL WAR, ISLAMISM, AND TURKEY

No doubt, Turkey's relationship with Lebanon improved dramatically following the Syrian withdrawal from Lebanon in 2005. Many Lebanese considered Turkey's role in Lebanon as cross-sectarian, fulfilled in the interest of Lebanon as a nation and a state. Notwithstanding abundant Turkish support to the Sunni community, especially the Turkish communities in Lebanon, Turkish participation in UNIFIL and increased humanitarian aid to Lebanon fostered a sociopolitical environment in which Turkish influence deepened. However, the outbreak of the Syrian civil war transformed the dynamics of the Lebanon-Turkey relationship.

After thirty years of Syrian occupation of Lebanon, Lebanese have mixed feelings about Syria. Strong anti-Syrian feelings have permeated the social landscape across communal lines. More specifically, Islamists and Salafists strongly opposed the Syrian regime that suppressed them and crushed their presence in northern Lebanon. Nevertheless, pro-Syrian feelings have been cultivated by Hezbollah as a means to support the rejectionist axis against Israel, comprising Tehran, Damascus, and Hezbollah. Significantly, many Lebanese had not associated their hostility toward the Syrian regime with their feelings toward Syrians. A history of Lebanese-Syrian interpersonal relations, intermarriages, and trade, save an endemic feeling of stoic resignation about Middle East politics, had tempered, on the personal level, the repercussions of the Syrian regime's policies and actions in Lebanon. This is the sociopolitical background in Lebanon against which the Syrian crisis erupted in Syria in 2011.

As the war continued unabated, the Syrian crisis has posed a multifaceted threat, considered existential by some, to Lebanon as a state and a nation. The massive influx of Syrian and Palestinian refugees from Syria and the polarization of Lebanon's major political camps have affected not only the demography but also the geographical and public space in confessional Lebanon. In principle, Lebanon pursued a policy of "disassociation" regarding the Syrian crisis; nevertheless, this policy, in practice, had been all but turning a blind eye to Lebanon's two major antagonistic political camps supporting either the Syrian regime or the Syrian opposition. Backed by Saudi Arabia, the pro-Western March 14 forces, led by Hariri's Future Movement, vocally supported the Syrian opposition and provided a tacit political and security cover for anti-Syrian groups, especially the Islamists and Salafists. Northern Lebanon, especially Tripoli and Akkar, emerged as a hub for anti-Syrian activities. Armed groups (and weapons) flowed into Syria, spearheaded by Salafi-jihadis. Makeshift hospitals and security zones were established to accommodate the Syrian opposition.[1]

On the other hand, backed by Iran, the pro-Syrian camp of March 8, led by Hezbollah, supported the Syrian regime. Initially, Hezbollah had vocally and logistically supported the regime. Before long, however, Hezbollah publicly and emphatically asserted its military involvement in Syria as a means to protect Lebanon from the Salafi-jihadis and to support the Syrian regime as an integral part of the "Resistance" and the anti-Israel rejectionist axis. Hezbollah Secretary General Hassan Nasrallah declared in May 2013 that Hezbollah "will not allow the Syrian regime to be defeated" and underscored that "Syria is the back of the Resistance [i.e., Hezbollah's Islamist resistance] and its support, and the Resistance cannot stand idly by."[2]

Hezbollah's military support of the Syrian regime poisoned the overall Turkish relationship with the Shi'a community and its backers in the state. Turkish leaders, in the same fashion as Lebanon's Islamists and Salafists, demonized Hezbollah as the party of Satan. In the same month Nasrallah affirmed his party's military involvement in the Syrian civil war, Turkish deputy prime minister Bekir Bozdag declared that Hezbollah, or "Party of God" in Arabic, should change its name to "Party of Satan," blaming the Islamist organization for killing thousands of civilians in Syria.[3] Meanwhile, Turkey, through its embassy in Beirut, TIKA, and the Turkish Red Crescent, assisted Syrian refugees in Lebanon, focusing on the Syrian Turkmen refugees who escaped to northern Lebanon. Whereas TIKA and the Turkish Red Crescent delivered humanitarian aid to refugees, the embassy, in concert with these organizations, supported and cooperated with Islamic aid organizations, mostly associated with the Islamist Jama'a Islamiyah (Islamic Association), to help refugees in Tripoli and Akkar.[4]

Founded in the 1950s, the Jama'a Islamiyah, the Muslim Brotherhood branch in Lebanon, has established an impressive social infrastructure to help the disadvantaged and deprived within the Sunni community. Nevertheless, this has not translated into representative political power. The traditional Sunni leadership, led by Hariri's Future Movement until the withdrawal of Saad Hariri from politics in 2022, represented Sunni political power in the state.[5] Following the withdrawal of Syria from Lebanon, the Jama'a courted the AKP party as a sister Islamist party and supported Turkish policy in Lebanon. Reportedly, members of the Jama'a were among the crowds that welcomed Davutoglu and Erdogan to Lebanon. In fact, by 2010, the Jama'a considered forging a strong relationship with Turkey a strategic objective. In its pivotal *Political Vision of the al-Jama'a al-Islamiyah in Lebanon* in 2010, the Islamist party stressed the importance of the Turkish role in the region:

> We see that our long term goal is to reach a real unity that will restore to the *Ummah* [Muslim community] its significance among the nations. . . . Therefore, we should read very carefully the regional transformations, in particular the entrance of Turkey, government and people, as an essential power to the region, profiting from various regional and international factors. It is expected that this Turkish role will have a strong influence on the region in the near future.[6]

Significantly, the Turkish support of the Islamist opposition parties in Syria and later its direct involvement in the Syrian civil war helped strengthen the Jama'a-AKP relationship as both shared ideological, social, and political goals and concerns. The Jama'a soon emerged as a strong defender of Turkish policy and legacy in Lebanon. This was reflected during the Armenian centenary commemoration of the 1915 genocide. As Armenians began to organize events marking the centenary anniversary of the genocide in April 2015, the Jama'a organized a three-day campaign defending Turkey against what the Islamist party considered the false claims of genocide by Armenians. Thousands crowded the streets in Tripoli waving Turkish flags. Lebanese parliamentarian Khaled al-Daher warned Armenians against "offending Turkey" and emphasized he would not tolerate what he described as "lies," "delusions," or "historical hatred" against Turkey. He described Turkey as a country of freedoms and justice and declared: "We salute the man behind Turkey's renaissance: [President] Recep Tayyip Erdogan."[7] This was a surprising—to some shocking—reality dawning on Lebanon's society as few Lebanese had been aware of deepening Turkish influence among Sunnis.

Paralleling Turkey's thriving relationship with al-Jama'a, Ankara mobilized the pro-Turkish civil society organizations by providing more humanitarian aid and enhancing the promotion of Turkish language, culture, and cultural identity among Sunnis. Significantly, Ankara began forging a strong relationship with Salafists (ultra-orthodox Muslims) in general and ***haraki*** (activist) Salafists in particular. Salafists, broadly speaking, hark back to the pristine purity of Islam as reflected in the application of the Prophetic model by emulating the companions of the Prophet and their followers. This bolsters their claim to the return to the authentic beliefs and practices of the first generations of Muslims (Righteous Salaf) as a paradigm to the *Ummah*. This entailed determining the methodology (*manhaj*) of **Salafism**, or the way by which **Salafists** can implement their beliefs and call to Islam (*da'wa*), which inadvertently raised questions about engaging politics. Consequently, three schools of thought—quietest, activist, and Salafi-jihadi—were identified with Salafism, which reflected their responses to and positions toward politics and political authority. Quietest Salafists are apolitical and favor creating a "Salaf" society through indoctrination and education. Activist (haraki) Salafists assert their claim to politics on account of what they consider the miserable failure of the politics of Muslim rulers, especially in the Saudi Kingdom. Salafi-jihadis believe that change could only come through jihad and that quietests and activists are wasting their time. As such, Salafi-jihadi organizations, such as the Islamic State (ISIS) and al-Qaeda, enforce their vision of Islam in belief and manifest action, and they endorse waging jihad against what they believe idolatrous regimes that do not govern according to God's rules.[8]

As Russian military involvement in Syria helped to turn the tide of the war in favor of the Syrian regime, activist Salafists, who publicly supported the rebellion, had grown disillusioned with Arab Gulf leadership and policies in Syria. Moreover, active Salafists had also become disheartened with Saudi Arabia and to less extent the United Arab Emirates for their slow but steady retreat from Lebanon. Saudi Arabia had supported the Future Movement as a bulwark against Hezbollah's growing power in Lebanon. However, their financial help and political support of Lebanon steadily dwindled as Hezbollah, and by extension its patron Iran, came to control the state. In response, in February 2016, the kingdom suspended a $3 billion aid package promised to the Lebanese Army to buy French weapons. Commenting on Mecca's suspension of the aid, Riad Kahwaji, CEO of the Institute for Gulf and Near East Military Analysis, a Dubai-based think tank, said, "This shows that there is a consideration from the kingdom that the Lebanese government has very little control over the country's affairs with Hezbollah and Iran having the majority control over affairs in Lebanon."[9] No less significant, Saudi-forced detention of Lebanese prime minister Hariri in November 2017 dampened the Lebanon Sunni-Saudi relationship.[10]

Nevertheless, notwithstanding the Saudi retreat from Lebanon and the fact that Saudi Arabia does not support the Muslim Brotherhood and activist

Salafists, the kingdom has continued to support the quietest Salafi network in Lebanon through the Ministry of Religious Endowments and private institutions. Similarly, two main networks have become associated with the quietest and haraki (activist) Salafist schools of thought. Significantly, the quietest-oriented Kuwaiti *Jam'iyat Ihya' al-Turath al-Islami* (The Society for the Revival of Islamic Heritage), along with wealthy Gulf individuals, namely from Saudi Arabia and Kuwait, has supported the network of quietest Salafists, and the activist-oriented Qatari Sheikh Eid Charity Organization, along with wealthy Gulf individuals, has supported the network of haraki Salafists.[11] The Saudi retreat and Qatar's support of active Salafists availed an opportunity for Turkey not only to fill the void left by the kingdom but also to partner with Qatar to promote its policy in Lebanon. Similarly, as argued by some astute observers, Turkish support of Islamists and Iran's attempts at sidelining the PLO in the Palestinian refugee camps have enhanced the power of HAMAS at the expense of the PLO's leadership there, thereby extending Turkish influence to the camps.[12]

Conversely, disillusioned with Saudi and Hariri leaderships, active Salafists, Islamists, and not an insignificant number of quietest Salafists have looked up to both Erdogan as the champion of Muslim causes and Turkey as the most potent force in the Arab world and the Middle East. Meanwhile, the failed coup d'état against Erdogan in July 2016, which was publicly condemned by large pro-Erdogan demonstrations organized by al-Jama'a and active Salafists, encouraged the Turkish government not only to deepen its relationship with both Islamists and Salafists but also to help bring about their unity and channel their efforts through an encompassing authoritative religious organization. At the same time, Qatar, which has been the main benefactor of the active Salafist network and active Salafist sheikhs, spearheaded by Sheikh Salem al-Rafi'i, has readily cooperated with Turkey to realign the Islamist and Salafist forces.[13] The Association of Muslim Scholars, a large group of Sunni clerics, emerged as the AKP's de facto religio-social outlet that supported and advocated Islamist causes and concerns.[14]

The Association of Muslim Scholars has toed the Turkish line and/or acted as a defender of Turkey. It has supported Turkish military involvement in Syria, harshly criticized the Hezbollah-controlled government of Lebanon, and severely condemned Israel's treatment of Palestinians and Arab-Israel peace agreements. In fact, with regard to the recent United Arab Emirates–Israel and Bahrain-Israel peace agreements, the association issued a statement in which it called normalization of relations with what it called the "rapists," in reference to Israel, as high treason.[15] It has even acted in the capacity of an international organization assembling Sunni religious scholars from across the Muslim world to advocate Muslim causes. For example, in July 2020, the association sponsored an online forum in support of Jerusalem and al-Aqsa mosque, presenting twenty-eight religious scholars from across the Muslim world. The main speakers included the head of religious affairs in Turkey, Ali Arbash, and the leader of Palestinian HAMAS, Ismael Haniyah.[16] It also applauded Erdogan's decision in July 2020 to convert the former Orthodox Christian cathedral, Hagia Sophia, into a mosque. Islamists have long called for the conversion.[17]

Significantly, as pro-Hezbollah and pro-Armenian criticism of Turkey amplified, the association defended Turkish and Ottoman policies by issuing a warning stating:

> We remind those . . . [who] revealed themselves and showed their hatred of the Ottoman Caliphate and the overall Muslim Turkish people, along committing a series of insolent acts against our symbols and sacrosanct things: This is a threat to national coexistence and societal security . . . We affirm that disparaging the Ottoman caliphate is a rebuffed assault on our *Ummah*, religion, religious symbols and glorious history.[18]

POST–OCTOBER 17 REBELLION

Reeling from an acute economic slowdown, high unemployment, and endemic corruption among the political class, Lebanese from across sectarian backgrounds took to the streets on October 17, 2019, calling for the replacement of the whole political leadership. At a time when Lebanon had been mired in economic and political crises, Turkish influence appeared to grow further within the Sunni community. Pro-Hezbollah Lebanese politicians and media outlets accused Turkish officials of making secret payments to Sunni leaders in northern Lebanon, encouraging anti-government protests, and enhancing their intelligence presence in northern Lebanon, all in the benefit of Ankara gaining support along sectarian lines. In an interview on the Lebanese Broadcasting Corporation (LBC) television station on July 27, 2020, the leader of Lebanon's Free Patriotic Movement (FPM) and former foreign minister Gebran Bassil accused Brigadier General Karam Murad of facilitating the creation of Turkish cells in Lebanon. Shortly after the interview, Bassil tweeted that "the relationship with Turkey is relevant to us but there are a political, economic and security expansion of Turkey. I warn the security chiefs who know about and facilitate it."[19]

Bassil's accusation came in the wake of Interior Minister Mohammed Fahmi's claim that funds from Turkey had been smuggled to Lebanon to fuel violent street movements.[20] Meanwhile, a report in the pro-Hezbollah outlet *al-Akhbar* underscored that Turkey has undertaken various efforts to reinforce its influence within the Sunni community, especially in northern

Lebanon, and to confront Saudi sway in the country. It also added that Turkish efforts are employed in a similar fashion as those of the Muslim Brotherhood to bolster public support, in reference to the brotherhood's use of a social infrastructure to help Sunnis.[21]

The campaign highlighting the growing and threatening Turkish role in northern Lebanon gained momentum following an article published by a pro-Saudi outlet (https://www.asasmedia.com) affiliated with former interior minister Nouhad al-Mashnouq. The article accused Turkey of planning to occupy Tripoli and listed the names of "conspirators" and organizations supported and funded by Ankara. The article underscored three statements casting a net of danger over Tripoli and its residents: the first statement issued by Interior Minister Fahmi in which he accused Turkey of fomenting instability in Tripoli; the second statement issued by a leader of the Free Syrian Army, General Mustapha al-Sheikh, in which he warned of security movements in Tripoli and northern Lebanon to be carried out by groups supported by Turkey in coordination with a Tripolitan politician; and the final statement issued by a "political reference" with a long history of political activism in which he emphasized that Turkey's Erdogan can occupy Tripoli in one minute because he has, through his propaganda and political performance, occupied the hearts and minds of Tripolitans.[22]

The article also underscored that, according to a security survey report, the map of Turkish activism in Lebanon, which aims at controlling the "file of northern Lebanon," rests on a three-pronged approach. The first involves the direct contact of former minister and retired general Ashraf Rifi, the Association of Islamic Charitable Projects (**al-Ahbash**), and the forums of Nabil al-Halabi with Turkish intelligence. The second involves the cooperation between the AKP and the Islamic Association. And the last involves the Turkish Embassy in Lebanon that oversees the support of civil organizations, the coordination with the Secretary General of the Future Current Baha' Hariri, and the collaboration with the municipality of Tripoli.[23]

Retired general Khalil Helou, who served in Tripoli and fought Salafi-jihadis in northern Lebanon, rejected all allegations and accusations brought about by pro-Hezbollah or pro-Saudi parties against Turkey. He admitted that "Turkey has indeed extended its influence to Tripoli, Akkar and northern Lebanon employing soft power. But all these allegations and accusations that Turkey is fomenting violence, arming groups, or creating a network of cells are baseless."[24]

Turkey denied and condemned all these claims. Turkish Foreign Ministry spokesman Hami Aksoy called the claims "malicious statements" and added they were "deprived of comprehension" and impossible to take seriously.[25]

It's debatable whether Turkey had supported anti-government protests or had fomented violence in Tripoli; however, it's hardly possible to deny growing Turkish influence in Lebanon in general and within the Sunni community in particular. In fact, Lebanon's communal dynamics have more or less shifted in favor of Turkey. Until recently Lebanese communities stood in solidarity with the Armenians during genocide commemorations. Armenians today are shocked to see counterdemonstrations, even in Beirut, and public justification of the genocide by Sunni activists and leading Lebanese Turkmen.[26] Thousands of Turkish flags flutter in major Sunni neighborhoods each time Turkey is criticized. Evidently, Turkey has grassroots support within the Sunni community, which has paid little attention to Armenian grievances. No less significant, many Lebanese, regardless of sect or political bias, have become spellbound by Turkish soap operas and news outlets. The deluge of Turkish soap operas into Lebanese homes have made Turkish social norms, ethos, and fashion trends widely popular, replacing the social traction of Egypt's once paradigmatic cinema and television entertainment culture.[27] Moreover, Turkey has become a favorable destination to many Lebanese visitors since the two countries lifted visa requirements for travel in 2010.

Pointedly, Turkey has gained the gratitude of many Lebanese. Turkish officials swiftly sent messages of sympathy to the Lebanese people and extended their helping hand to the country following the massive nuclear-like explosion at the port of Beirut on August 4, 2020. The Turkish government immediately mobilized both state-run aid organizations and charity foundations, including TIKA, AFAD, Turkish health ministry, and the Turkish Red Crescent to send medical and humanitarian aid and a team of twenty physicians; to deliver 400 tons of wheat; and plan the construction of field hospitals.[28] Before long, in a show of support and solidarity with the Lebanese, top Turkish officials, including Vice President Fuat Oktay and Foreign Minister Mevlut Cavusoglu, visited Lebanon on August 8. They toured the demolished port and nearby areas and met with President Michel Aoun, Prime Minister Hassan Diab, and other officials. They reiterated their full support of Lebanon in this time of crisis and offered to help rebuild Beirut port and demolished buildings, as well as provide as much humanitarian and health aid as possible. They also offered to use the Turkish port of Mersin to receive products that could be later sent to Lebanon in smaller ships. No less significant, the Turkish delegation met Sunni religious leaders, whereupon Foreign Minister Cavusoglu offered citizenship to Lebanese of Turkish origin.[29]

Commenting on Turkish relief efforts, Nazim Mavis, head of the Turkish-Lebanese Interparliamentary Friendship Group, said that "relief efforts have started a process which will further strengthen relations between Lebanon and Turkey." Emphasizing Turkey's unique ties with Lebanon, he said that "we've never been imperialists. We've never been in Lebanon to exploit it. We lived together as brothers for 400 years." And he added: "Lebanon's integrity is important for Turkey. For us, Lebanon is a whole with its Christians, Muslims, Assyrians and Armenians. Turkey is ready to do whatever it can to protect this integrity."[30]

On closer examination, however, it becomes clear that Turkey has not leveraged its soft power and assistance for Lebanon into a political attempt to resolve Lebanon's economic and political crises. This became apparent when French president Emmanuel Macron visited Beirut immediately after the blast. Besieged by angry and grief-stricken Lebanese who had lost their loved ones and/or their properties in the blast, President Macron promised support for the reconstruction of the city and called upon Lebanese politicians to adopt a "new political deal" to resolve the politico-economic crises spiraling the country into an abject failed state. Significantly, he accused regional countries of seeking to promote their interests in Lebanon at the expense of the country. He said that "If France doesn't play its role, Iranians, Turks and Saudis will interfere with Lebanese domestic affairs, whose economic and geopolitical interests are likely to be to the detriment of the Lebanese."[31] President Macron, as promised, returned to Lebanon in early September to seek a political solution. He presented the country's political establishment with a carrot or stick offer: "implement reforms, and vital international aid will flow plentifully, but continue on the same path, and the doors to assistance will slam shut—and the country's ossified political leadership may be directly targeted with sanctions." Coinciding with the centenarian anniversary of France's founding of Greater Lebanon, he emphasized: "I did not come today to give a warning, but I returned to help Lebanon and accompany it to its future."[32]

Turkish officials were swift in responding to President Macron's purported reason to visit Beirut and his statements. Turkish vice president Oktay retorted that "it is actually France that interferes with Lebanese domestic politics. . . . We shouldn't take Macron too seriously. He is like a spoiled child in the region." Accusing France of basing its foreign policy in colonialism and underscoring Turkey's humanitarian aid on altruistic grounds, Vice President Oktay underlined that "the main difference between the two countries is colonialism."[33]

Be that as it may, this French-Turkish exchange, juxtaposed against Turkey's policy in Lebanon, over a country both had played a historical part in shaping, revealed both the limits of Turkey's political reach with the country's political establishment and its thus far arm's-length approach to Lebanon's Byzantine politics. Turkey, unlike France, has neither offered a plan for helping Lebanon out of its crisis nor a structural reform package to help fix the political system.

It's noteworthy that at the height of the tense Hezbollah-Turkey relations over Syria's civil war, Ankara had consistently pursued a measured approach toward Hezbollah. In August 2012, the Shi'ite al-Meqdad clan kidnapped twenty members of the Free Syrian Army (FSA) and a Turkish national from Beirut in retaliation to both the detention of eleven Shi'a pilgrims in May in Aleppo and the subsequent arrest by the FSA of Hassan Salim al-Meqdad in Damascus for allegedly belonging to Hezbollah. Al-Meqdad's clan issued a statement blaming Qatar, Saudi Arabia, and Turkey, especially the latter in view of its close relationship with the Syrian opposition. Reportedly, another Turkish national was abducted by one of the families of the detained pilgrims. Notwithstanding the war of words and threats between al-Meqdad and the FSA, and the certainty that Hezbollah was behind the kidnappings, Ankara did not undertake any escalatory measure. Ankara opted to deal with the Lebanese government, especially with intelligence chiefs, some of whom were close to Hezbollah. As it turned out, the Turkish nationals were released even before the pilgrims and Hassan al-Meqdad were released.[34]

Similarly, in August 2013, two Turkish nationals, a pilot and copilot, were kidnapped by gunmen in the southern suburbs of Beirut, an area controlled by Hezbollah, on their way to their hotel from Beirut's International Airport. The Turkish nationals were taken hostages because the Lebanese Shi'a pilgrims detained in Aleppo had not been released. In much the same vein as the previous episode, Ankara chose to handle the situation quietly and to communicate with Lebanese intelligence chiefs. General Abbas Ibrahim, the director of Lebanon's military intelligence, who is close to Hezbollah, led the talks with Turkish security chiefs, who had contacts with the rebels holding the Lebanese pilgrims. In October, both the Turkish nationals and Lebanese pilgrims were released. The Lebanese pilgrims were taken to Turkey before coming home, and the Turkish nationals were flown on a private jet to Turkey.[35]

This measured Turkish approach toward Hezbollah has remained thus far consistent. So despite the vitriolic rhetoric and mutual hostility, neither Turkey nor Hezbollah has taken escalatory steps vis-à-vis each other that could lead to either direct warfare in Syria or to a proxy one in Lebanon. This can be partly explained in relation to the complex Iran-Turkey relationship and the fact that Hezbollah has acted as an Iranian proxy. The two countries, despite their historic rivalry and/or enmity in the Middle East and their current adversarial roles in Syria, have managed to cooperate on a range of shared regional concerns. Both are parties to the Astana peace process for Syria.[36] Iran has supported the Turkish-backed Libyan Government of National Accord, Turkey has criticized US sanctions against Iran, and both had been critical of the recent Arab peace agreements with Israel, the Abraham Accords.

At the heart of this Iran-Turkish cooperation, notwithstanding the complex relationship between the two major Sunni and Shi'a powers in the Middle East, has been shared domestic and regional concerns that virtually turned the two foes into practical friends. The Arab rebellions, which began in Tunisia at the end of 2010, spilled over into Syria in March 2011. The rebellion in

Syria spelled the possible collapse of the Asad regime and disintegration of Syria, the emergence of powerful radical elements as represented by Salafi-jihadis, and the secession of the Kurds from Syria and/or the creation of an independent or autonomous Kurdish region along the Turkish border. On the one hand, Iran and Turkey (and Russia) worried about their long-standing vulnerability to secessionist and radical movements. On the other, they worried about US foreign policy in the Middle East in general and in Syria in particular. Whereas Turkey has been concerned about American support of the Syrian Kurds, who Ankara considers as affiliates to the PKK, Iran has been concerned about American (and Israeli) plans to undercut and contain Tehran's regional role, especially in Syria. All of this coincided with the Trump administration (2017–2021) unilaterally withdrawing from the Iran nuclear agreement (2018), snapping back sanctions on Iran, imposing more sanctions on Russia, and leading an international effort to compel states, including allies, to abide by the American sanction regime against Iran. Both Ankara and Tehran believed then that the American goal was regime change in Iran. No less significant, the Turkish government blamed the United States for not only abandoning Ankara during a botched 2016 coup d'état, but also for being indirectly involved in the coup. Russia and Iran, unlike the United States, immediately expressed their support for Erdogan's government.[37]

Parallel to Turkish policy toward Iran and Hezbollah, Ankara has pursued more or less a similar measured policy toward Saudi Arabia and its proxies in Lebanon. Although the Saudi-Turkey relationship, unlike the Iran-Turkey relationship, has not been marred by historic enmity, the two countries have had a fluctuating relationship alternating between antagonism and friendliness. Historically, Turkey denounced the Hashemite-led Arab revolt against the Ottoman Empire during WWI. However, Turkish leader Kamal Atatürk, founder of modern Turkey, pursued cordial relations with the newly founded Kingdom of Saudi Arabia in 1932. Broadly speaking, both countries found themselves in the same political aisle until 2003. They shared their opposition to the Soviet Union during the Cold War, supported Iraq against Iran in the Iran-Iraq war, supported the United States against Iraq in the first Gulf War (1990–1991), and both opposed the US invasion of Iraq in 2003.

The inability of the United States to build a new regional order following its occupation of Iraq put Saudi Arabia and Turkey on a path of rivalry and in opposite camps. This became pronounced during the spring of Arab revolutions. Whereas Turkey supported the Islamists who perceived Ankara as the paradigm of democracy coexisting with Islamism, Saudi Arabia frowned upon the Islamists as the bellwether of disruptive regional change. The Egyptian army's forced removal of the first democratically elected president of Egypt and Muslim Brotherhood leader Mohammad Morsi in 2013 heightened Saudi-Turkish tension, which spilled over into Syria and Qatar.

True, both Ankara and Riyadh supported the Syrian opposition against the Asad regime; nevertheless, they were at odds in supporting different and in most cases rival camps. Broadly speaking, whereas Turkey supported the Free Syrian Army (FSA) and Islamists, Saudi Arabia supported Islamists and hardline Salafi-jihadis. More specifically, Ankara took a dim view of Riyadh supporting some Salafi-jihadi movements who on dogmatic grounds either opposed what they considered Turkey's self-centered involvement in Syria or resisted being part of Turkish-led efforts to unify the opposition under Turkish leadership. However, the emergence of the Islamic State (ISIS), Russian active military involvement in support of the Asad regime, Washington's pressure on Riyadh (and other Gulf capitals) to stop funding Salafi-jihadi movements, and the elimination of pro-Saudi Salafi-jihadi leader Zahran Alloush led the kingdom to gradually reduce its involvement in Syria.[38] Consequently, Saudi-Turkish tension decreased in Syria, while at the same time Turkey reinforced its military position in northern Syria. But tension between the two flared up again regarding Qatar.

In June 2017, Saudi Arabia, the United Arab Emirates, Bahrain, and Egypt severed their diplomatic relations with and blockaded Qatar. Tension between Qatar and the aforementioned states had been rising since the eruption of the Arab revolutions. Besides frowning upon Qatar's independent foreign policy as inimical to the Gulf Cooperation Council, Saudi Arabia and the UAE had been incensed by Qatar's support of the Muslim Brotherhood, especially during the Arab rebellions.[39] In response, Turkey immediately came to the rescue of Qatar, sending food shipments and thousands of troops to defend Doha should hostilities erupt. Approximately 5,000 Turkish troops were stationed in a Turkish military base, which was completed by 2019 and named after the famous Muslim Commander Khalid bin Walid, upon whom Prophet Muhammad conferred the title "Unsheathed Sword of Islam."

Saudi authorities perceived Turkish military presence in Qatar as part of Ankara's expansionist policy and a threat to the security of the Arab Gulf countries. Saudi Crown Prince Muhammad Bin Salman referred to Turkey as part of a "triangle of evil" alongside Iran and the Muslim Brotherhood.[40] The prince's comments lumping Iran and Turkey together clearly reflected the heated rhetorical battle among Saudi Arabia, Iran, and Turkey consequent upon the three major Middle Eastern countries jockeying for regional power and predominance. Before long, Saudi-Turkish relations further deteriorated when Saudi journalist Jamal Kashoggi was murdered in the Saudi Arabian Consulate in Istanbul and Turkish authorities blamed Crown Prince bin Salman.

Nevertheless, during all the ups and downs in the Iran-Turkey and Saudi-Turkey relationships (and France-Turkey relationship), Turkey kept to its pattern of not upping the ante against Iran or Saudi Arabia in Lebanon. The vying for regional predominance among Turkey, Iran, and Saudi Arabia has extended to Lebanon but remained within limits thanks to Ankara's policy in Lebanon. Ankara has consistently pursued its diplomacy in Lebanon based on its soft power approach and desistance from arming or funding a political pro-Turkish party to do Ankara's political bidding in the same way Iran has supported Hezbollah or Saudi Arabia has supported the Future Movement.[41] Moreover, Turkey, as already mentioned, has neither adopted any economic or political initiative to help address the politico-economic crises afflicting Lebanon nor has taken a position regarding the October 17 Revolution and its various rebel factions.

Clearly, Turkey, as demonstrated, has favored supporting the Sunni community in general and the Turkish communities in particular. But it has chosen to ground its relationship with Lebanon in supporting grassroots and civil movements and organizations (including Islamists), promoting Turkish culture and national identity, offering scholarships, enhancing free trade and tourism, providing humanitarian aid, funding and building vital institutions and projects, and assisting Lebanon in times of need on the popular and state levels, all more or less at a distance from Lebanon's Byzantine domestic politics and foreign meddling in the country's affairs. Moreover, Turkey has maintained its consistent approach to Lebanon with regard to the geopolitics of the eastern Mediterranean consequent to the discovery of large oil and gas reserves there.

LEBANON, TURKEY, AND THE GEOPOLITICS OF THE EASTERN MEDITERRANEAN

The discoveries of large gas reserves in the eastern Mediterranean by Israel in 2009 and 2010, Cyprus in 2011, and Egypt in 2015 have set off a multifaceted geopolitical conflict involving a number of Middle Eastern and European countries on one side and Turkey on the other. Turkey, which imports most of its energy, had become concerned no less about being excluded from the emerging huge east Mediterranean gas market than becoming the target of an alignment of states with which Ankara has geopolitical rivalry or conflicts.

The competition over hydrocarbon resources in the eastern Mediterranean ignited Turkey's maritime and geopolitical conflicts with both Greece and Cyprus. Turkey has a conflict with both Greece and Cyprus over their maritime boundaries and exclusive economic zones (EEZ), which comprise areas of the ocean, "generally extending 200 nautical miles (230 miles) beyond a nation's territorial sea, within which a coastal nation has jurisdiction over both living and nonliving resources." Turkey has claims to an EEZ in the eastern Mediterranean, part of which conflicts with Greek claims to the same areas including a sea zone next to the islands of Rhodes and Crete. Turkey, a non-signatory of the UN Convention on the Law of the Sea, has disputed Cyprus's EEZ on the grounds that no island should have a 200-nautical-mile EEZ. Turkey also asserts that the Turkish Republic of Northern Cyprus, which was created during the Turkish invasion of Cyprus in 1974 and is not recognized by the UN, has claims over parts of the EEZ claimed by the Republic of Cyprus.[42]

These conflicts grew from rising tensions over (a) Cyprus drilling for oil without, as Turkey perceived, consideration to the maritime rights of the Turkish Republic of Northern Cyprus; (b) the proposed route for the eastern Mediterranean gas pipeline project (EastMed pipeline); and (c) the creation of the Eastern Mediterranean Gas Forum. The envisioned €6.2 billion pipeline to Europe is the brainchild of Greece, Cyprus, and Israel's close coopera-tion, which excluded Turkey. In March 2019, the agreement on the proposed project was ceremoniously signed in the presence of US Secretary of State Mike Pompeo, where the parties to the agreement, leaving no room for doubt, pointed out that their cooperation intentionally excluded Turkey. Significantly, this tripartite cooperation gained an institutional form in January 2020 with the creation of the Eastern Mediterranean Gas Forum, which also included Egypt, Jordan, the Palestinian Authority, and Italy (which later withdrew).[43]

Fearing being sidelined from the emerging energy and security framework in the eastern Mediterranean, Turkey responded by sending ships, tagged by gunboats, to undertake energy exploration next to Cyprus, and signed a secu-rity and maritime border agreement with the UN-recognized Tripoli-based Government of National Accord (GNA) against the forces of General Khalifa Haftar, whose backers include the UAE, France, and Russia. Besides provid-ing sophisticated weapons to the GNA, the agreement created an EEZ cov-ering a sea area extending from Turkey's southern Mediterranean shore to Libya's northeast coast, which disrupted the plan for the proposed EastMed pipeline.[44]

No doubt, Turkey's gunboat and coercive diplomacy in the eastern Mediterranean underscored its intent to safeguard its geopolitical interests and disrupt plans meant to undermine its security. In fact, Turkey's diplo-macy may be connected to its geopolitical outlook as expressed in its Blue Homeland or "Mavi Vatan" doctrine. Though nebulous and not recognized as Turkey's official geopolitical doctrine, Blue Homeland has supporters in the Turkish bureaucracy and has recently gone mainstream. Broadly speaking, the doctrine envisions expansive maritime boundaries for Turkey in the Black Sea, the Aegean Sea, and the Mediterranean and power projection there.[45]

Conversely, Turkey's diplomacy pitted it against Greece, Cyprus, Egypt, Israel, the UAE, and France, which became a member and the strongest European supporter of the EastMed Gas forum.[46] This inflamed tension between Paris and Ankara, including over Lebanon. It was against this background that Paris and Ankara had bickered over Lebanon in the aftermath of the explosion of Beirut's port. However, and interestingly enough, Turkey's geopolitical imbroglio in the eastern Mediterranean had little to do with Lebanon. Notwithstanding Ankara's offer to rebuild the port of Beirut, Turkey, unlike France, Russia, and China, has not concluded any agreement with Lebanon to either undertake offshore oil and gas exploration or to manage Lebanon's ports. In addition, Turkey has played little, if any, role in the efforts led by the United States to demarcate Israel-Lebanon maritime and land borders.[47]

The answer to Turkey's disinclination to try to use Lebanon as a lever in its east Mediterranean diplomacy lay clearly in its consistent approach not to get involved in a regional conflict fought on Lebanese soil. This is reinforced, on the one hand, by the priority Turkey places on the geostrategic importance of countries that best serve its diplomacy and, on the other, by Lebanon's weak internal and regional position that could, under the pretext of a binding alliance, make Beirut the spark of regional confrontations.

From the vantage point of the Blue Homeland, the eastern Mediterranean straddles the Mediterranean basin, the Middle East, and the IndoPacific area. Being at the mouth of the Suez Canal, "it is a mandatory point of passage for trade routes linking Europe to the Indian Ocean and, by extension, to Southeast Asia." "It is also the main maritime interface of the near East and the Mashriq." As a result, Cyprus, not Lebanon, lies at the heart of the EEZ claimed by Turkey, thereby becoming a major strategic area. Cihat Yayci emphasizes that Cyprus is "the most important island in the Mediterranean in geopolitical and geostrategic terms." For him, Cyprus is the "veritable 'aircraft carrier,' providing easy access to Turkey, Syria, Lebanon, Israel, Jordan, Iraq and Egypt."[48]

From Lebanon's standpoint, a report published by the Lebanese National Defense, an outlet of the Lebanese Armed Forces, underscored that

> The geopolitical conflict in the region seems clear . . . and it seems more clear that the conflict for the control of energy resources and transmission lines, especially gas, is one of the main pillars of this ram . . . the fact that Lebanon does not have the ability to impose its conditions in any regional or international conflict due to its internal situation at the political and economic levels, therefore Lebanon must take advantage of the existing conflict by seizing the opportunities that arise as a result of the competition between regional and international countries. It should move away from "binding" its decisions in the field of gas to any external party so that no external party has the ability to exploit the country's domestic conditions and use internal tools to ignite a global conflict.[49]

Chapter 10

Erdogan's Principles and Praxis

ERDOGAN'S NEO-OTTOMANISM

Turkish foreign policy in the Middle East under the AKP-led governments, as expressed by neo-Ottomanism, greatly suffered by the dawning of the Arab autumn, the preferred designation of the collapse of Arab rebellions. The euphoria with which President Erdogan welcomed the rise of the Muslim Brotherhood in Egypt, Libya, and Tunisia transformed into a personal domestic apprehension and near isolation of his country in the Middle East.

Herein, it's noteworthy that Erdogan's neo-Ottomanism has partly unfolded differently from Davutoglu's neo-Ottomanism, bringing to the fore the doctrine's inherent contradictions. Central to this has been the drift from Davutoglu advocating a policy of "zero problem with neighbors" to Erdogan's employment of coercive, including military, diplomacy with nearly all of Turkey's neighbors. The rise and fall of Arab uprisings put in sharp relief Erdogan's application of neo-Ottomanism. Political expediency regarding Turkey's national security interests trumped the soft power approach inherent in neo-Ottomanism's "zero problem with neighbors." This has been reflected in how Erdogan dealt with the Kurdish, Libyan, GCC-Qatar, Cypriot, and Libyan disputes and/or conflicts. No less significant is how Erdogan promoted neo-Ottomanism. For him, as the case of the Egyptian uprising fully demonstrates, neo-Ottomanism also signified the promotion of democracy and Islamism as the twin ideological pillars of Turkey's foreign policy. In this respect, it is important to comprehend Erdogan's conceptualization of democracy and Islamism as contextualized within the framework of Turkish politics.

The democratization of Turkey under the doctrine of Kemalism entailed the secularization of modern Turkey by means of the full subjugation of Islam to the state and its eradication from the public sphere. Banning religious orders (*tarikats*) and public display of religious attire displayed the state's hostility to any religious form of expression. However, the rise of political Islam posed a threat to the state. The state perceived that active intervention and control were the best means to deflect the threat of political Islam and secure the state's secular ideals and goals. The state, in addition to continuing the ban of religious orders, established the Directorate of Religious Affairs (***Diyanet İşleri Başkanliği***), to serve as an ideological bulwark against political Islam.

However, this approach led to the transformation of Turkish political Islam. The state shut down Islamist or Islamist-leaning parties for violating the principles of laicism as laid down in the constitution.[1] It was against this background that a reformist camp in the Islamist Virtue party, which represented Turkish political Islam, undertook radical ideological transformation. Ioannis N. Grigoriadis perceptively observed that members of this camp, led by Erdogan, "attempted to break the vicious circle of state suppression by advocating a radical transformation of Islamist ideology. The establishment of an Islamic republic would no more be the ultimate aim. Allegiance to the secular principles of Western European democracy was instead adopted, and an amalgamation of Islamic values with Western political liberalism was attempted. The quest for Islamic religious freedoms was now framed in the language of political liberalism and multiculturalism."[2]

Members of this camp founded the Justice and Development party (AKP) following the closure of the Virtue party in 2001. The AKP leadership broke with its Islamist past and projected itself as a moderate conservative party loyal to secularism. In the words of Grigoriadis, "the new ideology of the party was an amalgam of conservativism, liberalism, Islamic values and rightist political ideas."[3] In other words, the AKP did not subscribe to the "Islam is the solution" ideological utopian fallacy that characterized Islamism in the Middle East. Islamism in its new formulation coexists with democracy because it is rooted in both democracy and Islamic values.

The fall of Tunisian leader Zine al-Abidine and Egyptian leader Hosni Mubarak in January and February 2011 respectively, followed by the rise of Rachid al-Channouchi, leader of the Islamist party al-Nahda, which won a plurality in the first free parliamentary elections in Tunisia's history in November 2011, and Muhammad Morsi of the Muslim Brotherhood as the first democratically elected president of Egypt in June 2012 waxed Ankara's political fortunes across the Middle East. Then– prime minister Erdogan tried to shape a new Middle Eastern order based on his neo-Ottomanism outlook whereby Islamism coexists with democracy. Ankara and Cairo had become the capitals from where Erdogan strove to export neo-Ottomanism as the aspirational model for the new regional order.

Erdogan envisioned an Ankara-Cairo strategic partnership to serve as the axis of his neo-Ottomanism vision of the new Middle East. Building his influence in Cairo and uniting Ankara, the heir seat of the Ottoman Empire that dictated Middle East politics for centuries, with Cairo, the seat that set the tone of contemporary Arab politics, underlay his strategic partnership. As part of a tour in support of the Arab uprisings to the North African countries of Libya, Tunisia, and Egypt, Erdogan landed in Cairo in September 2011 during its transitional period to democracy. He was welcomed as a hero by throngs of Egyptians and his pictures adorned the billboards and placards that spanned the Cairo airport highway. Whether in Tunisia, Libya, or Egypt, he was hailed as the "pride of the Muslim Ummah."

From the podium of Cairo University, Erdogan spoke about the importance of democracy. Significantly, in his comments to Egyptian media, Erdogan supported a secular state in Egypt, to the consternation and dismay of the Muslim Brotherhood. He emphasized that

I am a non-secular Muslim . . . but I am the prime minister of a secular state and I say, "I hope there will be a secular state in Egypt." One must not be afraid of secularism. Egypt will grow in democracy and those called upon to draw up the constitution must understand it must respect all religions, while also keep themselves equidistant from the followers of all religions so that people can live in security.[4]

ERDOGAN'S WELTANSCHAUUNG AND LEBANON

A year later, in November 2012, Erdogan made a second visit to Egypt. This time, from the same podium, he spoke about the potential of the strategic partnership between Egypt and Turkey, emphasizing that "should Egypt and Turkey unite peace and stability would prevail in the region, and should they hold together neither crying nor wailing would overwhelm the region."[5]

Significantly, Erdogan, besides congratulating the Egyptians on their free elections, spoke about the paramount role of the Islamic civilization and its values. He cited the 139th verse of the Koran, Surat Ali Imran: "So do not weaken and do not grieve, and you will be superior if you are [true] believers." He then proceeded: "In Egypt, in Turkey, in this entire geography, we need to feel this key principle every moment, carry it in our heart, in our mind and remember it each moment. . . . We, the people of this geography are believers, then we are superior. . . . We will continue on our path with full self-confidence and we will all together make history regain its course." He added that "The essence of the mentality of coexistence with diversities that constitutes the soul of democracy, again, finds its roots in our civilization."[6]

This part of Erdogan's speech is very revealing of his view of history, outlook of the future, and perception of the paramountcy of Muslim civilization. Clearly, Erdogan believed, as most Islamists, that Muslim society has lost its way and should Muslims unite as believers in the abode of Muslim civilization, where democracy finds its roots, history will go back on its right track and Muslims will thrive (as superior). But Erdogan, unlike most Islamists, does not believe that secularism negates Islamism. An Islamist, indeed, can rule a democratic, secular state because Muslim values undergird the diversity with which democracy and secularism provide the safety valve for social harmony where the democratic state respects the freedom of the individual and the secularist state respects the multiplicity of religions. No doubt, Erdogan shares with the Muslim Brotherhood Muslim values, but that does not mean he necessarily shares the Muslim Brotherhood's approach to governance. This, in Erdogan's view, forms the comprehensive picture of Muslim society as painted by the brushes of democracy and Islamism. In this respect, one could safely argue that Erdogan believed that Arab uprisings had been part of the process of Muslim history regaining its course under the guidance of Muslim unity and values. As such, Erdogan supported Egypt and cultivated a strong relationship with Morsi.

However, following large popular demonstrations against President Morsi, General Abdel Fatah el-Sisi ousted Morsi in July 2013, reportedly to save Egypt from the specter of civil war. Saudi Arabia and the UAE, both of which opposed the Muslim Brotherhood, supported el-Sisi. Erdogan's aspirations and vision for a strategic partnership with Egypt came to an abrupt end. He referred to el-Sisi as "a tyrant" and accused the interim Egyptian government of practicing "state terrorism."

Significantly, coinciding with the run-up to the Egyptian army's coup, Turkey faced a wave of demonstrations and civil unrest that began in late May 2013. Initially, the protests were to contest the urban development plan for Istanbul's Taksim Gezi Park, but they swiftly grew into major rallies challenging Erdogan's rule throughout Turkey. Erdogan's government was blindsided by the protests. Resilient and authoritative, Erdogan weathered the protests. But his fear of being ousted in the same manner as Morsi only reinforced his determination to nip in the bud any imaginary or real threat to his regime. Soner Cagaptay perceptively observed:

> Gezi Park and Morsi's ouster made Erdogan become more authoritarian in quashing any similar protests he feared could oust him in the future. Domestically, this decision increased Turkey's democratic backslide. . . . Furthermore, the failed July 15, 2016 coup against Erdogan . . . meant that Erdogan and his government were even more emboldened to clamp down on dissidents in the country. Erdogan had been a master of reading the global zeitgeist and responding to it

with a public relations executive's craftiness . . . However, after the summer of 2013 and the Gezi Park rallies, he lost this magic touch and ability to awe the international community. The image of Erdogan as an authoritarian leader belatedly started to take shape in many Western capitals and in financial circles. Investment into Turkey started to dry up, and rising anti-Erdogan sentiments in the West only fed into Erdogan's rooted resentment toward the West from his political past.[7]

Regionally, following the 2013 events, Turkey's relationships with Egypt and the Arab monarchies of the Gulf, with the exception of Qatar, deteriorated on account of Ankara's support of the Muslim Brotherhood. As mentioned (see previous chapter), Saudi Crown Prince Muhammad bin Salman described Turkey as part of a "triangle of evil" alongside Iran and the Muslim Brotherhood. Erdogan, besides welcoming Islamists to Ankara, augmented his support of the Islamists in Libya, Tunisia, and Syria. Turkey's tension with Egypt and UAE extended to the eastern Mediterranean and Libya. He also entrenched Turkey's military presence in Qatar, Iraq, and Syria, especially in the latter two countries in order to curb the power and reach of the PKK and their allies there. Turkey faced near isolation in the Arab world. Yet all parties in the Middle East, including Iran and Israel, whether grouped in blocs or axes, refrained from sparking regional wars. Theirs were either proxy confrontations fought in the weak or failed states of Syria, Yemen, and/ or Libya or attempts to settle scores mainly in Iraq. Inasmuch as these countries desired to have a say in shaping a new order in the Middle East, they were careful about preventing open and direct warfare among and between each other.

Interestingly enough, amid all this tension, proxy confrontations, and coercive geopolitical diplomacy, Turkey has not used Lebanon as a lever in its foreign policy. Turkey, unlike Saudi Arabia, Iran, Syria, and even Israel, has continued to pursue a consistent approach toward Lebanon based on soft power diplomacy on the popular, cultural, humanitarian, civil, and state levels. More specifically, Turkey has built on the popular level an unparalleled influence in Tripoli, Akkar, and northern Lebanon, focusing on the Sunni community in general and on the Turkish communities, Islamists, and the dispossessed in particular. Thanks to its efforts, Turkey has created a legion of defenders from across the sociopolitical, religious, civil, and cultural spectrum of Lebanon. Evidently, these communities, groups, and individuals have become Turkey's vessels of influence in Lebanon.

This has created some tension in intercommunal relations in Lebanon. The Maronite Church and the Armenian community's grievances with Turkey over the Great Famine and Armenian genocide during World War I have nurtured deep anti-Turkish feelings; yet they have been paling in comparison to Turkey's rising approval among Lebanese.

To be sure, some have raised the point that Turkey has failed to remove the Asad regime or act as a political patron or colonial power in Lebanon to curb the power of Hezbollah or stem the tide of Iran's expansion in the region. Some have sarcastically criticized Turkey for arming its supporters with the opium of "soap operas" in their households instead of arms. Some have disparaged Turkey for supporting Islamists and whitewashing its past in Lebanon through rewriting Ottoman history.[8] Some have decried Turkey's reluctance to offer solutions or reform plans to Lebanon's economic crises and confessional political system, respectively. Some have contended that Turkey's soft power diplomacy in Lebanon is none other than a tool of dissimulation to control northern Lebanon under certain circumstances in the near future. Yet a consensus emerges among many Lebanese that Turkey has not only helped Lebanon in its time of need and crises but has also kept Lebanon more or less out of Ankara's endeavors to vie for predominance in the Levant and the eastern Mediterranean.[9]

In turn, besides criticizing Turkey, the Hezbollah-controlled governments have been keen to curb the power of pro-Turkish, anti-Syrian regime activists. Nevertheless, Turkish influence in northern Lebanon has become so deep and popular that it has already become a barrier to Hezbollah's unreserved power. Notwithstanding the transformation of communal dynamics in Lebanon, Turkey has the power to mobilize the Sunnis in northern Lebanon against Hezbollah. However, this influence has not yet been reflected in the state's military and security apparatus.

Reflecting on the Turkish relationship with Lebanon, the prevalent view among Sunnis in northern Lebanon was asserted by a Tripolitan: "Erdogan is our 'Sword' and Turkey is the defender of our Ummah."[10] This view is not universally shared in Lebanon. But gradations of this view have been cutting across communal and bureaucratic lines in Lebanon.

Conclusion

Recent regional and global geopolitical developments have ushered in a new realignment of forces whose politico-economic impressions are not yet well defined. Yet the changes these developments have generated have already effected a qualitative turn in how the countries of the Middle East perceive their own security and how they perceive their national security vis-à-vis each other. In this respect, Turkey has reemerged at the intersection of these developments a regional and international country of note in need of redefining its political orientation to live up to its new position at home and abroad.

Since President Barack Obama's failure to enforce the "red line" that he himself had enunciated in 2012 to the effect that "if Assad used chemical weapons, it would warrant US military action," Arab rulers in the Gulf have become concerned about Washington's gradual geopolitical withdrawal from the Middle East.[1] In fact, the US reorientation toward Asia, which began under the Obama administration, has created an environment of uncertainty for the Arab Gulf countries about US foreign policy in the Middle East.[2] This became more pronounced by the way Arab rulers have come to see the unfolding of American foreign policy in Iraq, Afghanistan, Yemen, Syria, and Iran. From their standpoint, Washington's reorientation toward Asia not only signaled American withdrawal from the Middle East but also Washington's declining power.

In 2015, to the chagrin of the Arab Gulf, Washington signed the Iran nuclear agreement, formally known as the Joint Comprehensive Plan of Action (JCPOA). However, even when Washington withdrew from the JCPOA in 2018 and applied maximum pressure on Iran, Arab Gulf rulers have remained unsure whether Washington would confront Tehran for its proxy attacks on Saudi Arabia and most recently on the UAE. Washington has not only dampened its support for the Saudi-led offensive in Yemen against the Iranian-supported Houthis but also reversed former president Donald Trump's designation of the Houthis as terrorists. It's no secret that from the popular or governmental vantage point in the Middle East, Washington's withdrawal from Afghanistan and end of mission in Iraq have been the product of colossal American foreign policy failure.

Paralleling these developments, the Biden administration sanctioned the release of the US intelligence assessment that Saudi Crown Prince Mohammed bin Salman had approved the operation to kill journalist Jamal Khashoggi. This US message was explicitly perceived by bin Salman, the de facto ruler of the kingdom, as Washington's attempt to compromise his leadership and legitimate ascension to the throne. The kingdom's ministry of foreign affairs dismissed what it called the "negative, false and unacceptable assessment in the report pertaining to the kingdom's leadership."[3]

Clearly, US foreign policy has exacerbated the level of uncertainty in the future of the United States–Arab Gulf relationship and reinforced Arab belief that Washington is continuing with its gradual geopolitical withdrawal from the Middle East. Consequently, Arab Gulf countries have tried to recalibrate their relationship with the United States by seeking regional policy alternatives. Central to this shift were the end of the Arab Gulf blockade of Qatar; the readiness of UAE and Bahrain (and Morocco and Sudan) to sign peace treaties with Israel, known as the Abraham Accords; the determination of the Arab Gulf to promote trade and strategic cooperation with China (less so with Russia); and the resolve to reorient their policy toward Turkey (and Syria).[4] No less significant, the lack of Arab leadership, a Nasser, a Saddam, or even an Arafat, created a political and security void in the Middle East that underscored the importance of Turkey. Needless to say, the attempt to ascertain Saudi leadership, with support from UAE, did not pan out in Syria, Lebanon, or Yemen.

In the meantime, against the backdrop of American reorientation toward China, Turkey's deepening economic woes and near isolation in the Middle East following the collapse of the Arab rebellions and Erdogan's vision of a new regional order, save Erdogan's perennial fear of an army coup d'état or popular uprising, convinced Erdogan and the AKP leadership to reorient their policy vis-à-vis the Arab Gulf and Israel. One could argue that the reorientation of US national security strategy toward China and the perception of Washington's declining power amidst global geopolitical changes have served as the common denominator for the Arab Gulf and Turkey to improve their relationship.[5]

Before long, UAE officials visited Syria in November 2021 and, in turn, President Asad visited UAE in March 2022 in his first visit to an Arab country since the beginning of Syria's civil war in 2011.[6] Significantly, UAE National Security Adviser Sheikh Tahnoun bin Zayed al-Nahyan visited Turkey in August 2021. Sheikh Nahyan and President Erdogan discussed an array of issues ranging from UAE investment in Turkey, to bilateral security cooperation in the aftermath of American withdrawal from Afghanistan, to ending their rivalry in Libya and the eastern Mediterranean. The visit after nearly ten years of tension was described as "historic and positive."[7] Then following through on thawing the frosty UAE-Turkish relationship, UAE's de facto ruler, Crown Prince Mohammed bin Zayed al-Nahyan, visited Turkey in November 2021. In his meeting with President Erdogan, the crown prince promised substantial investments in Turkey. Commenting on the visit, President Erdogan said: "God willing, I will make a return visit to the UAE in February. . . . They (UAE) put up a $10 billion investment plan. By putting this $10 billion into place, we will have built a very different future."[8]

In a public display about how Turkey has reset its relationship with the UAE, President Erdogan stated that his forthcoming visit to UAE "would aim to shape the next 50 years of friendship and brotherhood with the UAE." And he added: "We do not consider the security and stability of all brotherly countries in the Gulf region separate from our own."[9] Signaling the importance placed on ties with the UAE, President Erdogan, in February 2022, traveled with a huge delegation, including Turkey's foreign, interior, economy, trade, industry and technology, transportation, culture and tourism, and agriculture ministers. President Erdogan was warmly received with signs of welcome in Turkish. Significantly, President Erdogan and Crown Prince al-Nahyan signed an array of agreements on defense, trade, climate change, industry, and the economy.[10]

In much the same vein, both Turkey and Saudi Arabia worked to mend their ties. Following months of mutual efforts, President Erdogan visited the kingdom in late April 2022. The warm embrace between President Erdogan and Crown Prince Muhammad bin Salman reflected that the previous cold relationship between the two countries had come to an end.[11] No doubt, Turkey's economic woes, high inflation, and forthcoming prospects of Turkish general elections in 2023 constituted a major driver in Erdogan's reset policy; nevertheless, both Turkey and Saudi Arabia had recognized that their cooperation on regional issues is beneficial to both. In fact, since Russia's invasion of Ukraine in February 2022, which ended the post–Cold War era, the two countries, along other Middle Eastern countries, have brooded over the unfolding shape of the new world order and the American global role. This has exacerbated the environment of uncertainty that Washington's foreign policy has created in the Middle East. This was reflected by the fact that most Middle Eastern countries have rejected American requests to sanction Russia. Consequently, both Saudi Arabia and Turkey, whose prominence has come to the fore of international politics as a major oil exporter and a major NATO member, respectively, internalized the importance of cooperation in the Middle East considering the nebulous environment of global politics.

In the meantime, President Erdogan's reset policy in the Middle East has continued with rapprochement with Egypt and Israel. All along, Lebanon has been no stranger to the ongoing realignment of forces in the Middle East and the prominent role Turkey could play regionally and globally. In February 2022, then prime minister Najib Miqati visited Turkey, accompanied by a large retinue of cabinet members including Tourism Minister Walid Nassar, Energy Minister Walid Fayad, Environment Minister Nasser Yassin, Agriculture Minister Abbas Hajj Hassan, Public Works and Transport Minister Ali Hamiyeh, and Economy Minister Amin Salam. President Erdogan and Prime Minister Miqati, along with Lebanese and Turkish officials, celebrated Lebanon-Turkish relations and the expansive agreements the two countries had signed to better their relations. The two leaders agreed to form a joint committee to address and cooperate on important issues such as the Syrian refugee crisis and renovation of the Beirut port, to expand the free trade agreement, and to continue cooperation in the energy, health, tourism, transport, and private sectors.

Considerably, Prime Minister Miqati underscored the importance of the Turkish regional role and virtually pleaded with President Erdogan to help Lebanon surmount its crises. Pointing out Turkey's key role in rehabilitating Lebanon, he emphasized,

> Your Excellency [President Erdogan], you said that a friend is one in time of need, and I say that a brother is always on the side of his brother, and we always feel that our relations are brotherly relations. . . . At all stations, you have been the first to extend a helping hand to Lebanon especially during the successive crises it has been going through. . . . Today we are in dire need of Turkey's cooperation and assistance, and your personal love for Lebanon and our close personal relations will open many doors for cooperation and assistance. . . . Lebanon is going through a crisis that is almost the worst in the world at all economic, financial and social levels. We need support and assistance in all fields.[12]

When all is said and done, it becomes clear that Turkey considers Lebanon its hinterland. The long Ottoman history in Lebanon that played a key role in shaping its society, politics, and political system is an integral component of Turkey's outlook and diplomacy in the Middle East under the AKP. Ottoman legacy and heritage, ranging from Ottoman historical sites, landmarks to Turkish customs, traditions, and language, are being reinvigorated and displayed in plain sight throughout Lebanon. Significantly, Turkish interest in Tripoli and northern Lebanon goes beyond Ankara's concern with and support of the Sunni community and Turkish communities. It is matter of strategic importance. Historically, on the one hand, the *wilaya* of Tripoli offered strategic depth and continuity to the wilaya of Syria, which protected the eastern approaches to Istanbul; on the other, the port of the city of Tripoli, the seat of power for the wilaya of Tripoli, protected and projected Ottoman power in the eastern Mediterranean. In fact, the Mamluks and Crusaders, among other powers, fortified Tripoli as a bulwark against their enemies from the East or West. Contemporaneously, although Turkey perceives Tripoli and northern Lebanon as culturally and traditionally connected to the heartland of Damascus; Ankara clearly considers this area a strategic post looking over the Syrian regime. No less significant, from Ankara's Sunni standpoint, Tripoli and northern Lebanon constitute the last bastion of Sunni power that is not influenced or overtaken by Iran's projection of power as symbolized by the Shi'a crescent.

Nevertheless, Lebanon is strategically secondary to Syria and Cyprus given their importance to Turkey's national security interest. Whereas the Kurds of Syria, given their affiliation with the PKK, pose the foremost threat to Turkey, Cyprus, given its maritime geostrategic location, poses an economic and security threat to Turkey's maritime and energy policy in the eastern Mediterranean. In this respect, Lebanon is too important to Turkey's outlook and diplomacy in the Middle East insofar as the cost of Ankara's interest and investment in Beirut remains on balance less costly than Ankara's investment in safeguarding its national security from internal and regional threats. This explains Ankara's thus far consistent measured, modulated approach to Beirut. However, this is not to say that Ankara will not use its influence in Lebanon under certain circumstances as a foil or tool of its coercive diplomacy should the need arise.

A former Lebanese ambassador to Turkey perceptively summed up the state of Lebanon-Turkey relations:

> Lebanon needs Turkey. Turkey today is a prominent regional and international country. Some Lebanese need to overcome the trauma of World War I. Turkey, unlike Saudi Arabia and Iran, has not involved Lebanon in the regional jockeying or vying for power or predominance. Yet I cannot say that Turkish support of Lebanon is born only out of altruistic reasons. Turkey has won the minds and hearts of many Lebanese, and surely can mobilize them, especially in Tripoli and northern Lebanon, in support of its foreign policy. But this does not mean that Lebanon should favor Turkey over its Arab brothers. This means welcoming Turkey as a lever of stability in Lebanon's never-ending Byzantine politics.[13]

Glossary

ACASR: American Committee for Armenian and Syrian Relief.

AFAD: The Disaster and Emergency Management Presidency.

Al-Ahbash: Organization of Islamic Philanthropic Projects.

Al-Jama'a al-Islamiyah: The Islamic Association.

Bilad al-Sham: The early Arabs referred to the area that comprises today's Lebanon, Syria, Jordan, Israel, and Palestinian territories as *Bilad al-Sham*. This designation is more or less synonymous with Greater Syria, a designation associated with Syria and *wilaya* of Syria under Ottoman rule. The Europeans referred to the Levant as the region along the eastern Mediterranean shores, roughly corresponding to Greater Syria.

caliph: Temporal and religious leader of the Muslim Ummah (community), regarded by Muslims as successor/deputy of Prophet Mohammad. Caliphs ruled the Abbasid dynasty until 1258 and then in Egypt until the Ottoman conquest of 1517. Ottoman sultans held the title until it was abolished in 1924 by Atatürk.

dhimmis: Christians and Jews protected under Islamic rule, known also by Muslims as people of the book, or recipients of divine revelations.

DFLP: Democratic Front for the Liberation of Palestine.

Din: Religion.

Diyanet: Diyanet İşleri Başkanlığı, Turkey's Directorate of Religious Affairs.

GCC: Gulf Cooperation Council.

haraki: Activist.

Hezbollah: The Shi'a Islamist Party of God.

Iqta': Also known as *Iltizam*, signifies feudalism whereby Ottoman authorities grant tax-farming and land tenure concession to *Muqata'jis* (*Iqta'* holders).

jihad: Literally "struggle." Broadly speaking, it is the struggle of Muslims to reform the self and/or one's community. It also refers to a war waged in defense of Islam, a war that could be offensive and/or defensive.

jizya: Head tax that *dhimmis* were required to pay to Muslim states for protection and exemption from military service.

millet system: The two-tiered Ottoman system made up of the higher Muslim community and the lower *dhimmi* community, which enjoyed a measure of social and religious freedom in return for paying the protection head tax, *jizya*.

muqata'jis: *iqta'* holders who can be classified as Emirs (local princes, rulers, commanders), Sheikhs (tribal chiefs or religious scholars), or *Muqaddams* (local chieftains).

mutasarifiyah: The reconstitution of Mount Lebanon by an organic statute (*règlement organique*) as an autonomous region (1861–1918) governed by a *mutasarif* (governor-general) of the Christian faith appointed by the Sublime Porte and approved by the major European powers. An administrative council of twelve members from the various religious communities in Lebanon was established to assist the *mutasarif*. Each of the six religious groups inhabiting Mount Lebanon (Maronites, Druzes, Sunnis, Shi'a, Greek Orthodox, and Melkite Catholics) elected two members to the council.

OIC: Organization of Islamic Countries.

ORSAM: The Center for Middle Eastern Strategic Studies.

PFLP: Popular Front for the Liberation of Palestine.

PLO: Palestine Liberation Organization.

Qa'im Maqamiyah: The political and administrative division of Mount Lebanon (1842–1861) into a northern district under a Christian *qa'im maqam* (sub-governor) and a southern district under a Druze *qa'im maqam*, both of whom answer to the *wali* of Sidon.

Salafism: A school of Islam whose adherents advocate the emulation of the first generations of Muslims (*al-salaf al-Salih*), the pious ancestors.

Salafists: Adherents of Salafism.

sanjak: An Ottoman district in a *wilaya*.

Shari'a: Islamic law.

sultan: An absolute ruler of a territory. Ottoman Sultan was both the head of state and government; his word was the law of the land.

tanzimat: A series of reformist edicts issued between 1839 and 1876 to safeguard the weakening Ottoman Empire. These reforms guaranteed life and property rights, instituted tax regulations, outlawed execution without trial, and abolished the *dhimmi* status accorded to Christians and Jews, thereby asserting the equality of Muslim and non-Muslim Ottoman subjects.

TIKA: Turkish Cooperation and Coordination Agency.

UNIFIL: United Nations Interim Force in Lebanon. UNIFIL is deployed in southern Lebanon.

'uqqal: Wise and religious Druzes.

wali: Governor of the *wilaya*.

wilaya: (plural *wilayat*), also known as *vilayet*, is an Ottoman Province.

Notes

SYNOPSIS AND METHODOLOGY

1. Residing in Hammana in the summer and in Hazmieh in the winter, I was bewildered by the grandeur of the Mezher palace in Hammana, whose owners were Druze *muqaddams* (holders of the tax-farming fief of Hammana), and terrified by the Ottoman cemetery in Hazmieh whose sight and mention tormented my great-grandmother, who endured the starvation of Mount Lebanon during World War I.

2. *Bilad al-Sham* comprised Lebanon, Syria, Israel, Jordan, and Palestinian territories, an area also known interchangeably at certain times in history as Syria or Greater Syria. This area is also referred to today as the Levant.

3. Philip K. Hitti, *Lebanon in History: From the Earliest Times to the Present* (London: Macmillan, 1962), 320.

4. Preceding the invasion of Tamerlane, the 1302 earthquake and several plagues, including the Black Death of 1348, ravaged many coastal and inland towns in Bilad al-Sham.

5. I hail from Hammana and am a member of the Facebook group "Hammana, la Fiancée d'Alphonse de Lamartine," which is, in principle, dedicated to Lamartine's visit to Hammana and its history and natural beauty: https://www.facebook.com/groups/219768226618588.

6. M. Eugène Poujade, *Le Liban et la Syrie, 1845–1860* (Paris: Librairie Nouvelle, 1860), 245–46. For the complete quote see chapter 2.

7. Lucius Ellsworth Thayer provided a proficient legalistic definition of Capitulations. He noted that "Extraordinary privileges and immunities have become so embodied in successive treaties between the great Christian Powers and the Sublime Porte that for most intents and purposes many nationalities in Turkey form a state within a state. This régime has come to be known as 'the capitulations': a code of legal reconciliation founded upon the immiscibility of Christianity and Islam; and a term of art alone descriptive of extraterritoriality in Turkey." Lucius Ellsworth Thayer, "The Capitulations of the Ottoman Empire and the Question of their Abrogation as it Affects the United States," *American Journal of International Law* 17, no. 2 (April 1923): 207.

8. On the concept of the correlation between "zero problems" and "soft power," see Adem Palabiyik, "Interpreting Foreign Policy Correctly in the East-West Perspective," *Today's Zaman*, June 3, 2010.

9. Ahmet Davutoglu, "The Clash of Interests: An Explanation of the World (Dis) Order," *Perceptions: Journal of International Affairs* 2, no. 4 (December 1997–February 1998).

10. Ahmet Davutoglu, "Turkey's Foreign Policy Vision: An Assessment of 2007," *Insight Turkey* 10, no. 1 (2008): 79. On reconfiguring Turkey's foreign policy on the basis of its optimal geographic location, Davutoglu emphasized:

Turkey's geography gives it a specific central country status, which defers from other central countries. For example, Germany is a central country in central Europe, which is far from Asia and Africa. Russia is another central country in the lands of Europe and Asia, which is far from Africa. Iran is a central country in Asia, which is far from Europe and Africa. Taking a broader, global view, Turkey holds an optimal place in the sense that it is both an Asian and European country and is also close to Africa through the eastern Mediterranean. A central country with such an optimal geographic location can not define itself in a defensive manner. It should be seen neither as a bridge country which only connects two points, nor a frontier country, nor indeed as an ordinary country, which sits at the edge of the Muslim world or the West.

Ibid., 78.

11. There are no books examining Ottoman/Turkey-Lebanon relations. There are reputable books examining Lebanon's history, including under Ottoman rule, foremost among which are Hitti, *Lebanon in History*; Kamal S. Salibi, *The Modern History of Lebanon* (London: Weidenfeld and Nicolson, 1965); and Fawwaz Traboulsi, *A History of Modern Lebanon* (London: Pluto Press, 2007). There are books on Turkish foreign policy. But there are no books on Turkish foreign policy toward Lebanon.

12. On the controversies surrounding neo-Ottomanism, see, among others, Merve Şebnem Oruç, "A Surreal View on Erdogan and neo-Ottomanism," *Daily Sabah*, February 16, 2021; Marwa Maziad and Jake Sotiriadis, "Turkey's Dangerous New Exports: Pan-Islamist, Neo-Ottoman Visions and Regional Instability," *Middle East Institute*, April 21, 2020; Nicholas Danforth, "The Nonsense of 'Neo-Ottomanism,'" *War on the Rocks*, May 29, 2020; and Marwan Kabalan, "Turkey's Foreign Policy and the Myth of neo-Ottomanism," *Al-Jazeera*, August 5, 2020.

13. "The 'Strategic Depth' that Turkey Needs," interview with Ahmet Davutoglu, *Turkish Daily News*, September 15, 2001.

14. Davutoglu, "Turkey's Foreign Policy Vision," 79.

15. See *Policy of Zero Problems with Our Neighbors*, Republic of Turkey, Ministry of Foreign Affairs, https://www.mfa.gov.tr/policy-of-zero-problems-with-our-neighbors.en.mfa.

16. Turkey's state institutions and civil society organizations have been an integral part of the AKP-led governments' religious outreach fusing AKP's version of Islam with Turkish nationalism, whereby Turkish language, identity, and culture are promoted alongside religious curricula. Turkey's version of Islam as related to the Hanafi school of jurisprudence, in contrast to Saudi Arabia's conservative Hanbali-Wahhabi school of Islam, is relatively liberal and therefore flexible in interpreting Islamic laws.

Turkey has financed the construction of mosques across the globe, solidified its relationship with Islamist movements, granted thousands of scholarships to students to enlist in Turkish institutions, and sponsored many seminars and forums on Islam and Islamic civilization. See Gonul Tol, "Turkey's Bid for Religious Leadership: How the AKP Uses Islamic Soft Power," *Foreign Affairs*, January 10, 2019.

17. Joseph S. Nye Jr., "Soft Power," *Foreign Policy* 80 (Autumn 1990): 168.

CHAPTER 1

1. Tyre and Byblos comprised the leading city-states in Phoenicia. Whereas Tyre emerged as a principal port famous for its Phoenician purple dye, Byblos was famed for its papyrus and first use of the Phoenician alphabet. The Phoenicians first founded Tripolis as a trading station. The Greeks gave these cities their time-honored appellations.

2. Philip K. Hitti, *Lebanon in History: From the Earliest Times to the Present* (London: Macmillan, 1962), 179. See also Helmut Koester, *Introduction to the New Testament: History, Culture and Religion of the Hellenistic Age*, Vol. I (New York: Walter De Cruyter, 1987), 42.

3. This is clearly stated in the New Testament. See Matthew 15:21; Mark 3:8 and 7:24, 31; and Luke 6:17 and 10:13, 14.

4. Hitti, *Lebanon in History*, 206–9.

5. Koester, *Introduction to the New Testament*, 362–71. On early Church fathers, see Henry Chadwick, *The Early Church* (London: Penguin Books, 1990).

6. For details on the Christological controversy, see Chadwick, *Early Church*, 192–212. See also Albert Hourani, *Minorities in the Arab World* (London: Oxford University Press, 1947), 1–14.

7. Although the theological rift has not been bridged throughout the centuries, relations between the two churches have improved following the Second Vatican Council (1962–1965). In 1979 the Joint International Commission for Theological Dialogue between the Catholic Church and the Orthodox Church was established to continue dialogue and better relations.

8. It's noteworthy that the term *Greek* in the Melkite Greek Catholic Church signifies the Byzantine Rite heritage of the church, the liturgy used by all the Eastern Orthodox churches. The term "Catholic" acknowledges communion with the Church of Rome.

9. See Hourani, *Minorities in the Arab World*, 1–14.

10. Hitti, *Lebanon in History*, 238–39. See also Abert Hourani, *A History of the Arab Peoples* (Cambridge, MA: Belknap, 1991), 22–24.

11. On details on the Pact of Omar, including on inconsistencies regarding its origins, see Mark R. Cohen, "What Was the Pact of 'Umar? A Literary-Historical Study," *Jerusalem Studies in Arabic and Islam* 23 (1999). See also the work of the ninth-century historian 'Abbas Ahmad ibn-Jabir al-Baladhuri, *Kitab Futuh al-Buldan* (The Book on the Conquests of Countries), ed. and trans. M. J. de Goege and Philip Hitti. Philip K. Hitti, *The Origins of the Islamic State: Kitab Futuh al-Buldan of*

'Abbas Ahmad ibn-Jabir al-Baladhuri, Vol. 1 (New York: Columbia University Press, 1916), 165–222, https://archive.org/details/originsofislamic01albauoft/page/n9/mode/2up.

12. The majority of Lebanon's approximately 1500 villages still carry their Phoenician and Aramaic names.

13. See Yusuf al-Dibs, *Al-Jami' al-Mufassal fi Tarikh al-Mawarinah al-Mu'assal* (The Detailed Collection of the True History of the Maronites) (Beirut: Dar Lahd Khatir lil-Tiba'ah wal-Nashr wal-Tawzi', 1987); Istifan al-Duwayhi, *Asl al-Mawarinah* (Origin of the Maronites) (Ihdin: Mu'assasat al-Turath al-'Ihdini, 1973); see also Bishop Yusuf al-Dibs, "Laysa al-Jarajima al-Marada" (al-Jarajima are not al-Marada) *al-Mashriq* (1903), cited first from Matti Moosa, "The Relation of the Maronite of Lebanon to the Mardaites and al-Jarajima," *Speculum* 44, no. 4 (October 1969): 597–608.

14. Henri Lammens, "Al-Marada," *al-Mashriq* (1902), cited first from Moosa's excellent analysis on Maronite origins and controversy: Moosa, "Relation of the Maronite of Lebanon."

15. Hitti, *Lebanon in History*, 246.

16. Ibid., 246–47.

17. See Istifan al-Duwayhi, *Tarikh al-Tai'fa al-Maruniyah* (The History of the Maronite Denomination) (Beirut, 1890); Istifan al-Duwayhi, *Tarikh al-Azminah* (History of Times) (Beirut: Dar Lahd Khatir lil-Tiba'ah wal-Nashr wal-Tawzi', 1985).

18. Kamal Salibi, *Maronite Historians of Medieval Lebanon* (Beirut: American University of Beirut, 1959), 94.

19. Ibid., 95.

20. Following the death of Prophet Muhammad in 632 CE, the question of his succession led to the split of the Muslim community between Sunnis and Shi'a. The Shi'a, or partisans of Ali, Prophet Muhammad's cousin and son-in-law, believed that the *khalifa* (successor/deputy) to the Prophet should always come from his lineage through the Ali family. They believe that the Imamate, the spiritual and temporal leadership of the Muslim community, which passed from the Prophet to Imam Ali, should be inhered in his family. Imams are considered infallible, and most Shiites believe that the Imamate died out with the twelfth Imam, who went into occultation. Most of the companions of the Prophet believed that the *khalifa* should be selected on the basis of his qualifications. Those who believed in choosing the *khalifa* became known as Sunnis, the upholder of the Sunna (tradition) of Prophet Muhammad. The Ismai'ilis supported the claim of Ismail's Imamate, the eldest son of the sixth Imam Ja'far al-Sadiq. Since Ismail died in 760 CE, five years before his father, the Ismai'ilis believe that Ismail had been irrevocably appointed as successor to his father, and that his son Muhammad had become Imam after him. Significantly, they regard Imam Muhammad as al-Mahdi, the divinely guided one in heaven. No less significant, Ismai'ilis developed doctrines, such as emanation, incarnation, and transmigration, that distanced them from orthodox Islam. See Hourani, *History of the Arab Peoples*, 40.

21. The Druzes favor to be called al-Muwahhidun (Unitarians). Their theology is based on an esoteric, inner meaning of the scriptures, divulged only to the initiated few *'uqqal* (wise). A disciple of Hamza, Baha' al-Din Muqtana, played a key role in

propagating the new faith following its persecution in 1021, writing epistles to the scattered and prospective adherents of the faith. He is highly esteemed and credited with writing four of the six books of the Druze scripture, the Epistles of Wisdom. For details on the Druze faith, see Philip K. Hitti, *The Origins of the Druze People and Religion* (Andesite Press, 2017, originally published in New York in 1928); Hourani, *Minorities in the Arab World*, 8–9; and Sami Nasib Makarem, *The Druze Faith* (Caravan Books, 2012, originally published in 1960). The earliest study on the Druze religion was made by Silvestre de Sacy, *Exposé de la Religion des Druzes*, 2 vols. (Paris, 1838).

22. Kamal S. Salibi, *The Modern History of Lebanon* (London: Weidenfeld and Nicolson, 1965), xiv–xvi; Hitti, *Lebanon in History*, 257–62.

23. For an excellent itinerary of the First Crusade based on primary sources, see Charles Foster, "The First Crusaders in Lebanon," *Archaeology and History* 16 (Autumn 2002): 2–10.

24. Matti Moosa, *The Maronites in History* (Syracuse: Syracuse University Press, 1986), 218–19; Mouannes Mohammed Hojairi, "Church Historians and Maronite Communal Consciousness" (PhD diss., Columbia University, 2011), 44–45.

25. For the text of the letter, see René Ristelhueber, *Traditions Françaises au Liban* (Paris, 1918), 65–66.

26. Salibi, *Modern History of Lebanon*, xx–xxii.

27. Kamal S. Salibi, "The Maronites of Lebanon under the Frankish and Mamluk Rule (1099–1516)," *Arabica* 4, no. 3 (September 1957): 291–94.

28. Ibid., 294–99.

29. Alawis were called Nusayris until the beginning of the twentieth century. An offshoot of Shi'a Twelver Islam, Alawis venerate Ali as the last manifestation of God on earth. According to their apotheosis of Ali, Ali ibn Abi Talib is the last and only perfect manifestation of God, in whom the Islamic religion and its *Shari'a* have been created. The origin of their name is still a matter of speculation. Supposedly, the name Nusayris bears the name of the Nusayri Mountains; derives from a diminutive of the Arabic word "Nasara" (Christians); or derives from the founder of the sect, Muhammad Ibn Nusayr. They believe in transmigration of souls and, similar to Ismai'li, an esoteric teaching of their religion. For excellent details on Alawis, see Matti Moosa, *Extremist Shiites: The Ghulat Sects* (New York: Syracuse University Press, 1988), 311–81.

30. See Hitti, *Lebanon in History*, 324–26; Salibi, "Maronites of Lebanon," 297–98; and Albert Hourani, "From Jabal 'Amil to Persia," *Bulletin of the School of Oriental and African Studies* 49, no. 1 (1986): 133–34: Henri Lammens, *La Syrie: Précis Historique* (Beyrouth: Impimerie Catholique, Deuxième Volume, 1921), 15.

31. Salibi, "Maronites of Lebanon," 301.

32. Hitti, *Lebanon in History*, 326–27.

33. Lammens, *La Syrie*, 15–16 and 38.

34. On Mongol invasions and Tamerlane's plundering and sacking of the Syrian interior, see Lammens, *La Syrie*, 19–22.

CHAPTER 2

1. Bernard Lewis, *The Middle East: A Brief History of the Last 2,000 Years* (New York: Scribner, 1995), 112–15; Philip K. Hitti, *Lebanon in History: From the Earliest Times to the Present* (London: Macmillan, 1962), 349–50.

2. Hitti, *Lebanon in History*, 357.

3. Ibid., 359.

4. In 1856 the term of *ra'iyah* was replaced by the less offensive term *taba'ah* (followers). Ibid., 360.

5. Fawwaz Traboulsi, *A History of Modern Lebanon* (London: Pluto Press, 2007), 4. See also Henri Lammens, *La Syrie: Précis Historique* (Beyrouth: Impimerie Catholique, Deuxième Volume, 1921), 66–69.

6. Ibid.

7. The history of the arrival of the Kurds to Lebanon is traced to the twelfth century during the rule of the Kurdish Ayyubid Dynasty founded by Saladin. The Mamluks also brought Kurdish tribes to Tripoli and Djun Akkar to protect their territories from local rebels and foreign invasions. Lammens, *La Syrie*, 66. Ahmad Muhammad Ahmad, *Akrad Lubnan wa-Tanzimuhum al-Ijtima'i wa-al-Siyasi* (The Kurds of Lebanon and their Social and Political Organization) (Beirut: Maktabat al-Fakih, 1995), 39–50. For details on Kurdish history in Lebanon see following chapters.

8. Lammens, *La Syrie*, 70; Traboulsi, *History of Modern Lebanon*, 6; Hitti, *Lebanon in History*, 372–72.

9. Traboulsi, *History of Modern Lebanon*, 5–9; Hitti, *Lebanon in History*, 374.

10. Lammens, *La Syrie*, 75–76.

11. Hitti, *Lebanon in History*, 377; Traboulsi, *History of Modern Lebanon*, 7.

12. Lammens, *la Syrie*, 77.

13. Hitti, *Lebanon in History*, 378–79; Traboulsi, *History of Modern Lebanon*. For details on Fakhr al-Din's experience during his exile, see Anis al-Nusuli, *Rasa'il al-Emir Fakhr al-Din* (The Letters of the Prince Fakhr al-Din) (Beirut, 1946).

14. Lammens, *La Syrie*, 79–80; Hitti, *Lebanon in History*, 380–82; Traboulsi, *History of Modern Lebanon*, 7.

15. Hitti, *Lebanon in History*, 383–85; Traboulsi, *History of Modern Lebanon*, 7–8.

16. Lammens, *La Syrie*, 71–90; Hitti, *Lebanon in History*, 382; Traboulsi, *History of Modern Lebanon*, 8.

17. Lammens, *La Syrie*, 80.

18. Ibid., 85.

19. Hitti, *Lebanon in History*, 386–87; Traboulsi, *History of Modern Lebanon*, 8–9; Kamal S. Salibi, *The Modern History of Lebanon* (London: Weidenfeld and Nicolson, 1965), 6–7.

20. Emir Bashir was allegedly poisoned by Emir Haydar, as cited by the chronicler of the Shihab Emirs, Haydar Ahmad al-Shihabi. See Haydar Ahmad al-Shihabi, *Lubnan fi 'Ahd al-Umara' al-Shihabiyyin* (Lebanon in the Era of the Shihabi Emirs), 3 vols., ed. Asad Rustum and Fouad E. Boustany (Beirut: Editions St. Paul, 1984), cited first by William Harris, *Lebanon: A History 600–2011* (London: Oxford University Press, 2012), 114.

21. Harris, *Lebanon*, 114–15; Hitti, *Lebanon in History*, 389–90; Lammens, *La Syrie*, 94–95.

22. Feudatories or *Muqata'jis* are subsidiary tax farmers who paid the Ottoman government, in this matter, via the Shihabs.

23. As noted earlier, the ancestor of this family is the Kurdish chieftain Ali Janbulad, the wali of Aleppo. Janbulad rebelled against the Ottomans and was supported by Fahkr al-Din II. The Ottomans crushed his rebellion and executed him. His family was forced to leave Aleppo and seek refuge in the Chouf, under the protection of Fakhr al-Din II. Known in Mount Lebanon as Jumblatts, they rose to prominence in the Chouf district following the demise of Ma'ni leadership in 1697. Other Kurdish families that settled in Lebanon for long periods of time and became fully assimilated in Lebanon's society include the Sayfas in Tripoli, the Mir'bis in 'Akkar, the 'Imads in Mount Lebanon, and the Hamiyehs in Ba'albeck. Lammens, *La Syrie*, 66; Ahmad Muhammad Ahmad, *Akrad Lubnan wa-Tanzimuhum al-Ijtima'i wa-al-Siyasi*, 39–61, first cited by Farah W. Kawtharani and Lokman I. Meho, "The Kurdish Community in Lebanon," *International Journal of Kurdish Studies* 19, no. 1–2 (January 2005).

24. Harris, *Lebanon*, 115–16; Hitti, *Lebanon in History*, 390; Salibi, *Modern History of Lebanon*, 9–10. *Muqaddam* is a rank between emir and sheikh.

25. Lammens, *La Syrie*, 101; Hitti, *Lebanon in History*, 392; Salibi, *Modern History of Lebanon*, 11.

26. The wali of Tripoli had problems with the Shi'a Hamade clan. Yusuf led a campaign against the Hamades and routed their forces in Amioun, Kura. Christians were enamored by Yusuf's courage and his empathy for Christians. Yusuf's guardian was a Maronite from Rashmayah, Sa'd al-Khuri. The Jumblatts also supported Yusuf. According to Henri Lammens, the Porte was happy to utilize the valor of the young emir and thus approved his nomination as the emir of the whole mountain. Once secure in his princely seat, Emir Yusuf elevated the status of the Khuri family to the rank of sheikhdom. This family gave Lebanon two presidents. Lammens, *La Syrie*, 102.

27. Lammens, *La Syrie*, 103–12; Hitti, *Lebanon in History*, 394–95.

28. Harris, *Lebanon*, 122; Hitti, *Lebanon in History*, 394–95.

29. Lammens, *La Syrie*, 112–17.

30. C. F. Volney, *Travels Through Syria and Egypt in the Years 1783, 1784, and 1785*, Vol. II (London: G.G. J. & J. Robinson, 1787), 32.

31. Hitti, *Lebanon in History*, 407. During this time also Maronites welcomed Catholic Syrian, Armenian, and Greek communities to North Lebanon and Kisrwan. Ibid.

32. Volney, *Travels Through Syria and Egypt*, Vol. I, 299–300.

33. Ibid., vol. II, 33.

34. Lammens, *La Syrie*, 117–19; Hitti, *Lebanon in History*, 412; Salibi, *Modern History of Lebanon*, 18–20.

35. Harris, *Lebanon*, 132; Hitti, *Lebanon in History*, 414; Lammens, *La Syrie*, 121–28.

36. Lammens, *La Syrie*, 130–31; Salibi, *Modern History of Lebanon*, 21–22.

37. The Maronite Church established a number of schools in the eighteenth century, the most prominent of which were the schools of Ayntura (1724), Zgharta (1735), and Ayn Waraqa (1789).

38. Greek Orthodox and Greek Catholics initially made up the Melkites who accepted the decrees of the Council of Chalcedon (451). When Constantinople split from Rome in 1054, the Melkites followed Constantinople and were therefore classified by Rome as schismatics. But when a group of Melkites entered into communion with Rome in the late seventeenth century, the Uniate Melkites became known as Greek Catholics and the non-Uniates as Greek Orthodox.

39. Harris, *Lebanon*, 128.

40. Lamens, *La Syrie*, 137.

41. Hitti, *Lebanon in History*, 416; Salibi, *Modern History of Lebanon*, 25.

42. Lammens, *La Syrie*, 144–46.

43. Ibid., 146–47; Salibi, *Modern History of Lebanon*, 26–27.

44. Alphonse De Lamartine, *A Pilgrimage to the Holy Land; Comprising Recollections, Sketches, and Reflections, Made During a Tour in the East*, Vol. 1 (New York: D. Appleton & Company, 1868), 155.

45. Lammens, *La Syrie*, 152–54; Hitti, *Lebanon in History*, 421–22; Salibi, *Modern History of Lebanon*, 28–29.

46. Lammens, *La Syrie*, 155–57; Hitti, *Lebanon in History*, 421–22; Salibi, *Modern History of Lebanon*, 28–29.

47. Lamartine, *Pilgrimage to the Holy Land*, 117.

48. Lammens, *La Syrie*, 158–65; Hitti, *Lebanon in History*, 423–24; Salibi, *Modern History of Lebanon*, 34–35; Fawwaz Traboulsi, *A History of Modern Lebanon* (London: Pluto Press, 2007), 12–13; Harris, *Lebanon*, 138–39.

49. The capitulations were initially treaties and trade agreements concluded between the Ottoman Empire and European powers to promote trade. Then, as the Ottoman Empire grew weaker, the capitulations evolved to include Ottoman concessions to European powers granting rights and privileges to their citizens living in the empire, as well as entitlements to protect the minorities of the empire. For example, France acted as the protector of the Catholics, Britain of Jews and Druzes, and Tsarist Russia of Greek Orthodox. For excellent details on the development of capitulations, see James B. Angell, "The Turkish Capitulations," *American Historical Review* 6, no. 2 (January 1901): 254–59.

50. Lammens, *La Syrie*, 166–68; Hitti, *Lebanon in History*, 424–25; Salibi, *Modern History of Lebanon*, 36–39; Traboulsi, *History of Modern Lebanon*, 12–13; Harris, *Lebanon*, 139–40.

51. Lammens, *La Syrie*, 118.

CHAPTER 3

1. Henri Lammens, *La Syrie: Précis Historique* (Beyrouth: Impimerie Catholique, Deuxième Volume, 1921), 169–71; Philip K. Hitti, *Lebanon in History: From the Earliest Times to the Present* (London: Macmillan, 1962), 433–35; Kamal S. Salibi,

The Modern History of Lebanon (London: Weidenfeld and Nicolson, 1965), 46–52; Fawwaz Traboulsi, *A History of Modern Lebanon* (London: Pluto Press, 2007), 12–18; William Harris, *Lebanon: A History 600–2011* (London: Oxford University Press, 2012), 140–41.

2. Colonel Churchill [Charles Henry Churchill], *The Druzes and Maronites under the Turkish Rule: From 1840–1860* (London: Bernard Quaritch, 1862), 66. The Khazins, Hubayshes, and Dahdahs of Kisrwan helped the Ottomans circulate their petition. The Ottomans also gained over Emir Bashir Ahmad Abou Lam', who fulfilled their biddings. Ibid.

3. Ibid., 65.

4. Richard Edwards, *La Syrie, 1840–1860, Histoire, Politique, Administration, Population, Religions et Mœurs, Événements de 1860 d'après des Actes Officiels et des Documents Authentiques* (Paris: AMYOT, Libraire Editeur, 1862), 69–70.

5. The Druze chiefs included Nu'man and Sa'id Jumblatt, Ahmad and Amin Arslan, Nasif Abu Nakad, Husyan Talhuq, and Dawud 'Abd al-Malik. Salibi, *Modern History of Lebanon*, 60; Churchill, *Druzes and Maronites*, 73.

6. Salibi, *Modern History of Lebanon*, 61–62; Churchill, *Druzes and Maronites*, 77–78.

7. Salibi, *Modern History of Lebanon*, 62; Churchill, *Druzes and Maronites*, 78–79.

8. Hitti, *Lebanon in History*, 435; Salibi, *Modern History of Lebanon*, 62–64; Churchill, *Druzes and Maronites*, 80–82.

9. According to official documents, the total population of Mount Lebanon was 213,070, of whom 95,350 were Maronites, 41,090 Greek Catholics, 28,500 Greek Orthodox, 35,600 Druzes, 12,300 Shi'ites, and 200 Jews. The Christian district had 74,700 Maronites. The Druze district had 25,450 Druzes, 17,350 Maronites, 5,200 Greek Orthodox, and 15,590 Greek Catholics. There were 10,150 Druzes in the Christian district and in Dayr al-Qamar. See Richard Edwards, *La Syrie, 1840–1860*, 71.

10. Salibi, *Modern History of Lebanon*, 66.

11. Churchill, *Druzes and Maronites*, 83.

12. Greek Orthodox chafed at Maronite disregard of their civil and ecclesiastical rights. Moreover, Greek Orthodox convents had been deprived of lands, and proselytism among their flock had been carried out by several means, including intimidation. Ibid., 81–82.

13. Ibid., 90–92; Salibi, *Modern History of Lebanon*, 68–69.

14. M. Eugène Poujade, *Le Liban et La Syrie, 1845–1860* (Paris: Librairie Nouvelle, 1860), 245–46.

15. Ibid., 247–48.

16. Richards, *La Syrie, 1840–1860*, 106–8; Salibi, *Modern History of Lebanon*, 71–72.

17. Salibi, *Modern History of Lebanon*, 71–72; for the complete French text of the *Règlement of Shakib Effendi*, see Richards, *La Syrie, 1840–1860*, 109–14.

18. Richards, *La Syrie, 1840–1860*, 119.

19. At the time, the Christian community was also affected by the apprehensive relationship between the Maronites and the Greek Orthodox, as well as by

the contestation over the *qa'im maqamiyah*, following the death of *qa'im maqam* Haydar abu al-Lam'. Salibi, *Modern History of Lebanon*, 74; Richards, *La Syrie, 1840–1860*, 122.

20. Antun Dahir al-'Aqiqi (and other documents), translated with notes and commentary by Malcolm H. Kerr, *Lebanon in the Years of Feudalism, 1840–1868: A Contemporary Account* (Beirut: American University of Beirut, Oriental Series no. 33, 1959), 45. Quote first cited by Salibi, *Modern History of Lebanon*, 84.

21. Colonel Churchill explained that the Khazins had committed the unpardonable offense of seeking the support of the British government to the representation of their grievances at the Porte. This glaring departure from the principle of Maronite allegiance to France had to be signally chastised. Churchill, *Druzes and Maronites*, 125.

22. Ibid., 47–53; Ussama Makdisi, "Corrupting the Sublime Sultanate: The Revolt of Tanyus Shahin in Nineteenth Century Ottoman Lebanon," *Comparative Studies in Society and History* 42, no. 1 (January 2000): 180–208. Salibi, *Modern History of Lebanon*, 85–86.

23. Henry Harris Jessup, *Fifty-Three Years in Syria*, Vol. I (New York: Fleming H. Revell Company, 1910), 166; Churchill, *Druzes and Maronites*, 132–33.

24. Jessup, *Fifty-Three Years in Syria*, 166.

25. Churchill, *Druzes and Maronites*, 138.

26. Jessup, *Fifty-Three Years in Syria*, 167.

27. Churchill, *Druzes and Maronites*, 158–59. See also al-'Aqiqi, *Lebanon in the Years of Feudalism, 1840–1868*, 55–57.

28. Jessup, *Fifty-Three Years in Syria*, 171.

29. Ibid., 171; Churchill, *Druzes and Maronites*, 143.

30. Jessup, *Fifty-Three Years in Syria*, 168–69.

31. Jessup, *Fifty-Three Years in Syria*, 172; Churchill, *Druzes and Maronites*, 144–45.

32. Churchill, *Druzes and Maronites*, 145–46.

33. Ibid., 146.

34. Ibid., 146–47.

35. Ibid., 159–60; Jessup, *Fifty-Three Years in Syria*, 177.

36. Churchill, *Druzes and Maronites*, 153–54.

37. Ibid., 155–57.

38. Ibid., 158.

39. Salibi, *Modern History of Lebanon*, 94.

40. Churchill, *Druzes and Maronites*, 157–58.

41. Ibid., 161.

42. Ibid., 163.

43. Ibid., 163; Jessup, *Fifty-Three Years in Syria*, 179.

44. Churchill, *Druzes and Maronites*, 167; Jessup, *Fifty-Three Years in Syria*, 180.

45. Churchill, *Druzes and Maronites*, 169; Jessup, *Fifty-Three Years in Syria*, 180.

46. Churchill, *Druzes and Maronites*, 171–72.

47. Ibid, 172–73.

48. Ibid., 174–75.

49. Ibid., 178.

50. Ibid.

51. Ibid., 183–88; Jessup, *Fifty-Three Years in Syria*, 184–86; Salibi, *Modern History of Lebanon*, 102–4.

52. Churchill, *Druzes and Maronites*, 190–91; Jessup, *Fifty-Three Years in Syria*, 187.

53. Jessup, *Fifty-Three Years in Syria*, 187.

54. Ibid., 187–88.

55. Churchill, *Druzes and Maronites*, 194–205.

56. According to Churchill: 11,000 Christians were massacred; 100,000 suffered; 20,000 became widows and orphans; 4,000 died from destitution; 3,000 Christian habitations burned; and 2,000,000 L (lira) property was destroyed. Ibid., 219. For other accounts, see Hitti, *Lebanon in History*, 438; Salibi, *Modern History of Lebanon*, 106; and Alexis Heraclides and Ada Dialla, *Humanitarian Intervention in the Long Nineteenth Century: Setting the Precedent* (Manchester: Manchester University Press, 2015), 137.

57. Churchill, *Druzes and Maronites*, 205–6; Jessup, *Fifty-Three Years in Syria*, 194.

58. Jessup, *Fifty-Three Years in Syria*, 195.

59. Ibid., 196; Churchill, *Druzes and Maronites*, 211–13.

60. Jessup, *Fifty-Three Years in Syria*, 204; Churchill, *Druzes and Maronites*, 214–16.

61. Ibid.

62. See letter in Edwards, *La Syrie, 1840–1862*, 179–80.

63. Representatives of Britain, France, Prussia, Austria, Russia, and the Porte held a conference in Paris on August 3, 1860, in which the parties agreed to two protocols. The protocols entailed that the sultan will take immediate measures to stop the effusion of blood and restore order; a body of European troops, which may be increased to 12,000 men, shall be sent to Syria to contribute toward the reestablishment of tranquility; and European powers promise to maintain on the coast of Syria sufficient naval forces to contribute toward the success of the common efforts to reestablish tranquility on the coast of Syria. For the text of the protocols see Thomas Erskine Holland, *The European Concert in the Eastern Question: A Collection of Treaties and Other Public Acts* (Oxford: Clarendon Press, 1885), 207–8.

64. Jessup, *Fifty-Three Years in Syria*, 206–7.

65. Churchill, *Druzes and Maronites*, 228–30.

66. Ibid., 232–43; Salibi, *Modern History of Lebanon*, 108–9.

67. For details on Lord Dufferin's (born Frederick Temple Blackwood) views, see his biographer Charles E. Drummond Black, *The Marquess of Dufferin and Ava* (London: Hutchinson & Co., 1903), 55–56. Although Lord Dufferin recognized Druze barbarism and Turkish treachery, he blamed the Maronite Church for creating an antagonistic attitude toward the Druzes. See also Jessup, *Fifty-Three Years in Syria*, 209; Churchill, *Druzes and Maronites*, 258–59.

68. The election of the twelve members of the administrative council was proportioned according to a sectarian formula in the following regions of Mount Lebanon: Kisrwan: two Maronites; Jizzin: one Maronite, one Druze, and one Sunni; Matn:

one Maronite, one Greek Orthodox, one Druze, and one Shi'ite; Chouf: one Druze; Koura: one Greek Orthodox; and Zahle: one Greek Catholic. The administrative council was charged with tax collection and controlling revenues and expenditures of Mount Lebanon *Mutasariyah*, and assisting the mutasarif in all governmental affairs. Holland, *European Concert in the Eastern Question*, 212. For the entire text of the *Règlement* see Holland, *European Concert in the Eastern Question*, 212–18.

69. Ibid., 212–18. See also Hitti, *Lebanon in History*, 442–43; and Salibi, *Modern History of Lebanon*, 110–11.

70. Holland, *European Concert in the Eastern Question*, 212–18.

71. Dawud Pasha was initially appointed for three years (1861–1864). His appointment was renewed for five years. He resigned in May 1868. Holland, *European Concert in the Eastern Question*, 209.

72. Jessup, *Fifty-Three Years in Syria*, 266–67; Hitti, *Lebanon in History*, 445.

73. Dawud Pasha was succeeded by Franco-Nasri Pasha (1868–1873), Rustum Pasha (1873–1883), Wassa Pasha (1883–1892), Na'um Pasha (1892–1902), Muzaffar Pasha (1902–1907), Yusuf Franco (1907–1912), and Ohannes Koyoumjian (1912–1915). Holland, *European Concert in the Eastern Question*, 209–10; Hitti, *Lebanon in History*, 446–47.

74. I am a graduate of the Convent of the Sisters of the Good Shepherd in Hammana and the School of the Carmelite Fathers in Hazmieh.

75. Black, *Marquess of Dufferin*, 59.

CHAPTER 4

1. For details on the Young Turks, see Feroz Ahmad, *The Young Turks: The Committee of Union and Progress in Turkish Politics 1908–1914* (New York: Columbia University Press, 2010, originally published by Oxford University Press in 1969); and M. Sükrü Hanioğlu, *The Young Turks in Opposition* (London: Oxford University Press, 1995).

2. Henry Morgenthau, *Ambassador Morgenthau's Story* (New York: Doubleday, Page & Company, 1919), 12–15.

3. The Eastern Question emerged as a result of the weakness and disintegration of the Ottoman Empire in the nineteenth century. The question revolved around the European contest for control of former Ottoman territories and potential political disarray within the empire that any European power could take advantage of to enhance its power vis-à-vis the other powers. This question arose periodically during the Greek revolution of the 1820s, the Crimean conflict (1853–1856), the Balkan crisis of 1875–1878, the Bosnian crisis of 1908, and the Balkan Wars of 1912–1913.

4. The Armenian-inhabited provinces, which Turkish newspapers called the Six Provinces of Eastern Anatolia, were divided into seven provinces split into two administrative regions. The first region comprised the Prefectures of Van, Paghesh, Diarbekir, and Kharpert. The second region comprised the Prefectures of Garin, Trebizond, and Sepasdia. Each region would be headed by a European inspector general, whose appointment had to be approved by the European powers. These officials

would be responsible for the supervision of the administration, justice, and police apparatus, as well as the governors and prefects of their regions. Their responsibility also included the equal distribution of government jobs between Muslims and non-Muslims. For excellent details, see Zaven Der Yeghiayan, Armenian Patriarch of Constantinople, 1913–1922, *My Patriarchal Memoirs*, trans. Ared Misirliyan (Barrington, RI: Mayreni Publishing, 2002, originally published in Armenian in Cairo, 1947), 25–27.

5. During the forced migration of Armenians from their homes in Eastern Anatolia, the Armenian Patriarch Zaven Der Yeghiayan had an audience with Grand Vizier Said Halim Pasha on June 27, 1915, who censured the patriarch: "Last year, when I was engaged in the project of Reforms, I said to Mr. Giers, 'The Armenian nation is ours, and we are quite capable of thinking about its prosperity.' I was sincerely engaged in that matter, but unfortunately your people did not allow us, thinking that a Dutchman can reform our country better that we can. I felt then that there was going to be a chill between the two [Armenian and Turkish] nations, which did indeed happen." Yeghiayan, *My Patriarchal Memoirs*, 77.

6. Morgenthau, *Ambassador Morgenthau's Story*, 26–27.

7. Ibid., 7.

8. Ibid., 102.

9. Ibid., 161.

10. Ibid., 171.

11. Ibid., 109–10.

12. Information on the operations of HMS *Doris* was gleaned from its log, which was declassified in 1966. See Edward J. Erickson, "Captain Larkin and the Turks: The Strategic Impact of the Operations of *HMS Doris* in Early 1915," *Middle Eastern Studies* 46, no. 1 (2010).

13. By Greater Syria I refer to the geography of what's today Lebanon, Syria, Israel, Palestinian territories, and Jordan.

14. L. B. Weldon, *Hard Lying: Eastern Mediterranean 1914–1919* (London: Herbert Jenkins Limited, 1925), 9–10.

15. A copy of the memorandum was retrieved from the private archives of Jesuit Fathers in Lebanon, which were compiled and published with commentaries by Presses De L'Université Saint-Joseph. See Christian Taoutel and Pierre Wittouck, *Le Peuple Libanais dans la Tourmente de la Grande Guerre 1914–1918, D'après les Archives des Pères Jésuites au Liban* (Beirut: Presses De L'Université Saint-Joseph, Deuxième edition, 2018), 113.

16. Morgenthau, *Ambassador Morgenthau's Story*, 173.

17. Taoutel and Wittouck, *Le Peuple Libanais*, 62.

18. See copy of declaration in Jesuit archives, ibid., 104.

19. Taoutel and Wittouck, *Le Peuple Libanais*, 108.

20. The entry is most likely by father superior Paul Mattern, head of the Syrian mission during the 1914–1918 War. See Taoutel and Wittouck, *Le Peuple Libanais*, 118.

21. Morgenthau, *Ambassador Morgenthau's Story*, 186–87.

22. Nicholas Z. Ajay, "Political Intrigue and Suppression in Lebanon during World War I," *International Journal of Middle East Studies* 5, no. 2 (April 1974): 143–44.

23. Captain Weldon underlined that "For the next six weeks [beginning in late January 1915] we were working up and down the Syrian coast reconnoitering with our planes, landing and picking up agents, and generally making ourselves useful in the ways our superiors thought fit." See Weldon, *Hard Lying*, 20.

24. T. F. Farman, "French Claims on Syria," *Contemporary Review* 108 (July–December 1915): 344–45. Jamal Pasha suspected the loyalty of Arab forces in the Ottoman Army; he, therefore, deployed approximately 16,000 Anatolian troops and kept them in Mount Lebanon throughout the Great War.

25. Emir Shakib Arslan had served as an Ottoman deputy and fought against the Italian invasion of Tripoli in 1912. He was a highly respected patriot and a friend of Enver Pasha. Louis Farshee, *Safer Barlik: Famine in Mount Lebanon During World War I* (Portland, OR: Inkwater Press, 2015), 37.

26. George Antonious, *The Arab Awakening: The Story of the Arab National Movement* (Royal Oak, New Zealand: Pickle Partners Publishing, 2015, originally published in Beirut in 1938), 220. Jamal Pasha knew about some incriminating documents seized in the French consulate before his military campaign against the British in Egypt, but he refrained from taking any action that may have whipped up the antagonism of his Arab troops. He approved only the political prosecution of Michel Mutran, a Francophile and well-known Christian, who was found guilty of enlisting French support to annex Ba'albeck to Mount Lebanon. Mutran died on his way to exile. See the entry of Father P. Louis Cheikho in the Jesuits' archives. Taoutel and Wittouck, *Le Peuple Libanais*, 120.

27. Antonious, *Arab Awakening*. See also Farman, "French Claims on Syria," 345.

28. Antonious, *Arab Awakening*, 221.

29. Ibid., 223–24.

30. Ibid., 224.

31. Taoutel and Wittouck, *Le Peuple Libanais*, 124.

32. A copy of Stanley Hollis's letter was compiled in the Jesuits' archives. Ibid., 148.

33. See Father Joseph Mattern's diary entry on April 12, 2015. Taoutel and Wittouck, *Le Peuple Libanais*, 28–30.

34. See Father Joseph Mattern's diary entry on June 28, 1915. Ibid.

35. Graham A. Pitts, in his dissertation "Fallow Fields: Famine and the Making of Lebanon," argues that Mount Lebanon's peculiarly intense reliance on flows of capital, grain, and humans, unlike other regions in Greater Syria that invested more in subsistence crops, was prone to face the catastrophe of starvation. Graham A. Pitts, "Fallow Fields: Famine and the Making of Lebanon" (PhD diss., Georgetown University, 2016), 38.

36. Whereas the British officially proclaimed the blockade on June 2, 1915, the French made their official proclamation on August 27, 1915.

37. Taoutel and Wittouck, *Le Peuple Libanais*, 34–38.

38. Nicholas Z. Ajay, "Mount Lebanon and the Wilayah of Beirut, 1914–1918: The War Years" (PhD diss., Georgetown University, 1972), 388.

39. According to a close friend of Jamal Pasha, Halidé Edib, "there was one single railway (that was not complete at the time) over which the entire military transport

and the entire provisioning of the country had to pass." See Halidé Edib Adivar, *House with Wisteria: Memoirs of Halidé Edib* (Charlottesville: Leopolis Press, 2003), 322. The last *Mutasarif* of Mount Lebanon, Ohannes Kouyoumdjian Pasha, emphasized that shipments of trainloads of wheat ordered by Jamal Pasha to Beirut and Mount Lebanon were obstructed by the military using trains and fuel to move troops and their supplies. See Ohannes Kouyoumdjian Pasha, *Le Liban á la Veille et au début de la Grande Guerre: Mémoirs d'un Gouverneur, 1913–1915* (Paris: C'entre d'Histoire Armènienne Contemporaine, 2003), 137. Both references were first cited by Melanie Tanielian, "The War of Famine: Everyday Life in Wartime Beirut and Mount Lebanon (1914–1918)" (PhD diss., University of California–Berkeley, 2012), 37.

40. By fall 2016 the bread situation had become so desperate that girls were selling themselves or their properties for a loaf of bread. Ajay, "Mount Lebanon," 394–95.

41. Christopher M. Andrew and A. S. Kanya-Forstner, *The Climax of French Imperial Expansion 1914–1924* (Stanford, CA: Stanford University Press, 1981), 107.

42. Ibid.

43. A copy of Father Boulos Akl's letter was included, along with its translation into English by Ajay, in the appendix of his dissertation. Ajay, "Mount Lebanon," 178–82.

44. Ibid., 183–96.

45. In May 1916, the governor of Mount Lebanon, Ali Munif Bey, established the Lebanon Wheat Company to locate and distribute wheat to the people of Mount Lebanon at a fair price. No wheat was delivered to the general population because of corruption and profiteering. The company was closed in October. Another effort by the local government to allow designated people to get food from Homs, Hama, and Dara' also failed because Ottoman authorities had already requisitioned mules, camels, and donkeys, making transportation of food hardly possible. Meanwhile, people could not afford soaring prices. See letter, ibid.

46. Reportedly Sharif Hussein of Mecca, who came to support the British against the Ottomans, denounced the behavior and policies of Jamal Pasha and called for his punishment by hanging. See letter in ibid.

47. Ibid., 195.

48. See Father Angélil's diary entry in Taoutel and Wittouck, *Le Peuple Libanais*, 40.

49. See Father Mattern's diary entry in ibid., 62.

50. Special Cable to the *New York Times*, "Famine Grips Syria, Beirut Devastated: Whole Levant Is Starving and Hopeless, American Woman Writer Says," *New York Times*, September 16, 1916.

51. See the American's letter (whose identity was not mentioned) in Taoutel and Wittouck, *Le Peuple Libanais*, 84–86.

52. See letter in ibid., 62.

53. Father Louis Cheikho cited this quote from his correspondence with a committee responsible for coming to the aid of the hungry, which comprised superiors of convents and religious houses. See excerpt of Father Cheikho's correspondence, dated October 5, 1916, in Taoutel and Wittouck, *Le Peuple Libanais*, 59.

54. See excerpt of letter in ibid., 94.

55. Ibid.

56. See Jesuits' diary entries in Taoutel and Wittouck, *Le Peuple Libanais*, 82. See also Tanielian, "The War of Famine," 40–42.

57. See entry in Taoutel and Wittouck, *Le Peuple Libanais*, 88.

58. See Father Mattern's entries in ibid., 42.

59. See entry in ibid., 84.

60. Morgenthau, *Ambassador Morgenthau's Story*, 288.

61. According to an official estimate received at the State Department from US Consul at Erzeroum, 50,000 Armenian children were made orphans by the massacres. See "Fifty Thousand Orphans. Made so by the Turkish Massacres of Armenians," *New York Times,* December 18, 1896. See also ibid., 289. For more information on the massacres, see Selim Deringil, "'The Armenian Question Is Finally Closed': Mass Conversions of Armenians in Anatolia during the Hamidian Massacres of 1895–1897," *Comparative Studies in Society and History* 51, no. 2 (April 2009): 344–71; and Ronald Grigor Suny, *"They Can Live in the Desert but Nowhere Else": A History of the Armenian Genocide* (Princeton, NJ: Princeton University Press, 2015), 129–31.

62. Morgenthau, *Ambassador Morgenthau's Story*, 290.

63. Yeghiayan, *My Patriarchal Memoirs*, 47–49 and 55–56.

64. See letters addressed to Armenian Patriarch Zaven Der Yeghiayan in ibid., 34–45.

65. Ibid., 61–63.

66. Ibid., 65.

67. See the two letters of June and July 1915 addressed by Patriarch Zaven Der Yeghiayan to the Prelate of Bulgaria Ghevont Turian, in which the patriarch detailed Ottoman extermination policy and asked Prelate Turian to solicit the help of the Prelate of the United States and His Holiness the Catholicos. Patriarch Yeghiayan emphasized in his letters that his appeals for help were unanswered and only the US and Bulgarian embassies took an interest in helping the Armenians, but their efforts had no impact on the Turkish government; ibid., 84–87. Many deportees traveling on foot across the Syrian Desert were killed, were robbed, or died from thirst and/or starvation, and young girls were raped and kidnapped.

68. See transcription of Patriarch Yeghiayan's audience with Talaat Pasha in ibid., 79–81.

69. Ajay, "Mount Lebanon," 413.

70. Rafael de Nogales, *Four Years Beneath the Crescent*, trans. Muna Lee (New York: Charles Scribner's Sons, 1926), 179.

71. Ajay, "Mount Lebanon," 505.

72. Ellen Marie Lust-Okar, "Failure of Collaboration: Armenian Refugees in Syria," *Middle Eastern Studies* 32, no. 1 (January 1996): 57.

73. John Ahmaranian, "The Armenians in Lebanon," *World Lebanese Cultural Union*, April 27, 2015, https://wlcui.com/2015/04/27/the-armenians-in-lebanon -history-and-demography-by-dr-john-ahmaranian/. See also Robert G. Rabil, "The Armenian Genocide, Maronite Starvation, and Lessons in Past Atrocities," *Fikra Forum- Washington Institute for Near East Policy*, May 12, 2021.

74. Ajay, "Mount Lebanon," 506.

75. According to Philip Hitti, thousands of Assyrian and Armenian refugees flocked into Lebanon. Beirut had 15,000 and its environs had an equal number. Philip K. Hitti, *Lebanon in History: From the Earliest Times to the Present* (London: Macmillan, 1962), 485.

76. I am familiar with Bourj Hammoud and other cities and towns where Armenians reside in Lebanon.

77. Yeghiayan, *My Patriarchal Memoirs*, 113.

78. Bayard Dodge, *The American University of Beirut: A Brief History of the University and the Lands which It Serves* (Beirut: Khayat's, 1958), 41.

79. Quote taken from Ajay, "Mount Lebanon," 508, as cited in Halidah Adib, *Memoirs of Halidé Edib* (New York: Century Company, 1926), 428–30.

80. See above including Patriarch Huwayek's appeal to the French that the whole Lebanese population was in danger of extinction.

81. See Ambassador Henry Morgenthau's telegram in Papers Relating to the Foreign Relations of the United States, 1915, Supplement, the World War, File No. 867.4016/117, Office of the Historian, Department of State, Constantinople, September 3, 1915. In a telegram to the US secretary of state, dated July 10, 1915, Ambassador Morgenthau wrote: "persecution of Armenians assuming unprecedented proportions. . . . Reports from widely scattered districts indicate systematic attempt to uproot peaceful Armenian populations and through arbitrary arrests, terrible tortures, wholesale expulsions and deportations from one end of the Empire to the other accompanied by frequent instances of rape, pillage, and murder, turning into massacre, to bring destruction and destitution on them." Ibid., File No. 867.4016/74, Constantinople, July 10, 1915. In a follow-up telegram on August 11, 1915, Ambassador Morgenthau wrote: "Turkish anti-Armenian activities continue unabated. . . . To advance immediate aid to these helpless people will in itself imply our protesting attitude." Ibid., File No. 867.4016/90, Constantinople, August 11, 1915.

82. American Committee for Armenian and Syrian Relief, *Minutes: 1915–1919*, 12, https://neareastmuseum.com/wp-content/uploads/2019/02/American-Committee -for-Armenian-and-Syrian-Relief-Meeting-Minutes-1915-1919.pdf.

83. Ajay, "Mount Lebanon," 453.

84. In summer 2018, the American government helped provide $5,000 to Lebanon Hospital for the Insane, $252,800 to ACASR, $50,000 to Individual Relief Societies for Lebanon Villages, and $100,000 in individual remittances to Syrian relatives. See message of acting secretary of state to the War Trade Board, in Papers Relating to the Foreign Relations of the United States, 1918, Supplement 2, the World War, File No. 867.48/959b, Office of the Historian, US State Department, Washington, July 22, 1918.

85. See Spanish ambassador telegram to assistant secretary of state, in Papers Relating to the Foreign Relations of the United States, 1918, Supplement 2, the World War, File No. 867.48/619, Office of the Historian, US State Department, Washington, March 27, 1917.

86. In May 1917, responding to the Spanish ambassador, the American government organized, in cooperation with the American Red Cross, a delivery of relief supplies onboard the collier USS *Caesar*. Supplies included 5,000 gallons cottonseed oil,

825,000 lbs. whole wheat, 1,000 cases of condensed milk, 200,000 lbs. sugar, 13,640 cu. ft. donated foodstuffs and clothing, 80,000 lbs. beans, 980,000 lbs. flour, 100,000 lbs. crushed wheat, 300,000 lbs. rice, 5,000 gallons kerosene oil, and 458 cases hospital supplies. See assistant secretary of state's telegram to the Spanish ambassador, in ibid., File No. 867.48/608, Washington, May 4, 1917.

87. See secretary of state's telegram to the American Committee for Armenian and Syrian Relief, in ibid., File No. 867.48/640, Washington, August 24, 1917.

88. See British ambassador's telegram to US assistant secretary of state, in ibid., File No. 867.48/698, Washington, December 3, 1917.

89. See telegram of Assistant Secretary of State Phillips to British Ambassador Spring Rice in Ibid., File No. 867.48/698, Washington, December 18, 1917.

90. American Committee for Armenian and Syrian Relief, *Minutes: 1915–1919*, 20.

91. Ajay, "Mount Lebanon," 459–60.

92. Dodge, *American University of Beirut*, 40–42.

93. Ibid., 43.

94. Ajay, "Mount Lebanon," 522–26.

95. Bayard Dodge estimated that 300,000 people had died in Beirut and Mount Lebanon. See Dodge, *American University of Beirut*, 46. Paul Du Véou, a captain in the Légion d'Orient, wrote that more than 180,000 Lebanese died from hunger. See Paul Du Véou, *La Passion de la Cilicie 1919–1922* (Paris: Librairie Orientaliste Paul Geuthner, 1937), 57. In his correspondence with me on May 8, 2021, Christian Taoutel, chair of the Department of History and curator of the Jesuits' archives at Saint Joseph University, put the number of dead according to the Maronite Church at 250,000, and according to Jesuits' sources between 180,000 and 200,000.

96. I grew up in Hazmieh, a suburb of Beirut, where a Turkish cemetery is located. My great-grandmother and grandfather often told stories about harsh Turkish rule in Mount Lebanon including the Great Famine. I viewed the film *Safar Barlik* during a special event at my middle school, the Carmelite Fathers in Hazmieh.

97. Commissioned by Saint Joseph University, Beirut, and writer Ramzi Toufic Salame, the Memory Tree commemorates the estimated 200,000 people who died in the famine between 1915 and 1918.

98. My interview on August 3, 2022, with a Maronite bishop and spokesperson of the Church who preferred to remain anonymous. To be sure, the Great Famine is still a focus of controversy among the Maronite clergy. Some priests have deep resentment toward Turkey and its legacy in Lebanon, including the massacres of 1860 and the Great famine. They frown upon Turkey's relationship with Lebanon. I held many discussions on Turkey with local priests in Baabda district, Mount Lebanon.

CHAPTER 5

1. Sylvia Haim, ed., *Arab Nationalism: An Anthology* (Berkeley: University of California Press, 1962), 7.

2. Bassam Tibi, *Arab Nationalism: A Critical Enquiry*, second edition (New York: St. Martin's Press, 1990), 92.

3. Zeine Zeine, *Arab-Turkish Relations and the Emergence of Arab Nationalism* (Beirut: Khayat's, 1958), 59.

4. H. A. R. Gibb, *Modern Trends in Islam* (Chicago: University of Chicago Press, 1947), 33.

5. Tibi, *Arab Nationalism*, 93.

6. Haim, *Arab Nationalism*, 21.

7. Ibid., 26.

8. Tibi, *Arab Nationalism*, 94.

9. George Antonius, *The Arab Awakening: The Story of the Arab National Movement* (Beirut: Librairie du Liban, 1969), 54.

10. Haim, *Arab Nationalism*, 81.

11. Antonius, *Arab Awakening*, 108–20; Eliezer Be'eri, *Army Officers in Arab Politics and Society* (New York: Praeger, 1970), 327; for a detailed account on Arab societies see Eliezer Tauber, *The Emergence of Arab Movements* (London: Frank Cass, 1993).

12. Tibi, *Arab Nationalism*, 111.

13. C. E. Dawn, "The Origins of Arab Nationalism," in *The Origins of Arab Nationalism*, ed. Rashid Khalidi, Lisa Anderson, Muhammad Muslih, and Reeva S. Simon (New York: Columbia University Press, 1991), 56; Philip S. Khoury, *Urban Notables and Arab Nationalism* (Cambridge: Cambridge University Press, 1983), 23.

14. See text of Sykes-Picot Agreement in Antonius, *Arab Awakening*, 428–30.

15. Walter Laqueur and Barry Rubin, eds., *The Israel-Arab Reader: A Documentary History of the Middle East Conflict*, 5th edition (New York: Penguin, 1995), 16.

16. Arab Office, *The Future of Palestine* (Westport, CT: Hyperion, 1976), 99.

17. See text of the agreement in Laqueur and Rubin, *Israel-Arab Reader*, 17–19.

18. Ibid., 19.

19. Yehoshua Porath, *The Emergence of the Palestinian-Arab National Movement: 1918–1929*, Vol. 1 (London: Frank Cass, 1974), 81.

20. Antonius, *Arab Awakening*, 287.

21. See text in ibid., 440–42.

22. See King-Crane Commission Recommendations in Laqueur and Rubin, *Israel-Arab Reader*, 21–28.

23. Kamal S. Salibi, *The Modern History of Lebanon* (London: Weidenfeld and Nicolson, 1965), 162.

24. See *Covenant of the League of Nations* (Geneva, 1924), https://www.ungeneva .org/en/library-archives/league-of-nations/covenant.

25. See the text of British Mandate in Laqueur and Rubin, *Israel-Arab Reader*, 30–36; see also Helen Miller Davis, *Constitutions, Electoral Laws, Treaties of the States in the Near and Middle East* (Durham, NC: Duke University Press, 1953), 328. For a comprehensive account on religion, national identity, and confessional politics in Lebanon, see Robert G. Rabil, *Religion, National Identity, and Confessional Politics in Lebanon: The Challenge of Islamism* (New York: Palgrave Macmillan, 2011).

26. Adel Ismail, *Le Liban, Documents Diplomatiques et Consulaires Relatifs a L'Histoire du Liban*, Vol. XIX (Beirut: Editions des Oeuvres Politiques et Historiques, 1979), 18.

27. See Kamal Salibi, "Islam and Syria in the Writings of Henri Lammens," in *Historians of the Middle East*, ed. Bernard Lewis and P. M. Holt (London: Oxford University Press, 1962), 330–42. See also Henri Lammens, *La Syrie, Precis Historique* (Beirut: Imprimerie Catholique, 1921).

28. Yusuf al-Sawda, *Fi Sabil Lubnan* (For Lebanon) (Alexandria: Madrasat al-Farir al-Sina'iyah, 1919), 15. Quote first cited from Asher Kaufman, "Phoenicianism: The Formation of an Identity in Lebanon in 1920," *Middle East Studies* 37, no. 1 (January 2001).

29. Maurice Barres's concept of nationalism was based on pride in tradition and heritage, patriotic spirit of Catholicism, and geographical determinism as a determinant of the unique national character of France. Barres's concept was an intellectual fodder to Phoenicianists, who took pride in the glory of their Phoenician heritage, Catholic Maronitism, and the unique national character of Lebanon. Even Corm's title apparently took its inspiration from *La Colline Inspirée*, by Barres. See Maurice Barres, *La Colline Inspirée* (Paris: Plon-Nourrit, 1922), and *Le Culte du Moi* (Paris: Plon-Norrit, 1922). See Charles Corm, *La Montagne Inspirée*; *Chasons de Geste*, second ed. (Beirut: Editions de La Revue Phenicienne, 1964).

30. See E. P. Hoyek, "Les Revendications du Liban, Memoire de La Delegation Libanaise a la Conference de la Paix," in *La Revue Phenicienne*, ed. David Corm & Fils (Beirut: Edition Maison D'Art, Juillet 1919). It's noteworthy that the notion of Mount Lebanon as a historical refuge for the persecuted manifesting its own national character uniqueness has been reconsidered by none other than Kamal Salibi and his student Abdulrahim Abu Husayn. Abu Husayn pointed out that Salibi, throughout the latter part of his career, sought to "understand and debunk the nationalist myths espoused by Lebanese nationalists and partisans of its individual communities alike." In his view, the critical assessment of Lebanese history and historiography was Salibi's opus, *A House of Many Mansions*, which challenged the entire field of Lebanese history, including Salibi's previous works. In *A House of Many Mansions*, Salibi wrote that

> The whole concept of Lebanon as a historical mountain refuge for the persecuted of Syria rests on the assumption that the Islamic state never succeeded in establishing full dominance over the rugged mountains. When the facts are examined, however, an entirely different picture emerges. Beginning from the time of the Arab conquest, Islamic control was never absent from the Lebanon mountains except at the time of the Crusades. . . . All things considered, the Muslim rulers of Syria, except for the Ottomans after 1841, did not recognize a special autonomous status for the Lebanon mountains. They simply accorded the local Maronites, Druzes and Shiites the treatment which the Islamic states normally reserved for tribes.

This opus, to use Abu Husayn's term, in which "facts are examined" does not include one single footnote citing Salibi's factual sources supporting his reconsidered history and historiography of Lebanon. A critical yet popular rationale about Salibi's revised work claims that Salibi was so distressed by the civil war that he sought to create a national myth shared by all antagonistic sects in Lebanon, which had neither unique history nor standing under Muslim rule. For Abu Husayn's quotes, see

Abudlrahim Abu Husyan, "Kamal Salibi, 1929–2011," *Review of Middle East Studies* 45, no. 2 (Winter 2011): 297–99; for Salibi's quote, see Kamal Salibi, *A House of Many Mansions: The History of Lebanon Reconsidered* (London: I. B. Tauris, 1988), 139–44.

31. On the formation of modern Lebanon, see Meir Zamir, *The Formation of Modern Lebanon* (London: Croom Helm, 1985).

32. Franck Salameh, *Language, Memory and Identity in the Middle East: The Case of Lebanon* (New York: Lexington Books, 2010), 47.

33. The French systematically amended some of these decrees and issued new ones so as to overhaul the system in line with their overall policies, including, for example, the abolition of the upper house (Senate) in the chamber of deputies (Representation Council). For French policies under the mandate, see Zamir, *Formation of Modern Lebanon*; and Edmond Rabbath, *La Formation Historique du Liban Politique et Constitutionnel* (Beirut: Librairie Orientale, 1973).

34. On the *Mutasarifiyah* see Asa'd Rustum, *Lubnan fi 'Ahd al-Mutasarifiyyah* (Lebanon under the Era of the Mutasarifiyyah) (Beirut: Dar al-Nahar Lil-Nashr, 1973); see also Kamal Salibi, *Modern History of Lebanon*.

35. Farid el-Khazen, *The Communal Pact of National Identities: The Making and Politics of the 1943 National Pact* (Oxford: Centre for Lebanese Studies, October 1991), 10.

36. On the most comprehensive account of Syria's Arab nationalist politics during the mandate, see Philip Khoury, *Syria and the French Mandate: The Politics of Arab Nationalism, 1920–1945* (Princeton, NJ: Princeton University Press, 1987).

37. See Rania Maktabi, "The Lebanese Census of 1932 Revisited: Who Are the Lebanese?" *British Journal of Middle Eastern Studies* 26, no. 2 (1999): 219–41.

38. See the communique addressed to the French High Commissioner by the Patriarchate on February 6, 1935, in Rabbath, *Formation Historique du Liban*, 407–8.

39. Khazen, *Communal Pact of National Identities*, 10.

40. Ibid., 34–37.

41. See Khoury, *Syria and the French Mandate*, 486–93.

42. See Raghid Solh, "The Attitude of the Arab Nationalists towards Greater Lebanon during the 1930s," in *Lebanon: A History of Conflict and Consensus*, ed. Nadim Shehadi and Dana Haffar Mills (London: I. B. Tauris, 1988), 149–61.

43. Out of a total resident population of 793,396, the Maronites numbered 227,800 (28.8 percent), the Sunnis 178,100 (22.4 percent), and the Shi'a 155,035 (19.6 percent). The Maronites, being the largest sect, were allocated the powerful office of the president of the republic; the Sunnis, the second largest sect, were allocated the premiership; and the Shi'a, the third largest sect, were allocated the position of speaker of parliament. The distribution of parliamentary seats was set up at Christian to Muslim ratio of six to five, and government positions were also distributed according to the six-to-five ratio. For the official results of the census, see a copy of the census as it appeared in the official gazette in Maktabi, "Lebanese Census of 1932," 223.

44. The celebrated term "Arab Face" was first mentioned in Solh's speech on October 7, 1943, which is considered the formal enunciation of the National Pact. See text of the speech in Basim al-Jisr, *Mithaq 1943, Limadha Kan? Wa Hal Saqat?* (National

Pact 1943, Why It Was Founded? Did It Collapse?) (Beirut: Dar al-Nahar lil-Nashr, 1978), 485–95; the other celebrated theme "No East, No West" was emphasized by Khoury, while advocating a special relationship with the Arab world. Al-Jisr, *Mithaq 1943, Limadha Kan?* 482–84. Both quotes were first cited from El-Khazen.

45. See A. B. Gaunson, *The Anglo-French Clash in Lebanon and Syria, 1940–1945* (London: Macmillan, 1987).

46. Georges Catroux, *Dans la Bataille de la Mediterranee, Egypte, Levant, Afrique du Nord, 1940–1944. Temoignages et Commentaires* (Paris: R. Julliard, 1949), 259.

47. See Pierre Rondot, *Les Institutions Politiques du Liban, des Communautes Traditionnelles a L'etat Moderne* (Paris: Imprimerie Nationale, 1947), 65–66.

48. Rodger Shanahan, *The Shi'a of Lebanon: Clans, Parties and Clerics* (London: I. B. Tauris, 2005), 29–32.

49. For a detailed account on the Shi'a during the French mandate see Tamara Chalabi, *The Shi'is of Jabal Amil and the New Lebanon: Community and Nation-State, 1918–1943* (New York: Palgrave Macmillan, 2006).

50. On Christian movements and currents during this episode in Lebanon's modern history, see Walid Phares, *Lebanese Christian Nationalism: The Rise & Fall of an Ethnic Resistance* (Boulder, CO: Lynne Rienner, 1995), 85–90.

51. For example, the Syrian Social Nationalist Party, founded by the Greek Orthodox Antun Sa'ada in the 1930s, advocated Syrian nationalism, as opposed to Arab nationalism. On Syrian Social Nationalist Party (SSNP) ideology, see Labib Zuwiyya Yamak, *The Syrian Social Nationalist Party: An Ideological Analysis* (Cambridge, MA: Harvard University Press, 1966). This party cofounded both Muslims and Christians.

52. Georges Naccache, *L'Orient*, March 10, 1949, reproduced in *Un Reve Libanais: 1943–1972* (Beirut: Editions du Monde Arabe, 1983), 57–58. Quote first cited from Salameh and Phares.

53. El-Khazen, *Communal Pact of National Identities*, 68.

54. Yusri Hazran, "The Origins of Sectarianism in the Fertile Crescent and Egypt," *British Journal of Middle Eastern Studies* 40, no. 2 (1917): 162–82.

CHAPTER 6

1. On Hashemite regional ambitions and postwar Arab politics, see Patrick Seale, *The Struggle for Syria: A Study of Post-War Arab Politics, 1945–1958* (Oxford: Oxford University Press, 1965).

2. For details on the opposition to President al-Khoury, see Nicolas Nassif, *Camille Chamoun: Akher al-'Amalikah* (Camille Chamoun: The Last of the Giants) (Beirut: Dar al-Nahar lil-Nashr, 1988), 31–52.

3. President Chamoun refused to form a cabinet mostly populated by members of the National Socialist Front, as its leader Jumblatt expected. Moreover, Chamoun and Jumblatt had different views about introducing reforms. Whereas the former supported reforms through the Lebanese system at the hands of meritorious officials, the

latter supported first and foremost reforming the confessional system. For details see Nassif, *Camille Chamoun*, 69–70.

4. Robert G. Rabil, "Lebanon-Turkey Relations: Reclaiming the 'Sword' and 'Crescent' of Islam," *Asian Journal of Middle Eastern and Islamic Studies* 15, no. 1 (2021): 86.

5. Camille Chamoun, *Crise Au Moyen-Orient* (Paris: Gallimard, 1963), 376.

6. Rabil, "Lebanon-Turkey Relations," 87.

7. Fawwaz Traboulsi, *A History of Modern Lebanon* (New York: Pluto Press, 2007), 132–33; see also Rabil, "Lebanon-Turkey Relations," 87.

8. Office of the Historian, "The Eisenhower Doctrine, 1957," US State Department, https://history.state.gov/milestones/1953-1960/eisenhower-doctrine.

9. John Foster Dulles, *Economic and Military Cooperation with Nations in the General Area of the Middle East* (Washington, DC: GPO, January 1957), 2–5.

10. Department of State, *AFP: Current Documents 1957* (Washington, DC: GPO, 1961), 816–17.

11. Nassif, *Camille Chamoun*, 87.

12. Ibid., 86–87.

13. Kamal Salibi, "Lebanon under Fuad Chehab, 1958–1964," *Middle Eastern Studies* 2, no. 3 (April 1966): 215.

14. Nassif, *Camille Chamoun*, 92–97; see also Office of the Historian, "Eisenhower Doctrine."

15. Nassif, *Camille Chamoun*, 98.

16. The Phalange party (Kata'ib) was founded by Pierre Gemayel in 1936. Its program rested on safeguarding the political autonomy and authority of the Maronites in Lebanon against Arab Muslim pretensions. The Phalange party defined Lebanon as a historical political community with Maronitism, which Gemayel equated with patriotism, as its basis. On the Phalange (later on Lebanese Forces) and Lebanon's domestic and regional politics, especially the Arab-Israeli conflict, see Robert G. Rabil, *Embattled Neighbors: Syria, Israel, and Lebanon* (Boulder, CO: Lynne Rienner, 2003), 46–47, 54–55, 59–62, and 68.

17. Chamoun, *Crise au Moyen-Orient*, 384–420.

18. My interview with senior Lebanese official and former ambassador to Turkey, who asked that his identity remain anonymous, on May 13, 2022.

19. Ibid.

20. Fouad Chehab served as president of Lebanon from 1958 until 1964. His reign was known for supporting state institutions as pillars of stability in a country and region buffeted by Cold War and Arab Cold War politics. Nicolas Nassif, *Joumhouriyat Fouad Chehab* (The Republic of Fouad Chehab) (Beirut: Dar an-Nahar, 2008).

21. Kamal Jumblatt, *Haqiqat al-Thawrah al-Lubnaniyah* (The Truth about the Lebanese Revolution) (Beirut: Dar al-Nashr al-'Arabiyah, 1959), 155.

22. Ibid., 173; quote cited first in Malcolm H. Kerr, "Book Reviews: Lebanese Views on the 1958 Crisis," *Middle East Journal* 15, no. 2 (Spring 1961), 213.

23. Ferenc A. Váli, *Bridge across the Bosporus: The Foreign Policy of Turkey* (Baltimore: Johns Hopkins Press, 1972), 314.

24. Ibid., 314.

25. Michael Bishku, "Turkey and Its Middle Eastern Neighbors since 1945," *Journal of South Asian and Middle Eastern Studies* 15, no. 3 (Spring 1992): 66.

26. Suha Bolukbasi, "Behind the Turkish-Israeli Alliance: A Turkish View," *Journal of Palestine Studies* 29, no. 1 (Autumn 1999): 26.

27. For details on the Cyprus crisis, see H. Salih, *Cyprus: Ethnic Political Counterpoints* (Lanham, MD: University Press of America, 2004).

28. Bolukbasi, "Behind the Turkish-Israeli Alliance," 27.

29. Váli, *Bridge across the Bosporus*, 308.

CHAPTER 7

1. For details, see Robert G. Rabil, *Embattled Neighbors: Syria, Israel, and Lebanon* (Boulder, CO: Lynne Rienner, 2003), 46–50.

2. Ibid.

3. For details on the program of the LNM, see Marius Deeb, *The Lebanese Civil War* (New York: Praeger, 1980), 74–77.

4. Kamal Jumblatt, *Lubnan wa Harb al-Taswiyah* (Lebanon and the War for a Settlement) (N.p.: Center of Socialist Studies, Progressive Socialist Party, 1977), 19–21. See also Kamal Jumblatt, *Hadhihi Wasiyati* (This Is My Will) (Paris: Stok, 1978), 12–16; and Kamal Jumblatt, *Fi Majra al-Siyasah al-Lubnaniyah* (In the Course of Lebanese Politics) (Beirut: Dar al-Tali'a, 1962), 42–60.

5. Fronted by the PLO, the Muslim Camp included the Lebanese National Movement (LNM), Progressive Socialist Party, Murabitoun, Syrian Social Nationalist Party (SSNP), and Leftist parties. The mainstay of the Christian Camp included the Phalange Party and the National Liberal Party (founded by Camille Chamoun). Under the Phalange leadership of Bashir Gemayel, the Christian camp was united under the Lebanese Forces.

6. For details, see Rabil, *Embattled Neighbors*, 50–53.

7. See *New York Times*, September 11, 1957; first quoted by Philip Anderson, "'Summer Madness': The Crisis in Syria, August–October 1957," *British Journal of Middle Eastern Studies* 22, no. 1–2 (1995).

8. Ibid. It's noteworthy that, in August 1957, Syria accused the United States, Turkey, and Iraq of plotting to overthrow the government, and consequently expelled three American officials the government believed were involved in the plot.

9. *New York Times*, September 17, 1957.

10. Anderson, "Summer Madness." Reportedly, the crisis was defused on account of Soviet domestic politics.

11. Majid Khadduri, "The Alexandretta Dispute," *American Journal of International Law* 39, no. 3 (July 1945): 406–25.

12. Philip K. Hitti, *Lebanon in History: From the Earliest Times to the Present* (London: Macmillan, 1962), 372–75.

13. Farah W. Kawtharani and Lokman I. Meho, "The Kurdish Community in Lebanon," *International Journal of Kurdish Studies* 19, no 1–2 (January 2005).

14. Ibid.

15. I served as chief of emergency of the Red Cross in Baabda region, including East Beirut, during the civil war. I visited most areas in East Beirut from which the Kurds were displaced.

16. Welcomed by President Asad, Ocalan took up residence in Damascus in 1980 following General Kenan Evren's military coup in Turkey. Then he established a PKK military and ideological base in the Beka' valley, which was under the control of Syrian intelligence. At the time, the Beka' valley served as a hotbed for Middle Eastern and international radical organizations, especially anti-Turkish and anti-Israeli groups. The PKK camp was near to both the Armenian Secret Army for the Liberation of Armenia (ASALA) and Democratic Front for the Liberation of Palestine's (**DFLP**'s) camps. The PKK convened two congresses in Lebanon, one in 1982 in which decisions were taken to plan PKK control of swaths of southeastern Turkey. At the time, Turkey had virtually no military presence in Lebanon. The only Turkish individual who came to enjoy wide respect and was considered as legendary and "Lebanese at heart" among Lebanese was Timur Goksel. He spent most of his thirty-five-year career with the United Nations at **UNIFIL**, first as a spokesman and then as a senior adviser. United Nations Interim Force in Lebanon (UNIFIL) is a UN peacekeeping mission initially established on March 19, 1978, in southern Lebanon by UN Security Council Resolutions 425 and 426 to confirm Israel's withdrawal from Lebanon, which Israel had invaded a few days prior as part of its military Litani operation to destroy PLO military bases south of the Litani river and to ensure that the government of Lebanon would restore its effective authority in the area (see more information on UNIFIL in the next chapter). Goksel liaised with most political and militant groups in Lebanon, which considered him as reliable and running a "bullshit-free" zone. Moreover, Goksel helped Turkish and international journalists tread the dangerous waters of Lebanon. Journalists found a warm welcome in his Naqoura headquarters. He also was a founding editor of *Al-Monitor's Turkey Pulse*. I was fairly informed about the radical organizations operating in the 1980s in the Beka' valley. See Aytac Kadioglu, "Not Our War: Iraq, Iran and Syria's Approaches towards the PKK," *Cesran International-Center for Strategic Research and Analysis* 9, no. 1 (Winter 2019), https://cesran.org/not-our-war-iraq-iran-and-syrias-approaches-towards-the-pkk.html. See also *The Workers' Party of Kurdistan (PKK)*, Ministry of Foreign Affairs–Turkey, 2008, https://irp.fas.org/world/para/docs/mfa-t-pkk-s.htm. On Timur Goksel see his interview with Jean E. Krasno on March 17, 1998, as transcribed by United Nations Digital Library, available at https://digitallibrary.un.org/record/503181?ln=en. Goksel succumbed to COVID-19 in his beloved Beirut, where he had lived since his retirement from UNIFIL in 2003. See Andrew Parasilit, "Timur Goksel, Former Al-Monitor Editor and UN Diplomat, Dies," *Al-Monitor*, February 23, 2021, https://www.al-monitor.com/originals/2021/02/timur-goksel-former-almonitor-editor-and-un-diplomat-dies.html.

17. Acting in my capacity as chief of emergency of the Red Cross in Baabda region, I was familiar with the policies and actions of the various domestic and regional actors in Lebanon. For details on the civil war and Syria's actions in Lebanon, see Rabil, *Embattled Neighbors*.

18. I often discussed off-the-cuff political conditions and actions by various militant groups in Lebanon with Christian and militia leaders. Christian leaders were more interested in Turkish illicit drug activity in Lebanon than in the PKK.

19. For details on the agreement and Israel-Turkish relations, see Mustafa Kibaroğlu, "Turkey and Israel Strategize," *Middle East Quarterly* 9, no. 1 (Winter 2002); and Michael Eisenstadt, "Turkish-Israeli Military Cooperation: An Assessment," *Policy Watch* 262 (July 24, 1997).

20. Michael B. Bishku, "Turkish-Syrian Relations: A Checkered History," *Middle East Policy* 19, no. 3 (Fall 2012).

21. Efraim Inbar, "Regional Implications of the Israeli-Turkish Strategic Partnership," *Turkish Studies* 3, no. 2 (Autumn 2002).

22. Kawtharani and Meho, "The Kurdish Community in Lebanon."

23. Avedis K. Sanjiah, *The Armenian Communities in Syria and under Ottoman Dominion* (Cambridge, MA: Harvard University Press, 1965), 59.

24. See ibid., 60–61; Scott Abramson, "Lebanese Armenians: A Distinctive Community in the Armenian Diaspora and in Lebanese Society," *Levantine Review* 2, no. 2 (Winter 2013): 189.

25. According to Bayard Dodge, following the independence of the Republic of Turkey and its embrace of the slogan "Turkey for the Turks," a population exchange took place between Turkey and Macedonia. More specifically, "Over 100,000 Armenians found their way into Syria, as they were obliged to leave their homes in Turkey. The Near East Relief brought down 7,000 of its orphans from the north and placed them in temporary quarters in Jbail, Ghazir, Sidon, Aleppo, and other places. Over 60,000 refugees lived in wretched wooden huts near the Beirut River." Bayard Dodge, *The American University of Beirut* (Beirut: Khayat's, 1958), 55.

26. Abramson, "Lebanese Armenians," 191. See also Hilmar Kaiser, "The Armenians in Lebanon during the Armenian Genocide," in *Armenians of Lebanon: From Past Princesses and Refugees to Present Day Community*, ed. Aida Boudjikanian (Beirut: Haigazian University & Armenian Heritage Press, 2009).

27. I am familiar with Armenian demography in Lebanon and have maintained personal relationships with a number of Armenians.

28. Ohannes Geukjian, "The Policy of Positive Neutrality of the Armenian Political Parties in Lebanon during the Civil War, 1975–90: A Critical Analysis," *Middle Eastern Studies* 43, no. 1 (January 2007): 65–66.

29. Ibid.

30. Ibid., 67.

31. I was familiar with some of the support the Armenian churches gave to the Christian community and Christian leadership. For example, the Mekhitarist (Mekhitarian) Church built a dispensary in Hazmieh, a suburb in East Beirut, on land owned by the church. The dispensary served as the headquarters of the Red Cross and the Fire Department in Baabda region. The church also provided food and temporary shelter to internally displaced Christians. I also knew a number of Armenian fighters and senior members in the Phalange party and National Liberal party. On the other hand, some Marxist Armenians joined the Communist party and fought among their ranks against Christian militias.

32. Suha Bolukbasi, "Behind the Turkish-Israeli Alliance: A Turkish View," *Journal of Palestine Studies* 29, no. 1 (Autumn 1999): 31. It was no secret in Lebanon that Syria provided military assistance to both the PKK and ASALA in the Beka' valley. Syria also endorsed the PLO's military training of both parties until President Asad had a falling out with PLO leader Yasser Arafat, who escaped to Tripoli from the Beka' before being forced to leave for Tunis in December 1983.

33. For the name and date of states that recognized the Armenian genocide, see the Ministry of Foreign Affairs of the Republic of Armenian, https://www.mfa.am/en/recognition/.

CHAPTER 8

1. Alexander Murinson, "The Strategic Depth Doctrine of Turkish Foreign Policy," *Middle Eastern Studies* 42, no. 6 (November 2006): 945–64; Joshua W. Walker, "Learning Strategic Depth: Implications of Turkey's New Foreign Policy Doctrine," *Insight Turkey* 9, no. 3 (2007): 32–47; Ahmet Davutoglu, "Turkey's Foreign Policy Vision: An Assessment of 2007," *Insight Turkey* 10, no. 1 (2008): 77–96.

2. F. Stephen Larrabee and Ian O. Lesser, *Turkish Foreign Policy in an Age of Uncertainty* (Santa Monica, CA: RAND Corporation, 2003), 127.

3. Much has been written on Mustafa Kemal (Atturk) and Kemalism as a state ideology; see Soner Cagaptay, *Islam, Secularism and Nationalism in Modern Turkey: Who Is a Turk?* (London: Routledge, 2006); Muammer Kaylan, *The Kemalists: Islamic Revival and the Fate of Secular Turkey* (Amherst, NY: Prometheus Books, 2005).

4. M. Ataman, "Özal Leadership and Restructuring of Turkish Ethnic Policy in the 1980s," *Middle Eastern Studies* 38, no. 4 (2002): 133.

5. Davutoglu, "Turkey's Foreign Policy Vision," 79. On reconfiguring Turkey's foreign policy on the basis of its optimal geographic location, Davutoglu emphasized:

> Turkey's geography gives it a specific central country status, which differs from other central countries. For example, Germany is a central country in central Europe, which is far from Asia and Africa. Russia is another central country in the lands of Europe and Asia, which is far from Africa. Iran is a central country in Asia, which is far from Europe and Africa. Taking a broader, global view, Turkey holds an optimal place in the sense that it is both an Asian and European country and is also close to Africa through the eastern Mediterranean. A central country with such an optimal geographic location can not define itself in a defensive manner. It should be seen neither as a bridge country which only connects two points, nor a frontier country, nor indeed as an ordinary country, which sits at the edge of the Muslim world or the West.

Ibid., 78.

6. For details on the Hariri assassination and its ramifications for Lebanese politics, see Robert G. Rabil, *Syria, the United States, and the War on Terror in the Middle East* (Westport, CT: Praeger Security International, 2006), 168–81.

7. Special Tribunal for Lebanon, August 18, 2020, https://www.stl-tsl.org/crs/assets /Uploads/ 20200818-F3840-PUBLIC-Summary-of-Judgment-FILED-EN-FINAL. pdf.

8. Özlem Tür, "Turkish-Syrian Relations—Where Are We Going?" The Research Unit on International Security and Cooperation (UNISCI) Discussion Papers Núm. 23, Mayo 2010 (Universidad Complutense de Madrid, Madrid, España), 163–75. Murinson, "Strategic Depth Doctrine of Turkish Foreign Policy," 956.

9. It's noteworthy that long-serving UN diplomat, spokesperson, and senior adviser of UNIFIL was Turkish Timur Goksel, who liaised with most political and militant groups active in Lebanon and was highly respected in Beirut and among journalists. He was viewed as a legendary figure for his honesty, diplomacy, and reliability, and was perceived as "Lebanese at heart." He passed away in 2021 in Beirut. See note 16 in chapter 7.

10. I was on a field research trip to Lebanon when the Hezbollah-Israel conflagration erupted. Turkish criticism of and popular demonstrations against Israel were broadcast on various Lebanese TV channels, such as LBCI, and Qatar's al-Jazeera.

11. According to Security Council resolutions 425 (1978) and 426 (1978) of March 19, 1978, UNIFIL was established to confirm the withdrawal of Israeli forces from southern Lebanon; restore international peace and security; and assist the government of Lebanon in ensuring the return of its effective authority in the area. According to Security Council resolution 1701 (2006) of August 11, 2006, UNIFIL, in addition to carrying out its mandate under resolutions 425 and 426, shall monitor the cessation of hostilities; accompany and support the Lebanese armed forces as they deploy throughout the South, including along the Blue Line, as Israel withdraws its armed forces from Lebanon; coordinate its activities referred to in the preceding paragraph (above) with the government of Lebanon and the government of Israel; extend its assistance to help ensure humanitarian access to civilian populations and the voluntary and safe return of displaced persons; assist the Lebanese Armed Forces (LAF) in taking steps toward the establishment between the Blue Line and the Litani river of an area free of any armed personnel, assets, and weapons other than those of the government of Lebanon and of UNIFIL deployed in this area; assist the government of Lebanon, at its request, in securing its borders and other entry points to prevent the entry in Lebanon without its consent of arms or related materiel. By this resolution, the council also authorized UNIFIL to take all necessary action in areas of deployment of its forces and as it deems within its capabilities, to ensure that its area of operations is not utilized for hostile activities of any kind. United Nations Interim Force in Lebanon (UNIFIL), United Nations, https://unifil.unmissions.org/unifil-mandate. See also Republic of Turkey, Ministry of Foreign Affairs, *Relations between Turkey and Lebanon*, http://www.mfa.gov.tr/relations-between-turkey-and-lebanon.en.mfa.

12. Reliefweb, OCHA Services, "Turkish Humanitarian Aid to Lebanon and Syria as of 8 August 2006," https://reliefweb.int/report/lebanon/turkish-humanitarian-aid -lebanon-and-syria-08-aug-2006.

The civil society organizations that provided aid to Lebanon included the Light House Organization, Humanitarian Aid Foundation, Turkish Kidney Foundation, and the International Istanbul Brotherhood and Cooperation Association. The Turkish government also provided humanitarian aid to Lebanese refugees in Syria, who numbered approximately 160,000. Even the Turkish ambassador to Israel, emphasizing Ankara's historical, geographical, and humanitarian responsibility to be at the forefront of emergency relief to the region, suggested that a humanitarian aid corridor be established between Damascus and Beirut, with the Mersin port in Turkey as the international center for humanitarian aid delivery.

13. This view was prevalent in Beirut during and after war, as I witnessed.

14. Cagil Kasapoglu, "Lebanon Mission Launchpad for Turkey's Foreign Policy Agenda," *Daily Star*, June 25, 2009.

15. Cagil Kasapoglu and Mohammed Zaateri, "Turkish Minister Highlights Need for Regional Peace and Stability," *Daily Star*, August 1, 2009. See also *an-Nahar* and *as-Safir*, July 31 and August 1, 2009.

16. Turkish authorities consider the Turkmen communities in Lebanon as Turkish communities. In this respect, the Turkish communities in Lebanon include the Akkar, Ba'albeck, and Dinneyeh Turkmen, the Cretan Turks, the Circassians, and the Anatolian and Mardini Turks.

17. The Center for Middle Eastern Strategic Studies (**ORSAM**) carried out two field research trips in Lebanon to locate the Turkish communities in Lebanon. One report was published in 2010 and the other in 2015. As per its reports, ORSAM was established on January 1, 2009 in order to provide relevant information to the general public and to the foreign policy community. The institute underwent an intensive structuring process, beginning to concentrate exclusively on Middle Eastern affairs. ORSAM's research is sponsored by the Turkmeneli Cooperation and Culture Foundation. Oytun Orhan, "The Forgotten Turks: Turkmens of Lebanon," ORSAM Report 11 (February 2010). Oytun Orhan, Bilgay Duman, M. Musa Budak, and A. Selcan Özdemirci, "Turkey-Lebanon Friendship Bridge: The Turkish Presence and the Ottoman Heritage in Lebanon," ORSAM Report 199 (June 2015).

18. Orhan, Duman, Budak, and Özdemirci, "Turkey-Lebanon Friendship Bridge," 26.

19. Saban Kardas, "Davutoglu Promotes Stability in Lebanon," *Eurasia Daily Monitor* 6, no. 149 (August 4, 2009).

20. Orhan, Duman, Budak, and Özdemirci, "Turkey-Lebanon Friendship Bridge," 26.

21. TIKA is a government agency within the office of the prime minister. It organizes the bulk of Turkey's official development assistance to developing countries, focusing on Turkic countries and Turkish communities. For information on TIKA and its projects, see its Arabic website, https://www.tika.gov.tr/ar.

22. Naim Bourjaoui, "Lubnan wa Turkiyah . . . 30 Itifaqiyat Ta'awun fi 7 'Uqud min al-Ukhuwah" (Lebanon and Turkey . . . 30 Agreements of Cooperation during 7 Decades of Brotherhood) *Anadolu Agency,* February 1, 2022.

23. In 2012, the Disaster and Emergency Management Presidency (**AFAD**), an agency of the Ministry of Interior, laid the foundation for a school in Akkar. A water supply network and a reservoir were constructed. Mosques and churches were repaired and sports fields were built. Most of the construction work took place in Akkar region.

24. The Beirut Yunus Emre Turkish Culture Center promoted the teaching of Turkish language in schools funded by Turkey, as well as "Turkish Science" at the Lebanese University, the Faculty of Arts and Humanities. See the center's Facebook page: https://www.facebook.com/yeeBeyrutt/.

For information on Presidency for Turks Abroad and Related Communities, see its official website: https://en.afad.gov.tr/about-us. For information on TIKA, including its work in Lebanon, see its official website: https://www.aa.com.tr/en/middle -east/turkeys-tika-provides-aid-to-families-in-lebanon-/1864389. Dozens of civil society organizations were established in Lebanon. Important organizations include "Lebanese Turkmen Association (Qawashra), Lebanon Turkish Fraternity Association (Qawashra), Lebanon Turkish Culture Association (Aydamun), Duris Social Solidarity Association (Duris), Lebanese Turkish Association (Tripoli), Uli Al Nuha (Tripoli), Lebanese Turkish Friendship Association (Tripoli), Lebanon Turkmani Association (Tripoli), Association for Developing Lebanon-Turkey Relations (Tripoli), Jil Mustakbel (Beirut), Lebanon Turkish Forum (Beirut), Lebanon Turkish Youth Association (Beirut), Saida Lebanese Turkish Friendship Association (Saida). All these associations work for improving the conditions of Lebanese Turkmen, preserving Turkmen culture and language, developing Turkey-Lebanon relations, increasing social interaction between Turkey and Lebanon, and enhancing Turkey's image in Lebanon." Orhan, Duman, Budak, and Özdemirci, "Turkey-Lebanon Friendship Bridge," 28.

25. Khaled Omar Tadmori received undergraduate, master's, and doctorate scholarships from the Turkish Ministry of National Education, Lebanese-Turkish Friendship. He received his master's degree in Architectural Restoration and Evaluation of Historical Urban Sites, Faculty of Architecture, Department of Restoration, Mimar Sinan University, Istanbul, Turkey and his PhD in Preservation and Renovation of Historical Urban Sites, Department of City Planning, Mimar Sinan University, Istanbul, Turkey. His CV is available at http://www.araburban.com/files/file/CDS/CV/ Khaled%20Tadmori%20CV.pdf.

Dr. Tadmori's current and future restoration projects include some of the most important Ottoman landmarks: المولوية الدراويش تكية (Mawlawiyah Darawish Lodge (of dervish order)), العظم حمام (Al-Azam Turkish Bath), السنجق بك محمود جامع (Mahmoud Bek al-Sanjak Mosque), الزعيم لطفي محمود جامع (Mahmoud Lutfi al-Za'im Mosque), الجامع الحميدي (Al-Hamidi Mosque), باشا محمد الوزير الباشا سبيل (Water Pasha Kiosk of Minister Muhammad Pasha), الزاهد سبيل (Al-Zahed Water Kiosk), القادرية التكية (Qadiriyah Dervish Order Lodge), التل ساعة (Al-Tal Clock). For details on the campaign to support Dr. Tadmori's urban planning and restoration projects to save Tripoli's landmarks and heritage, see his Facebook page at https://www.facebook.com/khaledtadmoury/.

26. "Foreign Minister Vows Turkish Citizenship for Lebanon's Turkmen," *Ahval*, August 8, 2020.

27. Bourjaoui, "Lubnan wa Turkiyah . . . 30 Itifaqiyat Ta'awun fi 7 'Uqud min al-Ukhuwah."

CHAPTER 9

1. My findings are based on a field research trip in northern Lebanon throughout June and July 2012, and on extensive discussions with former and current officials in the Lebanese army and intelligence apparatus. I also held discussions and interviewed Islamists and Salafists. I undertook further field research trips to Lebanon in summer 2015 and summer 2019. I visited dozens of refugee camps along the Syrian border, and met and interviewed many Lebanese and Syrian refugees from across the political spectrum. My research led to the publication of Robert G. Rabil, *Salafism in Lebanon: From Apoliticism to Transnational Islamism* (Washington, DC: Georgetown University Press, 2014); and Robert G. Rabil, *The Syrian Refugee Crisis in Lebanon: The Double Tragedy of Refugees and Impacted Host Communities* (Lanham, MD: Lexington Books, 2016).

2. See Secretary General of Hezbollah Nasrallah's speech on the party's Al-Ahed News website, http://www.alahednews.com.lb/essaydetails.php?eid=76648andcid =149.

3. Jessica Chasmar, "Hezbollah Should Change Name to 'Party of Satan,' Turkish Deputy PM Says," *Washington Times*, May 2, 2013.

4. The first wave of Syrian refugees to enter Lebanon from April 2011 until the beginning of 2012 settled in northern Lebanon, especially in Wadi Khaled, Tripoli, and Akkar. Many of the refugees moved in with their relatives while local communities supported the rest. Lebanese charitable organizations, mostly Islamic, such as Al-Bashaer, Beit al-Zakat, and al-Wifaq al-Khayri, along with UN and international organizations such as Caritas, UNHCR, and the International Committee of the Red Cross (ICRC), took the lead in assisting the refugees. Rabil, *Syrian Refugee Crisis in Lebanon*, 11–14, 23–24.

5. For details on the history, ideology, and politics of Jama'a Islamiyah, see Robert G. Rabil, *Religion, National Identity, and Confessional Politics in Lebanon: The Challenge of Islamism* (New York: Palgrave Macmillan, 2011).

6. See the English translation of the Jama'a's political outlook in Rabil, *Religion, National Identity, and Confessional Politics*, 153–60.

7. "Lebanese Deputy: Historical Hatred, Propaganda against Turkey Unacceptable," *Anadolu Agency*, April 25, 2015.

8. For details, see Rabil, *Salafism in Lebanon*, 21–57.

9. Awad Mustafa, "Saudi Arabia Cancels $3B Aid to Lebanon; French Weapons Deal Held," *Defense News*, February 19, 2016.

10. According to David Ignatius, "Lebanese officials worry that MBS [Muhammad Bin Salman], as the 32-year-old crown prince is known, wants to force Lebanon into his confrontation with Iran. Some Lebanese analysts complain that the Saudis treat the Hariri family, who have been bankrolled by Riyadh for decades, almost as a wholly owned subsidiary." David Ignatius, "Saudi Arabia Forcibly Detained Lebanon's Prime Minister, Sources Say," *Washington Post*, November 10, 2017.

11. Rabil, *Salafism in Lebanon*, 168.

12. This line of thought is perceptively advanced by former Lebanese parliamentarian Dr. Basem Shabb, with whom I have regular correspondence, including on

October 10, 2020, in which he expressed this view and added that Iran's attempts at eroding Arab nationalism in Lebanon has left Sunnis vulnerable to Turkish influence.

13. This is based on discussions and interviews with Islamists, Salafists, Tripoli residents, and former Lebanese officials in 2012, 2015, and 2019, including lengthy interviews with Sheikh Salem al-Rafi'I and Islamist Muhammad Ayubi on July 19, 2012.

14. A significant number of active Salafists are members of the Association of Muslim Scholars, including former president of the association, Sheik Salem al-Rafi'I, Sheikh Raed Hleihel, and Sheikh Bilal Baroudi.

15. On October 2, 2020, the association issued a statement asserting: "Palestine is an Ummah cause, and liberating and saving each grain of its land is a duty. Conceding a hand span [of Palestine] is a crime, and normalizing [relations] with the rapists is a high treason." Statement is available at https://www.facebook.com/muslimolama /photos/a.433159696812310/3118728434922076/.

16. For details on the event, see https://www.facebook.com/muslimolama/photos/ pcb.2804006373060952/28 04005646394358/.

17. The cathedral was converted into a mosque after the Ottoman conquest of Constantinople in 1453. But in 1934 the cathedral became a museum and thereafter a UNESCO World Heritage site. The association's statement is available at https:// www.facebook.com/muslimolama/photos/a.433159696812310/2891420824319506/.

18. Statement available at https://www.facebook.com/muslimolama/photos/a .433159696812310/2804932086301714/.

19. See LBC interview with Gibran Bassil, July 27, 2020. See Bassil's tweet: https: //twitter.com/Gebran_Bassil/status/1287836128549142528.

20. "Report: Lebanon Probes Millions of Dollars Brought from Turkey," *Naharnet*, July 7, 2020, http://www.naharnet.com/stories/en/273147.

21. Firas al-Shoufi, "Turkiya fi Lubnan 'ala Khat al-Ikhwan al-Muslimin: Al-Tamkin Awalan" (Turkey in Lebanon Following the Line of the Muslim Brotherhood), *al-Akhbar*, July 13, 2020.

22. Nahla Naser al-Din, "Bil-Waqae' wal-Asam': Hakaza Tuhader Turkeyah li 'Ihtilal' Tarablus" (Through Facts and Names: This Is How Turkey Prepares to 'Occupy' Tripoli), *Asasmedia*, July 12, 2020, https://www.asasmedia.com/news/386462.

23. According to the article, the first approach entailed the communication and coordination between Turkish intelligence and former internal security chief and minister of justice Ashraf Rifi; the collaboration between Turkish intelligence and al-Ahbash, which keeps it secret; and the collaboration with the forums of Nabil al-Halabi, which organizes training courses on how to mobilize the public under the supervision of Turkish intelligence. The second approach entailed the collaboration between the AKP and the Islamic Association, which focuses on educational and organizational channels. The educational channel emphasizes the Islamist ideology shared by the two parties. This channel is led in Lebanon by Dr. Chafiq Taleb, an expert in Ottoman history, who has led the campaign against Armenian claims of Turkish perpetration of Armenian genocide through a series of talks and forums. The last approach entailed the Turkish Embassy's support of civil organizations including al-Azm organization, which is affiliated with Prime Minister Najib Miqati;

collaboration with the Future Movement including with the Hariri's Foundation for Sustainable Development; and support of and coordination with the Municipality of Tripoli and the group the Guards of the City. Some of the activists involved include Dr. Jamal Badaoui, former council member of the municipality, Muhammad Showq, founder of the Guards of the City, and Nasr Mu'mari, a senior member of the Tripoli Forum. Ibid.

24. My interview with retired general Khalil Helou on May 22, 2022.

25. The *New Arab* Staff, "Turkey Denies Supporting Anti-Government Protests in Northern Lebanon," *New Arab*, July 29, 2020, https://english.alaraby.co.uk/english/news/2020/7/29/turkey-denies-supporting-anti-government-protests-in-northern-lebanon.

26. During an interactive television episode on al-Jadid (New TV) on June 10, 2020, hosted by known Armenian anchor Nshan Ter-Harutyunyan, a responder on WhatsApp called him a "refugee" and accused him of racism because he referred to Turkish president Recep Tayyep Erdogan as "an obnoxious Ottoman." Ter-Harutyunyan snapped back: "You refer to Lebanese people of Armenian descent as refugees. You son of a bitch, I am more Lebanese than you." He went on to say that people in Lebanon are horrendously racist and he defended his criticism of Turkey and President Erdogan by pointing out that Turkey had slaughtered 1.5 million Armenians. No sooner had he said that than a caravan of cars surrounded the TV station in Beirut, people chanting and shouting anti-Armenian slogans. In response, Mounir Hassan, a pro-Turkey activist, posted a video on social media in which he called Ter-Harutyunyan "gay," "dog," "stupid," and "obnoxious." Hassan added, "We and our Ottoman and Turkish ancestors are proud of the massacre that our Ottoman ancestors carried out against the Armenians." Mounir Hassan is the head of the Lebanese Mardelli Assembly, the goal of which is to preserve the heritage of people hailing from Mardin, Turkey. The incident shook the Armenian community to the core. See Edmond Y. Azadian, "Turkey's Ottomanist Ambitions Target Armenians in Lebanon," *Armenian Mirror-Spectator*, June 18, 2020. The clip is available with translation by Middle East Media Research Institute (MEMRI) at https://www.memri.org/tv/armenian-lebanese-host-neshan-haroutiounian-proud-people-here-racistcriticize-turkey-genocide.

27. Observations based on my visits to many households, including those related to me, that virtually sanctified their leisure time to watch Turkish drama shows.

28. Jeyhan Aliyev, "Turkey Extends Helping Hand to Lebanon in Wake of Explosion," *Andalu Agency*, August 5, 2020.

29. Major television stations in Lebanon, such as MTV, broadcast the visit of Turkish officials, August 8 and 9, 2020. See also *an-Nahar* and *al-Liwa*,' August 8, 9, 2020; and Reuters Staff, "Turkey Says It Is Ready to Help Rebuild Port of Beirut," *Reuters*, August 8, 2020.

30. Sivan Ozmus, "Turkish Aid after the Blast Strengthening Ties with Lebanon," *Andalu Agency*, August 15, 2020, https://www.aa.com.tr/en/politics/turkish-aid-after-blast-strengthening-ties-with-lebanon/1943049.

31. Rajib Soylu, "Beirut Explosion: Turkey Ridicules Macron's Lebanon Visit as Colonialism," *Middle East Eye*, August 11, 2020, https://www.middleeasteye.net/news/beirut-explosion-turkey-macron-lebanon-visit-colonialism.

32. Timour Azhari, "In Lebanon: Macron Offers the Carrot or Stick," *al-Jazeera*, September 2, 2020, https://www.aljazeera.com/news/2020/9/2/in-lebanon-macron-offers-the-carrot-or-the-stick.

33. Soylu, "Beirut Explosion."

34. My interview with a Lebanese army general on September 14, 2014. According to the general, who asked that his identity remain anonymous, and a report by the Lebanese Center for Research and Consulting, Hezbollah was behind the kidnappings. Hezbollah controls the area from which the Syrians were kidnapped. Moreover, only Hezbollah's intelligence knew the identity and political affiliations of the hostages. The Al-Meqdad clan does not have the intelligence-gathering capabilities to identify the political affiliations and/or membership of the hostages. Hezbollah ordered the kidnapping because Hassan al-Meqdad was a senior member of the Islamist party, which wanted him released. See "Amn Hezbollah Khataf al-Raha'en wa Salamahum li-Al al-Meqdad" (Hezbollah Security Kidnapped the Hostages and Handed Them over to al-Meqdad), *Al-Markaz al-Lubnani lil-Abhath wal-Istisharat* (Lebanese Center for Research and Consulting), August 17, 2012, http://www.center-lcrc.com/news/6368.

For details, see also "Itlaq Sarah al-Makhtouf al-Turki lida Al al-Meqdad" (Release of the Abducted Turkish from al-Meqdad), *al-Mayadeen*, September 11, 2012; and Layal Abu Rahal, "Ashirat al-Meqdad Takhtouf 30 Surian and Muwaten Turki Ba'd I'tiqal 'al-Jaysh al-Hur' li-Ibniha" (Al-Meqdad Clan Kidnaps 30 Syrians and a Turkish National After the Detention of Her Son by the Free [Syrian] Army), *Ash-Sharq al-Awsat*, September 11, 2012.

35. Martin Chulov, "Turkish Airlines Pilot and Co-pilot Kidnapped in Beirut," *The Guardian*, August 9, 2013. See also "Turkish Pilots Kidnapped in Beirut Are Released and in Turkey," *Daily Sabah*, October 20, 2013.

36. The Astana peace process, sponsored by Russia, Turkey, and Iran in the Kazakh capital of Astana in early 2017, endeavored to bring about a cease-fire in Syria by creating de-escalation zones and to solve humanitarian issues as a prelude to a peace settlement. For details, see Sinem Cengiz, "Assessing the Astana Peace Process for Syria: Actors, Approaches, and Differences," *Contemporary Review of the Middle East* 7, no. 2 (2020).

37. Robert G. Rabil, "Donald Trump is Reshaping the Middle East—In Russia's Favor," *Washington Post*, August 22, 2018.

38. For details on Turkish and Saudi support of different opposition groups in Syria, see Engin Yüksel, *Strategies of Turkish Proxy Warfare in Northern Syria: Back with a Vengeance* (Clingendael, Netherlands: Clingendael Institute, November 2019); Aaron Lund, "The Syrian Rebel Who Tried to Build an Islamist Paradise," *Politico Magazine*, March 31, 2017.

39. In 2013, following mass demonstrations in response to political and economic crises in Egypt, Egyptian armed forces overthrew the first democratically elected president, Mohamed Morsi, a senior member of the Muslim Brotherhood. Whereas

Saudi Arabia and the UAE supported the ouster of Morsi, Qatar condemned it. Soon thereafter, Doha's relations with Cairo deteriorated, and Egyptian authorities shuttered Qatar's Al Jazeera television station. In March 2014, Saudi Arabia, UAE, Bahrain, and Egypt withdrew their ambassadors from Qatar, citing Qatar's "interference in their internal affairs, which Qatar denied." Tension continued to build up until June 2017, when Saudi Arabia, UAE, Bahrain, and Egypt blockaded Qatar. For details, see Alex MacDonald, "Qatar Blockade: What Caused It and Why Is It Coming to an end?" *Middle East Eye*, January 5, 2021; and Samuel Ramani, "The Qatar Blockade Is Over, But the Gulf Crisis Lives On," *Foreign Policy*, January 27, 2021.

40. Reuters Staff, "Saudi Prince Says Turkey Part of 'Triangle of Evil': Egyptian Media," March 7, 2018.

41. Since his detention (and fallout) in Saudi Arabia, Saad Hariri has tried to improve his relationship with Turkish president Erdogan. Following his nomination as prime minister–designate, approximately a year after his resignation as prime minister in October 2020, Hariri made an unannounced visit to Turkey in January 2021. He met with President Erdogan for two hours. The Turkish presidency stated that the private meeting focused on regional security issues and "deepening and strengthening ties." Observers in Lebanon reported that Hariri's real objective was both to seek President Erdogan's help in forging a government and to try to persuade the Turkish government to replace Saudi Arabia as the benefactor of Hariri and his Future Movement. Hariri had thus far failed to forge a coalition government, which some had chalked up to Saudi reservations about Hariri. Reportedly, President Erdogan offered his support of Lebanon but refrained from championing Hariri as Turkey's man in Lebanon. In fact, Hariri faced angry reactions from some Turkish officials. Owned by the Hariri family, Oger Telecom acquired 55 percent of Turk Telecom for $6.5 billion through loans from Turkish and international lenders. In 2018, Oger Telecom defaulted on paying an installment on a $4.5 billion loan and thereafter was accused of siphoning off billions of dollars to Lebanon as profit shares from Turk Telecom. According to Turkish officials, this constituted one of the largest corruption cases in Turkey. See "Lebanon's Hariri Pays Unannounced Visit to Erdogan," *Arab News*, January 8, 2021; and "Erdogan-Hariri Surprise Meeting Angers Turkish Opposition," *Arab News*, January 12, 2021.

42. "Greece's Maritime Claims 'Maximalist,' Violate International Boundaries Laws," *Daily Sabah*, May 13, 2019.

43. Galip Dalay, "Turkey, Europe, and the Eastern Mediterranean: Charting a Way out of the Current Deadlock," *Brookings*, January 28, 2021. Asli Aydintaşbaş, "Turkey: A Deal Is Possible," *European Council on Foreign Relations*, May 2020.

44. Dalay, "Turkey, Europe, and the Eastern Mediterranean"; Aydintaşbaş, "Turkey."

45. For details on the Blue Homeland doctrine, see its homepage: https://mavivatan .net/mavi-vatan-kavrami-ve-onemi/.

46. Furious with Ankara, Athens responded to the Libyan-Turkish agreement by signing a similar agreement with Egypt to delimitate their maritime jurisdictions. See Hacer Baser, "Egypt, Greece Sign Maritime Demarcation Deal," *Anadolu Agency*, June 8, 2020.

47. For details on the history of the disputed Israel-Lebanon borders and US-led efforts to mediate a solution, as well as on Russia's and China's agreements and interest in the port of Tripoli, see Robert G. Rabil, "Bordering on a Solution," *National Interest* 163 (September/October 2019) and "The Future of Non-State Actors in the Middle East: Hezbollah and al-Hashd al-Sha'bi," *Palm Beach Center for Democracy and Policy Research*, July 21, 2021.

48. Aurélien Denizeau, "Mavi Vatan, the 'Blue Homeland': The Origins, Influences and Limits of an Ambitious Doctrine for Turkey," Études de l'Ifri, *Ifri*, April 2021, 10–12.

49. Captain Hassan Safa, "Ghaz Lubnan Tharwa Wataniyah Wasat Sira' Geopolitiki 'Amiq" (Lebanon's Gas Is a National Fortune amid a Deep Geopolitical Struggle), *Al-Difa' al-Watan al-Lubnani* (Lebanese National Defense), 116 (April 2021).

CHAPTER 10

1. The Islamist National Order party was shut down in 1971, the National Salvation Party was banned in 1980, the Welfare party was outlawed in 1998, and the Virtue party was banned in 2001, all for carrying out anti-secular activities. Necmettin Erbekan led these parties and represented the leadership of political Islam in Turkey.

2. Ioannis N. Grigoriadis, "Islam and Democratization in Turkey: Secularism and Trust in Divided Society," *Democratization* 16, no. 6 (2009): 1198–99.

3. Ibid., 1199.

4. Nicola Mirenzi, "Erdogan and Secularism," *Reset Dialogues*, September 27, 2011; Ayla Albayrak and Muneef Halawa, "Islamists Criticize Turkish Premier's 'Secular' Remarks," *Wall Street Journal*, September 15, 2011.

5. Erdogan's full speech in Turkish is available at https://www.youtube.com/watch ?v=7qKm8F_DpKY. For quotes in Arabic from Erdogan's speech, see Bahi Hassan, "Erdogan fi Jami'at al-Qahira: La Aqbal al-'Udwan 'ala Ghaza . . . wa-Uhayi Morsi 'ala Sahb al-Safir" (Erdogan from Cairo University: I Don't Accept the Aggression against Ghaza . . . and I Salute Morsi for Pulling out the Ambassador), *Al-Masry Al-Youm*, November 17, 2012, https://www.almasryalyoum.com/news/details /244939.

6. Hassan, "Erdogan fi Jami'at al-Qahira"; and Sedat Ergin, "Major Blow to the Plea to Change the Course of History," *Hürriyet Daily News*, July 19, 2013.

7. Soner Cagaptay, "Erdogan's Failure on the Nile," *Washington Institute for Near East Policy*, May 28, 2019.

8. TIKA has funded forums to glorify Ottoman history. See "TIKA Tad'um Nadwa Tahta 'Unwan '1516 Sanat Taghyir al-Sharq al-Awsat wal-'Alam'" (TIKA Supports a Forum under the Headline "1516 Is the Year that Changed the Middle East and the World"), TIKA, December 23, 2016, https://www.tika.gov.tr/ar/news/detail-31634. In the year 1516, the Ottoman Empire conquered the Middle East.

9. This is based on my discussions with many Lebanese, including in the diaspora, from across Lebanon's communal and political spectrum, especially from 2017 until 2022.

10. Robert G. Rabil, "Lebanon-Turkey Relations: Reclaiming the 'Sword' and 'Crescent' of Islam," *Asian Journal of Middle Eastern and Islamic Studies* 15, no. 1 (2021).

CONCLUSION

1. Derek Chollet, "Obama's Red Line, Revisited," *Politico Magazine*, July 19, 2016; Daniel Harper, "Kerry: Obama's Failure to Enforce Red Line in Syria Came at a Cost," *New York Post*, December 5, 2016.

2. See White House, *National Security Strategy*, February 2015, https://obamawhitehouse.archives.gov/sites/default/files/docs/2015_national_security_strategy_2.pdf; and US Department of Defense, *Summary of the 2018 National Defense Strategy of the United States*, 2018, https://obamawhitehouse.archives.gov/sites/default/files/docs/2015_national_security_strategy_2.pdf.

3. Ismaeel Naar, "Saudi Arabia 'Completely Rejects' US Report's Assessment on Murder of Jamal Khashoggi," *Alarabiya News*, February 27, 2021, https://english.alarabiya.net/News/gulf/2021/02/27/Saudi-Arabia-categorically-rejects-US-report-on-murder-of-Jamal-Khashoggi-Statement.

4. Robert G. Rabil and Francois Alam, "The Biden Administration Needs a Viable Foreign Policy Multilateral Approach," *Eurasia Review*, March 23, 2021.

5. According to the US Department of Defense 2022 National Security Strategy: "The Defense priorities [of USA] are: 1. Defending the homeland, paced to the growing multi-domain threat posed by the PRC. . . . The Department will act urgently to sustain and strengthen deterrence, with the People's Republic of China (PRC) as our most consequential strategic competitor and the pacing challenge for the Department." US Department of Defense, *DOD Transmits 2022 National Defense Strategy*, March 28, 2022, https://www.defense.gov/News/Releases/Release/Article/2980584/dod-transmits-2022-national-defense-strategy/.

6. The UAE has disapproved of American foreign policy toward Syria. UAE has perceived the Caesar Act and sanctions against Damascus as harmful to the Syrian people, as well as obstacles to the UAE's cooperation with Syria. Moreover, both Saudi Arabia and UAE have consistently perceived that the US interest in Syria, as reflected in the presence of a small contingent of American forces, has not been about helping foster a solution to the Syrian civil war but more about denying a Russian victory in Syria. In response to President Asad's visit to UAE, a US state department spokesperson said that Washington was "profoundly disappointed and troubled by this apparent attempt to legitimise Bashar al-Assad, who remains responsible and accountable for the death and suffering of countless Syrians, the displacement of more than half of the prewar Syrian population, and the arbitrary detention and disappearance of over 150,000 Syrian men, women and children." See "Syria's Assad Visits UAE in First Trip to Arab State since 2011," *al-Jazeera*, March 18, 2022, https://www.aljazeera.com/news/2022/3/18/syrias-assad-visits-uae-in-first-trip-to-arab-state-since-2011.

7. See "Senior UAE Official Visits Turkey as Frosty Relations Thaw," *Arab Weekly*, August 19, 2021, https://thearabweekly.com/senior-uae-official-visits-turkey-frosty-relations-thaw.

8. "Has Abu Dhabi Crown Prince's Visit to Ankara Prompted Erdogan to Operate a Foreign Policy Reset?" *Arab Weekly*, November 30, 2021, https://thearabweekly.com/has-abu-dhabi-crown-princes-visit-ankara-prompted-erdogan-operate-foreign-policy-reset.

9. "Erdogan Visits UAE to Bolster Political, Economic Ties," *al-Jazeera*, February 14, 2022, https://www.aljazeera.com/news/2022/2/14/erdogan-to-visit-uae-to-bolster-political-economic-ties.

10. Ibid. See also "Erdogan Visits UAE to Strengthen Economic, Political Ties," *Daily Sabah*, February 14, 2022, https://www.dailysabah.com/politics/diplomacy/erdogan-visits-uae-to-strengthen-economic-political-ties.

11. "Erdogan Meets Saudi Leaders in First Visit since Kashoggi Murder," *al-Jazeera*, April 28, 2022, https://www.aljazeera.com/news/2022/4/28/turkeys-erdogan-to-visit-saudi-arabia-relations-warm.

12. Wassim Seif al-Din, "Miqati fi Ankara: Lubnan fi Amas al-Haja lil-Ta'wun wal-Musa'da min Turkiyah" (Miqati in Ankara: Lebanon Is in Most Need of Cooperation and Assistance from Turkey), *Anadolu Agency*, February 2, 2022.

13. My interview with retired senior Lebanese diplomat and former ambassador to Turkey, May 22, 2022. I conducted several interviews with the aforementioned official among other retired and current officials who asked that their identity remain anonymous.

Selected Bibliography

Abramson, Scott. "Lebanese Armenians: A Distinctive Community in the Armenian Diaspora and in Lebanese Society." *Levantine Review* 2, no. 2 (Winter 2013): 188–216.

Adib, Halidah. *Memoirs of Halidé Edib*. New York: Century Company, 1926.

Adivar, Halidé Edib. *House with Wisteria: Memoirs of Halidé Edib*. Charlottesville: Leopolis Press, 2003.

Ahmad, Ahmad Muhammad. *Akrad Lubnan wa-Tanzimuhum al-Ijtima'i wa-al-Siyasi* (The Kurds of Lebanon and their Social and Political Organization). Beirut: Maktabat al-Fakih, 1995.

Ahmad, Feroz. *The Young Turks: The Committee of Union and Progress in Turkish Politics 1908–1914*. New York: Columbia University Press, 2010, originally published by Oxford University Press in 1969.

Ahmaranian, John. "The Armenians in Lebanon." *World Lebanese Cultural Union*, April 27, 2015. https://wlcui.com/2015/04/27/the-armenians-in-lebanon-history-and-demography-by-dr-john-ahmaranian.

Ajay, Nicholas Z. "Mount Lebanon and the Wilayah of Beirut, 1914–1918: The War Years." PhD diss., Georgetown University, 1972.

———. "Political Intrigue and Suppression in Lebanon during World War I." *International Journal of Middle East Studies* 5, no. 2 (April 1974).

Al-'Aqiqi, Antun Dahir (and other documents). Translated with notes and commentary by Malcolm H. Kerr. *Lebanon in the Years of Feudalism, 1840–1868: A Contemporary Account*. Beirut: American University of Beirut, Oriental Series no. 33, 1959.

Al-Baladhuri, 'Abbas Ahmad ibn-Jabir. *Kitab Futuh al-Buldan* (The Book on the Conquests of Countries). Edited and translated by M. J. de Goege and Philip Hitti. Philip K. Hitti, *The Origins of the Islamic State: Kitab Futuh al-Buldan of 'Abbas Ahmad ibn-Jabir al-Baladhuri*. Vol. 1. New York: Columbia University Press, 1916. https://archive.org/details/originsofislamic01albauoft/page/n9/mode/2up.

Al-Dibs, Yusuf. *Al-Jami' al-Mufassal fi Tarikh al-Mawarinah al-Mu'assal* (The Detailed Collection of the True History of the Maronites). Beirut: Dar Lahd Khatir lil-Tiba'ah wal-Nashr wal-Tawzi,' 1987.

———. "Laysa al-Jarajima al-Marada" (al-Jarajima are not al-Marada) *al-Mashriq* (1903).

Al-Duwayhi, Istifan. *Asl al-Mawarinah* (Origin of the Maronites). Ihdin: Mu'assasat al-Turath al-'Ihdini, 1973.

———. *Tarikh al-Azminah* (History of Times). Beirut: Dar Lahd Khatir lil-Tiba'ah wal-Nashr wal-Tawzi', 1985.

———. *Tarikh al-Tai'fa al-Maruniyah* (The History of the Maronite Denomination). Beirut, 1980.

Al-Jisr, Basim. *Mithaq 1943, Limadha Kan? Wa Hal Saqat?* (National Pact 1943, Why It Was Founded? Did It Collapse?). Beirut: Dar al-Nahar lil-Nashr, 1978.

Al-Nusuli, Anis. *Rasa'il al-Emir Fakhr al-Din* (The Letters of the Prince Fakhr al-Din). Beirut, 1946.

Al-Sawda, Yusuf. *Fi Sabil Lubnan* (For Lebanon). Alexandria: Madrasat al-Farir al-Sina'iyah, 1919.

Al-Shihabi, Haydar Ahmad. *Lubnan fi 'Ahd al-Umara' al-Shihabiyyin* (Lebanon in the Era of the Shihabi Emirs). 3 vols., edited by Asad Rustum and Fouad E. Boustany. Beirut: Editions St. Paul, 1984.

American Committee for Armenian and Syrian Relief. *Minutes: 1915–1919*, 12. https://neareastmuseum.com/wp-content/uploads/2019/02/American-Committee -for-Armenian-and-Syrian-Relief-Meeting-Minutes-1915-1919.pdf.

Anderson, Philip. "'Summer Madness': The Crisis in Syria, August–October 1957." *British Journal of Middle Eastern Studies* 22, no. 1–2 (1995).

Andrew, Christopher M., and A. S. Kanya-Forstner. *The Climax of French Imperial Expansion 1914–1924*. Stanford, CA: Stanford University Press, 1981.

Angell, James B. "The Turkish Capitulations." *American Historical Review* 6, no. 2 (January 1901).

Antonius, George. *The Arab Awakening: The Story of the Arab National Movement*. Beirut: Librairie du Liban, 1969.

Arab Office. *The Future of Palestine*. Westport, CT: Hyperion, 1976.

Ataman, M. "Özal Leadership and Restructuring of Turkish Ethnic Policy in the 1980s." *Middle Eastern Studies* 38, no. 4 (2002).

Barres, Maurice. *La Colline Inspiree*. Paris: Plon-Nourrit, 1922.

———. *Le Culte du Moi*. Paris: Plon-Norrit, 1922.

Be'eri, Eliezer. *Army Officers in Arab Politics and Society*. New York: Praeger, 1970.

Bishku, Michael. "Turkey and Its Middle Eastern Neighbors since 1945." *Journal of South Asian and Middle Eastern Studies* 15, no. 3 (Spring 1992).

———. "Turkish-Syrian Relations: A Checkered History." *Middle East Policy* 19, no. 3 (Fall 2012).

Black, Charles E. Drummond. *The Marquess of Dufferin and Ava*. London: Hutchinson & Co., 1903.

Bolukbasi, Suha. "Behind the Turkish-Israeli Alliance: A Turkish View." *Journal of Palestine Studies* 29, no. 1 (Autumn 1999).

Cagaptay, Soner. "Erdogan's Failure on the Nile." *Washington Institute for Near East Policy*, May 28, 2019.

————. *Islam, Secularism and Nationalism in Modern Turkey: Who Is a Turk?* London: Routledge, 2006.

Catroux, Georges. *Dans la Bataille de la Mediterranee, Egypte, Levant, Afrique du Nord, 1940–1944. Temoignages et Commentaires*. Paris: R. Julliard, 1949.

Cengiz, Sinem. "Assessing the Astana Peace Process for Syria: Actors, Approaches, and Differences." *Contemporary Review of the Middle East* 7, no. 2 (2020).

Chadwick, Henry. *The Early Church*. London: Penguin, 1990.

Chalabi, Tamara. *The Shi'is of Jabal Amil and the New Lebanon: Community and Nation-State, 1918–1943*. New York: Palgrave Macmillan, 2006.

Chamoun, Camille. *Crise Au Moyen-Orient*. Paris: Gallimard, 1963.

Churchill, Colonel [Charles Henry Churchill]. *The Druzes and Maronites under the Turkish Rule: From 1840–1860*. London: Bernard Quaritch, 1862.

Cohen, Mark R. "What Was the Pact of 'Umar? A Literary-Historical Study." *Jerusalem Studies in Arabic and Islam* 23 (1999).

Corm, Charles. *La Montagne Inspiree; Chasons de Geste*. 2nd edition. Beirut: Editions de La Revue Phenicienne, 1964.

Covenant of the League of Nations (Geneva, 1924). https://www.ungeneva.org/en/library-archives/league-of-nations/covenant.

Danforth, Nicholas. "The Nonsense of 'Neo-Ottomanism.'" *War on the Rocks*, May 29, 2020.

Davis, Helen Miller. *Constitutions, Electoral Laws, Treaties of the States in the Near and Middle East* (Durham, NC: Duke University Press, 1953).

Davutoglu, Ahmet. "The Clash of Interests: An Explanation of the World (Dis)Order." *Perceptions: Journal of International Affairs* 2, no. 4 (December 1997–February 1998).

————. "Turkey's Foreign Policy Vision: An Assessment of 2007," *Insight Turkey* 10, no. 1 (2008).

Dawn, C. E. "The Origins of Arab Nationalism." In *The Origins of Arab Nationalism*, edited by Rashid Khalidi, Lisa Anderson, Muhammad Muslih, and Reeva S. Simon. New York: Columbia University Press, 1991.

Deeb, Marius. *The Lebanese Civil War*. New York: Praeger, 1980.

Denizeau, Aurélien. "Mavi Vatan, the 'Blue Homeland': The Origins, Influences and Limits of an Ambitious Doctrine for Turkey." Études de l'Ifri, *Ifri*, April 2021.

Deringil, Selim. "'The Armenian Question Is Finally Closed': Mass Conversions of Armenians in Anatolia during the Hamidian Massacres of 1895–1897." *Comparative Studies in Society and History* 51, no. 2 (April 2009).

Dodge, Bayard. *The American University of Beirut: A Brief History of the University and the Lands which It Serves*. Beirut: Khayat's, 1958.

Du Véou, Paul. *La Passion de la Cilicie 1919–1922*. Paris: Librairie Orientaliste Paul Geuthner, 1937.

Dulles, John Foster. *Economic and Military Cooperation with Nations in the General Area of the Middle East*. Washington, DC: GPO, January 1957.

Edwards, Richard. *La Syrie, 1840–1860, Histoire, Politique, Administration, Population, Religions et Mœurs, Événements de 1860 d'après des Actes Officiels et des Documents Authentiques*. Paris: AMYOT, Libraire Editeur, 1862.

Eisenstadt, Michael. "Turkish-Israeli Military Cooperation: An Assessment." *Policy Watch* 262 (July 24, 1997).

El-Khazen, Farid. *The Communal Pact of National Identities: The Making and Politics of the 1943 National Pact*. Oxford: Centre for Lebanese Studies, October 1991.

Erickson, Edward J. "Captain Larkin and the Turks: The Strategic Impact of the Operations of '*HMS Doris*' in Early 1915." *Middle Eastern Studies* 46, no. 1 (2010).

Farman, T. F. "French Claims on Syria." *Contemporary Review* 108 (July–December 1915).

Farshee, Louis. *Safer Barlik: Famine in Mount Lebanon During World War I*. Portland, OR: Inkwater Press, 2015.

Foster, Charles. "The First Crusaders in Lebanon." *Archaeology and History* 16 (Autumn 2002).

Gaunson, A. B. *The Anglo-French Clash in Lebanon and Syria, 1940–1945*. London: Macmillan, 1987.

Geukjian, Ohannes. "The Policy of Positive Neutrality of the Armenian Political Parties in Lebanon during the Civil War, 1975–90: A Critical Analysis." *Middle Eastern Studies* 43, no. 1 (January 2007).

Gibb, H. A. R. *Modern Trends in Islam*. Chicago: University of Chicago Press, 1947.

Grigoriadis, Ioannis N. "Islam and Democratization in Turkey: Secularism and Trust in Divided Society." *Democratization* 16, no. 6 (2009).

Haim, Sylvia, ed. *Arab Nationalism: An Anthology*. Berkeley: University of California Press, 1962.

Hanioğlu, M. SüKrü. *The Young Turks in Opposition*. London: Oxford University Press, 1995.

Harris, William. *Lebanon: A History 600–2011*. London: Oxford University Press, 2012.

Hazran, Yusri. "The Origins of Sectarianism in the Fertile Crescent and Egypt." *British Journal of Middle Eastern Studies* 40, no. 2 (1917).

Heraclides, Alexis, and Ada Dialla. *Humanitarian Intervention in the Long Nineteenth Century: Setting the Precedent*. Manchester: Manchester University Press, 2015.

Hitti, Philip K. *Lebanon in History: From the Earliest Times to the Present*. London: Macmillan, 1962.

———. *The Origins of the Druze People and Religion*. Andesite Press, 2017, originally published in New York in 1928.

Hojairi, Mouannes Mohammed. "Church Historians and Maronite Communal Consciousness." PhD diss., Columbia University, 2011.

Holland, Thomas Erskine. *The European Concert in the Eastern Question: A Collection of Treaties and Other Public Acts*. Oxford: Clarendon Press, 1885.

Hourani, Albert. "From Jabal 'Amil to Persia." *Bulletin of the School of Oriental and African Studies* 49, no. 1 (1986).

———. *A History of the Arab Peoples*. Cambridge, MA: Belknap, 1991.

———. *Minorities in the Arab World*. London: Oxford University Press, 1947.

Hoyek, E. P. "Les Revendications du Liban, Memoire de La Delegation Libanaise a la Conference de la Paix." In *La Revue Phenicienne*, edited by David Corm & Fils. Beirut: Edition Maison D'Art, Juillet 1919.

Inbar, Efraim. "Regional Implications of the Israeli-Turkish Strategic Partnership." Turkish Studies 3, no. 2 (Autumn 2002).

Ismail, Adel. *Le Liban, Documents Diplomatiques et Consulaires Relatifs a L'Histoire du Liban* (Beirut: Editions des Oeuvres Politiques et Historiques, Vol. XIX, 1979).

Jessup, Henry Harris. *Fifty-Three Years in Syria*. Vol. I. New York: Fleming H. Revell Company, 1910.

Jumblatt, Kamal. *Fi Majra al-Siyasah al-Lubnaniyah* (In the Course of Lebanese Politics). Beirut: Dar al-Tali'a, 1962.

———. *Hadhihi Wasiyati* (This Is My Will). Paris: Stok, 1978.

———. *Haqiqat al-Thawrah al-Lubnaniyah* (The Truth about the Lebanese Revolution). Beirut: Dar al-Nashr al-'Arabiyah, 1959.

———. *Lubnan wa Harb al-Taswiyah* (Lebanon and the War for a Settlement). N.p.: Center of Socialist Studies, Progressive Socialist Party, 1977.

Kaiser, Hilmar. "The Armenians in Lebanon during the Armenian Genocide." In *Armenians of Lebanon: From Past Princesses and Refugees to Present Day Community*, edited by Aida Boudjikanian. Beirut: Haigazian University & Armenian Heritage Press, 2009.

Kardas, Saban. "Davutoglu Promotes Stability in Lebanon." *Eurasia Daily Monitor* 6, no. 149 (August 4, 2009).

Kaufman, Asher. "Phoenicianism: The Formation of an Identity in Lebanon in 1920." *Middle East Studies* 37, no. 1 (January 2001).

Kawtharani, Farah W., and Lokman I. Meho. "The Kurdish Community in Lebanon." *International Journal of Kurdish Studies* 19, no. 1–2 (January 2005).

Kaylan, Muammer. *The Kemalists: Islamic Revival and the Fate of Secular Turkey*. Amherst, NY: Prometheus Books, 2005.

Khadduri, Majid. "The Alexandretta Dispute." *American Journal of International Law* 39, no. 3 (July 1945).

Khoury, Philip S. *Syria and the French Mandate: The Politics of Arab Nationalism, 1920–1945*. Princeton, NJ: Princeton University Press, 1987.

———. *Urban Notables and Arab Nationalism*. Cambridge: Cambridge University Press, 1983.

Kibaroğlu, Mustafa. "Turkey and Israel Strategize." *Middle East Quarterly* 9 no. 1 (Winter 2002).

Koester, Helmut. *Introduction to the New Testament: History, Culture and Religion of the Hellenistic Age*. Vol. I. New York: Walter De Cruyter, 1987.

Kouyoumdjian Pasha, Ohannes. *Le Liban á la Veille et au début de la Grande Guerre: Mémoirs d'un Gouverneur, 1913–1915*. Paris: C'entre d'Histoire Armènienne Contemporaine, 2003.

Lamartine, Alphonse De. *A Pilgrimage to the Holy Land; Comprising Recollections, Sketches, and Reflections, Made During a Tour in the East*. Vol. 1. New York: D. Appleton & Company, 1868.

Lammens, Henri. "Al-Marada," *al-Mashriq* (1902).

———. *La Syrie: Précis Historique*. Beyrouth: Impimerie Catholique, Deuxième Volume, 1921.

Laqueur, Walter, and Barry Rubin, eds. *The Israel-Arab Reader: A Documentary History of the Middle East Conflict*. 5th edition. New York: Penguin, 1995.

Larrabee, F. Stephen, and Ian O. Lesser. *Turkish Foreign Policy in an Age of Uncertainty*. Santa Monica, CA: RAND Corporation, 2003.

Lewis, Bernard. *The Middle East: A Brief History of the Last 2,000 Years*. New York: Scribner, 1995.

Lust-Okar, Ellen Marie. "Failure of Collaboration: Armenian Refugees in Syria." *Middle Eastern Studies* 32, no. 1 (January 1996).

Makarem, Sami Nasib. *The Druze Faith* (Caravan Books, 2012, originally published in 1960).

Makdisi, Ussama. "Corrupting the Sublime Sultanate: The Revolt of Tanyus Shahin in Nineteenth Century Ottoman Lebanon." *Comparative Studies in Society and History* 42, no. 1 (January 2000).

Maktabi, Rania. "The Lebanese Census of 1932 Revisited: Who Are the Lebanese?" *British Journal of Middle Eastern Studies* 26, no. 2 (1999).

Maziad, Marwa, and Jake Sotiriadis. "Turkey's Dangerous New Exports: Pan-Islamist, Neo-Ottoman Visions and Regional Instability." *Middle East Institute*, April 21, 2020.

Moosa, Matti. *Extremist Shiites: The Ghulat Sects*. New York: Syracuse University Press, 1988.

———. *The Maronites in History*. Syracuse: Syracuse University Press, 1986.

———. "The Relation of the Maronite of Lebanon to the Mardaites and al-Jarajima." *Speculum* 44, no. 4 (October 1969).

Morgenthau, Henry. *Ambassador Morgenthau's Story*. New York: Doubleday, Page & Company, 1919.

Murinson, Alexander. "The Strategic Depth Doctrine of Turkish Foreign Policy." *Middle Eastern Studies* 42, no. 6 (November 2006).

Naccache, Georges. *L'Orient*, March 10, 1949; reproduced in *Un Reve Libanais: 1943–1972*. Beirut: Editions du Monde Arabe, 1983.

Nassif, Nicolas. *Camille Chamoun: Akher al-'Amalikah* (Camille Chamoun: The Last of the Giants). Beirut: Dar al-Nahar lil-Nashr, 1988.

———. *Joumhouriyat Fouad Chehab* (The Republic of Fouad Chehab). Beirut: Dar an-Nahar, 2008.

New Testament. Matthew 15:21; Mark 3:8 and 7:24, 31; and Luke 6:17 and 10:13, 14.

Nogales, Rafael de. *Four Years Beneath the Crescent*. Translated from Spanish by Muna Lee. New York: Charles Scribner's Sons, 1926.

Nye, Joseph S. Jr. "Soft Power." *Foreign Policy* 80 (Autumn 1990).

Office of the Historian. "The Eisenhower Doctrine, 1957." US State Department. https://history.state.gov/milestones/1953-1960/eisenhower-doctrine.

———. US Department of State, 1915, 1916, 1917, and 1918.

Orhan, Oytun. "The Forgotten Turks: Turkmens of Lebanon." *Center for Middle Eastern Strategic Studies* (ORSAM), Report 11 (February 2010).

Orhan, Oytun, Bilgay Duman, M. Musa Budak, and A. Selcan Özdemirci. "Turkey-Lebanon Friendship Bridge: The Turkish Presence and the Ottoman Heritage in Lebanon." *Center for Middle Eastern Strategic Studies* (ORSAM), Report 199 (June 2015).

Palabiyik, Adem. "Interpreting Foreign Policy Correctly in the East-West Perspective." *Today's Zaman*, June 3, 2010.

Phares, Walid. *Lebanese Christian Nationalism: The Rise & Fall of an Ethnic Resistance*. Boulder, CO: Lynne Rienner, 1995.

Pitts, Graham A. "Fallow Fields: Famine and the Making of Lebanon." PhD diss., Georgetown University, 2016.

Porath, Yehoshua. *The Emergence of the Palestinian-Arab National Movement: 1918–1929*. Vol. 1. London: Frank Cass, 1974.

Poujade, M. Eugène. *Le Liban et la Syrie, 1845–1860*. Paris: Librairie Nouvelle, 1860.

Rabbath, Edmond. *La Formation Historique du Liban Politique et Constitutionnel*. Beirut: Librairie Orientale, 1973.

Rabil, Robert G. "The Armenian Genocide, Maronite Starvation, and Lessons in Past Atrocities." *Fikra Forum—Washington Institute for Near East Policy*, May 12, 2021.

———. "Bordering on a Solution." *National Interest* 163 (September/October 2019).

———. *Embattled Neighbors: Syria, Israel, and Lebanon*. Boulder, CO: Lynne Rienner, 2003.

———. "The Future of Non-State Actors in the Middle East: Hezbollah and al-Hashd al-Sha'bi." *Palm Beach Center for Democracy and Policy Research*, July 21, 2021.

———. "Lebanon-Turkey Relations: Reclaiming the 'Sword' and 'Crescent' of Islam." *Asian Journal of Middle Eastern and Islamic Studies* 15, no. 1 (2021).

———. *Religion, National Identity, and Confessional Politics in Lebanon: The Challenge of Islamism*. New York: Palgrave Macmillan, 2011.

———. *Salafism in Lebanon: From Apoliticism to Transnational Islamism*. Washington, DC: Georgetown University Press, 2014.

———. *Syria, the United States, and the War on Terror in the Middle East*. Westport, CT: Praeger Security International, 2006.

———. *The Syrian Refugee Crisis in Lebanon: The Double Tragedy of Refugees and Impacted Host Communities*. Lanham, MD: Lexington Books, 2016.

Reliefweb, OCHA Services. "Turkish Humanitarian Aid to Lebanon and Syria as of 8 August 2006." https://reliefweb.int/report/lebanon/turkish-humanitarian-aid-lebanon-and-syria-08-aug-2006.

Republic of Turkey, Ministry of Foreign Affairs. *Policy of Zero Problems with Our Neighbors*. https://www.mfa.gov.tr/policy-of-zero-problems-with-our-neighbors.en.mfa.

———. "Relations between Turkey and Lebanon." http://www.mfa.gov.tr/relations-between-turkey-and-lebanon.en.mfa.

Ristelhueber, René. *Traditions Françaises au Liban*. Paris, 1918.

Rondot, Pierre. *Les Institutions Politiques du Liban, des Communautes Traditionnelles a L'etat Moderne*. Paris: Imprimerie Nationale, 1947.

Rustum, As'ad. *Lubnan fi 'Ahd al-Mutasarifiyyah* (Lebanon under the Era of the Mutasarifiyyah). Beirut: Dar al-Nahar Lil-Nashr, 1973.

Sacy, Silvestre de. *Exposé de la Religion des Druzes*. 2 vols. Paris, 1838.

Safa, Hassan. "Ghaz Lubnan Tharwa Wataniyah Wasat Sira' Geopolitiki 'Amiq" (Lebanon's Gas Is a National Fortune amid a Deep Geopolitical Struggle). *Al-Difa' al-Watan al-Lubnani* (Lebanese National Defense) 116 (April 2021).

Salameh, Franck. *Language, Memory and Identity in the Middle East: The Case of Lebanon*. New York: Lexington Books, 2010.

Salibi, Kamal S. *A House of Many Mansions: The History of Lebanon Revisited*. London: I. B. Taurus, 1988.

———. "Islam and Syria in the Writings of Henri Lammens." In *Historians of the Middle East*, edited by Bernard Lewis and P. M. Holt. London: Oxford University Press, 1962.

———. "Lebanon under Fuad Chehab, 1958–1964." *Middle Eastern Studies* 2, no. 3 (April 1966).

———. *Maronite Historians of Medieval Lebanon*. Beirut: American University of Beirut, 1959.

———. "The Maronites of Lebanon under the Frankish and Mamluk Rule (1099–1516)." *Arabica* 4, no. 3 (September 1957).

———. *The Modern History of Lebanon*. London: Weidenfeld and Nicolson, 1965.

Salih, H. *Cyprus: Ethnic Political Counterpoints*. Lanham, MD: University Press of America, 2004.

Sanjiah, Avedis K. *The Armenian Communities in Syria and under Ottoman Dominion*. Cambridge, MA: Harvard University Press, 1965.

Seale, Patrick. *The Struggle for Syria: A Study of Post-War Arab Politics, 1945–1958*. Oxford: Oxford University Press, 1965.

Shanahan, Rodger. *The Shi'a of Lebanon: Clans, Parties and Clerics*. London: I. B. Tauris, 2005.

Solh, Raghid. "The Attitude of the Arab Nationalists towards Greater Lebanon during the 1930s." In *Lebanon: A History of Conflict and Consensus*, edited by Nadim Shehadi and Dana Haffar Mills. London: I. B. Tauris, 1988.

Special Tribunal for Lebanon, August 18, 2020. https://www.stl-tsl.org/crs/assets /Uploads/ 20200818-F3840-PUBLIC-Summary-of-Judgment-FILED-EN-FINAL.pdf.

Suny, Ronald Grigor. *"They Can Live in the Desert but Nowhere Else": A History of the Armenian Genocide*. Princeton, NJ: Princeton University Press, 2015.

Tanielian, Melanie. "The War of Famine: Everyday Life in Wartime Beirut and Mount Lebanon (1914–1918)." PhD diss., University of California–Berkeley, 2012.

Taoutel, Christian, and Pierre Wittouck. *Le Peuple Libanais dans la Tourmente de la Grande Guerre 1914–1918, D'après les Archives des Pères Jésuites au Liban*. Beirut: Presses De L'Université Saint-Joseph, Deuxième edition, 2018.

Tauber, Eliezer. *The Emergence of Arab Movements*. London: Frank Cass, 1993.

Thayer, Lucius Ellsworth. "The Capitulations of the Ottoman Empire and the Question of their Abrogation as it Affects the United States." *American Journal of International Law* 17, no. 2 (April 1923).

Tibi, Bassam. *Arab Nationalism: A Critical Enquiry.* 2nd Edition. New York: St. Martin's Press, 1990.

Tol, Gonul. "Turkey's Bid for Religious Leadership: How the AKP Uses Islamic Soft Power." *Foreign Affairs*, January 10, 2019.

Traboulsi, Fawwaz. *A History of Modern Lebanon.* New York: Pluto Press, 2007.

Tür, Özlem. "Turkish-Syrian Relations—Where Are We Going?" The Research Unit on International Security and Cooperation (UNISCI) Discussion Papers Núm. 23, Mayo 2010. Universidad Complutense de Madrid, Madrid, España.

United Nations Interim Force in Lebanon (UNIFIL). United Nations. https://unifil .unmissions.org/unifil-mandate.

US Department of Defense. *DOD Transmits 2022 National Defense Strategy.* March 28, 2022. https://www.defense.gov/News/Releases/Release/Article/2980584/dod -transmits-2022-national-defense-strategy/.

———. *Summary of the 2018 National Defense Strategy of the United States*, 2018. https://obamawhitehouse.archives.gov/sites/default/files/docs/2015_national _security_strategy_2.pdf.

US Department of State. *AFP: Current Documents 1957.* Washington, DC: GPO, 1961.

Váli, Ferenc A. *Bridge across the Bosporus: The Foreign Policy of Turkey.* Baltimore: Johns Hopkins Press, 1972.

Volney, C. F. *Travels Through Syria and Egypt in the Years 1783, 1784, and 1785.* Vol. I and II. London: G.G. J. & J. Robinson, 1787.

Walker, Joshua W. "Learning Strategic Depth: Implications of Turkey's New Foreign Policy Doctrine." *Insight Turkey* 9, no. 3 (2007).

Weldon, L. B. *Hard Lying: Eastern Mediterranean 1914–1919.* London: Herbert Jenkins Limited, 1925.

White House. *National Security Strategy.* February 2015. https://obamawhitehouse .archives.gov/sites/default/files/docs/2015_national_security_strategy_2.pdf.

Yamak, Labib Zuwiyya. *The Syrian Social Nationalist Party: An Ideological Analysis.* Cambridge, MA: Harvard University Press, 1966.

Yeghiayan, Zaven Der, Armenian Patriarch of Constantinople, 1913–1922. *My Patriarchal Memoirs.* Translated from Armenian by Ared Misirliyan. Barrington, RI: Mayreni Publishing, 2002, originally published in Armenian in Cairo, 1947.

Yüksel, Engin. *Strategies of Turkish Proxy Warfare in Northern Syria: Back with a Vengeance.* Clingendael, Netherlands: Clingendael Institute, November 2019.

Zamir, Meir. *The Formation of Modern Lebanon.* London: Croom Helm, 1985.

Zeine, Zeine. *Arab-Turkish Relations and the Emergence of Arab Nationalism.* Beirut: Khayat's, 1958.

SELECTED NEWSPAPERS

Al-Ahed News (Beirut)
Al-Akhbar (Beirut)
Al-Diyar (Beirut)
Al-Hayat (London)

An-Nahar (Beirut)
Anadolu Agency (Ankara)
As-Safir (Beirut)
Ash-Sharq al-Awsat (London)
Daily Sabah (Ankara)
Haartez (Jerusalem)
Hürriyet Daily News (Ankara)
Jerusalem Post (Jerusalem)
Le Monde (Paris)
L'Orient-Le Jour (Beirut)
Türkiye (Ankara)

Index

www.ingramcontent.com/pod-product-compliance
Lightning Source LLC
Chambersburg PA
CBHW031415270326
41929CB00010BA/1471